AF287617

Michael Kuperberg

Quantifying and Predicting the Influence of Execution Platform on Software Component Performance

The Karlsruhe Series on Software Design and Quality

Volume 5

Chair Software Design and Quality
Faculty of Computer Science
Karlsruhe Institute of Technology

and

Software Engineering Division
Research Center for Information Technology (FZI), Karlsruhe

Editor: Prof. Dr. Ralf Reussner

Quantifying and Predicting the Influence of Execution Platform on Software Component Performance

by
Michael Kuperberg

Dissertation, Karlsruher Institut für Technologie
Fakultät für Informatik
Tag der mündlichen Prüfung: 4. November 2010
Referenten: Prof. Dr. Ralf Reussner, Prof. Dr. Walter F. Tichy

Impressum

Karlsruher Institut für Technologie (KIT)
KIT Scientific Publishing
Straße am Forum 2
D-76131 Karlsruhe
www.ksp.kit.edu

KIT – Universität des Landes Baden-Württemberg und nationales
Forschungszentrum in der Helmholtz-Gemeinschaft

KIT Scientific Publishing 2011
Print on Demand

ISSN 1867-0067
ISBN 978-3-86644-741-7

Abstract

Software engineering is concerned with the cost-efficient construction of applications which behave as specified, are well-designed and of high quality. Among software quality attributes, performance is one of most prominent and well-studied. Performance evaluation is concerned with explaining, predicting and preventing long waiting times, overloaded bottleneck resources and other performance problems.

However, performance remains hard to evaluate because it depends not only on software implementation, but also on several other factors such as the workload and the execution platform on which the software runs. The execution platform comprises hardware resources (CPU, networks, hard disks) and software resources (operating system, middleware). In former approaches, the influence of the execution platform was a hard-wired part of the model, and not an adjustable parameter. This meant that to answer sizing and relocation questions, a performance model had to be recreated and quantified for each candidate execution platform.

The resulting **challenge** addressed by this thesis is to devise an effective approach for quantifying and predicting the influence of the execution platform on software performance, using Model-Based Performance Evaluation (MBPE) at the level of software architecture. The primary targeted benefit is a decrease of the effort needed for performance prediction, since answering sizing and relocation questions no longer needs the deployment and measurement of the considered application on every candidate execution platform.

The application of MBPE starts at design time since delaying performance evaluation until the implementation of the software is not desirable: the refactoring costs increase with the degree of completeness and deployment. To model the artefacts of the software application, MBPE builds upon the well-studied concept of software components and their required and provided services as exchangeable building blocks which facilitate recomposition and reuse. In most MBPE approaches, the atomic behaviour actions of components carry timing values. On the basis of these timing values, an analysis of the overall application behaviour (e.g. prediction of response times) is then performed.

Unfortunately, such timing values are platform-specific and the resulting architectural model is also platform-specific. Therefore, the model needs to be rebuilt for each considered execution platform and for each usage profile. Additionally, the durations of atomic component actions often amount to just a few nanoseconds, and measuring such fine-granular actions is challenging because conventional timer methods are too coarse for them.

The **contribution of this thesis** is a novel approach to quantify and to predict both platform-independent and platform-dependent resource demands on the basis of performance models. Using automated benchmarking of the execution platform, the approach is able to make precise, platform-specific performance predictions on the basis of these models, without manual effort. By separating the performance evaluation of the application from the performance evaluation of the execution platform, the effort to consider different platforms (e.g. for relocation or sizing scenarios) is significantly decreased, since it is no longer needed to deploy the application on each candidate platform. To select the timer methods used in measurements, this thesis introduces a novel platform-independent algorithm which quantifies timer quality metrics (e.g. accuracy and overhead).

Building on the Palladio Component Model (PCM) and its tooling, the implementation of the approach provides a convenient user interface and a validated theoretical foundation. The resource demands are parametrised over the usage (workload) of the considered components, and are expressed as annotations in the PCM-based behaviour model of the component.

To integrate the presented approach into the PCM, new meta-model concepts have been introduced into the PCM, and corresponding tooling has been added. The enhanced PCM workbench allows for automated creation of PCM model instances from black-box bytecode components, and also includes concepts and tools to convert benchmarking results into PCM resource models.

The presented approach focuses on applications that will run as platform-independent bytecode on bytecode-executing virtual machines (BEVMs) such as the Java VM. It accounts for dynamic and static optimisations performed in modern BEVMs, e.g. just-in-time compilation (JIT) and inlining. To translate the platform-independent resource demands into timing values, this thesis introduces a benchmark suite for BEVMs. This benchmark suite addresses both fine-granular bytecode instructions (e.g. integer addition or array initialisation) and platform API methods provided by BEVM's base libraries, e.g. by the Java Platform API.

Unlike existing approaches, the contribution of this thesis

- does not require modification or instrumentation of the execution platform

- quantifies the performance speedups of the execution platform (e.g. just-in-time compilation) and reflects them during performance prediction

- deals with API and library methods in an atomic way, providing method-level benchmarking results which are more intuitive than per-instruction timings

- provides more detailed per-invocation performance results than conventional profilers, and supports stochastic distributions of performance values, which are more realistic and information-richer than conventional average or median metrics

An extensive **validation** of performance prediction capabilities offered by the new approach was performed on a number of Java applications, such as widely used SPECjvm2008, SPECjvm98, SPECjbb2005 and Linpack benchmarks. The validation demonstrated the prediction accuracy of bytecode-based cross-platform performance prediction, and showed that it has significantly better results than prediction based on CPU cycles. The validation used one execution platform as a basis to obtain platform-independent resource demands, and predicted the performance of the application on other execution platforms (which were significantly different from the basis platform) without deploying and benchmarking the application on them. The validation also addressed individual parts of the presented approach: the precision and the overhead of the resource demand quantification were studied, and the heuristics-based approach for automated method benchmarking was evaluated w.r.t. its effectiveness, coverage and precision of the benchmarking results. A large comparison of timer methods on the basis of quality attributes was performed on several Java and .NET platforms.

Zusammenfassung

Software Engineering beschäftigt sich mit kosteneffektiver Konstruktion von qualitativ hochwertigen Softwareanwendungen, deren Verhalten einer vorgegebenen Spezifikation folgt und denen ein zielgerichteter Entwurf zugrundeliegt. Unter den Qualitätsattributen von Software nimmt die Performance eine zentrale Rolle ein und wird dementsprechend intensiv erforscht. Der Forschungsbereich Performance-Analyse beschäftigt sich mit Messung, Modellierung und Vorhersage von Performance, um Performance-Probleme wie z.B. überlastete Ressourcen zu erklären und ihnen vorzubeugen.

Performance-Analyse bietet zahlreiche Herausforderungen und offene Forschungsfragen, da die Performance einer Applikation in komplexer Weise von Faktoren wie Implementierung, Nutzlast und Ausführungsumgebung abhängt. Die Ausführungsumgebung beinhaltet Hardware-Ressourcen wie z.B. CPU und Festplatte, aber auch Software-Ressourcen wie das Betriebssystem oder die Middleware. In früheren Modellierungsansätzen war der Einfluss der Ausführungsumgebung als ein konstanter und fixierter Faktor enthalten, sodass das Modell für Vergleiche der Ausführungsumgebungen oder für Fragestellungen zur Ressourcendimensionierung mehrfach neu aufgestellt werden musste.

Daraus ergibt sich die in dieser Doktorarbeit angegangene **Herausforderung,** einen effektiven Ansatz zur Vorhersage des Einflusses der Ausführungsumgebung auf Software-Performance zu entwickeln. Der zu entwickelnde Ansatz soll ohne Installation und Messung der analysierten Applikation auf jeder der betrachteten Ausführungsumgebungen auskommen. Dieser Ansatz soll als Bestandteil von modellbasierter Performance-Analyse auf der Ebene der Software-Architektur zum Einsatz kommen, während also nur einzelne Teilkomponenten der Anwendung zur Verfügung stehen. Der Nutzen des neuen Ansatzes liegt darin, dass weniger Zeit und Kosten für modellbasierte Performance-vorhersagen in Dimensionierungs- und Verlegungsszenarien aufgewendet werden müssen.

Die Anwendung der modellbasierten Performance-Vorhersage beginnt bereits zur Entwurfszeit, da das Hinauszögern von Performance-Analysen bis zur Implementierungsphase dazu führt, dass die Behebung der aufgedeckten Performance-Probleme mit umso höheren Kosten verbunden ist, je weiter die Implementierung fortgeschritten ist. Die Anwendungen werden dabei mit Hilfe von Software-Komponenten modelliert, welche als austauschbare und unabhängig einsetzbare Einheiten mit schnittstellenbasierter Kommunikation einen gegliederten Entwurf und nichtmonolitische Umsetzung erlauben. Die zur Entwurfszeit bereits implementiert vorliegende Komponenten werden dabei mit dem beschriebenen Ansatz analysiert; fr̈ noch nicht implementierte Komponenten werden Schätzungen und Performance-Vorgaben (z.B. über Service Level Agreements) verwendet. Die Modellierung der Performance wird in den meisten komponentenbasierten Ansätzen über die Annotation von Zeitwerten an Elemente von Verhaltensmodellen bewerkstelligt, welche anschließend durch einen analytischen oder simulationsbasierten Ansatz ausgewertet werden. Der signifikante Nachteil der Verwendung von Zeitwerten zur Performance-Modellierung ist allerdings deren plattformspezifische Natur, sodass das resultierende Modell auch plattformspezifisch bleibt. Deshalb muss das Modell für jede betrachtete Ausführungsumgebung dupliziert und neu annotiert werden. Erschwerend kommt hinzu, dass die Dauer von Komponentendiensten oft im Nanosekundenbereich liegt und mit zur Verfügung stehenden Bibliotheksmethoden zur Zeitmessung nicht akkurat gemessen werden kann, da diese zu grobgranular dafür sind.

Der **wissenschaftliche Beitrag** der vorliegenden Doktorarbeit ist ein neuer modellbasierter Ansatz für Messung und Vorhersage von plattformunabhängigen Ressourcenverbräuchen und plattformspezifischen Ausführungszeiten von Software-Komponenten. Der vorgestellte Ansatz ist auf Anwendungen ausgerichtet, die in Bytecode vorliegen und damit von virtuellen Maschinen (VMs, z.B. Java VM) plattformübergreifend ausgeführt werden können. Der Ansatz berücksichtigt dabei statische und dynamische Optimierungen, die in modernen VMs eingesetzt werden, wie z.b. die Kompilierung von Bytecode nach Maschinencode zur Laufzeit (Just-in-Time compilation, „JIT") oder das Inlining von Methoden.

Durch weitestgehende Automatisierung der einzelnen Schritte (und vor allem durch automatisches Benchmarken der Ausführungsplattform) ist der Ansatz dabei in der Lage, den manuellen Aufwand für die Performancevorhersage zu minimieren. Das Benchmarken der virtuellen Maschine umfasst sowohl die feingranularen Bytecodebefehle (z.B. Addition oder Arraybenutzung) als auch die Bibliotheksmethoden der Plattform-API. Indem die Performance der Anwendung von der Performance der Ausführungsplattform getrennt wird, sinkt auch der Aufwand für die Betrachtung verschiedener Plattformen in Dimensionierungs- und Verlegungsszenarien. So ist es nicht länger notwendig, die Anwendung auf jeder der betrachteten Plattformen zu installieren und durchzumessen.

Für die Auswahl der Bibliotheksmethoden für die Messung der Zeit entwickelt die vorliegende Arbeit einen neuen plattformunabhängigen Ansatz, der die Qualitätsattribute dieser Methoden quantifiziert und durch eine neue aggregierende Metrik den Vergleich zwischen diesen Bibiotheksmethoden erleichtert.

Die Implementierung des Ansatzes erweitert das Palladio-Komponentenmodell (Palladio Component Model, PCM), und kann damit über dessen Werkzeuge für Performance-Vorhersagen benutzt werden. Um die neu eingeführen plattformunabhängigen Ressourcenverbräuche in PCM-Modellen verwenden zu können, wurde das PCM-Metamodell und die entsprechenden Modelltransformationen erweitert. Zudem wurden Werkzeuge für die Generierung von Modellinstanzen aus Ressourcenbenutzung durch Komponenten und aus Benchmarking-Ergebnissen von Ausführungsplattformen entwickelt.

Im Unterschied zu existierenden Ansätzen zeichnet sich der Beitrag der vorliegenden Arbeit durch folgende Eigenschaften aus:

- Die Ausführungsplattform muss weder instrumentiert noch verändert werden.

- Die Performance-Erhöhungen durch Laufzeitoptimierungen der Ausführungsplattform (z.b. JIT) werden quantifiziert und bei der Performance-Vorhersage berücksichtigt.

- Bibliotheksmethoden wie z.b. diejenigen der Java Platform API werden als atomare Einheiten während der Benchmarking-Phase betrachtet und nicht in Bytecodeinstruktionen aufgespalten, da ihre Performance auf Methodenebene besser handhabbar und für Nutzer leichter verständlich ist.

- Während Profiler die gemessenen Zeitenwerte als Durchschnitt oder Median zur Verfügung stellen, unterstützt der vorgestellte Ansatz stochastische Verteilungen von Bytecode-basierten Ressourcennutzungswerten und hat damit einen höheren Informationsgehalt.

Eine umfangreiche **Validierung** des neuen Verfahrens zur Performancevorhersage untersucht die Güte der Vorhersageergebnisse mit Hilfe weit verbreiteter Benchmarks wie SPECjvm2008, SPECjbb2005 und Linpack. Die Validierung zeigt die Genauigkeit der Vorhersagen und die Überlegenheit des vorgestellten Verfahrens gegenüber dem bisher in PCM benutzten Ansatz, der auf Zählung von CPU-Zyklen basiert. Die Validierung benutzt eine Ausführungsplattform als Basis für die Quantifizierung plattformunabhängiger Ressourcenverbräuche, und sagt dann die Performance der betrachteten Applikationen auf anderen Ausführungsplattformen voraus, ohne diese Applikationen dort zu installieren und zu messen.

Die Validierung umfasst ebenso die einzelnen Bestandteile des Ansatzes, also die Bestimmung der Bytecode-orientierten Ressourcenverbräuche sowie das applikationsunabhängige Benchmarken der virtuellen Maschinen. Das im Rahmen der Dissertation entwickelte Verfahren zur Quantifizierung von Qualitätattributen der Timermethoden wird auf zahlreiche Methoden unter Java und .NET angewandt und die Ergebnisse werden anhand der neu eingeführten Metrik verglichen.

Acknowledgements

This thesis has one author but many people to thank for – colleagues and collaborators, students and staff, family and friends.

First and foremost, the vision and wisdom of my parents Valentina and Ilya have inspired me for many years, and I've learned a lot more from them than can fit into any PhD thesis. Their unconditional love and support but also fair and pointed criticism provided me with a framework for which I am endlessly grateful. Therefore, I dedicate this thesis to them.

Prof. Ralf Reussner has been a great PhD advisor, research group leader and a wonderful person to work with. Ralf has provided me with an environment to explore, to invent and to publish and he has supported my work in every manner. I'm especially grateful for his trust and his patience at the beginning of my work, and for providing me with numerous opportunities to teach. Ralf has managed to bring good mood, a sense of belonging together and a common vision to a team of people with different backgrounds and individual research interests. Despite his increasingly tight schedule, Ralf always found time for advising me and his critical reviews helped to shape this thesis.

Prof. Walter F. Tichy has provided helpful feedback even before the thesis writing phase, and his comments during IPD seminars and during oral examinations have given me several useful insights. I'm very grateful for his involvement as the second advisor of my thesis, and for his suggestions on how to improve it.

Over the years, many members of the Software Design and Quality research group (SDQ) have scrutinized my work, reviewed my publications, and gave a lot of much-appreciated advice on my research, presentations and implementations. Klaus Krogmann has been a great officemate, a demanding co-author of papers and an engaged reviewer of this thesis – and we also had a lot of fun for over four years! Steffen Becker, Heiko Koziolek and Jens Happe gave me useful advice and provided much-valued reviews at the beginning of my PhD research. Samuel Kounev has inspired me with his enthusiasm, and invited me to participate in the visionary work of the SPEC Research Group. Thomas Goldschmidt reviewed this thesis and gave me useful advice on its readability. Erik Burger, Jörg Henß, Heinz Herrmann, Elena Kienhöfer, Anne Koziolek and many, many others at the KIT and at the FZI supported me in various organizational, technical and scientific matters.

Advising students was a great and rewarding part of my PhD work, and particular gratitude goes to Martin Krogmann for his work on bytecode instrumentation, to Fouad Omri for his work on benchmarking, as well as to Michael Hauck, Sebastian Bauer, and all others who influenced the work described in this thesis.

My family and relatives, spread over countries and continents, kept reminding me that there is life outside of Eclipse and TexMakerX, and their constant inquiries about my progress and the applicability of my work were an additional inspiration. During my PhD work and the writing of this thesis, many friends had to cut back on our joint hobbies and interests. Now that their waiting is over, I look forward to all the other activities and dreams which we had put in hibernation mode.

Karlsruhe, November 2010
Michael Kuperberg

Contents

Chapter 1.

Introduction

This chapter motivates the work pursued in this thesis, sets the context and the preconditions for the research that is performed, and states the problems that the thesis addresses. The shortcomings of existing approaches are presented to support the focus of the thesis, and to make the targeted field of research more precise. After formulating the resulting scientific challenges and goals, the contributions of the thesis are summarised and the validation of the developed approaches is sketched. Finally, the organisation of the thesis is explained.

1.1. Motivation

Software engineering is concerned with efficient and systematic development and evolution of software applications, following customer requirements and existing best practices. In addition to functional requirements which target the *results* of the application execution, non-functional requirements such as performance or reliability are of substantial importance to the software users. Non-functional requirements and software properties describe the quality of the software, and how *effective* the software is in performing its tasks.

Software performance has been a major concern and a field of intense research, with scientific publications on it appearing in 1969 [1, 2] and possibly even earlier. Yet as the software and underlying hardware have grown and become increasingly complex and concurrent, performance has remained a focal point for researchers and engineers. Performance problems and associated costs have received public attention [3, 4, 5, 6], and have lead to significant expenses [7] to correct the underlying issues in the design and implementation of the concerned software products. To provide approaches for dealing with these challenges, performance engineering [8] has established itself as a subfield of software engineering.

However, when facing budgetary and time constraints in projects, practitioners deal with performance only at the end of software development projects, which means that the "fix it later" approach is followed. But this delay is problematic since performance flaws are often caused by the *architecture* and the overall *design* of an application, in addition to performance-unconscious implementation. Attempting to solve the problem by replacing the originally planned execution platform with one having higher performance causes additional costs, and is ineffective when the software does not scale, as exemplified in [6]. In such cases, correction of performance issues requires architecture-level changes, which turn out to be very expensive since the completed implementation has to be corrected as well.

Consequently, *design-time* analysis and prediction of software performance is required to address potential performance issues as early as possible. As the implementation progresses, performance predictions can be compared to measurements, allowing timely corrective actions of need arises. To allow design-time prediction of software performance, several architecture-level approaches (e.g. [9, 10, 11, 12], see [5, 13] for an overview) have emerged and continue to flourish. However, design-time performance analysis is challenging, since no measurable implementation but only an architectural view exists at that time.

Making performance analysis a part of already happening design-time activities is particularly practical and promises effort savings through synergies. When an explicit software architecture is being modelled, its artefacts are static as well as dynamic models, which serve as a blueprint during later development. Enriching these models with performance information is especially attractive when the model can be executed (e.g. by simulation), since the model execution then can provide a performance prediction.

Rather than developing applications as large, monotonic blocks, decomposition into smaller entities has established itself as a maintainability "best practice". The prevalent kind of entities in architectural models are *software components* [14] and their connectors. Software components encapsulate design decisions and interact with other components over interfaces, while exposing their functionality as *services*.

Examples of well-known and popular implementations of the software components paradigm are Enterprise Java Beans [15] and Common Object Model (COM [16]). At the same, many advanced software component *metamodels* (i.e. formal descriptions of components, their roles and properties) have been developed in academia, as surveyed in [17].

Among existing component metamodels targeting business software applications, the Palladio Component Metamodel (PCM [9]) has a particularly extensive support for performance predictions. It explicitly parametrises the dynamic performance model of a component over the four performance-influencing factors which are shown in Figure 1.1. These factors are the usage profile [18], the component implementation, external components (addressed over required interfaces) and the execution platform.

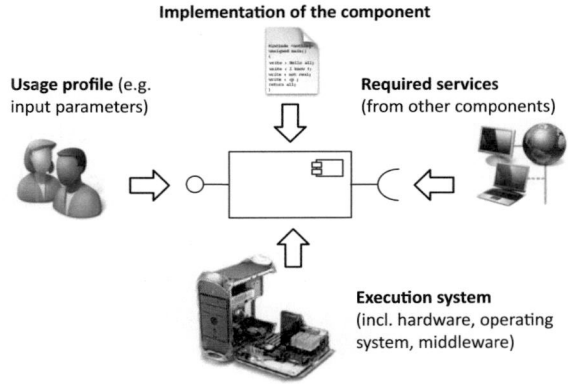

Figure 1.1.: Performance of software components: influencing factors

Since a PCM model of a component is parametrised over these factors, the model can be reused in different assembly and deployments scenarios, reducing the effort for modelling component-based applications. To model a component's usage of the execution platform, the Palladio Component Model uses technology-independent abstractions such as *CPU cycles* and other *low-level* usage metrics for hardware resources. PCM considers CPU cycles as a platform-independent metric, and CPU cycles are a convenient simplification as the software layers between the component and the hardware are included transparently in the metric values.

1.2. Problem Statement and Scientific Challenges

Direct counting of CPU cycles has become unreliable with the increasing popularity of concurrent programming and multi-core CPUs, as will be shown in Chapter 7. Additionally, most execution platforms do not support obtaining the precise number of CPU cycles spent executing a given thread or method. Instead, only the total number of executed CPU cycles across all processes and threads can be queried.

As an alternative, measuring the CPU demands of a component's work request could be done on the basis of timing measurements. However, inferring CPU cycles from timing measurements leads to imprecise results due to low timer method accuracy [19] and due to interruptions in execution caused by CPU interrupts and context switches. In general, there exists no approach to select among available techniques for time measurements, as accuracy differs between them and no approach is available to quantify it. Additionally, it is not clear whether further relevant quality attributes exist for selecting time measurement techniques, and whether it is possible to quantify them, too.

Even worse, the prediction accuracy with resource demands based on CPU cycles is unsatisfactory when predicting performance for execution platforms which have different hardware and software characteristics. This problem is aggravated by the fact that modern business applications are compiled to portable bytecode rather than hardware-specific machine code. Such bytecode is executed by virtual machines since neither operating systems nor conventional CPUs can execute bytecode directly, and these virtual machines perform runtime program optimisations to speed up the bytecode interpretation, which is quite slow.

For example, the Just-in-Time compilation of the Java Virtual Machine detects hot methods and compiles their bytecode into machine code, which leads to a speedup of more than an order of magnitude when compared to conventional bytecode interpretation. The achieved speedup depends on the Just-in-Time compiler and the execution platform, but also on the structure and behaviour of the compiled software, and these factors are hard to capture and to predict.

Performance *prediction* is needed and beneficial in scenarios where performance *measurement* is not possible or not rational due to resulting costs and complexity. For the **relocation** scenario shown in Figure 1.2, the component's performance is known for the current platform where it runs, but not on the target platform to which the relocation is planned. Conventional performance analysis requires the component (or even the entire application containing it) to be deployed and measured on the target platform. However, this incurs substantial effort for deploying the application and measuring its performance, and a more effective approach that makes use of the known performance on the original platform is needed.

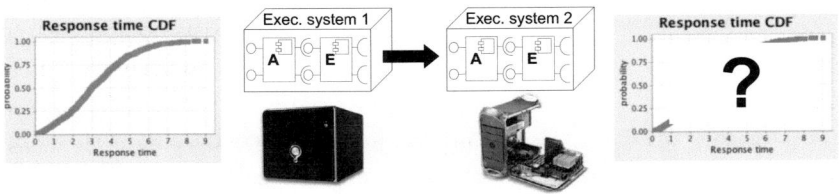

Figure 1.2.: Relocation scenario: predicting changes in component performance

For the **sizing** scenario shown in Figure 1.3, performance requirements such as "reponse time <6 ns in 90 % of cases, and <10 ns in 99 % of cases" are violated

5

for the current execution platform, and a new platform must be chosen so that the requirements are fulfilled again. As for the relocation scenario, conventional treatment of the sizing scenario requires either human estimation or the costly deployment and measuring the application on the execution platform. However, for sizing questions, *several* candidate platforms lead to an even higher effort than for the relocation scenario.

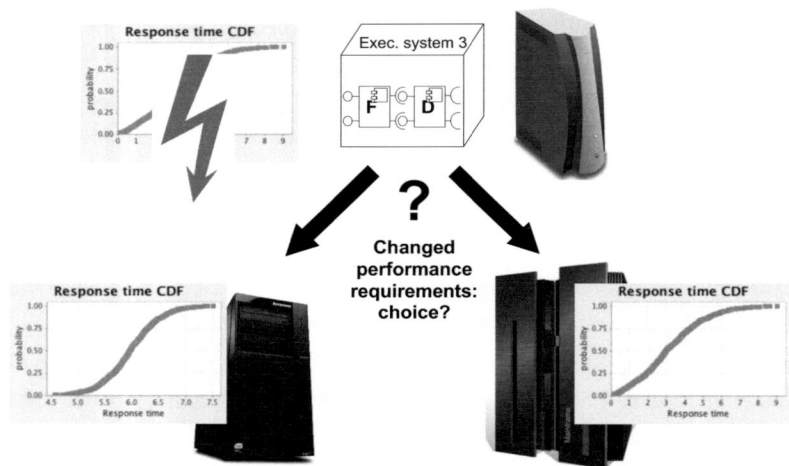

Figure 1.3.: Sizing: choosing an appropriate execution platform to fulfil performance requirements

Performance prediction is also needed in other scenarios, such as selecting among component implementations, making architectural design decisions, studying the impact of application workload, and others. For the presented thesis, the relocation and sizing scenarios are of particular interest because the performance model of the execution platform is of central importance for them, while other influencing factors shown in Figure 1.1 remain fixed.

Unlike in embedded systems and real-time environments, performance prediction for business applications is not interested in worst case execution durations, but rather in the average and median execution durations. To capture and to predict the performance variations using stochastic distributions, the Palladio Component Model and its tooling consider resource contention, request scheduling and other factors that impact the execution durations of individual work requests. Still, the key to accurate performance prediction in Palladio is the accurate quantification of the "raw" resource demands of the request, which form the focus of this thesis.

Summarising these requirements in the field of software performance engineering and shortcomings of existing approaches in one sentence, the following **problem statement** serves as the starting point for the presented thesis:

> Devise an approach for accurate cross-platform model-based performance prediction for bytecode-based components, utilising an application-independent resource demand metric instead of timing values and CPU cycles.

This problem statement leads to the following **scientific challenges** for the presented thesis:

- To allow more accurate performance predictions than when using CPU cycles, define a new application-independent and platform-independent metric for expressing resource demands of components.

- Devise and implement an approach for quantifying the resource demands on the basis of the new metric so that the approach can be applied to generic applications/components and does not require a specialised execution platform or modification of existing execution platforms.

- Create benchmarks that translate the new platform-independent resource demand units into platform-specific timing values.

- Extend the Palladio Component Model to support the new resource demand metric using first-class model entities, without having to convert them into CPU cycles or other existing resource demand units.

7

- Demonstrate that the new resource demand metric indeed results in better cross-platform performance prediction accuracy.

- For the cases where the new resource demand metric cannot be used and timing measurements have to be performed, identify quality attributes for selecting timer methods to support accurate time measurements.

- Devise an approach for quantifying the quality attributes of timer methods without having to inspect the implementation of the timer method, and devise a process for selecting the most appropriate method for timing measurements.

1.3. Shortcomings of Existing Solutions

Traditional approaches to model-based performance prediction rely on manual or semi-automated creation of queuing networks [20, 21], Petri nets [22, 23, 24] and other fine-grained models. However, the resource demands in the elements of these model need to be specified, and this requires measurements which incur large effort. Additionally, these resource demands are usually expressed as platform-dependent timing values, which leads to the need to perform the measurements and benchmarks on each considered platform, further increasing the modelling effort.

To address the problem that timing measurements are platform-dependent, several approaches separate the application performance from execution platform performance by identifying *work units*, such as *application building blocks* or resource-specific demand units. However, most attempts to find resource demands metric other than timing values are specific for an application, specific for an implementation platform or a technology [25, 26, 27], and often require a specialised toolset to work [28]. Therefore, they do not fulfil the requirement of being both platform-independent and application-independent. Most of these approaches are concerned with performance *analysis* rather than with performance *prediction*, and no validated cross-platform performance prediction technique that addresses the challenges from Section 1.2 has been published.

Meyerhöfer and Lauterwald [29, 30] propose platform-independent component measurement for Java components. However, their approach does not address the challenge of Just-In-Time compilation, which needed for performance modelling of today's bytecode-executing virtual machines. The benchmarking part of the approach in [29] quantifies the performance of bytecode instructions and methods in the context of one application, rather than in an application-independent way. Additionally, [29] does not validate the prediction results in cross-platform scenarios, and does not quantify the prediction error. The quantification of the application workload in [29] is also platform-specific: for example, EJB interceptors and JVMPI (Java Virtual Machine Profiling Interface) are used. However, JVMPI has been deprecated since 2004 and has been removed from Java 6. In contrast to the choice made in [29], the approach chosen in this thesis is both application-independent and platform-independent.

Binder et al. [28] use bytecode instructions as application building blocks, but do not quantify the execution duration of the instructions and thus cannot predict the performance of the bytecode-based components. In [28], performance of all bytecodes is assumed to be equal and parameters of individual instructions (incl. names of invoked methods) are ignored, which is not realistic.

Performance *prediction* on the basis of bytecode benchmarking has been proposed by several researchers [31, 32], but no validated cross-platform prediction has been presented and no libraries or tools are available.

Execution durations of individual bytecode instructions have been studied independently from performance prediction by Lambert and Brown in [33], however, their approach to *instruction timing* was applied only to a subset of the Java instruction set, and has not been validated or used for predicting the performance of a real application. Hu et al. derive worst-case execution time of Java bytecode in [34], but their work is limited to real-time JVMs.

Cost analysis of bytecode-based programs is presented by Albert et al. in [35], but neither bytecode benchmarks not actual realistic performance values can be obtained, since the performance is assumed to be equal for all bytecode instructions.

Although benchmarking and performance prediction depend heavily on the quality of the used timer methods, there exists no definition of quality metrics beyond accuracy. Even for accuracy, it is known that it differs across methods and execution platforms, but no approach exists which is capable of quantifying it on a given platform. Books on performance measurement, evaluation and benchmarking (e.g. [36], [37]) discuss the importance of timer accuracy for quantifying the errors in measurements, but do not provide algorithms for *computing* the accuracy or other quality metrics. Also, the role of the timer method invocation costs is not discussed and no platform-specific data is provided.

In [38], Buble et al. denote imprecise timing information as the first cause of imprecision in CORBA benchmarking. They state that in their experience, the RDTSC (read Timestamp Counter) instruction is "a good source of timing information on the Intel platforms", but do not provide any proof or numbers to justify their opinion. In [39], Holmes provides an overview of clocks, timers and scheduling events accessible from Java, but does not provide any reusable means to obtain precise characteristics of timer methods. In [33], Lambert and Power build on [40] and [41] to obtain platform-independent timings of Java Virtual Machine bytecode instructions, using the RDTSC (read time stamp counter) instruction of the Intel Pentium processors. However, they also do not try to obtain the accuracy or the invocation cost of RDTSC calls.

Concluding, existing attempts for cross-platform performance analysis do not allow the *prediction* of the performance of business applications. In particular, they ignore the runtime optimisations such as Just-in-Time compilation, although this optimisations have significant impact on application performance in realistic environments. Existing solutions also cannot be used in a platform-independent and application-independent way, because they rely on techniques which are vendor-specific, or which require a significant modification of the execution platform. Finally, no approach exists that provides metric-based selection among techniques for time measurements, which is needed because accuracy of benchmarking part of performance prediction depends on the accuracy and other properties of the measurement techniques.

1.4. Thesis Approach

The basic idea of the approach that is presented in this thesis is to separate the performance behaviour of an application into a platform-specific part and an application-specific, platform-independent part. The two parts are expressed using models and then combined by performing model-based performance prediction that uses bytecode-level application building blocks. The principle of the approach is shown in Figure 1.4, and explained in the following.

In particular, the presented approach automates both the creation of a platform-independent performance profile of the considered application, and the creation of an application-independent performance profile of execution platforms. Of course, it also automates the prediction of platform-specific execution durations (timings) of a given application on a particular execution platform, with a given application usage profile.

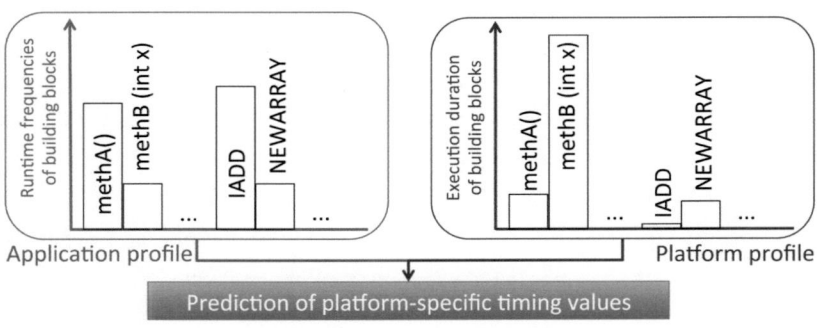

Figure 1.4.: Overview of the cross-platform performance prediction approach of this thesis

A simplified analogy for the presented prediction approach is that of a shopping cart: a purchase that consists of several items can be quantified either through the total cost of the purchase or by listing the type and quantity of individual items. The total cost is *vendor-specific* if the cost of the items varies from vendor to vendor – but it is also easier to grasp and requires less "memory" to remember. Instead, describing the contents of the shopping cart in a *vendor-independent* way by listing the items and their quantity in detail is a vendor-independent representation, but it still allows customers to compare the cost of the shopping cart across vendors but computing the total cost of the purchase.

Application Profile

An *application profile* as used in this thesis consists of *runtime frequencies* of application building blocks (Chapter 4 discusses the selection of the application building blocks for this thesis). The execution of the application building blocks by the execution platform can be seen as the processing of resource demands issued by the application to the execution platform. In this thesis, the term *resource demands* is therefore applied to the application building blocks when the execution platform is considered as a single, complex resource.

The term "application" can denote an entire, multi-component application – but also a single component, or a single class/module. Correspondingly, an "application profile" applies to the set of services/methods offered by the interface(s) of a given application/component/module/class. The application profile can encompass private (non-exposed) services/methods in addition to those services/methods which are accessible over public interfaces.

The application profile consists of *runtime* (i.e. dynamic) frequencies and not of static frequencies because loops, branches and other control flow constructs impact the execution of the application at runtime. In some simpler cases, it would be possible to use static code analysis or symbolic execution to approximate the runtime frequencies without actually running the application. However, Chapter 4 of this thesis introduces a more universal, instrumentation-based solution for obtaining *real* and precise runtime frequencies of bytecode instructions and method invocations.

Since the runtime execution of a service/method depend on its parameters, the performance profile of a service/method needs to be quantified individually for each relevant "input", i.e. for each parameter assignment. Instead of specifying the performance profile of a service individually for each relevant parameter combination, it is possible to generate *parametrised performance profiles* which contain functions (rather than constants) as counts of individual application building blocks. One possibility to do so is through machine learning with genetic algorithms, as exemplified in the PhD dissertation of Klaus Krogmann [42].

The application profile is not a trace but an aggregated account of the runtime frequencies of building blocks. Therefore, it abstracts from the effects of execution order: executing building blocks BB_1 and BB_2 in the sequence BB_1 BB_2 BB_2 BB_1 is assumed to have the same contribution to the performance profile as BB_1 BB_1 BB_2 BB_2. A consequence of this assumption is that the kind of building blocks must be chosen appropriately: selecting CPU instructions as building blocks means that CPU pipelining, out-of-order execution and other effects will violate the implicit additivity and commutativity properties of the proposed application profile definition.

So far, the application profile is not a performance profile in the classic sense, since neither timing values nor resource demands are attached to the elements of the application profile. While the individual application building blocks can be seen as the application's *resource demands* to the execution platforms, it is more usual to express resource demands in terms of hardware/software resources (CPU, hard disk drives, threads in a thread pool, etc.) or in timing values than in "building blocks". Translating the application profile into application *performance metric values* is achieved by using a *platform performance profile*.

Platform Performance Profile

In short, the platform performance profile consists of resource demands or timing values of a given application building block. For example, if an API method is an application building block, its execution duration can be the resource demand, or its use of resources (expressed in CPU cycles, bytes written to an HDD, etc.) can be used for the platform performance profile. Of course, the resource demands of an application building block depend on its usage, i.e. on its parameters: for example, the performance of an API method that implements reversing the sorting order of an array depends on that array's length (and, of course, on the implementation of the method and on the execution platform).

Therefore, obtaining the platform performance profile means *benchmarking* the execution platform and accounting for parametric performance dependencies. A significant challenge in platform benchmarking is to perform it in a setting that is as close as possible to the setting in which the actual application will be run. As any measurement impacts the measured system, so does benchmarking, and obtaining a representative platform performance profile should be carried out in a systematic, controlled environment.

It should be noted that the platform is considered as a *black box*, i.e. only its externally visible properties, behaviour, configuration and interfaces are used. In particular, the approach does not build a *model* of the platform's internals, and does not quantify the performance of the individual platform parts. A further aspect is that this thesis targets business applications, rather than embedded applications or scenarios with real-time requirements. Additionally, the prediction approach of this thesis is to be used during the design phase and for the applications which are built from components which are only partially available at that time.

There are several reasons to build a black-box performance profile/model rather than a detailed behavioural performance model which requires detailed ("white-box") knowledge of the execution platform:

- a detailed behavioural performance model of an execution platform is very hard to build for today's multi-layered, self-optimizing platforms, and requires human expertise (i.e. it is hard to automate)

- the detailed model requires substantial computing efforts to be used during performance prediction (e.g. using simulation): today's CPU simulators execution time is several orders of magnitude larger than the duration of the simulated work

- as layers of the execution platform can be exchanged independently, behavioural performance models would have to be built for each layer, and
  corresponding interfaces between the models would have to be established

Consequently, in this thesis, the modeling of execution platforms will follow the
"black box" approaach, rather than the "white-box" approach.

Predicting the Platform-specific Timing Values and Resource Demands

The simplest way to predict the performance of a given application on a particular platform is to combine the application profile and the platform performance
profile using element-wise multiplication and computation of the sum. In the
following, we use definitions which will be reused and expanded in Chapter 6:

- $Freq(BB_i, WL_j, App_k)$ is the runtime frequency of building block BB_i when
  workload WL_j is exercised on application App_k

- $Perf(BB_i, Plat_m)$ is a performance metric value of BB_i on platform $Plat_m$
  (e.g. execution duration, number of CPU cycles, etc.)

- $PP(WL_j, App_k, Plat_m)$ is the *predicted* platform-specific performance of App_k
  with workload WL_j on execution platform $Plat_m$

$Pred(WL_j, App_k, Plat_m)$ is computed as the sum of products over all building
blocks found in application App_k:

$$Pred(WL_j, App_k, Plat_m) = \sum_i Freq(BB_i, WL_j, App_k) \cdot Perf(BB_i, Plat_m) \qquad (1.1)$$

An important assumption manifested in Formula 1.1 is that of non-parallel
execution of building blocks: by computing the sum over the $Freq$ and $Perf$
values, the performance is predicted for the case where the building blocks
are executed in a non-overlapping manner and without optimisations, i.e. in
a sequence. To explain this assumption, *intra-application parallelism* and *intra-
platform parallelism* must be considered separately.

The intra-application parallelism is not a limitation of the performance prediction methodology itself, since an application behaviour model can be built that

explicitly models the parallelism at the level of concurrently executed services or methods. In fact, the Palladio Component Model that serves as the foundation of this thesis (and whose prediction tooling is extended by this thesis) provides exactly the needed capabilities. Therefore, Formula 1.1 can be applied individually to the application/component parts or services which have no inner concurrency, and the partial performance prediction results can then be fed into a behaviour model that captures the intra-application concurrency and accounts for potential speedup.

The intra-platform parallelism is harder to capture when a black-box platform performance model/profile is used. Here, further research is needed that must combine application analysis and platform analysis. In this thesis, we assume that the building blocks are chosen at such granularity that benchmarking them on the execution platform reveals the intra-platform parallelisation effects *individually for each building block*, so that the effects are then captured through the performance metric values for a given building block. This assumption means that the *ordering* of building blocks in an application does not impact the intra-platform parallelisation – the task of finding the limitations of this assumption are considered to be future work which should build on the findings of this thesis.

1.5. Contributions

In line with the problems and challenges outlined in Section 1.2, this thesis makes the following contributions:

- **Quality metrics and attributes for timer methods**: this thesis formalises the relations between central timer quality metrics such as accuracy and invocation costs, and studies their *combined* impact on measurement accuracy. Additionally, new quality attributes such as epoch stability and stability in multi-threaded scenarios are defined and their importance for reliable timing measurements is demonstrated.

- A **platform-independent approach for quantification of timer method quality attributes** is developed and allows the analysis of timer methods as black boxes, i.e. without having to inspect their implementation or technical details of the underlying execution platform. The approach is implemented in different programming languages and validated on different operating systems and middleware platforms.

- **Quality-driven timer method selection**: a new unified metric is developed which aggregates different quality attributes into a one-valued metric. The new metric allows for easier comparison and selection of timer methods, and it is applied to a large variety of timer methods from different sources and on different execution platforms to provide a quantitative survey of existing timer methods.

- **Platform-independent and application-independent performance metrics**: This thesis establishes bytecode instruction counts *and* method invocation counts as platform-independent performance metrics, and demonstrates the importance of their runtime parameters. This performance metric is used to quantify resource demands of bytecode-based components and applications.

- **Resource demand quantification**: A novel approach for effective, transparent and application-independent quantification of bytecode-level resource demands is developed. The new approach works without requiring specialised/modified execution platform or manual modification of application source code. It is implemented and validated for the Java bytecode.

- **Execution platform benchmarking**: To translate the duration of bytecode-based resource demands into platform-specific timing values, a novel approach for automated benchmarking of bytecode-executing virtual machines is presented. The central contribution of this approach is the *automated* construction of benchmarks to quantify the performance of the execution of Java bytecode instructions and methods on the Java Virtual Machine.

- **Cross-platform performance prediction**: using bytecode-based application resource demands and platform benchmarking results, performance prediction can be performed for several platforms without having to deploy the considered application on all of them. The performance prediction mechanism only requires the application-independent benchmarks to be run on the execution platforms. The prediction addresses the performance effects of Just-in-Time compilation and other runtime optimisations performed by modern execution platforms. The prediction accuracy of the bytecode-based performance prediction is validated for several real-life applications and workloads on several execution platforms with substantially different capabilities and architectures. The validation also shows that the prediction accuracy is better than for prediction based on CPU cycles.

- **Integration into model-based architecture-level performance analysis**: An extension of the Palladio Component Metamodel and its tools has been performed to integrate bytecode-based performance prediction into it. This extension introduced explicit resource interfaces for access of hardware resources and infrastructure components, such as middleware or virtual machines. As a result, the Palladio Component Model can use bytecode-based resource demands of components for its existing capability to predict the performance of concurrent and multi-user application usage scenarios.

In the next section, the validation of these contributions is described.

1.6. Validation

As this thesis makes several contributions, each of them requires a thorough validation to show the contributions' benefits, scope and also their limitations. The validation follows the Goal-Question-Metric approach, which guides the selection of the validation criteria by imposing a top-down process for selection of validation metrics.

For the time-oriented performance indicators, their quality attributes such as reliability, accuracy and overhead are examined in a large study that spans several platforms with different hardware architectures, operating systems, virtual machines, and programming languages. This study demonstrates that the approach developed in this thesis allows educated decisions despite lacking or imprecise documentation, and the tools presented in this thesis eliminate the guesswork on which indicator selection is based in state-of-the-art.

The core contribution of this thesis is the platform-independent performance prediction of black-box bytecode based components, and its validation is performed using several applications and components. These applications include file compression, audio file decoding, encryption as well as several workloads which are used in software and hardware benchmarking and comparison. The applications and workloads originate in widely used, industry-developed, benchmarks such as SPECjbb2005, SPECjvm2008, SPECjvm98, Linpack and JavaGrande, but also include self-written algorithms.

The instrumentation-based resource demand quantification is shown to be precise, and it is validated in terms of overhead and scalability. The benchmarking of methods and APIs is validated with a focus on the novel heuristics that it uses to facilitate finding valid, benchmarking-suitable parameters and invocation targets. Additionally, the quality of benchmarking results and the duration of benchmark generation are discussed. Finally, it is shown that the approach integrates well into the Palladio Component Model.

1.7. Thesis Organisation

Chapter 2 explains the foundations, concepts and terminology that is relevant for this thesis, and explains the relation of existing techniques and tools to the presented thesis and its contributions.

Chapter 3 presents a novel approach for selecting timer-oriented performance indicators, using a well-defined set of quality criteria and test-based techniques for detecting unreliable indicators.

Chapter 4 introduces a framework for instrumentation-based quantification of instruction-precise runtime resource demands made by black-box, bytecode-based components and applications. The distinguishing characteristic of the new framework is that it instruments the applications in a transparent (behaviour-neutral) and portable way so that the instrumented application runs on any standard-compliant bytecode-execution virtual machine. Using basic block analysis and bytecode invariant analysis, the instrumentation overhead is significantly reduced.

Chapter 5 presents a generative approach for creating benchmarks that quantify the performance of bytecode instructions and object-level methods. The results of the benchmarks allow us to predict the performance of applications which use these instructions and methods as building blocks. In particular, the benchmarking results are more than characterisations of the execution platform.

Chapter 6 explains how the platform-specific performance prediction is calculated from platform-independent resource demand quantification results and platform-specific benchmarking results. It also discusses the changes in the Palladio Component Model and its tooling to accommodate the approach introduced in this thesis, in particular the bytecode-oriented resource demands.

Chapter 7 contains the extended, multi-platform validation which uses several applications and workloads as well as different timer methods and performance counters. Chapter 8 discusses related work, and compares it to this thesis and its contributions. Chapter 9 concludes with a summary, discussion of the results and lessons learned, and provides an outlook in the form of future work and possible extensions to the presented approach.

Chapter 2.

Foundations and State-of-the-Art

This chapter lays the foundations for the contributions in the forthcoming chapters, by presenting the context and areas of research targeted by this thesis. The terminology and the current state of research are described, including the limitations of existing solutions. The chapter is structured as follows: Section 2.1 gives an introduction to the field of software performance. Section 2.2 presents the foundations of performance engineering. Section 2.3 provides an overview of benchmarking research and existing benchmarks.

Section 2.4 describes the different techniques for time measurements. Section 2.5 contains an overview of bytecode-executing virtual machines and related middleware concepts. Section 2.7 describes the foundations of bytecode engineering. Section 2.8 explains the notion of instrumentation in the context of this thesis.

Section 2.9 briefly introduces ahead-of-time compilation. Section 2.10 describes resource demand quantification and profiling. Section 2.11 provides an overview of software components and performance analysis in that field of research. Finally, Section 2.13 introduces the Palladio Component Model.

2.1. Software Performance

Performance is a collective term for quantifying how efficiently execution resources are used by an application to perform its tasks. Performance is characterised by setting the amount of accomplished work in relation to the amount of time and resources used during the task processing. Thus, the definition of performance resembles the definition of power in physics, which is computed as the ratio of accomplished work and processing time.

Quantifying performance involves considering both the view of the entity which issues a work request (the client) and the entity which processes that work request (the server). One server can receive and concurrently handle several work requests from distinct clients, and the work requests usually differ in size and complexity.

Performance metrics [43] frequently used in computer science include

- *response time* (i.e. the time needed to accomplish the work requested by a client from a server, measured from client's perspective)

- *utilisation* of a resource, i.e. the percentage of a defined time interval during which the resource is busy performing work

- *throughput*, i.e. the (average) number/size of work items processed in a considered time interval

A short response time is desired because the software user is interested in receiving the answer to her request quickly, as quick request processing by the server makes the client's own work more efficient. When a server receives several requests concurrently, response times increase because incoming requests have to wait until currently processed request(s) complete. Another reason for response time increase during concurrent request processing are switching times between requests. In general, the response time of a work request is determined not only by its size and complexity, but also by the state and the load of the execution platform, which results in resource contention and waiting times. The maximum processing capability of the server is usually limited, and the utilisation of resources cannot grow beyond 100 %.

The server can consist of several hardware and software parts, and it can issue work requests to other servers for processing sub-tasks of the original work request. A client can dispatch work requests in synchronous manner (blocking until work requests processing is completed) and asynchronous manner (continuing while the work request is processed by the server). Note that the client side and the server side can be located on the same physical computer (execution platform): the distinction is only made to explain the different views and roles relevant for performance assessment.

The throughput of a system is usually measured in requests per time unit, and can be computed both for the entire request-processing application (or execution platform) and for individual resources. Of course, the value of the throughput depends on the size and complexity of the requests used for its calculation (smaller requests allow a higher throughput). Therefore, a precise specification of the throughput requires that a characterisation of the requests used for the calculation is specified with it.

The maximum throughput of a system is often called *capacity*, and it is limited by those resources for which the utilisation reaches 100 % and which thus become bottlenecks. Finding bottlenecks and alleviating their impact on the system performance is one of the primary tasks in performance engineering. Note that the utilisation is defined over a time *interval* because for a given time *instant*, the utilisation has a binary value: a resource is either utilised or idle. Thus, computing resource utilisation for a time interval requires sampling of the resource state, and the sampling interval influences the value and the accuracy of the resulting utilisation value. Resource utilisation can also be computed for a given request or a given application, by analysing which request/application is being processed at the time a sample is taken.

The different performance metrics are relevant for different stakeholders: resource utilisation and throughput are relevant for the performance specialists and administrators on the server side, while the response time is relevant both for the client (customer) and the server (which strives to satisfy the customer's expectations). Additionally, developers use these metrics to enhance the performance of the request processing and to control the costs, since an underutilised execution platform means that processing capacities are being wasted.

All of the above metrics have in common that they are based on time values and time intervals. Therefore, accurate measurement of time is essential for accurate measurement of performance metrics. Section 2.4 will address this challenge in more detail.

2.2. Performance Evaluation, Engineering, Optimisation, Modelling and Prediction

Measuring performance metrics requires a deployed, running system (both the client side and the server side) or a running prototype of it, and a workload which makes the client issue work requests to the server. When direct measurements are not precise enough or (technically) impossible or infeasible, indirect measurements (e.g. using Kalman filters [44]) can be used. Indirect measurements derive the desired metric from other metrics, sometimes with a loss of accuracy.

For direct measurements, a large variety of techniques and tools exists, from performance indicators to benchmarks and profilers, which will be covered in the following sections. Still, measuring performance metrics remains a non-trivial task because of lacking support for accurate measurements on execution platforms, and because the measurement and its overhead impact the measured entity. Additionally, traditionally used wall-clock timers become unreliable as the parallelism of applications increases: on multi-core execution platforms, threads and processes of an application can be executed concurrently. On multi-core platforms, concurrent execution results in a speedup of application's execution, although the underlying resource demands remain the same or even increase due to synchronisation overhead. Unfortunately, the granularity of timer methods for measuring thread-individual CPU usage times is too coarse-grained on many platforms [19].

In systematic software engineering, addressing the performance of an application *at the end* of the development phase is too late, because fixing performance issues and bottlenecks is more expensive for a completed application than during the design phase. Therefore, design-time performance evaluation and performance prediction allows software authors to anticipate performance issues and to address them early, before the issues find their way into the application's implementation. Design-time performance evaluation and prediction must operate on performance models of the application, as no measurable implementation exists at that time.

Creating design-time *performance models* requires setting the design model (architectural model) into a relation to the performance information, which can originate from different sources. When applications are built top-down, projected response times for requests are decomposed (usually by estimation) into response times and processing times for sub-requests. While approximative, such an approach allows the developers to monitor whether the projected request response time is later violated by the implementation of a sub-task, and countermeasures can be taken (e.g. exchanging or enhancing the implementation of the task, or adjusting the planned performance metric values for other sub-tasks). Thus, *design-time architectural performance models* can serve as guidelines ("blueprints") for application development.

On the other hand, when an application is developed bottom up (from existing and planned components), an architectural performance model can serve for monitoring the performance of the entire application. Here, too, performance metric values originate from different sources: measurements, estimations and requirements. Regardless of the development approach, design-time architectural performance modelling allows predicting the influence of the four influence factors from Figure 1.1 on the performance of the application.

2.2.1. Model-based Performance Prediction

There are several approaches for performance prediction on the basis of architectural performance models, and they involve *analytical* or *simulation-based* solving of the performance model.

Analytical modelling is represented by queuing networks [21], Petri nets [22], process algebras [11], Markov chains [45] and other formalisms. The performance model can be an instance of such a formalism, or can be translated into it, for example through model transformations. An analytical model is solved using mathematical techniques, which can be both exact and heuristic-based.

While analytical models offer the advantages of fast model solving and a well-studied theoretical underpinnings, they are often too limited for real-life architectural models [46] and too complex for being used by practitioners.

Simulation-based modelling differs from analytical modelling in that it mimics the execution of the modelled system, but introduces simplifications and abstractions. Instead of executing a work step of the simulated scenario directly, a simulation accounts the time needed to execute that work step, adjusts the state of the resources, and proceeds with the next work step immediately after this. Such condensed execution allows simulating request scheduling as well as resource usage and contention, but runs faster than a real execution of the simulated scenario would. Simulations can be derived (e.g. through model transformation) from architectural performance models, and evolve together with application's architectural model and implementation.

Both analytical modelling and simulation-based modelling allow studying design decisions and answering trade-off questions at architectural level. Once parts of the developed application become available, they can be supported by measurements, which are usually more accurate and thus more convincing than estimations.

While the *formalisms* of model-based performance prediction approaches are well-developed and usually very details, the challenge of obtaining resource demands is not addressed by them, and manual measurements are usually assumed to supply resource demand aspects of the modelling.

2.2.2. Software Performance Engineering

To bridge the semantic gap between software development (in particular architectural models) and formal performance modelling, the Software Performance Engineering approach (SPE) was developed by Smith et al. [47]. SPE brings together modelling of the application, application workload, application's resource requests and the modelling of the execution platform and its resources. Additionally, SPE encourages the definition of performance goals and key performance scenarios, which are revisited, refined and reassessed during the design and development phases of the studied product.

SPE covers the software execution modelling (i.e. the static *and* dynamic aspects of architectural modelling) as well as execution platform modelling (called system execution model). SPE encourages focussing on performance-relevant parts of the models and on performance-critical usage scenarios, which can be expressed as service level agreements (SLAs). From usage scenarios (i.e. workloads), an annotated control flow graph has to be created manually, and annotated with resource demands for each of the graph nodes.

The annotations of graph nodes include hardware resource demands which are expressed in a platform-independent way, e.g. as the number of CPU cycles or the number of hard disk accesses. The platform-specific timing values of the platform-independent resource demand units are specified separately, in the so-called *overhead matrix*. The SPE-ED tooling [48, 49] combines several control flow graph into a system execution model, which is translated into a queuing network. The resulting queuing network is solved analytically to obtain performance metrics such as response time or utilisation.

As with model-based approaches, SPE assumes that resource demands are specified by the user – thus, the contribution of this thesis can be useful for SPE, too.

2.3. Benchmarking and Performance Measuring

There exist many approaches and tools for measuring software performance. The simplest, but least scalable way is to modify an application's source code by manually inserting statements for performance measurement. Such statements can make use of timer method, performance indicators, hardware performance counters, etc. Aspect-oriented programming can be used instead of manual insertion, and it allows separating the measurement-related aspects (and code) from the actual measured application.

In contrast to such "white-box" measurements (the application internals have to be known), "black-box" measurements address externally visible interfaces and behaviour of the application. Black-box measurements can be performed manually (by writing performance tests, workload drivers, measurement testbeds etc.) or using supporting tools such as profilers. Performance measurement artefacts are usually developed in an ad-hoc manner and evolve together with the measured product. Yet often, a stable and self-contained artefact is required to measure and to compare a product type (category) or different implementations of a technology. Such artefacts are usually called *benchmarks* and are described in the following.

The term *benchmark* originates from marks made on a workbench since these marks enabled the workers to compare the length of created products, e.g. to ensure their uniformity. As it is hard to compare hardware and software just be analysing their static specifications, dynamic behaviour needs to be analysed to expose the runtime performance (and other quality attributes) of the considered hardware and software. For example, a higher CPU frequency does not mean that that the CPU will execute a given workload faster, e.g. because the cache and the RAM are critical resources for the execution.

In computing, *benchmarking* means running a program or a workload (called *benchmark*) to obtain one or several numeric values (*benchmarking results*) for comparing software and hardware products. For example, performance benchmarking can produce absolute or relative results, e.g. a time value or a score in percent. As multidimensional benchmarking results are harder to compare than a single metric, benchmarks tend to produce a central "key" value which is used for comparison, plus a hierarchy of sub-results which can be used for in-detail comparison. A benchmark can produce aggregate result(s) for a system as a whole, i.e. without addressing the services and capabilities of the system in isolation – but there are also benchmarks that address each system functionality individually.

2.3.1. Benchmark Types

Depending on its composition and origin, a benchmark is called *application benchmark* if it is a real-life application, while a *synthetic* benchmark is a specifically-created workload targeting a sub-part of the benchmarked system. For example, Whetstone [50] is a synthetic benchmark originating in 1972 which targets the floating-point unit of the CPU and which is aware of and protected against compiler optimisations; its result metric is "thousands of Whetstone instructions per second" (kWIPS).

Another synthetic benchmark is Dhrystone [51] from 1984, which can be considered as an ancestor of SPECint2000 [52], but has a rather small codesize, allowing it to fit into the instruction cache of modern CPUs. The output metric of Dhrystone is the number of iterations of the main code loop per second, which is a more meaningful metric than MIPS (million instructions per second) because instruction counts between CISC and RISC should not be compared.

It is also common to extract the "performance hotspots" of an application benchmark into a separate, small benchmark, which is easier and faster to execute but will still give a helpful preview on the performance of the full application. Beyond comparisons of existing (already released) hardware and software, benchmarks are also used often during design and development, to ensure that the developed product will perform well, and to detect issues in design and implementation.

Unfortunately, to obtain good benchmarking results, purposeful and unrealistic "fitting to benchmarks" was performed by some vendors, resulting in strict benchmark *run rules* issued by benchmark authors, e.g. in 1992 for the SPEC CINT92 benchmark [53]. These run rules prescribe which tuning settings, optimisations and configurations are allowed, to ensure that the benchmark results are representative and realistic, and also repeatable by third parties (for verification, etc.). Some benchmark products allow submitting benchmarking results both for the prescribed case, and for an "unlimited" scenario where the benchmark user can optimise and tune at her discretion.

As benchmark authoring and publishing is neither licensed nor controlled, benchmarks can be created both by vendors and independent parties, and their expressiveness, informative value, scope, refinement and other properties vary significantly. A particular product can produce excellent benchmarking results for one benchmark and rank miserably in another.

Correspondingly, vendors tend to publish only those benchmarking results which display their products favourably, and may contest benchmarks where their products do not perform well. Then, it is the task of independent parties (journals and magazines, scientists and consumer protection agencies) to cover both well-performing and under-performing contestants. Also, the cases of *benchmarketing* [54] should be avoided, which occurs benchmarks are created to "make the benchmark numbers as high as possible, regardless of whether they actually have any predicting power".

Benchmark authoring is a challenging task which requires in-depth knowledge of the benchmarked system, benchmarking "best strategies" (patterns) and pitfalls (anti-patterns). Thus, benchmark authoring is a task which needs human thinking and human intelligence during design and development. Still, a few researchers try to generate benchmarks in an automated way (e.g. using model-driven techniques [55]), but their approaches require a formalisation of the system to benchmark, e.g. an architectural model in the case of [55].

While performance is the primary focus of benchmarking in computing, other quality attributes such as security and reliability are also important, but applications and workloads to assess them are rarely called benchmarks, but rather *tests*. Increasingly, energy efficiency (energy costs being one of constituents for cost of ownership) receive attention, resulting in energy ("power") benchmarks from performance evaluation authorities such as SPECpower_ssj2008 [56]. Energy efficiency also leads to performance-dependent metrics, such as "operations per watt".

When a performance benchmark returns just one key value (the benchmark metric), other important performance-related metrics, such as scalability, standard deviation etc. are omitted. Scalability quantifies the performance behaviour of a benchmark when the workload increases, the number of execution system nodes increases, or both. Additionally, it is important how the performance degradation of the benchmarked system looks like when the utilisation of the execution system increases and approaches the saturation point (which may be well below 100 % utilisation). However, for the end user, having stable performance behaviour (e.g. response times of 0.5 seconds with a standard deviation of 0.1 second) may be more important than having low response time with a large standard deviation.

A *microbenchmark* does not benchmark an entire application or system, but rather focuses on a small function or service offered by the system. For example, benchmarking a CPU should stress all components of the CPU (ALU, cache, etc.), while a microbenchmark for floating-point operations can focus on those and does not have to be concerned with memory operations, etc. A kernel-based benchmark such as the Linpack benchmark [57] contains an algorithm (which can be synthetic or extracted from a real application), and usually returns a single metric, such as the MFLOPs (millions of floating-point operations per second).

2.3.2. Overview of Benchmarks

More than a hundred benchmarks of various types, targets, sizes, origins, licensing and ages exist, and there is unfortunately no authority or council to collect and systematise them. Benchmarks developed as industry standards are well-regarded, and usually driven by multi-vendor councils and consortia, such as Standard Performance Evaluation Corporation (SPEC), Transaction Processing Performance Council (TPC), Business Applications Performance Corporation (BAPCo) and Embedded Microprocessor Benchmark Consortium (EEMBC). Existing collections (databases) of benchmarks are limited to separate research fields, e.g. DisCo benchmark database [58] for distributed computing.

Industry-standard benchmarks for desktop and enterprise Java include SPECjvm2008 [59], SPECjbb2005 [59], SPECjAppServer2004 [60], as well as their predecessors. SPECjvm2008 is a benchmark for client JVMs (i.e. local application execution), and it contains several workloads, such as audio file decoding, file compression, mathematical computations, Monte Carlo algorithm, Fourier transform, and others.

SPECjbb2005 models a three-tier distributed enterprise system with ware-houses and stresses XML processing and precise numeric calculations using Java's `BigInteger` class. SPECjAppServer2004 addresses benchmarking of Java Enterprise Edition implementations, i.e. it targets Java EE application serv-ers. SPECjAppServer2004 is an end-to-end benchmark which exercises the web container (incl. servlets and JSPs), the EJB container, container-managed persist-ence, messaging services and transaction management.

Other Java benchmarks are JavaGrande [61, 62], DaCapo [63], HBench:Java [32], UCSD Benchmarks for Java [64], and a benchmark from JavaWorld [65]. Surprisingly, there exist no industry-standard .NET bench-marks, and only a few research-grade benchmarks, e.g. [66, 67].

For benchmarking end-user personal computers in their entirety (rather than a technology or a hardware/software component), third-party benchmarks such as PCmark [68, 69] are available. Some operating system vendors even supply their products with built-in benchmarks which can be run by end users and serve to compare the performance of an operating system across execution plat-forms. For example, the Windows System Assessment Tool (WinSAT) is a com-ponent of the Microsoft Windows Vista and Windows 7 operating systems.

WinSAT measures various performance characteristics and capabilities of the hardware and reports them as a Windows Experience Index (WEI) score. This score has a decimal point range between 1.0 and a version-specific upper bound that is slated to increase in future operating system versions. The WEI expli-citly lists five sub-scores (CPU, hard disk, main memory, 2D and 3D graphics), the reported WEI value is the minimum of the sub-scores. The WEI has differ-ent usage scenarios: finding the least powerful hardware resource of a system, comparison between hardware configurations, specifying the hardware require-ments of a software product, etc.

2.3.3. Summary

Summarising the current state of benchmarking, it can be said that while there exists an overwhelming number of benchmarks, none of them is able to quantify the performance of *individual services* offered by a Java Virtual Machine, or a (generic) Java API. Similarly, no benchmark exists that quantifies the perform-ance (execution duration) of bytecode instructions.

In particular, it is not possible to predict the performance of an arbitrary Java application from the results of an existing Java benchmark, except when the considered application is identical or very similar to an existing benchmark. However, defining and quantifying similarities between a benchmark and a real-world application is a separate challenge.

While some approaches to quantify the performance similarities between app-lications are available (e.g. [70, 71]), their require the applications to be character-ised at microarchitecture level (i.e. CPU instruction mix, behaviour of branches, register allocation). Thus, these similarity-based approaches are not platform-independent, and must be performed on each candidate hardware type.

Thus, existing benchmarks are not suitable as a basis for cross-platform per-formance prediction.

2.4. An Overview of Timer Methods, Timers and Counters

Time is a fundamental one-dimensional physical quantity (according to Interna-tional System of Units, SI [72, p. 105]), with normed units such as second, milli-second, minute, etc. Measuring time is quintessential for quantifying and com-paring software and hardware performance, since performance metrics such as throughput, response *time*, utilisation etc. are based on time. While philosoph-ers disagree on whether time *per se* can be measured (claiming what is con-sidered as time is in fact the occurrence of periodic events), this thesis treats time as a measurable entity. Additionally, the assumption is made that the con-sidered systems are not measurably affected by time dilation and other effects resulting from relativity theory.

2.4.1. Hardware Performance Counters and Monitors

Given that time units are normed (one second is defined using the amount of radiation emitted by caesium), it is possible to measure the time by repeating the underlying experimental setup. However, it is more convenient to resort to simpler (albeit less precise) techniques: in modern computers and electronic clocks, crystals oscillating under voltage with a known, stable frequency are used. A hardware register is then keeping track of the number of oscillations (or a derived, proportional value).

A *hardware performance counter* is a generic term for a hardware register that can store the value a performance metric (the term *hardware performance monitor* is also widely used). It is expected that the usage of hardware performance counters does not impact the execution of the actual workload. This counter-stored metric may or may not increase at constant rate: a hardware performance counter can contain the number of CPU cache misses, the number of executed CPU cycles, etc. Especially for CPU cycles, it should be noted that multi-core CPUs with individually deactivatable cores, but also variable CPU speeds (as provided by SpeedStep and other technologies) can lead to the situation where the number of executed CPU cycles does not exhibit linear correlation with time.

The quantity of registers that can store hardware performance counter values is limited, and varies between CPU models and manufacturers. Thus, it is only possible to obtain a limited selection of performance counter values at the same time, and multiplexing is used when more counter types are available than registers to save their values. When more counter types are needed than can fit into the available registers, a measurement must be repeated until all requested counter types have been covered – however, this also requires the measurement runs to be identical so that counter values can be considered as if they would originate from a single measurement.

The hardware performance counters provide the advantage of (supposedly) low-overhead access to the performance indicators of the CPU, but they require software to aggregate and to interpret the obtained values. For example, if a register contains CPU cycles count, obtaining timing values requires to convert the register value using CPU frequency, which may vary over time, e.g. depending on CPU load or OS energy saving settings. Additionally, to map the work request to the values of performance counters, it must be analysed whether the work request shape and characteristics remain the same when it arrives at the hardware level, i.e. at the CPU.

For example, one source of imprecision associated with direct usage of hardware performance counters comes into play in the context of out-of-order instruction processing, or when CPU pipelining is adjusted due to pipeline stalls, cache misses and other events. In such cases, the hardware performance counter value may refer to different parts of the workload than planned. *Instruction-Based Sampling* [73] is a performance analysis technique introduced by AMD in 2007 to mitigate the pipelining-caused problems with hardware performance counters, and used in performance profiling and optimisation on multi-core platforms [74, 75] and for memory subsystems [76].

Also, the basic question of *how precise* hardware performance counters are requires attention and investigation, and needs to be repeated as new CPU architectures and generations appear.

Hardware performance counters are widely used in current research, especially in the area of operating systems and multi-core performance [77, 78, 79]. They have superseded earlier technology, such as programmable profiling coprocessors [80]. Of course, the main use of hardware performance counters (apart from the operating system and the hardware itself) is made by tools for performance analysis, debugging, prediction, and optimisation.

Time-oriented hardware performance counters such as the timestamp counter (TSC) or the high-precision event timer (HPET) are complicated or impossible to be used directly by the performance-measuring applications for various reasons. To obtain timing values, the TSC values must be compensated for changes in CPU frequency; on platform supported by PAPI library, TSC can be accessed using a C API, instead of assembler instructions. As PAPI offers no access to HPET, it must be read using assembler instructions. Also, support for HPET is not available in a substantial number of operating systems, e.g. in Windows XP.

TSC (the Time Stamp Counter) is a 64-bit register present on many, but not all, x86 and x64 processors [81]. Although the TSC is considered to have a high accuracy and a low overhead, its use is problematic when the CPU clock rate changes (e.g. in energy-saving CPU modes), when out-of-order execution of instructions happens, or on multi-core/multi-CPUs machines (due to unsynchronised TSCs). Relying on TSC may also reduce portability, and a number of Intel processors include a constant-rate TSC, i.e. it is read at the CPU's *maximum* clock rate regardless of the *actual* CPU clock rate, invalidating measurements where execution is partially performed at a lower clock rate. TSC counts the number of CPU ticks since the last CPU reset, and is accessible through the RDTSC ("read TSC") assembler instruction. The RDTSC can be wrapped for Java access using JNI, but the code needed for wrapping differs between operating systems. For the case study, the Linux and Mac OS X versions were self-written, while Windows version was based on a DLL and associated JNI code provided by Roedy Green [82].

HPET (High-Precision Event Timer) is a newer timer that has appeared around 2005. Its minimum update frequency of 10 MHz and is often considered as a more modern alternative to TSC or the real-time clock (RTC). However, HPET's use is restricted: it is not available from Windows XP, Windows Server 2003 or Linux with Kernel 2.4 and older. Therefore, HPET hasn't been evaluated, but its usage by the timer methods will become visible as evaluation results of JVM-provided timer methods are interpreted.

PIT (Programmable Interval Timer) is an older periodic counter originally implemented on a separate chip (e.g. Intel 8253/8254, value stored using 16 bits). The PIT was designed to update at a constant frequency of 1.193182 MHz (i.e. an update each 838 ns) , but the system clock accuracy would be much more coarse, as the system clock would be updated once every 65536 ($=2^{16}$) PIT ticks. In any case, the PIT is inferior to HPET and TSC, and has not been evaluated in this thesis. Hence, the only hardware counter considered during the validation will be the TSC, as it is the only hardware timer broadly available and widely used. Still, the algorithms developed in the next chapter can be applied to the other counters timers, e.g. using a JNI implementation accessing them. Thus, programmers should use functionality and performance indicators provided by operating systems, virtual machines etc., which are presented in the next sections.

Profilers with documented use of hardware performance counters include VI-Prof [83, 84], LIKWID [85], KOJAK [86], ScALPEL [87]. Performance-related research using hardware performance counters includes [79, 88, 89, 90, 91, 92, 81, 93] and hundreds of others, with some work in the combined area of performance and energy efficienty.

The wide usage of hardware performance counters means that their accuracy and other quality characteristics (usage overhead, dependability, stability, etc.) are critical for the tools depending on the counters. Given the large number or hardware performance counters, and the progress in hardware development, only a very limited amount of research on the *quality* of hardware performance counters is documented. This may be due to the complexity of the undertaking (fine-granular counter information, complex CPU behaviour), but also due to the *trust* into the manufacturer's capability to provide dependable hardware counters.

Araiza et al. [94] have developed a cross-platform microbenchmark suite for evaluating hardware performance counter data. They compared predicted counts with measured counter values and concluded that for the studied counters and hardware (i.e. in 2005), the results did match. However, Araiza et al. did not analyse the accuracy and other quality attributes of the counters, and no follow-up work on the proposed microbenchmark has been reported.

Zaparanuks et al. [95] have performed a comparative study of the accuracy of three measurement infrastructures (PAPI, perfctr and perfmon2) on three CPUs (Core 2 Duo, and AMD Athlon 64 X2 and Pentium D). The work in [95] is focused on cycle counts, and provides an in-detail analysis *at sub-OS level*, which is not useful for selecting performance indicators to use in application-level benchmarking. [95] does not address the accuracy of OS-provided and VM-provided hardware counter interface and performance counter interfaces.

Dongarra et al. analyse [96] describe accuracy estimation among the experiences and lessons learned with an older version of PAPI (from around 2002, [97]). PAPI is a portable interface to hardware performance counters that is also used by Zaparanuks et al. in [95], and which has been significantly expanded and redesigned since then [98].

Summarising the state of research concerning hardware performance counter, it becomes obvious that despite wide usage of the counters, little is known about their accuracy and other quality attributes. Furthermore, there is a semantic gap between the application performance metrics (such as response time) and hardware performance counters such as CPU cycles or cache misses.

2.4.2. Software-Provided Performance Indicators

In the software layers above hardware, different performance indicators are maintained and exposed by different applications and components. Each operating system maintains a collection of performance indicators about itself, which are used for scheduling and other core operating tasks, e.g. detection of hanging applications, CPU mode switching, etc. As a service to OS-hosted applications and to the human user, some of these performance indicators are exposed, either in the context of an API, or using an application (either with or without a GUI).

For example, the Activity Monitor of Mac OS X is a GUI application that shows (for each running process) its CPU time (i.e. the time the CPU spent executing this process), current CPU and memory usage, number of threads, number of system and kernel calls, context switches, etc. Additionally, it shows system-wide CPU usage (broken up into per-core information), system-wide disc and network activity, etc.

A similar command-line tool is `top` (also available on Linux). The recent editions of the Windows operating system offer a feature-rich GUI application that is called Process Explorer, which offers a superset of the functionality provided by the Task Manager application. For detailed profiling of HDD accesses on Mac OS X, the command-line tool `iosnoop` is available, which depends on DTrace.

DTrace [99, 100] is a comprehensive dynamic tracing framework created for use in the Solaris operating system. Its original task was to assist in troubleshooting kernel and application problems since it allows getting a global overview of a running system. This overview includes per-process usage of system's resources such as main memory, CPU, file system and network connections. It can also provide very fine-grained logging details, e.g. the arguments with which a specific function is being called, or a list of the processes possessing handles to a specific file.

Despite its award-winning power and careful minimisation of tracing's effects on performance, DTrace has found only a limited popularity. Possible reasons may be the requirement to learn a separate language called D, and the fact that the market share of the Solaris operating system is limited. Still, open-sourcing of DTrace has allowed for porting to FreeBSD, NetBSD and Mac OS X (introduced in version 10.5); the latter also provides a GUI called Instruments. For Linux, SystemTap [101] provides an approach similar to DTrace, and ProbeVue [102] targets the AIX operating system.

2.4.3. Timer Methods

All timer methods discussed in this section return 64 bit values, but not all of them can use the entire range, as explained in Section 7.2.5. The timer methods fall into two categories: OS-provided ones and those provided by middleware such as virtual machines.

OS-provided timer methods abstract away from hardware timer problems and the intricacies described above. However, the OS-provided timers introduce additional overhead when compared to the underlying counter, and they often rely on TSC, leading to issues with CPUs not properly implementing it [103], [104]. Furthermore, many applications are built on top of virtual machines (VMs) which provide their own timer methods that should (or must) be used instead of the specific timer methods provided by operating systems.

VM-provided timer methods provide uniform timer access independent of the underlying hardware/software platform. In this thesis, bytecode-executing virtual machines such as the Java Virtual Machine and the .NET Common Language Runtime (CLR) are considered.

In the following, the timer methods that will be studied during the validation are presented, starting with OS-provided methods.

- QPC (`QueryPerformanceCounter()`) is the Windows API method accessible from C/C++, which returns the underlying counter's state, and not time units. The separate `QueryPerformanceFrequency()` method reports the update frequency of the counter used by the `QueryPerformanceCounter()` method. Using Java Native Interface, these methods have been made accessible from Java; for .NET, the `System.Runtime.InteropServices` mechanism has been used for accessing them from the C# programming language.

- GTOD (`gettimeofday`) is the Linux API method that allows querying the current time, down to a microsecond. `gettimeofday` has been made accessible from Java for evaluation in this thesis using JNI. Also for Linux, the methods `clock_gettime` and `clock_getres` (defined in `time.h` C header file) are available, which allow the method user to select (using method parameters) which clocks are accessed. Accessible clocks include the system-wide realtime clock, a monotonic clock that cannot be reset, a high-resolution per-process timer from the CPU, and a thread-specific CPU time clock. `clock_gettime` and `clock_getres` haven't been analysed in the scope of this thesis.

- CTM (`java.lang.System.currentTimeMillis()`) is a static wall-clock timer method with milliseconds as units, thus being a rather coarse-grained time method

- NANO (`java.lang.System.nanoTime()`) is a wall-clock timer method (available since Java 1.5) with nanoseconds as units, but with the official API documentation saying that it has "nanosecond precision, but not necessarily nanosecond accuracy"

- CTCT (`java.lang.management.ThreadMXBean.getCurrent-ThreadCpuTime()`) is a method of the Java platform's management API which returns the calling thread's used CPU time (in nanoseconds, covering both system mode and user mode). It must be enabled with `java.lang.management.ThreadMXBean.setThreadCpuTime-Enabled(true)` provided that it is supported at all (which can be checked with `isThreadCpuTimeSupported()`).

- CTUT (`....ThreadMXBean.getCurrentThreadUserTime()`) is similar to CTCT, but returns only the time spent in user mode, not in system mode. Note that while it appears logical that the time spend *only* in system mode can be computed as the difference of values returned by these two methods, the invocation cost and the delay between the two calls can render the computation imprecise when the measured intervals are short.

- CPCT (`com.sun.management.OperatingSystemMXBean.getProcessCpuTime()`, `com.sun.management.UnixOperatingSystemMXBean.getProcessCpuTime()`) belong to the JMX API as do CTCT and CTUT. These two classes implement the `java.lang.management.OperatingSystemMXBean` interface, but unfortunately, the interface itself does not provide the `getProcessCpuTime()` method, and neither do any public classes in the Java Platform API. As can be seen by their package names, the two classes are not part of the public Java Platform API – still, the `com.sun` package is available on many JVMs beyond the market-defining JVM of the Oracle Inc. (which bought Sun Microsystems, the inventor of Java). For example, the JVM shipped with Mac OS X operating system contains `UnixOperatingSystemMXBean`. The method `getProcessCpuTime()` returns "the CPU time used by the process on which the Java virtual machine is running" in nanoseconds, but the returned value can be -1 if the platform does not support CPU process time accounting. Such a case (negative returned results) is checked in the implementation of algorithms from this thesis to prevent the algorithm from running too long as it would be the case if the timer interval values of 0 $((-1) - (-1))$ would be interpreted as "very large accuracy, and work between timer method invocations needs to be increased until the timer interval length reaches 1 accuracy".

- HRC (`sun.misc.Perf.highResCounter()`) is a proprietary (and un-documented, but `publicly` accessible) high-resolution timer method. It is located among the classes implementing the Java Platform API, and is notably different from Platform API methods in that it returns values in ticks and not (nano-/milli-) seconds. Additionally, it is not a static method, requiring the programmers to instantiate an instance of `sun.misc.Perf`. This class is shipped with JDK 1.5 and later not only with the official Or-acle/Sun distributions of the JRE/JDK, but also with the version 1.6 of JRE/JDK bundled with Mac OS X (tested with Mac OS X 10.6.4). Using the method `highResFrequency()`, the frequency of this timer can be queried, which allows converting the ticks into (nano-)seconds. Due to low visibility and portability concerns, this timer is rarely used directly, and be-fore the `nanoTime()` method was added to the Java platform API in ver-sion 1.5, many third-party tools were created to provide timers with better precision (and, thus, better accuracy) than `currentTimeMillis()`' *mil-liseconds*. Some of these tools are still used today, e.g. for systems that run on pre-1.5 JVMs.

Several *third-party tools* that provide Java-accessible timer methods exist. The validation in Chapter 7 will only consider timer methods that are available *both* for Windows *and* Linux operating systems; thus, PAPI [105] and PCL [106] will not be considered, though the algorithms presented in the next chapter (and their Java implementations) can be applied to them as well. Also, while PAPI is being developed and updated, the last version of PCL dates from January 2003.

Instead, the JETM (Java Execution Time Measurement Library [107]) and GAGEtimer (Genuine Advantage Gaming Engine timer [108]) have been con-sidered as candidates:

- `JETM`: the JETM library selects the "best" available timer using `bestAvailableTimer()` helper method of its class `EtmMonitorFactory`. The timer method used on the obtained timer class type/instance was `getCurrentTime()`.

- `GAGE`: from the GAGEtimer library, the method `getClockTicks()` in class `AdvancedTimer` is used; the clock's frequency can be queried using `getTicksPerSecond()`.

.NET is a software framework developed by Microsoft Corporations for Windows platforms, with parts of the framework being accepted as standards by ECMA and ISO, thus allowing cross-platform implementations by other parties. The algorithms presented in Chapter 3 have been applied to the timer methods provided by the .NET API to show the algorithms' benefits beyond Java applications. In particular, the application of the algorithms will show that the vendor-specified update frequency of .NET timer methods can be misleading, and the timer method accuracy is an order of magnitude larger than one timer tick.

The .NET framework makes use of a *Common Type System*, which allows the applications to access the .NET API (implemented by the so-called *Base Class Library*) from different languages, such as C#. The virtual machine of the .NET framework is called Common Language Runtime (CLR), and it executes .NET bytecode (*Common Language Infrastructure*). The Mono framework [109] is an alternative implementation of the .NET framework which runs on Windows, Mac OS X, Linux and other platforms.

The .NET API provides just two timer methods which return results in ticks rather than as timing values, but with the bonus that their update frequency (at least for the Microsoft implementation) is either fixed and specified, or platform-dependent but queryable.

- `.DAT`: The first studied timer method is the `DateTime` structure in the `System` namespace, which represents an instant in time, stored as a 64-bit number of ticks. The .NET documentation states that each tick corresponds to 100 ns; this unit information was verified and confirmed with the

43

algorithm described in Section 3.4. `DateTime` has a property called `Now` that denotes *current* local time of the used computer, with values ranging from midnight, January 1st, 0001 through the end of December 31st, 9999. The .NET API documentation states that the accuracy of this property depends on the system timer, and specifies that the accuracy is 55 ms on Windows 98 and 10 ms on Windows NT and newer versions. This means that the `DateTime.Now` values should increase in steps of 100,000 ticks. Note that there is no method or field in `DateTime` to query the accuracy, and that the invocation cost is not queryable, too.

- `.STO`: The second studied timer method is `StopWatch` class in the `System.Diagnostics` namespace, which is described as a means to provide "a set of methods and properties that you can use to accurately measure elapsed time". It is possible to query its update frequency using `Stopwatch.Frequency`, and whether it offers a high resolution (using `IsHighResolution`). The documentation states that `StopWatch.GetTimestamp()` method can be used in place of the unmanaged Win32 APIs `QueryPerformanceFrequency` and `QueryPerformanceCounter()`. Note that `StopWatch` should me more precise (or, in the worst case) as precise as `DateTime.Now`.

2.4.4. Summary

A large number of timer methods, hardware performance counters and software performance indicators exists. Many of them are specific to a hardware architecture, an operating system, or a middleware product. In platform-independent environments such as the Java Virtual Machine, platform API methods shield the user from platform-specific details. Unfortunately, most timer methods do not provide the information on the accuracy and other quality attributes of the measurement results.

Even when APIs that access performance counters expose the update frequency of the underlying counter, quality metrics such as invocation cost remain unresolved. For a performance engineer, the selection among timer methods and performance counters remains a guessing-based task when confronted with black-box, platform-independent APIs. Therefore, an approach to support this selection is needed, as the accuracy of techniques used in performance measurements is critical for the accuracy of the measurement results.

2.5. Middleware, Virtual Machines and Bytecode

Middleware is a term which describes "plumbing" software residing in the layer above the operating system and below the application, i.e. in the *middle* between the latter. Middleware encapsulates the functionalities required by more than one application, but not offered by the operating system, for example inter-application communication (also across physical machines, e.g. using CORBA for remote procedure calls), object-relational persistance (e.g. Hibernate), etc.

Another role played by the middleware is to be the broker between the different (and often incompatible) applications, which could not exchange information directly due to mismatches in formatting, etc. Additionally, middleware supports distributed computing, especially in the case where newer software has to been connected to older ("legacy") software, e.g. using message-passing brokers. Transaction coordinators and transaction monitors are also considered as middleware, especially when the coordinate transactions spanning several participants.

Distributed, interoperability-centred computation paradigms such as service-oriented computing (SOA), grid computing as well as cloud computing require middleware, too. Over time, the term "middleware" has come to describe software products that provide *interoperability* layers, making applications OS-independent and often also hardware-independent. The interoperability role of middleware has led to the development of technologies for *writing portable applications*, in particular using virtual machines.

A *virtual machine* is a software-implemented instruction set (usually defined by a specification) and a facility for executing the instructions from this set, as long as they adhere to the specification and are packaged in a documented format. A well-known example of virtual machine middleware is the Java Virtual Machine [110], whose instruction set is known as Java bytecode.

The instruction set of a virtual machine can be similar to the instruction set of a hardware CPU, but usually has a higher level and abstracts from hardware details such as registers, machine code format, etc. For example, the Java bytecode is stack-centred and the Java Virtual Machine has been implemented on many different hardware architectures (ARM, x86, x86-64, etc.) and many different operating systems. The Java slogan "write once, run everywhere" reflects the fact that an application compiled to Java bytecode can run on any Java Virtual Machine (at least as long as no platform-specific native code is part of the application).

A middleware product usually exposes its functionality through services which can be used by applications – but for virtual machines, the "interface" between the application and the middleware is the bytecode-executing program that is part of the middleware. For example, the Java Virtual Machine provides a platform-independent program launcher whose name, parameter set and the basic properties are fundamentally the same across implementations – again, this is mandated by the Java technology creator (Sun Microsystems, acquired in 2010 by Oracle Corporation). By devising a Technology Compatibility Toolkit that must be passed by JVM implementations to gain compliance confirmation, Sun Microsystems has ensured that the JVM implementations follow the specification.

Beyond the program launcher and the bytecode format, virtual machines provide a collection of utility classes, accessible over an application programming interface (API). For example, the Java Virtual Machine provides the Java Platform API, which offers platform-independent functionality such as data structures ("collections"), file system access, etc. The platform API greatly simplifies application programming, and can be implemented and ported by JVM vendors, while the the interfaces of the API serve as the contract between the application programmer and API provider.

The term virtual machine has obtained a second, distinctive meaning with the increasing popularity of operating system virtualisation, where an instance of an operating system that runs in a virtualised platform is called virtual machine. OS virtualisers (such as Xen, VirtualBox, etc.) shield running virtual machines from each other, allow users to assign fixed or variable resource shares to virtual machines, etc. OS virtualisers are not considered in this thesis.

2.6. Just-in-Time Compilation

Java programs run on any standard-compliant Java Virtual Machine (JVM) because they are compiled to platform-independent bytecode. However, Java bytecode must be *interpreted*: each bytecode instruction is parsed at runtime and mapped to one or several platform-specific instructions (CPU instructions), or even API/OS calls. One-by-one instruction interpretation is slow, and initially (in early JVMs), Java programs were found to be substantially slower than the same program/algorithm written in C/C++ and compiled to native, platform-specific code.

Execution of bytecode can be sped up without sacrificing the "compile once, run everywhere" property when programs (or parts thereof) are *dynamically translated* to platform-specific instructions *at runtime*. When runtime translation of bytecode to machine code is possible, the interpretation overhead can be removed and optimisations (e.g. constant folding and loop unrolling) can be applied to entire methods. Since the dynamic compilation of bytecode is often scheduled so that its results will become available at a certain point of time (or when a particular program location is reached), it is often called *just-in-time* (JIT) compilation, analogously to the just-in-time delivery of parts in car manufacturing, where it eliminates the costs of stock-keeping and overstocking.

As Section 2.14 will demonstrate, such optimisations can result in speedups well over an order of magnitude. The work presented in this thesis explicitly deals with the performance-relevant optimisations performed by the Java Virtual Machine at runtime. These runtime optimisations are the distinctive features showcased by the JVM vendors and the runtime optimisations are a subject of continuous enhancements. The central role is usually taken by the *Just-In-Time compiler* (JIT compiler), which analyses a running Java application to find "hot spots" (frequently executed or performance-heavy methods) for which the bytecode recompilation is most beneficial.

The JIT compiler then recompiles the hot spots *concurrently*, i.e. while the non-optimised bytecode of the application is executed. Once the hotspot is available in a native (platform-specific) version, the JVM replaces the bytecode of the hotspot implementation through the native implementation. It is important to highlight that this replacement takes place while the application continues to run.

The challenges of dealing with JIT compilation in JVMs arise when the indeterminism and gradualness of the JIT compilation must be considered. The main questions here are following:

- the **speedup** of the compiled method and its effect on the overall performance of a component service or even on an entire application

- **"what"**: which methods are compiled and which are interpreted

- **"when"**: the minimum number of executions that JIT compiler sees as sufficient for JIT compilation of a method

- **"how far"**: modern JIT compilers are capable of multi-staged compilation, where a method is further optimised as it is "getting hotter"

- **"permanence"**: the JVM can revert to the interpretation of a method if some assumptions done during the compilation, e.g. assumptions on method usage in polymorphic environments, change and the JIT-compiled code becomes incorrect

Some JIT compilers (such as the Oracle HotSpot JIT compiler) can be run in different modes. For example, the HotSpot compiler has a *client mode* tuned for end-user, workstation JVMs where short startup times are more important than higher speedup, and a *server mode* tuned for long-running applications where large-scale optimisations pay off.

The speedup effect of JIT compilation varies between programs, depending on how much *can* be optimised, and on how much *is* optimized and *when*. In particular, the internal structure of a program is a key factor – this includes the coding style and the efficiency of the code.

For example, consider a simple example where a method contains the loop which two additions of two different but constant value to a variable (the variable is used by the method so that the addition is not an instance of "dead code" which can be eliminated without side effects):

```
for(int i=0; i<max; i++){globalvar+=13; globalvar+=15;}
```

In this very simple example, not only the two additions can be merged into one, but modern JIT compilers can perform program analysis and if max is found to be a constant value on each run of the method containing the loop, the *entire* loop can be replaced by a *single* operation on GLOBALVAR. Current JIT compilers offer adaptive recompilation, on-stack replacement and other sophisticated techniques [111].

Compared to ahead-of-time compilation (cf. Section 2.9 for a discussion of AOT compilation), JIT has both advantages and disadvantages. The advantages are that JIT compilation does not prevent the program from starting *immediately*, and the compilation of the program is focusing on areas where a substantial performance gain is expected, which leads to lower compilation costs. Additionally, JIT can make use of profile-guided optimizations, which are based on profile data collected at runtime. AOT compilation has the disadvantage of higher upfront costs and a delayed program startup, as well as potential issues with polymorphism and runtime bindings (unless supported by checks in the generated native code or by the execution platform). The advantage of AOT is that the compilation results can be serialised (stored persistently) and reused on next program startup, whereas JIT compilation is usually starting all over again on each program start (although, conceptually, JIT compilation could store and re-use behaviour/hints/results as long as the program/bytecode of the considered method remains unchanged. Other bytecode-based execution environments use AOT compilation and precompilation – for example, the .NET Native Image

Generator [112] precompiles not only the bytecode of the applications, but also the bytecode of the classes implementing the .NET platform API.

The JIT compilation is not limited to bytecode-based environments: for example, JavaScript engines of contemporary browsers also speed up the execution of JavaScript, as does the Nanojit library [113] of the Mozilla Foundation for the Firefox browser.

2.7. Bytecode Engineering

Compiling source code into bytecode is not the only way to create bytecode. *Bytecode engineering* denotes direct dealing with bytecode, without decompiling it into source code. Bytecode engineering is an aggregate term for bytecode operations such as direct bytecode creation (without source code of the created application), modifying existing source code, obfuscating it, etc.

Usage scenarios for bytecode engineering [114, 115] include aspect-oriented programming (the aspects are woven into the compiled bytecode of the application), refactoring (e.g. Retrotranslator for Java [116]), automated test generation [117], code generation in application servers [118], object-relation data mappings, and many more. Bytecode engineering is not limited to research and experimental applications, but is an established technique in enterprise applications and commercially available software.

To allow the creation and manipulation of bytecode classfile contents, a bytecode engineering framework usually provides an object-oriented representation of the classfile contents. After the framework user has modified this representation as intended, the framework creates the executable bytecode from the representation. To simplify the dealing with bytecode, a bytecode engineering framework usually introduces simplifications and assistive tooling: for example, Java bytecode engineering frameworks such as ASM [114] tend to shield the framework user from the tedious tasks of calculating maximum stack height, administrating the constant pool, etc.

There exist many bytecode engineering frameworks for different bytecode languages, but only a couple of them enjoy maturity, stability, up-to-date sup-

port of bytecode standards, continued development as well as support and feedback by developers and the user community. For the Java implementation of the
concept of this thesis, the ASM framework [114] has been chosen on the basis of
these criteria.

2.8. Instrumentation

An instrument is a tool with a technical, scientific or medical purpose, usually
for measuring a quantifiable property such as speed, temperature, time, etc.
The term *instrumentation* encompasses instruments as well as infrastructure to
initialise them, read their values etc. In computing, instrumentation is used to
measure software and hardware performance, but also to trace and log program
execution and values of variables, as well as to diagnose errors.

An example of instrumentation in computing is the appropriately-named
Apple Mac OS X application INSTRUMENTS, which is performance analyser
and visualiser integrated with XCode, the vendor-provided multi-language free
IDE. INSTRUMENTS is built on top of the DTrace tracing framework [119, 99]
and shows graphs and statistics of events occurring in the studied application.
The events are displayed arranged on a time axis, and include CPU activity,
memory allocation, file activity, etc.; is is also possible to record user-generated
events and replay them as required to see the effect of code modifications.

The instrumentation itself consists of instructions, which can be both inserted
into the original application, or be separate from it and called by the execution
platform as it executes the application. Often, the instrumentation can be configured ("managed") and augmented using a service provider interface (SPI);
instrumentation also often provides applications and users access to hardware
performance counters which are otherwise complicated to use. Note that instrumentation and *profiling* are different but related terms: profiling aggregates,
interprets and visualises "raw" performance data, which can originate from instrumentation, but also from sampling, indirect measurements and other techniques. On the other hand, instrumentation is not limited to providing data for
profiling.

Instrumentation can be implemented as source code instrumentation (e.g. by inserting code to read and save timer values) or binary instrumentation (where the instrumentation is inserted into the compiled application, e.g. using bytecode engineering or machine code engineering [120]. The term *bytecode instrumentation* is used in a more broad term than for tracing/logging/measuring/profiling/monitoring [121, 122, 123]: bytecode instrumentation can add facilities for security [124, 125], help in implementing "design by contract" paradigm [126, 127], etc. Note that while bytecode engineering is a more general technique to augment *and modify* bytecode, bytecode *instrumentation* generally refers to *additive* changes, i.e. the original semantics are to be preserved.

A number of different tools and techniques for instrumentation exists, both for source-code instrumentation and binary code (e.g. bytecode) instrumentation. Early bytecode instrumentation approaches include BIT [128]; over time, bytecode instrumentation has become one of the tasks performed by bytecode engineering tools.

Instrumentation can be supported in a programming language (e.g. `System.Diagnostics.Trace` in $C\#$), or by the execution system (e.g. the Instrumentation API in the `java.lang.instrument` package of the Java Platform API). The latter allows instrumenting programs running on the JVM, by providing `ClassFileTransformer` and `Instrumentation` interfaces which can be implemented by a programmer.

The result of implementing these interfaces is an *instrumentation agent* which can instrument all loaded Java classes *except* classes belonging to the implementation of the Platform API (which, if allowed, could subvert the security mechanisms of the JVM). An instrumentation agent can be used both when a JVM is started up, and attached to a running JVM, research to allow instrumentation of classes belonging to the platform API is underway [129].

2.9. Ahead-Of-Time Compilation (AOT)

An alternative solution to bytecode interpretation (which is slow, simple but universal) and Just-In-Time compilation (which is faster but complicated and selective) is Ahead-Of-Time compilation (AOT) [130, 131]. AOT compilers translate platform-independent bytecode into platform-specific machine code, with the expectation of better performance than pure interpretation or than runtime JIT compilation. Of course, AOT-compiled programs lose their platform independence and the Java idea of "compile once, run everywhere" no longer holds for them.

AOT compilers can be standalone tools for use by application programmers or by end users, but AOT compilers can be also integrated into JVMs to provide transparent, seamless bytecode execution experience. The AOT compilation can be performed right on the execution platform before the application is executed, and the binary form of the application can be persisted for faster startup. In principle it is also possible to perform AOT cross-compilation [132], i.e. to perform the compilation of bytecode for a specific platform on a different platform.

Despite its promise, AOT has not found such a broad use in Java platforms as did JIT compilation. One possible reason may be that major desktop/enterprise JVM vendors (Sun Microsystems, Oracle/BEA, IBM) do not provide end-user AOT compilers. In other Java settings with higher importance of performance, AOT has gained a stronger foothold: some Java Micro Edition JVMs for portable devices and JVMs for real-time Java come with an integrated AOT compiler.

Other reasons for the slow (or under-publicised) adoption of AOT in the enterprise sector may be the following:

- The performance differences between JIT-compiled code and AOT-compiled code are either unknown or considered not significant enough for specific applications

- JVM-based and JVM-oriented tools such as Java profilers, memory usage analysers or Java heap inspectors cannot be applied easily to native code

- Applications servers which create bytecode classes through direct bytecode engineering (e.g. using AOP compilers), are hard to integrate with AOT compilation (which is more suitable for end-user "desktop" applications)

- Unlike the managed execution of bytecode which provides exception handling mechanisms, garbage collection etc., purely native (unmanaged) code is harder to control and is potentially more dangerous for the stability of a software system

- The runtime complexity of class loading and virtual methods in Java (where classes implementing an interface may be loaded dynamically)

- The (user-perceived) startup of the application is delayed by AOT compilation time; additional memory is required for AOT compilation

- Enterprise-grade AOT compilers require payment, while Java compilers and JVMs are free – many budget-restricted project thus choose not to afford an AOT compiler

In the scope of this thesis, AOT compilation will not be considered due to lack of relevance in enterprise applications.

2.10. Workload Quantification, Resource Demand Quantification and Profiling

To quantify the workload that an application puts onto the execution system, different approaches and techniques are available. To start with, the application can be analysed statically, but this strategy is complicated in light of parallelism, control flow constructs (conditional jumps, loops) and also randomisation and the behaviour of external components. Therefore, the workload of an application is usually analysed in a dynamic way, i.e. by executing the application or by simulating it. The dynamic performance analysis is usually called *profiling*, because it provides an aggregated view (summary, "profile") rather than a full trace of the application's behaviour.

Profiling serves to find bottlenecks, hot spots, but also deadlocks, memory leaks and other performance-impacting behaviour artefacts. Different approaches to implement profilers include hardware counter reading, making used of interfaces provided by the OS and the middleware, application sampling, application instrumentation, execution platform instrumentation, etc. Profiling information is destined not only for human users (program authors, execution platform engineers, etc.), but also for the executed programs themselves: using profiling information, programs become self-aware [133] and can make decisions on reconfiguration, execution scheduling etc.

Profiler development started in the 1970s [134], and new products emerge continuosly, fueled by new programming languages, new middleware, and increasing parallelism in applications and executions platforms. Beyond manual profiling (at source code level), profilers provide automated collection and evaluation of raw performance indicator values. Examples of profilers include Eclipse TPTP, CodeAnalyst, gprof, IBM Rational PurifyPlus, JProb, JProfiler, Oracle JRockit Mission Control, Oracle VisualVM, Oracle NetBeans, JetBrains dotTrace, NProf, Intel VTune, and many others.

Profilers differ in feature set, price, availability, overhead, level of detail (e.g. average values per method vs. full call graphs), precision/accuracy [135], scope (e.g. only application classes vs. execution system co-analysis), etc. Some profilers take full control of the application (they work as a layer between the application and the execution platform), while others depend on the (instrumented) application, the OS or the middleware to obtain raw profiling data.

Profiling interfaces are often offered by the OS or the middleware: for example, Java Virtual Machine Tools Interface (JVMTI) [136] allows registering listeners for events such as method entry, method exit, class loading, etc. Profiling support without the need for programming is also built into some operating systems, so that the performance of an OS-hosted application or processes can be profiled with "on-board means", e.g. with the Mac OS X Activity Monitor (see Section 2.4).

Sampling profilers are in principle less precise than instrumentation-based profilers, but incur less overhead; newer profiling products such as JProfiler [137] provide both mode (but not at the same time), at the programmer's discretion. While measuring the performance of short-running methods, profilers need to ensure that the profiling overhead does not outweigh the method itself – for example, JProfiler provides an "autotuning" option which attempts to detect such methods and to include them from auto-tuning. However, neither the thresholds used for identifying such methods, nor the information about timer accuracy/overhead (on which these decisions are based) are exposed.

Workload quantification and profiling are preconditions for *extraction of performance models* from application execution. After the static architecture of the application has been extracted into a model (e.g. using reverse engineering [138]), the dynamic model of the application's behaviour and performance has to be extracted. Given the variety of performance models (cf. Section 2.2.1), there exists no "universal" approach or technique for performance model extraction. To reverse engineer performance models based on layered queuing networks (LQNs), Hrischuk et al. [139] use traces obtained from instrumentations, as do Israr et al. [140]. These traces include timestamped events with unique IDs, where the IDs can be established using request ID propagation, or through correlating of the events during application execution.

Most of the described approaches for profiling and resource demand quantification return platform-specific results. None of them is both a platform-independent and application-independent approach that is accurate down to bytecode instructions.

2.11. Software Components and their Performance

Already introduced in Section 1.1, software components appeared as early as 1968 [141] and are seen as an approach that helps to decompose programs into reusable entities which encapsulate design decisions, provide explicit interfaces for access, and can be deployed independently. Component-based software engineering (CBSE) [142] continues to be in the focus of attention for industry and academia.

Meanwhile, new approaches such as OSGi [143, 144] are gaining popularity and industry acceptance, and with new research research questions such as componentisation in agile development [145] being addressed. Established, older component models such as Enterprise Java Beans (EJBs [15]), Microsoft Component Object Model (COM [146]) and others remain relevant and enjoy continued use.

2.11.1. Component Basics

In CBSE, an *interface* is a collection of *services*, where each service has a signature that contains input and output parameters (note that the interface contains only the descriptions of services, but no implementations of them). An interface is a first-class entity, i.e. it can exist independently from a component (e.g. in a *repository*), and it can be used by different components. To avoid confusion, a component should provide only one instance of a given interface.

When an interface is bound to a component using a *provided role*, it means that the component is offering the functionality (the services) of this interface. When an interface is bound to a component using *required role*, it means that the interface-provided functionality is used, i.e. an implementation of this interface is a precondition for the working of the component. The relation between provided and required roles/interfaces can be expressed through *contracts* and *protocols*, which provide an abstraction of the actual component execution.

Note that programming languages without component support do not have an exact counterpart of required interfaces even at object-oriented level: for example, Java classes can use any classes and methods by directly calling them in bytecode. In particular, it is the task of the execution platform to satisfy the operating requirements of classes at runtime; if the resulting class loading or resource loading fails, the execution platform throws an exception or stops with an error.

Also note that the granularity of a component is not fixed or prescribed: an implemented component can consist of 1 or 100 classes, provide 1 or 20 interfaces – still, the encapsulation property means that in the normal case, component allocation is *atomic*. Atomic deployment means that a component instance is deployed on exactly one execution platform node (computer), and if a component consists of several classes/modules, all intra-component communication is local, i.e. no remote calls are required.

At the same time, there exist approaches to inject component concepts such as explicit specification of dependencies into applications built using component-unaware languages for component-unaware execution platforms. For example, the modularisation efforts in the context of OSGi [147] are met with enthusiasm by developers and scientists. On the other hand, not every technology that describes itself as component-based indeed offers all concepts from component theory: for example, composed components are not possible in Enterprise Java Beans.

Reusability and redeployability of components have encouraged researchers to devise work processes that provide separation of concerns during component development and deployment. For example, Koziolek et al. have devised a development model for components that includes the roles of the component developer, the software architect (which assembles an application from components), the deployer (which installs and configures the application) and the performance analyst. The details of this development model are given in the next section, in the context of explaining the Palladio Component Model.

2.11.2. Component Modelling

The reuse of components requires not only the specification of functional properties at an interface level, but also information on the behaviour and extra-functional properties of components. Speaking more broadly, *models* of components are required to express different views: architectural models, behavioural models and extra-functional models need to be expressed, extracted, compared, stored and visualised. To regulate the contents of such model instances, *meta-models* formalise which entities are allowed and how they can be arranged, connected, named, etc.

Recognising the need for standardisation in component modelling, version 2.0 of the Unified Modelling Language (UML) contains model elements such as roles, interfaces, components, etc. UML 2.0 also contains a concrete graphic syntax for component model instances. Still, inadequacies and insufficiently strong semantics in UML 2.0 have led to the development of a range of component models. A *component model* (see a survey in [17]) formalises the artefacts of components, and often comes with tools for creation, analysis and editing of models.

Component-based and component-oriented performance prediction approaches are usually based on a given component model and interoperability with other models is rather rare (the KLAPER approach [148] contains an intermediate language for model-driven prediction of performance and reliability). Internally, component-based performance modelling and prediction approaches utilise generic performance modelling techniques and tools such as Petri nets, Markov models, process algebras, (Layered) Queuing Networks (cf. Section 2.2). [149] contains a survey on performance evaluation of component-based software systems, an older survey by Becker et al. [150] considers component models from the performance perspective.

An essential requirement for functioning of component-based performance prediction approaches is the availability of performance metric values for the elements of the performance model (a component-oriented performance model is rarely monolithic). In particular, if atomic component actions (i.e. their model counterparts) are annotated with performance metric values, these values must have been obtained in a systematic way. While obtaining these values, the modelled component can either be available (and thus can be measured), or the modelling phase precedes the implementation phase, and the performance value can only be guessed. Guessing (often called "estimation" or "approximation") is considered as acceptable when it is based on strong similarity measures or long experience.

When a component implementation is already available, its performance model should be obtained, for example when a new application is built from some existing and some planned components. The performance model for an existing component consists of sub-models for each of the services provided by the component, and the performance of provided interfaces depends on the performance of required interfaces.

However, as the implementors of required interfaces change from deployment to deployment, so does the performance of the required services utilised by a component (recall the component performance influences from Figure 1.1). Consequently, these performance dependencies must be expressed, and many components offer support for expressing such dependencies, e.g. as done by the Palladio Component Model introduced in the next section.

The internal work performed by a component implementation while processing an invocation of a provided service needs to be reflected in the performance model of that service. To quantify these internal work in terms of performance metrics (e.g. execution duration), it is intuitive to consider the *direct measurement* as the solution. However, in reality, the internal work performed by the implementation of a component service can have a complex behaviour, parametric dependencies, usage of different hardware resources and software layers, etc. On the other hand, the internal work can consist of a large number of very short actions which are hard to measure using existing performance indicators, e.g. timer methods.

2.11.3. Component Performance Modelling

At the beginning of a component lifecycle [14], a component is specified with its provided and required interfaces, and performance requirements (e.g. SLAs) can be specified. However, since no implementation exists at that point, no resource demands or performance values for offered interfaces can be specified. Only after a component implementation becomes available, an abstracted behaviour model can be derived together with resource demands.

These resource demands depend on the implementations of component's required interfaces, since in general, a component's implementation makes use of provided interfaces' implementations. Thus, only after the component implementation has been deployed and required interfaces have been bound, the dependencies can be resolved so that the resource demands become concrete value metrics and no longer contain unresolved references to the performance metrics and resource demands of required services.

At runtime, the application workload determines how the provided services of a component are involved, and the resulting service parameters have a significant impact on the performance metric values of that service. Resource contention and component state are important runtime impacts, too – note, however, that component state is often abstracted and not modelled, since it is hard to quantify and increases the complexity of performance models.

While measurement the internal component work is non-trivial per se, additional challenges appear when the scenarios detailed in Section 1.2 need to be addressed. These scenarios (application relocation, execution platform sizing) would require the measurement of the component implementation on each of the considered execution platforms, which can be a time-consuming task involving a significant amount of manual work to deploy and to measure the component. Additionally, to measure the component, its preconditions/requirements (e.g. required interfaces) must be satisfied, which means than more than just the components itself has to be deployed on each execution platform. Such a "performance test bed" needs to be deployed on each candidate execution platform where measurements need to be taken.

An extensive survey of performance evaluation and prediction approaches for component-based software systems is presented by Koziolek in [14]. The survey covers a large number of approaches, incl. CB-SPE (component-based software performance engineering) [151], CBML [152], PECT/PACC [153, 154, 155], COMQUAD [156, 157, 158] and others.

However, only few of them have tool support for measuring resource demands, and those with existing tool support have significant limitations. For example, The Prediction Enabled Component Technology (PECT) by Hissam, Wallnau, et al. PACC Starter Kit V2.0 is only available for the Windows operating system. The COMQUAD tooling targets C++ and Java components and provides tooling for measuring platform-specific and platform-independent resource demands. Unfortunately, it is based on vendor-specific technologies and has not been validated for performance prediction in realistic scenarios where applications are subject to runtime optimisations such as Just-in-Time compilation.

2.12. Platform-independent Resource Demands

Component performance is usually measured using *platform-specific* metrics, mostly response time. Response time contains the actual execution time plus the waiting times spent while execution platform is busy with other, concurrent requests. Less frequently, resource utilisation *by a process* (or by thread) is measured for resources such as hard disk or CPU, since the utilisation depends on other, concurrent resource demands issued by other components.

When several platforms are considered, performance measurements which use platform-specific timing values and metrics must be repeated on each of the platforms. If it would be possible to measure the component performance in terms of *platform-independent* metrics, it would suffice to measure these metrics on one platform. Still, the conversion from the platform-independent metric values into platform-specific timing values needs to be specified, and it is far from trivial.

The underlying problem is that performance metrics such as response time or resource utilisation depend on the four factors shown in Figure 1.1, which means that the resources which constitute the execution platform have individual shares in the platform-specific, *aggregated* performance metric value for a given execution of a work request (i.e. component service invocation). This, in turn, means that one value (e.g. execution time) needs to be split in *several* values, and their order and parallelism need to be addressed, too.

The complexity of splitting the value of one performance metric into several values of different metrics depends on the granularity used for modelling the execution platform. For example, modelling CPU caches and the RAM as separate entities requires many more measurements than when the CPU and RAM are modelled as one "black box" (but still separately from the hard disk).

The idea of platform-independent performance metrics has been implemented in the form of *resource demands* in several component models and associated tools, e.g. COMQUAD/COMAERA [158] or NICTA's unnamed component model [25]. For example, the Palladio Component Model (see next section for details) selects CPU cycles and bytes read/written from/to the hard disk as platform-independent resource demands – the processing speed of the corresponding resources forms the bridge between the platform-independent and platform-specific resources. The number of CPU cycles can be obtained by setting the execution time into relation to the CPU frequency.

2.13. Palladio Component Model

The Palladio Component Model (PCM) is a domain-specific language for modelling component-based software. PCM model instances are constructed at design time as architectural models, and can also be be extracted from existing components using reverse engineering [138]. On the basis of PCM model instances, the PCM tool chain predicts performance metrics such as execution time, response time, throughput and resource utilisation, using a variety of approaches (e.g. event-based simulation, queuing networks, Petri nets and analytic approaches).

The PCM focuses on design-time, model-driven performance prediction to assist software architects with design and deployment decisions, as well as with the reuse of existing components. It is implemented on the basis of several Eclipse technologies, incl. Eclipse Modelling Framework (EMF), Graphical Modelling Framework (GMF) and others. The development of the PCM started in 2003 at the University of Oldenburg, and since 2006 continues at the Karlsruhe Institute of Technology.

The formal foundation of the PCM is described using a metamodel [159], which covers component entities such as interfaces, roles as well as basic and composed components. The metamodel also covers a formalisation of component deployment, i.e. the relation between component instances and execution platforms. The modelling of execution platforms comprises hardware resources such as CPUs, hard disks and network connections (called linking resources), whereas the modelling of infrastructure-oriented software (e.g. middleware) is not formalised.

The PCM also defines a development process and associated roles for stakeholders, together with process artefacts and tasks. The process distinguishes between the following roles:

- The **component developer** addresses individual components and does not deal with their assembly into an application and their allocation on execution platforms. The component developer specifies the performance properties of her components' internal actions while all influencing factors from Figure 1.1 (except the component implementation) are still open and flexible. Such a parametrised performance specification enables reuse of the component and its performance model by third parties, independently from the component developer.

- The **software architect** composes the application from existing components (bottom-up), but also perform top-down design refinements. During the design phase, the software architect can model unavailable components (which will be created later during the development) and estimate their performance properties. According to the PCM development process, the software architect does not study the performance of the entire application, as separate roles for this task exist, which are described in the following.

- The **system deployer** is responsible for deploying the application on the execution platform and for configuring it accordingly. The system deployer contributes a performance model of the execution platform to the performance-predicting workflow. The performance model of the execution platform comprises processing rates of the CPU and hard disk resource, the throughput of the network connections, etc.

- The **domain expert** is familiar with the workloads and usage scenarios to which the application will be subjected. For modelling using the PCM, the domain expert specifies the usage profile which comprises the number of concurrent users, think time between requests, the parameter values for the application's public interfaces, etc.

- The **performance analyst** uses information provided by the four other roles, and executes performance prediction on the basis of it. The performance analyst can thus study the impact of relocating the application to other execution platform, exchanging component implementations, introducing load balancing, etc.

2.13.1. Component Modelling

Each interface declares one or several services, which are implicitly public; interfaces are created by component developers and sorted in repositories. A component which provides an interface must include an implementation of that interface, unless the component is a composed component and delegates the provided interface to one of its inner components. For each service of a provided component that it implements, the corresponding component model must provide an *RDSEFF* (resource demanding service effect automaton).

Figure 2.1 shows how components and their required and provided interfaces are represented by the elements of the PCM metamodel. Figure 2.1 uses a graphical concrete model syntax, but textual concrete syntaxes for the PCM also exist. A `DelegationConnector` connects the interfaces of the composed component with the interfaces of its inner components. An `AssemblyContext` allows distinguishing component instances by specifying their place and wiring (using an `AssemblyConnector`) in a `System` (i.e. the model of a software application) or in a `CompositeComponent`. A `ProvidedRole` respectively `RequiredRole` binds an interface instance to a component instance. For other parts and concepts of the Palladio Component Model, see [160, 159, 161].

The RDSEFF is of central importance to this thesis, since it specifies the resource demands issued by a component implementation. An example RDSEFF is shown in Figure 2.2 and is described in the following.

The RDSEFF describes the behaviour of the service implementation including the resource demand of the component service's internal work. An RDSEFF has one initial state and one terminal state, and it can contain several action types, including the following:

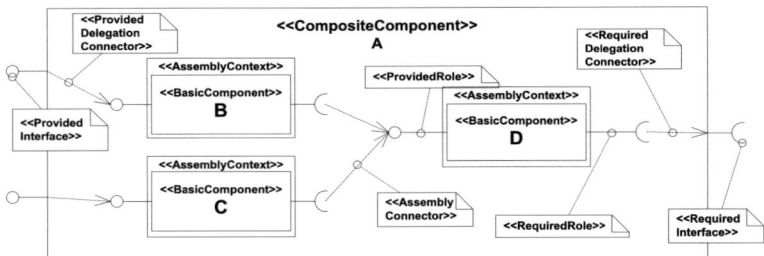

Figure 2.1.: A Composite Component Model Instance in the Palladio Component Model [46]

- an `InternalAction` describes component-internal work and is annotated with resource demands

- an `ExternalCallAction` models the invocation of a service provided by any other component which provides the corresponding interface; since the external component is exchangeable, annotating an external call action with resource demands is not possible because the model should reflect the fact that the component can be deployed independently

- a `BranchAction` evaluates a condition and depending on the result, one of the two conditional branches is taken

- a `LoopAction` evaluates a condition and repeats the loop body, which itself can contain further actions

The RDSEFF has further concepts, such as forking the parallel execution of two actions, acquiring and releasing passive resources, but its most important property is that it abstracts the behaviour of the modelled component service. The abstraction allows the modeller to concentrate on the performance-relevant behaviour and targets both control flow, data flow and the resource demands.

Also, note the evaluation of the service's input parameters and their relevance for the data flow: since the usage profile of the application translates to input parameters of component services, it is important to evaluate them and to propagate the input parameters to individual internal and external actions.

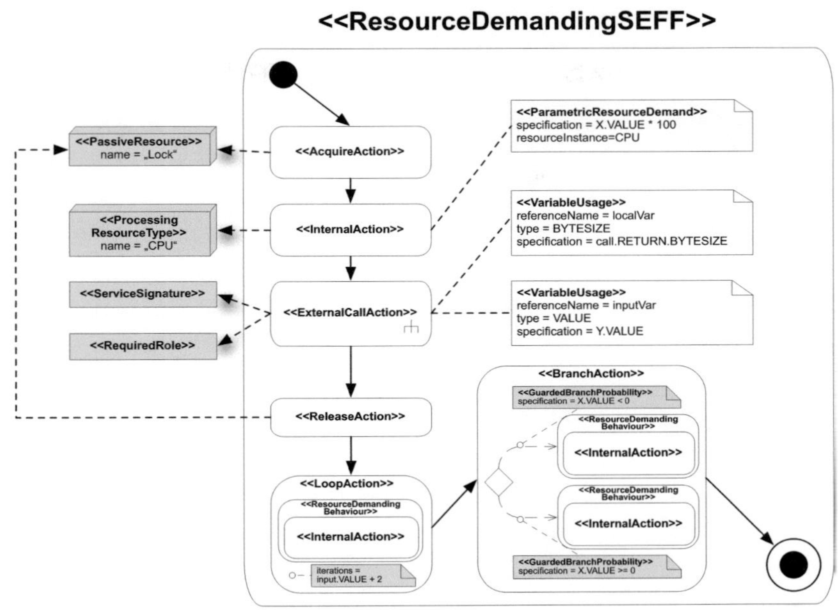

<<ResourceDemandingSEFF>>

Figure 2.2.: An example RDSEFF

Analysis of this dependencies leads to the parametrisation of the performance model over the usage profile, and supports scalability analysis and performance prediction.

Of the RDSEFF elements, only AcquireActions/ReleaseActions and InternalActions are relevant w.r.t. resource demands and resource usage. The next section describes the resource modelling in the PCM, and explains why this thesis focuses on InternalActions.

2.13.2. Execution Platform and System Usage Modelling

An AcquireAction/ReleaseAction references a PassiveResource. Passive resources are quantity-constrained resources such as monitors or semaphores. Their influence on the performance is given when a component service is waiting to acquire an instance of a passive resource (which is in use by another request), and thus the waiting request is blocked. Once the passive resource becomes available, the costs of acquiring it are so negligible that they can be ignored, and thus the costs of acquiring them are not even modelled in the PCM. Since the PCM tooling already deals successfully with passive resources, they are not considered in this thesis. Note that the correct modelling of the available quantity of a passive resource, as well as of `AcquireActions` and `ReleaseActions`, is the responsibility of the model creator. Alternatively, reverse engineering approaches can be used to reconstruct passive resource usage from existing components.

Network connections are modelled as `LinkingResources` in the PCM, and their modelling employs a strong abstraction to keep complexity at a manageable level. Still, validation experiments [160] have demonstrated sufficiently accurate performance prediction for network-using applications. Thus, `LinkingResources` are not addressed by this thesis, and is left to future work. It remains to be studied whether a more detailed network modelling would indeed increase the accuracy of performance prediction, or whether the increase in modelling effort and model complexity would be hard to justify.

In the PCM terminology, *active resources* are hardware resources which have a processing rate, such as CPU or hard disk. The modelling of active resources is split into `ProcessingResourceType` (which as an ID and name) and a `ProcessingResourceSpecification` which carries the processing rate and the request scheduling policy. Supported scheduling policies include First Come First Served (FCFS), processor sharing (all requests using an active resource are executed at the same time, and have the same share of its processing rate), and others.

Active resources reside in `ResourceContainers`, and `ResourceContainers` are connected by linking resources. Components are assigned to resource containers using deployment connectors (which form `AllocationContexts`).

2.14. Quantitative Impact of JVM Optimizations

In this section, we first demonstrate that execution duration of Java bytecode instructions on different execution platforms cannot be predicted simply by relating them to CPU frequency. Then, to show that even very "basic" (elementary) bytecode instructions have different execution durations and be benchmarked individually, we compare two different algorithms w.r.t. bytecode instruction counts and execution durations. Finally, to show the importance and non-linear impact of JVM optimizations, we study the quantitative impact of JIT compilation and JVM optimizations on the performance of the two algorithms.

For our study, we have designed two algorithms which have similar structure but use different bytecode operations in the measured section; we first discuss what is computed by the algorithms, and then lay out the design decisions and the configuration options of the algorithms. Afterwards, we compare their bytecode (as compiled using the Sun Microsystems JDK 1.6.0_08 with default settings), and finally compare their performance in interpreted and JITted mode.

Alg_1 is shown in Figure 2.3(a) as Java source code: it iteratively computes `nr` numbers in Fibonacci-like way, allowing two arbitrary `int` values as starting numbers. Alg_1 stores all computed Fibonacci values into `number`, an `int` array, so that no iteration of the algorithm can be "optimised away" by the JVM. The duration of the core computation of Alg_1 is measured using `System.nanoTime()`, the most precise timer method in the Java platform API.

Alg_2 is listed in Figure 2.3(b): it computes the first `nr` digits (incl. decimals places) of the ratio between the numbers *dividend* and *divisor*, which are passed to the algorithm externally and are expected to be non-zero and different. Computing a predefined number of decimal places (controlled through the `nr` field) would not be possible using Java operators or platform APIs. For example, when simply computing the `double`-typed result of dividing `dividend` and `divisor`, the number of decimal places is controlled by the precision of `double`.

To repeat Alg_1 and Alg_2 many times without the danger of JVM caching the results (the `results` array) and skipping the repeated execution of Alg_1, the

```
                                      int dividend = inputA;
                                      int divisor = inputB;
      results[0] = inputA;            results[0] = dividend;
      results[1] = inputB;            results[1] = divisor;

      int i=2;                        int i=2;
      start = System.nanoTime();      start = System.nanoTime();
      while (i<nr) {                  while (i<nr) {
        results[i] =                    results[i] = dividend/divisor;
          results[i - 1] +              dividend = 10*(dividend -
          results[i - 2];                 results[i]*divisor);
        i++;                            i++;
      }                               }
      end = System.nanoTime();        end = System.nanoTime();
      [...]                           [...]
            (a)                               (b)
```

Figure 2.3.: Java source code for (a) Alg_1 (to compute nr numbers in a Fibonacci-like way) and for (b) Alg_2 (to compute first nr digits of $\frac{dividend}{divisor}$), incl. decimal places

starting values `inputA` and `inputB` (initialised outside of the measured section) can be chosen differently for each run of Alg_1 / Alg_2 in our implementation.

We consider only the measured sections of the algorithms, i.e. the `while` loops. When the same value of nr is passed to Alg_1 and Alg_2, the loop *head* (`while(i<nr)`) is executed the same number of times, and thus is irrelevant for our comparison. The bytecode of the loop *bodies* of Alg_1 and Alg_2 is similar but not exactly the same: Alg_1 contains 15 instructions: 3·ALOAD, 1·IADD, 2·IALOAD, 1·IASTORE, 2·ICONST, 1·IINC, 3·ILOAD and 2·ISUB. Alg_2 contains 17 instructions: 2·ALOAD, 1·BIPUSH, 1·IALOAD, 1·IASTORE, 1·IDIV, 6·ILOAD, 1·IINC, 2·IMUL 1·ISTORE and 1·ISUB.

First, Alg_1 and Alg_2 are executed in interpretation mode (`-Xint` JVM flag), which means that no JIT compilation is performed by the JVM. Executing Alg_1 100 times with `nr` being 50000 gives a median duration of the measured section (`end-start`) of 1,498,000 ns. Executing Alg_2 under the same condition and with the same input gives a median duration of the measured section of 1,621,000 ns.

Setting these numbers in relation, we obtain $\frac{1,621,000}{1,498,000} \approx 1.08$, which is close to the ratio of the number of bytecode instructions in the loop bodies: $\frac{17}{15} \approx 1.13$.

Note that the overhead of the timer method `System.nanoTime` (invocation cost of 1000 ns) is negligible in comparison to the algorithm runtime: it is less than 0.1% of the latter. Computing the average duration (in nanoseconds) of bytecode instruction for the interpretation-only modus, we obtain $\frac{1,498,000}{15\cdot50,000} \approx 2.00$ for Alg_1 and $\frac{1,621,000}{17\cdot50,000} \approx 1.91$ for Alg_2. On the computer where the experiments were run, 2 ns correspond to 5.6 CPU cycles.

The numbers look quite differently when the JIT compilation is enabled, and encouraged by repeating 50,000 method invocations as warmup. Since the `-Xint` flag lets the JVM output the JIT compilation to the console, we verified the the two studied methods were indeed JIT-compiled.

Then, with the same inputs as before, the median duration of Alg_1 is measured to be 58,000 ns, and the median duration of Alg_2 is measured to be 513,000 ns. Not only is the speedup very different (25.83 for Alg_1, 3.16 for Alg_2), but the resulting average duration of an instruction is also very different. This proves that Java bytecode instructions must be benchmarked individually, and that JIT speedup is not a constant value.

Chapter 3.

Evaluating and Selecting Methods for Time Measurement

In physics, to express the power of a working entity, the relation between the performed work and the time spent performing the work is established. In informatics, performance (which is evaluated by setting the *amount of accomplished work* into the relation to the *used time* and the *used resources*) also requires precise, dependable measurement of time.

In particular, both Chapter 4 (resource demand quantification) and Chapter 5 (JVM benchmarking) will require solid, evaluated techniques for measuring time. This chapter addresses the fundamental question for computing performance metrics: *"how to measure time in a reliable way?"*, and develops an engineering approach to selecting time-measuring techniques and tools based on their quality. For example, a quality metric for a timer method is the accuracy of its results, and another one is the invocation cost of the method.

The approach presented in this chapter solves the following **scientific challenges**:

- what are the quality criteria for selecting the techniques and tools for measuring very short (sub-millisecond) durations?

- how to quantify these quality criteria, and which techniques and tools for time measurements are suitable for this thesis?

- how to detect issues of legacy timer methods, such as inadequate behaviour in multi-threaded contexts?

The resulting contributions include

- the identification of *quality properties* to evaluate and to compare time-oriented performance indicators, and derivation of a unified quality metric that encompasses these properties

- a platform-independent approach to quantify these quality attributes without inspecting the implementation of the indicators

The remainder of this chapter is structured as follows: Section 3.1 describes issues and challenges with obtaining timing values for benchmarking, performance analysis and performance prediction. Section 3.2 presents the foundations of timer methods. Section 3.3 describes a new approach (called TIMERMETER in the remainder of this thesis) for quantifying accuracy and invocation cost of timer methods. Section 3.4 contains algorithms for analysing units, monotonicity and stability of timer methods Section 3.5 sets epochs and maximum measurable time intervals into relation and shows how to compute them. Section 3.6 develops a new quality metric for timer methods, which unifies the different quality attributes of timer methods into a single value, making timer methods much easier to compare, especially across execution platforms. Section 3.7 summarises the contents of the chapter and concludes.

3.1. Issues and Challenges with Obtaining Timing Values for Performance Analysis

In order to obtain timing values, scientists and engineers are accustomed to calling *timer methods* provided by APIs of operating systems, virtual machines, third-party frameworks, etc. The API methods build on the underlying hardware and software, which can differ in capabilities and characteristics. At the same time, the API methods abstract from these underlying layers, shielding the user from their complexity and platform specifics. Thus, the API timer methods often must provide only the "greatest common denominator" timing functionality among the supported execution platforms. Therefore, differences between the properties of timer methods and the hardware that provides the timing information can be expected.

When using timer methods to perform fine-granular or accuracy-sensitive measurements, scientists naturally strive to select the best suitable timer method to measure time. Of course, "best" depends on the concrete setting, and concerns aspects such as *accuracy* of the timer method, its *invocation costs*, *non-interference* (with the measured system), presence in current and future execution platforms, etc. These factors have a great impact on the accuracy and statistical validity of their measurements. For example, to measure an operation that takes 250 ns, a timer method that uses a counter which is updated once every 15 ms is not appropriate.

Unfortunately, quantitative properties of timer methods are often not specified in their documentation because these properties are platform-specific: they depend on the underlying hardware, and on the software stack that processes the hardware signals. Also, no platform-independent algorithms or tools exist to quantify quantitative timer method properties. Additionally, the operating system performs the management of CPU throttling and multi-core CPUs in a transparent way, and existing timer methods must be tested for reliable and correct functionality under the new circumstances. The increased popularity of virtualisation poses an additional challenge: if the virtualisation layer must emulate the CPU and its counters/registers, the quantitative properties of the emulated CPU (update frequency of counters, etc.) can differ from the "real" one.

Hence, when precise performance measurements need to be performed, timer method users have to guess the accuracy and invocation costs of timer methods or have to perform ad-hoc experiments to estimate these values. Published values as in [162] or [163] are mostly vague and provided without the code that produced them, so it is not possible to transfer these platform-*specific* results to other hardware/software platforms without re-running the original code. For example, the official documentation [164] for the `nanoTime()` method in the Java platform API only states that the method provides "nanosecond precision, but not necessarily nanosecond accuracy" (the documentation does not define the terms "precision" and "accuracy", see next sections for definitions adopted in this thesis).

The remainder of this chapter presents a thorough, evaluated solution for these problems, and establishes a one-stop quality metric for timer methods by assembling in one formula different quality properties of timer methods. The following section lays the foundations by defining the terms used in this chapter.

3.2. Foundations of Timer Methods

A *timer method* is a software method that accesses a hardware *timer*, i.e. a periodic counter which is updated at regular intervals, so that the counter's value can be converted to timing values. Such a periodic counter is a hardware register that is incremented by a non-negative constant value, with a fixed timespan between two subsequent increments. An example of a periodic counter is the Time Stamp Counter (TSC) [165, 166], which is provided by newer CPUs.

The constant value of the increment is usually an integer value (mostly 1), but its unit may not be a standardised time unit such as nanosecond. For example, the Intel 64 and IA-32 Architectures Software Developer's Manual [166] states that for Pentium M processors, the TSC "increments with every internal processor clock cycle". For a CPU frequency of 2.5 GHz, a TSC increment would correspond to 0.4 ns.

A *counter tick* corresponds to the atomic action of updating the counter's value, usually increasing it by 1. To use a counter for time measurements, the time between two counter ticks need to be known, which corresponds to the inverse of the counter update frequency. The relationship between update frequency of a counter, and the `counter unit` (time corresponding to the counter value of 1) can be expressed as follows:

$$counter\ unit := \frac{time\ between\ ticks}{|increment|} = \frac{1}{(|increment|) \cdot (update\ frequency)} \qquad (3.1)$$

However, the time between two counter ticks is often unspecified or varying among hardware platforms, making it hard to transform counter values into time units. For some counters, the counter unit corresponds to a floating-point multiple of a "normal" time unit such as nanosecond. For such counters, Section 3.4 provides a uniform, black-box approach to calculate the units of timers and counters.

Timer method unit is the amount of time corresponding to 1 of the value returned by the timer method on a given platform with given dynamic and static settings. Examples of timer method units are 1 ns (e.g. `java.lang.System.nanoTime()` method), 1 ms (e.g. `java.lang.System.currentTimeMillis()` method), or 0.5468 ns (1 *tick* of the TSC on Intel T2400 at full clock frequency, where the TSC is updated every CPU clock tick).

The *value type* of a timer method refers to the value type of its returned value. For example, the `java.lang.System.nanoTime()` method of the Java platform APU returns `long` values. Timer methods can return signed or unsigned, floating-point or integer values; some timing frameworks define their own classtypes to encapsulate timing values (e.g. JavaSimon [167] defines a `Split` as a notion of a interval measurements). The value range of a counter/-timer depends on the number of bits used to store its values, and of course on its value type. For example, in Java, the maximum value for a `long` is $2^{63} - 1$, and the minimum value is -2^{63}, since a `long` is a *signed* 8 byte value, with 1 bit to store the sign and 63 bits to store the value.

The *method type* of a timer method can be either static or instance, where instance (i.e. non-static) means that the invocation target of the timer method needs to be initialised. If the method is of instance type, it should be tested whether an instance can be passed around and reused without unexpected side effects, even if the CPU core affinity of the thread using a timer instance changes. Note that the method type does not depend on the quantity of the underlying timer: a singleton timer can be reused by many instances of a class offering instance-typed timer method, and a static-typed timer method can be a facade to a per-core timer whose quantity is ≥ 1 on multi-core platforms.

Wall-clock time is a globally advancing monotonic time. Wall-clock time can be reported in a *globally absolute* way, e.g. `java.lang.System.currentTimeMillis()` which returns "the difference, measured in milliseconds, between the current time and midnight, January 1, 1970 UTC", independent of the timezone where the computer operates. Wall-clock time can also be reported in a *measurement-local* way, e.g. `java.lang.System.nanoTime()` which starts from 0 each time a computer is restarted or each time the a JVM process starts.

Thread time is a valuable metric in performance evaluation, where wall-clock time measurements in multi-threaded setting would be implausible due to very short OS scheduling timeslices. Thread time is the time spent by a thread in the active state, rather than in the "ready" or "suspended" state. For example, the interface `java.lang.management.ThreadMXBean` provides methods such as `getThreadCpuTime(long id)`.

Process time is defined for processes as thread time for threads, and corresponding timer methods are offered by the Java platform API as well.

A *countdown timer* is a software or hardware mechanism to signal an event or to start a task after a certain time has passed. Countdown timers may be one-shot or periodic and are often used to simulate concurrent behaviour and workload. An example of a countdown timer is the Java platform API class `java.util.Timer`.

An *epoch* is a (calendar) date which corresponds to the value 0 for a given timer, e.g. when the counter is initialised. When timer values are stored using a limited-range type, the monotonic increase of timer values means that the timer value will reach the maximum of the value type at some point in time. Once the maximum value has been reached, the value of the timer can either stop increasing or it can *overflow*, i.e. it restart from 0 or from the minimum value of value type (which can be negative). For example, an epoch of the aforementioned Java API timer method `System.currentTimeMillis()` is "midnight, January 1,

1970 UTC" (as stated in its documentation [164]). If the timer method overflows, it will again reach 0 some time after the overflow, which is yet another epoch. Correspondingly, for a given timer value, the *last epoch* defines the most recent date at which the counter/timer value was 0, while the *next epoch* defines the next recent date where the value is 0. If there are several instances of a counter, using them in a multi-process (or multi-thread) setting requires that their epochs are aligned – otherwise, the epoch offsets will distort measurements.

3.2.1. Quality Properties for Counters, Timers and Timer Methods

Based on the introduced definitions, this section presents a set of quantifiable quality properties for timer methods. Figure 3.1 shows the quality properties and some of the timer properties introduced above. The quality properties are explained below in clockwise order of Figure 3.1.

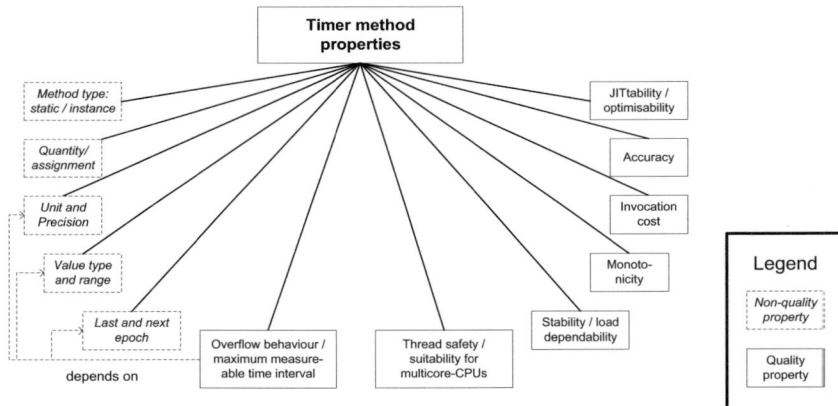

Figure 3.1.: Properties of counters/timers and timer methods

JITtability means the following: in Java Virtual Machine and similar bytecode-executing platforms, the interpreted bytecode can be just-in-time compiled

("JITted") to machine code to speed up its execution. If this happens, the invocation cost of a timer method can decrease, which must be reflected in the evaluation of measurements and in the evaluation of timer method quality. Hence,
to detect whether a timer method is JITtable, a sufficient warmup is needed to
make the method a candidate for JIT compilation, and to quantify the difference between the pre-JIT and post-JIT invocation cost. This quality property is
addressed during the evaluation of the presented approach (see Section 7.2).

For the following definitions that describe quality properties of timers, the
terminology from the official Java platform API documentation [164] serves as
a starting point and thus provides a terminology familiar to many scientists and
engineers. The timer method properties such as accuracy are considered as they
are seen at the API level by the application which invokes the timer method.

Accuracy (synonymously: *resolution* or *granularity*) of a given timer method is
the smallest measurable positive non-zero difference between two time intervals
measured with the counter, i.e.

$$precision := min\left\{(t_4 - t_3) - (t_2 - t_1)|t_4 > t_3, t_2 \geq t_1, (t_4 - t_3) > (t_2 - t_1) \geq 0\right\} \quad (3.2)$$

For example, the precision of `java.lang.System.nanoTime()` is 1 ns (=its
unit), although in practice, its resolution is often hundreds of ns. It holds that
accuracy $\geq$ *precision* because durations smaller than *precision* are measured as
0 (see Sections 3.2.2 and 3.2.3 for a more formal treatment of accuracy). Accuracy can be a floating-point multiple of a time unit when the timer/counter
as a floating-point type, or when the unit ("tick") of counter corresponds to a
floating-point multiple of a time unit.

Invocation cost of a timer method is a synonym for *execution duration* of that
timer method and spans the interval from the timer method invocation until it
returns a value, as seen by the method's invoker. The invocation cost may vary
from call to call due to CPU scheduling and other runtime influences, as well as
due to JIT (see above). The invocation cost can be smaller than the accuracy or
larger than it, and it depends on the way in which the timer method is invoked:
for example, in Java, a method can be invoked directly, using polymorphism, or

using the Java platform API's reflection capability. An algorithm to quantify the invocation cost is presented in Section 3.3 and its results are part of the evaluation in Section 7.2.

Monotonicity means that for two wall-clock time instants t_1, t_2 with $t_2 > t_1$, the retrieved timing values $value(t_1)$ and $value(t_2)$ will fulfil $value(t_2) \geq value(t_1)$. This is a very basic requirement to perform reliable timing measurements, and practitioners expect this requirement to be fulfilled by default. Therefore, it is usually not checked – however, especially in multi-threaded or multi-core platforms, it may be non-trivial to implement, and therefore deserves attention. For example, consider a situation where each CPU core maintains an own instance of its counter but cores can pause the counter incrementation during inactivity periods. Then, a thread/process that is relocated from one $core_i$ to $core_j$ ($j \neq i$) can encounter a situation where the counter value on $core_j$ is smaller than that on $core_i$, due to $core_j$'s inactivity at an earlier moment.

Stability (incl. *load dependency*) of a timer/counter is a boolean-typed value ("stable" vs. "unstable"). An example of unstable counter behaviour are *skipped compensated increments*: for example, instead of increasing the counter value by 1 each 10 ns, a counter may decide to increase the counter value by 100 each 1000 ns if the processor is under low load (e.g. to save energy). In such a case, the monotonicity is maintained but accuracy suffers and the measured values will be unstable if the CPU changes between low-load and heavy-load states. As this thesis takes a black-box view on the execution platform (and its timer/counter), the stability of a counter/timer must be tested from outside. Of course, testing can only reveal the presence of issues, and it cannot prove their absence. A first approach to test the stability of counters (see Section 3.4) shows that the Timestamp Counter (TSC) is an unstable counter even though it is monotonic, has high accuracy and low invocation cost.

Thread safety and *suitability for multi-core CPUs* are two further boolean-typed properties that encompass monotonicity and stability when a timer/counter is used concurrently by several threads, which can be spread over several CPU cores if available. For instance-typed timer methods and non-singleton timers/counters, thread safety and suitability for multi-core CPUs must be tested for different usage patterns (common shared instance, one instance per thread, etc.).

Overflow behaviour describes how the timer method behaves once it reaches the maximum value of its return type. The overflow behaviour thus depends on the value type of the method, and how soon the next overflow happens depends on how far back the last epoch dates, as well as on how fast the timer method values increase (i.e. on the timer method unit).

The *maximum measurable time interval* depends on the value type of the timer method. A precise mathematical definition of this term and a formula to compute it are given in Section 3.5, as the effects of overflow must be taken into account to compute it.

3.2.2. The Influence of Quantisation, Accuracy and Method Invocation Costs on Measured Timing Values

The quantisation effect is the effect shown in the left part of Figure 3.2: it occurs because the values U_i, U_{i+1}, ... stored by a timer are discrete, but the time value t_x to be measured can fall between two discrete values and a discrete value U_x is returned instead of t_x. In the following, $U_{i+1} - U_i$ will be called accuracy and shown as A in formulas.

The quantisation error $QE_{single}(t_x)$ of a single time measurements is defined as $QE_{single}(t_x) := U_x - t_x$ and is a floating-point value equally distributed along the range $[0.0, 1.0)$. Therefore, and the expected value of the quantisation error is

$$E\left[QE_{single}\right] = 0.5 \cdot (U_{i+1} - U_i) = 0.5 \cdot A \quad with \quad i \geq 0 \qquad (3.3)$$

since the location of t_x between two adjacent U_i is equally distributed. Note it holds $U_x \leq t_x$, i.e. single measurements are either precise or underestimated, but never overestimated.

To compute the duration of a time interval, two time values must be measured, i.e. two quantisation errors are involved in the measurement error of the time interval. Contrary to single measurements and also contrary to intuition,

Figure 3.2.: Effects of quantisation on measuring time values and time intervals

quantisation errors for time intervals can also lead to *over*estimation, as shown by the right part of Figure 3.2. Thus, the quantisation error can result in a measured value that is either $U_{i+1} - U_i$ *longer* or $U_{i+1} - U_i$ *shorter* than the real value of the time interval. Additionally, for a single given time interval measurement, the worst case quantisation error can be $\pm A$, which can be as much as 15 ms (more than 15 Million CPU cycles) on modern Windows systems, as shown in Section 7.2.

The remainder of this section shows which issues with timer methods need to be considered w.r.t. accuracy. It assumes that (i) during the considered measurements, no jumps in wall-clock time happen (e.g. no switch from summer to winter time occurs) (ii) no timer overflow happens (i.e. all timer values grow monotonically) (iii) the same timer instance is used throughout an example (i.e. on multi-core platforms, hardware counters and registers that are used belong to the same core).

The most straightforward way to measure the duration of a method call meth() is to place it between two invocations of the timer method time() and to compute their difference as in Listing 3.1.

```
1  long time1 = time();
2  meth();
3  long time2 = time();
4  long duration = time2 - time1;
```

Listing 3.1: Oversimplified measurement of method execution duration

To compute the time value to return, a timer method like time() reads a counter which is updated (increased) at regular intervals of the same length. This means that several subsequent timer method invocations can return the same value if the counter value has not been increased in between. Specifically, consider the case shown in Figure 3.3: when the timer method reads the counter value in the interval $[U_k, U_{k+1})$, it will use U_k as the counter value. This means that a measurement at time point t_x is not necessarily returned as t_x: the timer method returns the *last stored* timer value U_k instead of the (precise) value of t_x, this is hinted by the dashed line in Figure 3.3 and in the following figures. In the best case, the returned value U_k is equal to t_x while in the worst case, the returned value U_k is smaller than t_x by almost the entire size of A.

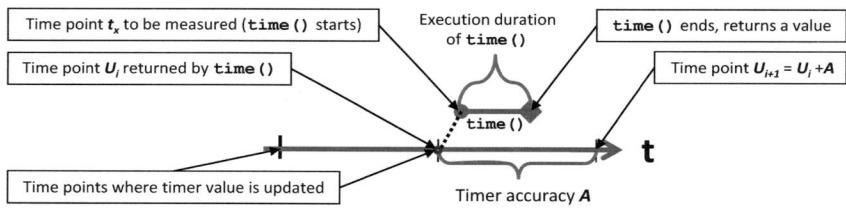

Figure 3.3.: Effects of timer accuracy on measurements (Legend: t_x: actual time to be measured; U_i: counter updates; A: timer method accuracy)

The influence of the accuracy on the measurements differs between the two following cases:

- **Case 1**: accuracy is larger than the invocation cost

- **Case 2**: accuracy is equal to or smaller than the invocation cost

For **Case 1**, consider Figure 3.4 and Figure 3.5. In Figure 3.4, the duration of the operation `meth()` is measured to $d = 0 \cdot A$ although its duration is closer to $1 \cdot A$ and should rather be measured to $1 \cdot A$. In Figure 3.5, the duration of the operation `meth()` is measured to $d = 1 \cdot A$ although its duration is closer to $0 \cdot A$ and should rather be measured to $0 \cdot A$. For both Figure 3.5 and Figure 3.5, the lack of knowledge about the relation of A and the invocation cost of `time()` leads to wrong conclusions about d and `meth()`.

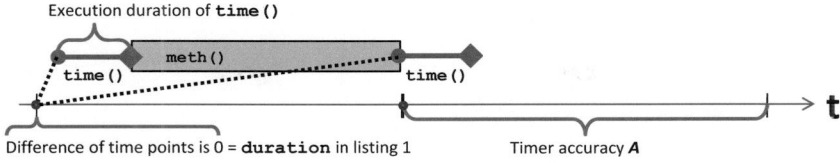

Figure 3.4.: Accuracy is larger than timer method execution duration, measured duration too small

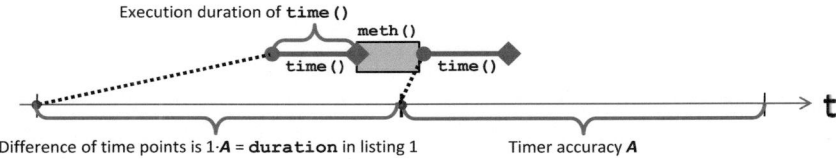

Figure 3.5.: Accuracy is larger than timer method execution duration, measured duration too large

For **Case 2**, consider Figure 3.6 where the accuracy is smaller than the timer method invocation cost. The measured duration is dominated by the timer invocation cost, and making conclusions about the duration of meth() from the measured duration is not permissible.

Thus, for Case 1 *and* Case 2, *both* the accuracy and the timer invocation cost need to be quantified to allow precise measurements and to enable the setup of statistically controlled experiments. An algorithm to calculate both quality properties is presented in Section 3.3.

3.2.3. The Effects of Rounding and Truncating

This subsection contains an in-depth consideration that will be needed in Section 3.3 to compute accuracy and invocation costs from the values returned by a timer method.

Consider an example counter that is updated with a fixed frequency of 3,579,545 Hz. Section 7.2 discusses such an OS counter, which is used by

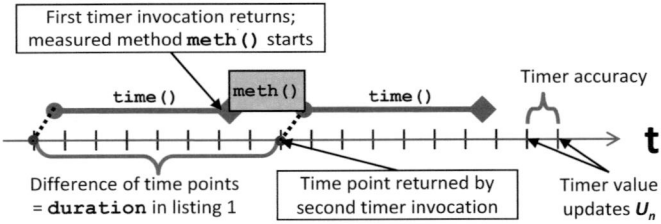

Figure 3.6.: Accuracy is smaller than timer method execution duration, measured duration too large

the `QueryPerformanceCounter` method of the Windows API, and by the `System.nanoTime()` Java Platform API timer method of Windows XP. The counter's accuracy $(= \frac{1}{frequency})$ is then ≈ 297.4 ns (rounded to one decimal place); in the remainder of this subsection, time units are omitted to simplify the discussion. Yet most timer methods, such as `java.lang.System.nanoTime()`, return values as whole-numbered `long`s and not as `double`s, i.e. without any decimal places.

Therefore, the timer method implementation has two choices to convert `double` values such as 297.4 to `long`s: (i) truncating (e.g. using Java casting operator) and (ii) rounding (e.g. using Java API method `java.lang.Math.round(double d)`), both of which introduce numerical errors. As this thesis considers the timer methods as "black boxes" (i.e. it does not analyse their implementations), one cannot know beforehand whether truncation (or rounding) is used or not.

Yet for devising our algorithm in Section 3.3, the effects of rounding and truncating on timer values and time intervals will play a crucial role. Thus, in this section, we prove that when using truncation or rounding to record `double`-typed time points as whole-numbered `long`-typed values, it is possible that two time intervals of the *same* actual length will be recorded as `long`-typed intervals whose lengths *differ* by 1.

3.2.3.1. Truncating

For *truncating*, consider a timer interval $E - S$ that starts at S and ends at E. Let A be the accuracy of the timer, $trunc(S)$ be the truncated value of S and $trunc(E)$ the truncated value of E. Due to truncation, the computed time intervals can appear larger than they are in some cases and smaller than they are in others.

As an example, consider a case with $A = 297.4$ and two intervals of length $3 \cdot A$ each ($= 892.2$ without truncation): the first interval starts at $7 \cdot A$ and ending at $10 \cdot A$, and the second interval starts at $10 \cdot A$ and ending at $13 \cdot A$. With truncation, the duration of the first interval is computed to

$$trunc(10 \cdot 297.4) - trunc(7 \cdot 297.4) = trunc(2974.0) - trunc(2081.8) = 893 \qquad (3.4)$$

Therefore, in this case, truncation leads to a result which is *larger* than the actual duration of 892.2. In contrast to that, the duration of the second interval appears *shorter* due to truncation:

$$trunc(13 \cdot 297.4) - trunc(10 \cdot 297.4) = trunc(3866.2) - trunc(2974.0) = 892 \qquad (3.5)$$

The definition of *truncation-caused interval measurement error* IME_{trunc} is as follows:

$$IME_{trunc}(E, S) := (E - S) - (trunc(E) - trunc(S)) \qquad (3.6)$$

$IME_{trunc}(E, S)$ is equivalent to $(E - trunc(E)) - (S - trunc(S))$. It holds that

$$0 \leq (E - trunc(E)) < 1 \qquad (3.7)$$

and

$$0 \leq (S - trunc(S)) < 1 \qquad (3.8)$$

The largest value of $IME_{trunc}(E, S)$ is achieved when $S - trunc(S) = 0$ and $E - trunc(E)$ is maximised (yet still $E - trunc(E) < 1$). Correspondingly, the smallest value of $IME_{trunc}(E, S)$ is achieved when $S - trunc(S)$ is maximised (yet still $S - trunc(S) < 1$) and $E - trunc(E) = 0$.

Finally, we can summarise that

$$-1 < IME_{trunc}(E, S) < +1 \qquad (3.9)$$

As the open interval $(-1, +1)$ contains at most *two* `long` values (i.e. without decimal spaces), we can conclude that trunctation can cause a time interval of a given length to be measured in at most two versions, in the above example 892 and 893.

3.2.3.2. Rounding

For *rounding*, again consider time interval start S and end E and assume that time values with decimal values of 0.5 and larger are rounded *up*, while smaller decimal values are rounded *down*. Using above example accuracy of 297.4, consider the time interval between $S = 1 \cdot 297.4$ and $E = 2 \cdot 297.4 = 594.8$. S is rounded to 297 while E is rounded to 595, the resulting interval $E - S$ is 298. At the same time, for $S = 2 \cdot 297.4 = 594.8$ and $E = 3 \cdot 297.4 = 892.2$, the same underlying time interval $(1 \cdot 297.4)$ after rounding is computed to $892 - 595 = 297$. Thus, an interval can appear both longer and shorter due to rounding.

For the rounded value $round(S)$ and $round(E)$, it holds that

$$-0.5 < (round(S) - S) \le 0.5 \qquad (3.10)$$

and

$$-0.5 < (round(E) - E) \le 0.5 \qquad (3.11)$$

We define the *rounding-caused interval measurement error*

$$IME_{round}(E, S) := (E - S) - (round(E) - round(S)) \qquad (3.12)$$

Note that $IME_{round}(E, S)$ is equivalent to $(E - round(E)) - (S - round(S))$.

$IME_{round}(E, S)$ achieves its largest (positive) value $E - round(E)$ is maximized and $S - round(S)$ is minimised. Let ϵ be an arbitrarily small value with $0 < \epsilon < 1$. The maximum value of $E - round(E)$ is $0.5 - \epsilon$ (when E is rounded down) and the minimum value of $S - round(S)$ is -0.5 (when S is rounded up). Hence, the maximum value of $(E - round(E)) - (S - round(S))$ is $1 - \epsilon$, which is smaller than 1.

In a similar way, the minimum value of $IME_{round}(E, S)$ is achieved when $E - round(E)$ is minimised (i.e. it is -0.5) and $S - round(S)$ is maximised (i.e. $0.5 - \epsilon$). Thus, the minimum value of $(round(E) - E) - (round(S) - S)$ is $-1 + \epsilon$. Altogether, it holds that

$$-1 < IME_{round}(E, S) < 1 \tag{3.13}$$

Therefore, the open interval $(-1, +1)$ contains at most *two* long values (i.e. integer values without decimal spaces).

Combining results of Section 3.2.3.1 and Section 3.2.3.2, we conclude that *both* truncation *and* rounding of timer values can cause two time intervals of the same actual length to be saved as two different whole-numbered long values, which have a difference of 1. This conclusion will be used in our algorithm presented in the Section 3.3.

3.3. Quantifying Accuracy and Invocation Cost of Timing Methods

Among the properties described in the previous section, accuracy and invocation cost are important and frequently considered quality properties. A platform-independent approach to quantify them has been introduced in [168], and constitutes an initial step for the work described in this chapter.

3.3.1. A Naive Approach to Estimating Timer Invocation Costs

Trying to obtain the invocation cost of the method time(), the straightforward way is to remove the call to meth() from Listing 3.1, and re-run the measurement as in Listing 3.2.

```
1  long time1 = time();
2  long time2 = time();
3  long timerInvocationCost = time2 - time1;
```

Listing 3.2: Oversimplified measurement of timer method invocation cost

However, for timers where the invocation cost is smaller than half of the accuracy (e.g. `java.lang.System.currentTimeMillis()` in Java – cf. Section 7.2), `timerInvocationCost` is likely to be zero. Meyerhöfer's code [30] repeats the measurements in Listing 3.3 (which discards the cases where `time2==time1`) a number of times and analyses the maximum and the average value of timerInvocationCost:

```
1  long time2 = time1;
2  while(time2==time1){
3    time2 = time();
4  }
5  long timerInvocationCost = time2 - time1;
```

Listing 3.3: Measuring timer method invocation costs according to [30]

However, Listing 3.3 does not analyse how many times the `while` loop was executed before the value of `time2` becomes larger than `time1`, and therefore `time2-time1` can include more than one invocation cost of `time()`. An enhancement of the code in Listing 3.3 will be presented in Section 3.3.2 in Listing 3.5. However, neither the code in Listing 3.3 nor the code in Listing 3.5 can compute both the accuracy and the invocation cost.

Another possibility would be a stochastic approach (see [40, 41, 33]), as sketched in Listing 3.4:

```
1  long sum = 0, time1=0, time2=0;
2  for(i=0...s){
3    time1 = time(); //first of s measurements
4    time2 = time();
5    sum = sum+(time2-time1);
6  }
7  long timerInvocationCost = sum/s;
```

Listing 3.4: Stochastic measurement of timer method invocation cost

As with the preceding algorithms, the code in Listing 3.4 cannot compute both the accuracy and the timer invocation cost.

A novel solution that covers both accuracy and invocation cost is presented in the next section.

3.3.2. Using Clustering for Quantifying Accuracy and Invocation Cost

As discussed in Section 3.3.1, if the invocation cost of the timer method is smaller than its accuracy, the two timer method calls as in Listing 3.2 are likely to return the same value for `time1` and `time2`, which is not helpful in finding the timer method's accuracy using clustering. Hence, we must "force" the second timer invocation to return a value which is one accuracy "step" higher. A visual explanation of this principle is shown in Figure 3.7 and Figure 3.8.

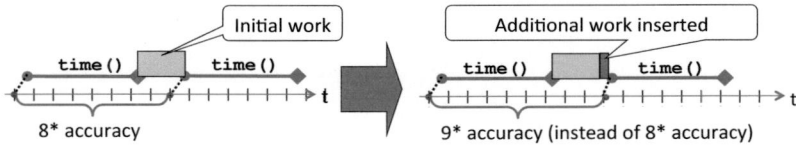

Figure 3.7.: Quantifying the accuracy (for the case accuracy < invocation cost)

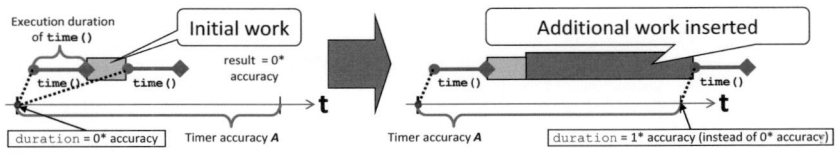

Figure 3.8.: Quantifying the accuracy (for the case accuracy ≥ invocation cost)

So, instead of invoking the second timer call immediately after the first one, a very small task should precede the second timer call so that the inserted task cannot be optimised away by the execution platform. If the inserted task is too small for a non-zero difference to appear, it should be enlarged until `time2-time1`≥ 0 (cf. Algorithm 3.1). Further enlargement of the inserted task shall lead to `time2-time1` becoming another accuracy "step" larger.

In reality, however, this idea is still too simple to work, as the results of running a Java implementation of this idea for the timer method `java.-lang.System.nanoTime()` show. Executing this implementation on Sun JDK 1.6.0_07 (default JIT and JVM settings, Windows XP Professional OS, Intel T2400 CPU), the following statistics for the measured time interval emerge: minimum value is 1676 ns, median value is 1956 ns, and the maximum value is 4190 ns. The initial interpretation of these results can be the following: the lower values are the *minimal* costs of invoking `nanoTime()`, the larger median values are due to delays caused e.g. by CPU scheduling, and the largest values are outliers caused by garbage collection etc.

However, a closer look at the individual measured results reveals that there are a few results that yield 1676 ns or 1677 ns, and the remaining majority yields 1955 ns or 1956 ns. In particular, there are no measurements between 1677 ns and 1955 ns, and the measurements following 1956 ns have a significant distance (278 ns and 279 ns, as well as multiples of those) to 1956 ns, which is very similar to the distance between 1676 ns/1677 ns and 1955 ns/1956 ns. Thus, the results are forming "clusters" with small intra-cluster element distances of 1 ns and larger inter-cluster distances of ca. 279 ns. A plausible explanation of intra-cluster differences is given by the effects of rounding and truncating (cf. Section 3.2.3). The inter-cluster differences appear to be due to the accuracy of the timer method, i.e. the values of 1955 ns/1956 ns equal "minimum timer invocation cost + 1 timer method accuracy".

An additional challenge arises for computing the invocation cost of timers whose accuracy is significantly larger than the invocation cost. One possibility is to perform an approximative, stochastic computation: repeat the code in Listing

4.2 n times (with $n \gg 1000$), and then assume that $invocationCost_{approximate} :=$ $\frac{\sum_{i=1}^{n} timerInvocationCost_i}{n}$. However, CPU scheduling, garbage collection and other effects can have a negative impact on the quality of the results.

Another possibility would be to use stochastic approach as in Listing 3.4 or repeat a significant number s of timer method invocations, and to divide the time distance between the result of the first and the last invocation by s, as shown in Listing 3.5. However, in practice, the accuracy is larger than the invocation cost by the factor of $5 \cdot 10^5$ (cf. the method `currentTimeMillis()` in Section 7.2). This would make the computation run for a long time if `time2-time1` should be more than just $1 \cdot accuracy$ of the method.

```
1  long time1 = time(); //first of s measurements
2  long time2;
3  for(int i=1; i<s; i++){
4  time2 = time();
5  }
6  long timerInvocationCost = (time2 - time1)/s;
```

Listing 3.5: Oversimplified measurement of timer method invocation cost

Instead of stochastic approximation or the approach in Listing 3.5, this thesis makes use of "helper" timer methods which have already known small (i.e. good) accuracy and low (i.e. well-suitable) invocation costs. First, it is checked whether the accuracy of the considered timer is larger than its invocation cost: this is visible by the minimum timer invocation being 0. Then, the invocation cost of the considered method is quantified using a "helper" timer method, since it holds that helper's invocation cost and accuracy are less than the accuracy of the considered timer.

In practice, for the timer methods with the best accuracy, the invocation cost is usually a multiple of the accuracy. For example, in Section 7.2, to compute the invocation cost of the Java platform API timer method `java.lang.System.-currentTimeMillis()` (unit: 1 ms, accuracy on the above platform: 15 ms), the helper method `java.lang.System.nanoTime()` is used (unit: 1 ns, accuracy on the above platform: 279 ns, median invocation cost: 1955 ns). This results in $0.0002\ ms$ as invocation costs of `currentTimeMillis()` on the above platform, which is equal to $0.2 \ \mu s$ or $200 \ ns$. Note that the accuracy of `currentTimeMillis()` is ca. 53763 times the accuracy of `nanoTime()`.

Algorithm 3.1 illustrates the data collection for cluster-based computation of accuracy and invocation costs. In Part A of Algorithm 3.1, the timer invocation cost is computed, if possible (if the smallest value of $\mathcal{R}$ (results) is 0, the minimum timer invocation cost is set to $undefined$, and needs to be computed in the way defined earlier in this section).

In Part B of Algorithm 3.1, the work performed between the timer invocations is gradually increased, to allow the time interval to grow by one duration of timer accuracy. Note that the `globalVariable` incremented in Algorithm 3.1 is globally visible (i.e. non-private) and is read after the computation is finished. The objective of this is to ensure that the incrementation task will not be "optimised away" by the dead-code analysis and similar techniques, and that each iteration of the loop will be executed. While this solution works pretty well for current execution platform such as Java Virtual Machine, the computation performed between the timer invocations can be replaced by another, more complicated algorithm (such as Fibonacci computation) if needed. Some efficiency-increasing techniques (not shown in Algorithm 3.1) have been implemented in this scope of this thesis to let Algorithm 3.1 terminate as soon as a predefined number of *distinct* values have been saved into $\mathcal{R}$.

The solution continues in Algorithm 3.2, which computes the accuracy and invocation cost from the measured values, using clustering. Part C of the solution (see Algorithm 3.2) creates clusters which contain at most two values of measured time intervals. The motivation for using clustering is that *one* interval value may have up to *two* `long`-typed values due to rounding/truncation, as shown in Section 3.2.3. Thus, a cluster can contain at most two values (a value stores a measured time interval); if an value with distance 1 to the *larger* element in a given cluster appears, it starts a new cluster. For the aforementioned example of `nanoTime`, 1676 ns and 1677 ns would belong to the same cluster, and 1955 ns and 1956 ns to another one.

Algorithm 3.1: Collecting values for computing accuracy and invocation cost

---

Data: numberOfMeasurements, numberOfWorkIncreaseSteps,
      workIncreaseStepSize
Result: $\mathcal{R}$, minimumTimerInvocationCost, medianTimerInvocationCost,
      maximumTimerInvocationCost

```
/* R is a set of time intervals */
```
$\mathcal{R} \leftarrow \emptyset$;

// A. compute timer method invocation costs
for $i \leftarrow 0$ ... *(numberOfMeasurements-1)* **do**
| start $\leftarrow$ Timer.timer(); finish $\leftarrow$ Timer.timer(); $\mathcal{R} \leftarrow \mathcal{R} \cup (finish - start)$;
end
sort($\mathcal{R}$);
if $\mathcal{R}.get(0)>0$ **then**
| minimumTimerInvocationCost $\leftarrow \mathcal{R}$.get(0);
else
| minimumTimerInvocationCost $\leftarrow$ undefined;
end
if $\mathcal{R}.get(\mathcal{R}.length/2)>0$ **then**
| medianTimerInvocationCost $\leftarrow \mathcal{R}$.get($\mathcal{R}$.length/2);
else
| medianTimerInvocationCost $\leftarrow$ undefined;
end
if $\mathcal{R}.get(\mathcal{R}.length-1)>0$ **then**
| maximumTimerInvocationCost $\leftarrow \mathcal{R}$.get($\mathcal{R}$.length-1);
else
| maximumTimerInvocationCost $\leftarrow$ undefined;
end

// B. further measurement data for computing accuracy
for $k \leftarrow 0$ ... *(numberOfWorkIncreaseSteps-1)* **do**
| workAmount $\leftarrow$ workAmount + workIncreaseStepSize;
| **for** $i \leftarrow 0$ ... *(numberOfMeasurements-1)* **do**
| | start $\leftarrow$ Timer.timer();
| | **for** $a \leftarrow 0$ ... *(workAmount-1)* **do**
| | | globalVariable++; a++;
| | **end**
| | finish $\leftarrow$ Timer.timer(); $\mathcal{R} \leftarrow \mathcal{R} \cup (finish - start)$;
| **end**
end
sort($\mathcal{R}$);
[...] // read the global variable to prevent dead-code elimination;

Finally, in Part D, the first two clusters are used to compute the accuracy of the timer method as the distance between their *cluster centers*. The cluster center is defined as the average of the two (or one) value(s) contained in the cluster, independently from the frequency of each value. For example, the cluster center for a cluster with 224 values of 1676 ns and 101 values of 1677 ns is still 1676.5 ns. With the cluster center of 1955 ns/1956 ns being 1955.5 ns, the timer accuracy would be computed to 1955.5 ns-1676.5 ns=279 ns.

For the solution shown in Algorithms 3.1 and 3.2 to work, several constraints and assumptions must be fulfilled (in addition to those listed at the beginning of this section). This constraints and assumptions, along with some limitations of the solution, are discussed in the remainder of this section.

Firstly, there must be *at least* two clusters, and the centers of the first two neighbouring clusters indeed have to be *one* timer method accuracy apart. The implementation of the approach can fulfil this constraint by either creating clusters on-the-fly, or by a sufficiently high `numberOfWorkIncreaseSteps` (e.g. 1000) and other inputs, for which the current implementation already provides suitable defaults. Using them, the constraint is fulfilled in practice by *all* studied timer methods (cf. Section 7.2).

Secondly, the solution cannot distinguish between the two cases "accuracy=1" and "accuracy=2": for example, with accuracy being 1, the first created cluster will contain the values x and $x+1$, and the second cluster will contain the values $x+2$ and $x+3$. With $x = 5$, the accuracy will be computed to

$$\frac{(x+3)+(x+2)}{2} - \frac{(x+1)+(x)}{2} = (x+2.5) - (x+0.5) = 7.5 - 5.5 = 2 \qquad (3.14)$$

while for the case with accuracy being 2, the first cluster will contain x (as the only value) and the second will contain $x+2$ (as the only value), which again results in the computed accuracy of $\frac{x+2}{1} - \frac{x}{1} = \frac{7}{1} - \frac{5}{1} = 2$. A simple but sufficient remedy to this problem is to detect the presence of the pattern $(x),(x+1),(x+2),(x+3)$ before the clustering begins, and to assume that the underlying accuracy is 1 (the pattern $x,x+1,x+2,x+3$ cannot occur when the accuracy is 2 or greater).

Algorithm 3.2: Computing Counter Accuracy and Invocation Cost

---

Data: $\mathcal{R}$ from Algorithm 3.1 (sorted in ascending order)
Result: accuracy

// definition of the Cluster class class Cluster(firstElement,secondElement);

// C. compute clusters from values/frequencies
List<Cluster> $\mathcal{C} \leftarrow \emptyset$;
$\mathcal{R} \leftarrow \mathcal{R} \setminus 0$ **for** *currentValue* $\in \mathcal{R}$ **do**
    if *C contains cluster whose firstElement == (currentValue-1)* **then**
       | add currentEntry as secondElement to that cluster
    end
    else
       | $\mathcal{NC} \leftarrow$ new cluster with currentValue as firstElement
       | $\mathcal{C} \leftarrow \mathcal{C} \cup \mathcal{NC}$
    end
end
//$\mathcal{C}$ is sorted and stores ≥ 2 clusters

// D. compute accuracy from the first two clusters
// (this is a simplified view of the algorithm)
Cluster clusterA $\leftarrow \mathcal{C}$.get(0);
Cluster clusterB $\leftarrow \mathcal{C}$.get(1);
if *clusterA.secondElement* $\neq$ *null* **then**
    | clusterCenterA $\leftarrow$ (clusterA.firstElement.timingValue+
    | clusterA.secondElement.timingValue)/2;
else
    | clusterCenterA $\leftarrow$ clusterA.firstElement.timingValue;
end
if *clusterB.secondElement* $\neq$ *null* **then**
    | clusterCenterB $\leftarrow$ (clusterB.firstElement.timingValue+
    | clusterB.secondElement.timingValue)/2;
else
    | clusterCenterB $\leftarrow$ clusterB.firstElement.timingValue;
end
accuracy $\leftarrow$ clusterCenterB - clusterCenterA;

Thirdly, when the first cluster contains one value and the second cluster contains two values (or vice versa), the computed accuracy will be a floating-point value, ending with .5. However, during the evaluation (see Section 7.2), such cases did not occur, and thus these cases are not investigated further in this thesis. In the implementation of the presented approach, if such a cases occurs, the accuracy is returned as a range whose width is 1 timer unit (e.g. "the accuracy is between 5 ns and 6 ns"). Such precision is usually sufficient for most performance measurement cases in practice.

Finally, both the first and the second cluster could contain just one value. The optimistic view of this case is that there is neither rounding nor truncation involved in the implementation of the timer method, and all timing values (and, therefore, time intervals) are multiples of the integer-typed accuracy which is 2 units or larger. The pessimistic view of this case is that rounding or truncation are involved, and each of the two clusters is missing one value that was not measured due to runtime disturbances or other reasons. One possible pessimistic scenario for the above example of nanoTime() would occur if 1677 ns would be missing in the first cluster (1676, 1677) and 1955 ns would be missing in the second cluster (1955, 1956). In such a scenario, the timer method accuracy would be computed as 1956 ns-1676 ns=280 ns. In a different case, if 1676 ns would be missing in the first cluster and 1956 ns would be missing in the second, the timer method accuracy would be computed to 1955 ns-1677 ns=278 ns. Thus, having only one value in the first and one (other) value in the second cluster means that the real accuracy is within ±2 precision units (for nanoTime(), this means ±2 ns).

3.3.3. Timer Method Invocation in Detail

To read the value of performance indicators (e.g. a timer or the CPU cycle counter) in Java, they must be accessed by invoking *methods*, as there are no "elementary" bytecode-level instructions to access performance indicators. There are several ways to call a method in the source code of a Java program:

1. invoke the method directly (i.e. choice of the timer method is fixed inside source code)

2. use polymorphism or delegation (e.g. define a facade or a wrapper using interfaces, the implementing class can be chosen flexibly)

3. use Java Reflection API (e.g. to find out whether a given timer method is available at runtime)

4. use AOP or bytecode engineering to define insertion points for concrete timer methods (which are weaved at loading time or at compile time into the bytecode)

There are several reasons for using the alternative 2. through 4.:

- The first reason is that since using a timer is a cross-cutting concern, the timer accesses are often spread over several components and classes of the source code, and programmers tend to prepare source code for quick and easy replacement of timers. For example, a given timer method needs to be replaced when a better counter becomes available, or when the application is ported to a platform where certain counters are not available. However, timer methods rarely implement an interface (the JMX beans provided by the package `java.lang.instrument` are a notable exception), and it's usually not possible to change the inheritance/implementation relations of timers (cf. `java.lang.System` class that defines two of the most widely used Java timers is final). Thus, a straightforward solution is to provide a facade/wrapper to the actual timer or counter.

- Another reason is that unlike logging, there is no "log level" mechanism for timer methods, at least in the standard Java Platform API (but also, at the time of writing, in no other timing library compatible with Java SE). Therefore, to distinguish "fine-granular" time measurements from "info-level" time measurements, programmers tend to introduce several facades, where one facade corresponds to one level in logging mechanism. By configuring the individual facades, developers can "rewire" unneeded "tim-

ing levels" to empty methods, allowing the JVM to perform runtime optimisations similar to what is done in logging libraries.

- The third reason is that runtime reconfiguration has become commonplace
  in today's system, allowing to change settings without shutting down the
  application. More generally, the configuration of a system is often separate
  from its actual implementation (cf. deployment descriptor in Enterprise
  Java Beans). To allow runtime reconfigurations w.r.t. timer methods (especially given the fact that they are often implemented in system classes or in
  classes implementing the Platform API), additional steps must be taken.

Therefore, the accuracy and the invocation cost of a timer method should be
quantified for all four of the above method invocation techniques. A further
aspect is added by instance-typed timer methods (cf. Section 3.2.1): the duration
of the creating/initialising the invocation target needs to be measured as well.
This is done in a way which is very similar to the quantification of the invocation
costs.

Finally, to address *JITtability* (cf. Section 3.2.1), the algorithms from Section 3.3.2 needs to be run (a) without warmup and (b) after sufficient warmup.
How much warmup is *sufficient* depends on the concrete virtual machine implementation and its setting; for the Java Virtual Machine, 20000 invocations
are usually thought to be sufficient, but the warmup mechanism itself must be
implemented properly [169]. Alternatively, the Algorithms 3.1 and 3.2 can be
modified in such a way that a sudden drop in the values of measured time intervals is detected, and interpreted as "JIT has completed" signal, leading to a
second run of the Algorithms 3.1 and 3.2. The current implementation of the
Algorithms 3.1 and 3.2 includes this enhancement, which can be activated as an
option.

3.4. Analysing Units, Monotonicity and Stability

Often, the timer unit is known or (implicitly) specified (e.g. *nano*seconds for
Java platform API's `System.nanoTime()`, as confirmed by the method's doc-

umentation). However, hardware counters such as TSC are often more precise, yet their implementation may be different between CPU manufacturers and models, leading to different update frequencies and thus to different units.

At the same time, the update frequency of counters is often aligned with CPU clock frequency and thus is not a power of 10 (typical CPU frequencies are 1.83 GHz, 2.8 GHz etc.). Thus, the counter time unit is not integer-typed multiple of time unit such as 1 ns or 1 ms. To use the high-resolution TSC and similar counters for measuring time intervals, the value of the unit must be obtained in a platform-independent way. In particular, by assuming a black-box view, the presented approach does not need to inspect the implementation of a counter to quantify its unit.

Sometimes, the timer methods accessing "unitless" counters are accompanied by a method that exposes the counter's update frequency. This implies that the counter's accuracy (resolution), which is the inverse of the update frequency, is exactly one "tick". For example, the `QueryPerformanceCounter` method (exclusively available on Windows) is accompanied by the method `QueryPerformanceFrequency`. Yet for those counters (TSC, HPET) where the update frequency cannot be queried, the need still exists for a platform-independent way to quantify the unit of the counter or, more precisely, of the method accessing it.

To quantify a counter's unit, a novel algorithm was developed in this thesis, and it is outlined in Algorithms 3.3 and 3.4 using pseudocode. In the following, we assume that a method to access the counter/timer is available, and that it returns monotonically increasing values during the execution of algorithm (in particular, the timer method's results do not "overflow"). An evaluation of the algorithm is provided in Section 7.2.

The algorithms use three methods:

1. `sleep(int r)` is a method that will pause the execution or the calling thread for (at least) r milliseconds

2. `t1()` is a timer method whose unit is known (e.g. `nanoTime()` in Java)

3. `t2()` is the actual timer method whose unit has to be quantified

3.4.1. Quantifying Units of Counters and Timers

The *central idea* behind our solution is to measure the executing thread's sleep durations (induced by `sleep(r)`) using both `t1()` and `t2()`, and to correlate the resulting interval durations so the relation between the known unit `t1unit` of `t1()` and unknown unit of `t2()` can be established.

We use `t1()` in addition to `sleep(r)` because in reality, the *requested* sleep duration `r` can differ significantly from the real sleep duration *measured* by `t1()` (in other words, we use `sleep(r)` as a measurement driver). This issue [170] is particularly visible on certain Linux distributions for the Java method
`Thread.sleep(int r)` when parametrised with small `r`, where the values of `r` are in milliseconds. Measurements that demonstrate this issue and show the need for `t1()` are presented later in this section, after the overall algorithm is presented and explained.

The Algorithm 3.3 makes use of two helper functions, `findOutliers` and `getLinearCorrelationSlope`. While `findOutliers` is shown in Algorithm 3.4 and detailed in Section 3.4.1.1, `getLinearCorrelationSlope` is a standard algorithm for getting linear regression using least square error [171, p. 730], and is not detailed here.

Note that the slope of the linear function that expresses the regression is non-zero, and therefore the counter unit (which is the inverse of the slope) can be computed safely. Also note that the correlation coefficient and the y-axis offset will be used later in this chapter to evaluate the quality of a counter with respect to its stability.

Note that in Algorithm 3.3, the calls to `t1` do *not* "wrap" the invocations to `t2()`. Instead, `t1` and `t2` are arranged in an interleaved way, which helps to compensate for potentially different invocation costs of `t2()` and `t1()`.

Algorithm 3.3: Computing Counter Unit

Data: t1unit,numberOfIncreases, numberOfIterations, initialSleepDuration,
sleepDurationIncrease, sleepOutlierThreshold,
groupOutlierThreshold

Result: counter unit (as a multiple of t1()'s counter unit)

for $i = 1 \ldots$ *nrOfIncreases* **do**
   | $\quad sleepTime_i \leftarrow initialSleepDuration + i \cdot sleepDurationIncrease$
end

for $j = 1 \ldots$ *numberOfIterations* **do**
   for $k = 1 \ldots$ *numberOfIncreases* **do**
      t1start $\leftarrow$ t1();
      t2start $\leftarrow$ t2();
      sleep($sleepTime_k$);
      $m1_{k+j \cdot numberOfIncreases} \leftarrow$ (t1() - t1start);
      $m2_{k+j \cdot numberOfIncreases} \leftarrow$ (t2() - t2start);
   end
end

outlierIndexes $\leftarrow$ findOutliers(m1, m2, sleepOutlierThreshold,
groupOutlierThreshold);

correlationSlope $\leftarrow$ getLinearCorrelationSlope(m1, m2, outlierIndexes);

counterUnit $\leftarrow$ t1unit/correlationSlope; //relative

3.4.1.1. Filtering Outliers

Linear correlation is suitable because with monotonic and stable timers, the measurements of the time interval (induced through sleep) *should* be similar between `t1()` and `t2()`.

Of course, there will be differences between them:

- the accuracy of `t1()` and `t2()` influences the accuracy of `measurementT1` and `measurementT2`

- `measurementT1` includes the invocation costs of `sleep(r)`, `t1()` and `t2()`, as does `measurementT2` – yet the invocation costs can vary from invocation to invocation by one or several accuracies (see [19])

- CPU scheduling, memory management, thread affinity scheduling of the execution platform etc. can lead to interruptions at any point of Algorithm 3.3, which can in turn lead to outliers.

To prevent such outliers from overimpacting the algorithm, two filters are used (the need for them is shown later in this section). The filters, encapsulated in Algorithm 3.4, accomplish the following:

1. if the `t1()`-measured sleep time is more than `sleepOutlierThreshold` % longer than the requested sleep time, the measurement point is skipped (i.e. it is not saved into `m1`/`m2`)

2. among the `numberOfIterations` measurements for a concrete value of `sleepTimes[k]`, we find the measurement with the minimum value of `m2`, and skip those of `numberOfIterations` measurements where `m2` is `groupOutlierThreshold` % or more above the minimum value of `m2`

We discuss the impact of choosing the values for `sleepOutlierThreshold` and `groupOutlierThreshold` during the evaluation in Section 7.2.

Algorithm 3.4: Identifying outliers: `findOutliers` method

Data: m1, m2,sleepOutlierThreshold, groupOutlierThreshold
Result: outlierIndexes
outlierIndexes $\leftarrow \emptyset$;
for $k = 1 \ldots$ *numberOfIncreases* **do**
    minSleep $\leftarrow +\infty$;
    for $j = 1 \ldots$ *numberOfIterations* **do**
        if $m1_{k+j \cdot numberOfIncreases} > (1 + \frac{sleepOutlierThreshold}{100}) \cdot sleepTime_k$ **then**
            outlierIndexes $\leftarrow outlierIndexes \cup (k + j \cdot numberOfIncreases)$;
        end
        if $m2_{k+j \cdot numberOfIncreases} < minSleep$ **then**
            minSleep $\leftarrow m2_{k+j \cdot numberOfIncreases}$
        end
    end
    for $j = 1 \ldots$ *numberOfIterations* **do**
        if $m2_{k+(j \cdot numberOfIncreases)} > (1 + \frac{groupOutlierThreshold}{100}) \cdot minSleep$ **then**
            outlierIndexes $\leftarrow outlierIndexes \cup (k + j \cdot numberOfIncreases)$;
        end
    end
end

3.4.2. Analysing Monotonicity during Concurrent Access to Timing Methods

In single-threaded scenarios, testing the monotonicity of a timer can be done by repeating a large number of timer method invocations with minimal work (i.e. saving of the timer values) performed between two adjacent timer method invocations. But for concurrent access to timers in multi-threaded platform, a more elaborate technique is needed.

For example, consider an unsynchronised (i.e. unprotected) static timer method which retrieves a value from a counter with an update frequency of 1 MHz and converts the retrieved value to nanoseconds, using a static field. As one counter tick equals 1 microsend (=1000 nanoseconds), the counter value is multiplied with 1000. Assume that a first thread starts executing the code in Listing 3.6, but is interrupted right after the second line when a second thread kicks in.

The second thread executes the code in lines 2 and 3, before it pauses and the execution of the first thread continues. As the value of the variable a (which is shared among the threads as it is static) has already been multiplied by 1000, the second multiplication (performed by the first thread) leads to a wrong result being stored in a. Not only does the first thread return the wrong result (the second and thus wrong value of the counter, and it is multiplied with 1000000 instead of 1000), but so does the second thread (the correctly read value of counter is multiplied with 1000000 instead of 1000).

```
1  long getTime(){
2    a=Counter.value; //a is a static field of type long
3    a = a*1000;
4    return a;
5  }
```

Listing 3.6: Example concurrency-unsafe timer method

When dealing with timer methods from public interfaces, clients must make smallest possible assumptions, i.e. they must treat the methods of these interfaces as possibly concurrency-unsafe, as in the above example. Assuming that the used implementation of the public interface is a black box and thus unmodifiable, clients should at least try to test whether the considered timer method is concurrency-(un)safe, with the option to switch to concurrency-safe alternatives. In this section, we describe a heuristic for studying whether a timer method is suitable for concurrent access.

To provoke concurrency issues, concurrent accesses to the timer method should "fire" (almost) simultaneously. But depending on the programming language, scheduling a task to run at a specific timepoint may or may not be available. In Java, the `java.util.Timer` class includes different methods to schedule `java.util.TimerTasks`, both one-shot and periodic ones. However, it uses the `java.util.Date` class to specify times, which "represents a specific instant in time, with millisecond precision" – such precision might be insufficient to deal with nanosecond-level timers.

Thus, a simpler technique which is independent of a programming language is employed (cf. Listing 3.7): `phaseLength` calls to the timer method are executed in a loop, and the shortest-possible pause between two calls is being inserted afterwards. The pause is inserted to change the shift (offset) between the timer method invocation starts for the cases where several instances of this algorithm are executed concurrently without external disturbances.

Each value returned by the timer method is recorded individually for later analysis, which is described below. The difference between the two neighbouring values corresponds to the timer invocation costs plus the overhead of recording the returned value (and additionally the time paused, where applicable).

```
1   int  phases  =  100;
2   int  phaseLength  =  200;
3   int  currPhase =0;
4   int  currCall ;
5   while (currPhase  <  phases ) {
6      currCall =0;
7      while ( currCall <phaseLength ) {
8         this . record ( timer . getValue ( ) ) ;  // record  value
9         currCall ++;
10     }
11     pause ( shortestSupportedTimeInterval ) ;

13     // phase  length  randomised  to  yield  different  method  start  times
14     phaseLength=100+Math . random (100 ); // uniformly  distributed  in
          [100 ,200)
15     currPhase ++;
16  }
```

Listing 3.7: Code for testing timer monotonicity in concurrent setting

The load on the execution platform is minimised, and a warmup phase precedes the actual measurements. We assume that no overflow (cf. Section 3.5) happens during a run, with the resulting expectation that the recorded timer method values are monotonically increasing. While the suggested test is just a heuristic, it is motivated by the observations of the TSC counter (cf. Section 7.2). The TSC counter exhibited frequent but unsystematic jumps of its values (resulting in values which are several times higher than those expected) though for *the single-threaded case*, the TSC fulfils the monotonicity requirement.

While many timer methods are static (e.g. those in the `java.lang.System` class of the Java platform API), some are not (e.g. `sun.misc.Perf.highResCounter()`). For the timer methods which are non-static (i.e. instance-typed, see Section 3.2.1), one cannot see from the signature whether there is just one instance of the implementing class (i.e. the implementation uses a singleton pattern). To check at runtime whether each call to the constructor (or factory method) returns a singleton or a new instance of the implementing class, the Java implementation of our approach can use object IDs.

Altogether, in Section 7.2, the following degrees of freedom will be explored when running the code in Listing 3.7:

- the number of concurrent threads running the algorithm in Listing 3.7

- for non-static methods, the usage of the implementing class instance:
  (a) same instance for all threads as opposed to
  (b) individual instance for each thread

3.4.3. Analysing Stability of a Timer

Section 3.2.1 introduced the notion of *timer stability* to express that the timer values indeed correspond to what is being measured. In this section, an approach to test and to quantify the stability of a timer method is suggested, based on the idea of *correlation* that was already employed in Section 3.4.2.

To see why stability is not a trivial property and needs to be assessed systematically, consider Figure 3.9. It shows the duration of a `Thread.sleep(long millis)` operation (the parameter is the requested sleep time in milliseconds), measured using the `System.nanoTime()` Java Platform API timer method. Each requested sleep time was measured 20 times to visualise the differences between individual measurements. It can be seen that `nanoTime()` is a stable timer as the measured values are very close to the requested sleep values, and only minor differences between the measurements for a given sleep time are observed.

In the same algorithm run, `TSC` was used to measure the sleep times, and the resulting co-measured values (in TSC ticks) are plotted in Figure 3.10. The TSC is accessed from Java using JNI; it returns the number of CPU ticks after an epoch that remains fixed during a program run. The experiment was run on a computer with CPU frequency of 2.8 GHz, i.e. 2.8 CPU cycles are executed in a nanosecond, and one cycle takes ≈ 0.357 ns (rounded to 3 decimal places). The x axis values in Figure 3.10 carry the requested sleep time (converted to ns), the

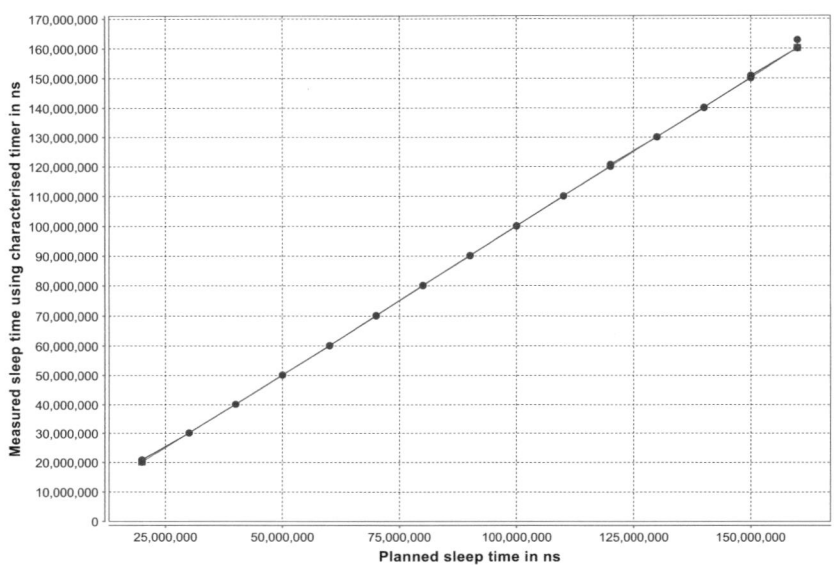

Figure 3.9.: Relation of requested sleep times (x-axis, in ns) to values measured with
nanoTime (y-axis, in ns)

zigzagged line carries the measured TSC values (y axis in TSC ticks). The red
line carries the *minimum* number of TSC ticks that *should* have been measured
(since the parameter of the `sleep` method has the semantic of "at least", the real
sleep duration can be higher).

In contrast to Figure 3.9, the sleep times measured with TSC and shown in
Figure 3.10 exhibit large jumps, which means that TSC is not a stable timer
method. In Figure 3.10, there seems to be no useful correlation between the
requested and TSC-measured sleep times despite the almost-perfect correlation for `nanoTime()`-based measurements in Figure 3.9. As the invocations
of `nanoTime()` seem not to suffer from outliers as much as TSC does, it seems
that the outliers of TSC are not caused by external factors and disturbances.

It should be noted that the shown measurements were performed on a dual-
core computer with no external load (only the measurements and the OS were

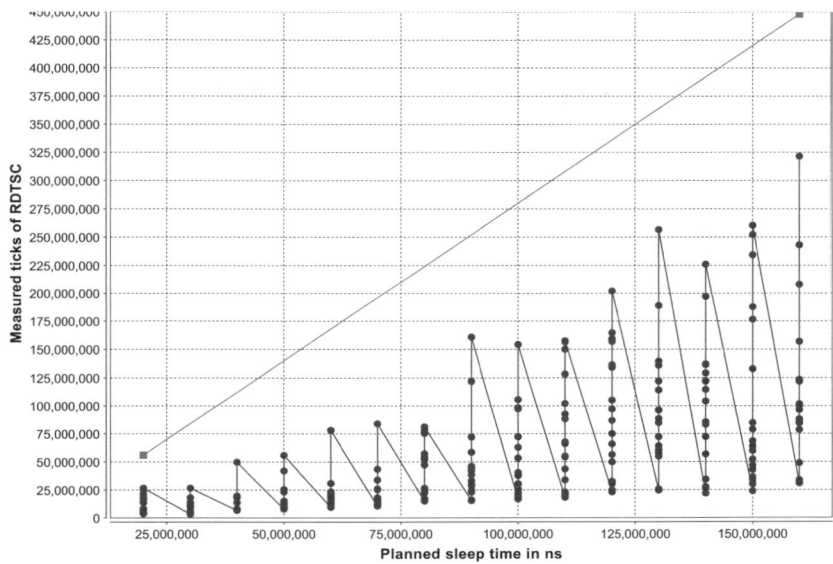

Figure 3.10.: Zigzagged line with round shapes: requested sleep times (x-axis, in ns) and values measured with TSC (y-axis, in ticks); straight line with square shapes: number of CPU cycles (y-axis) corresponding to the requested sleep time (x-axis)

running), yet repeating the measurements on the same computer but with CPU load close to 100% (caused by a parallel thread) showed that nanoTime() kept its stability while TSC got even worse. These results suggest that TSC is not a reliable and stable timer for measurements on this platform. But what are the reasons for it? Is it still possible to obtain the unit of TSC?

To formalise the notion of stability, one needs to quantify *how far* and *how often* the measurements can deviate from what is expected to be measured. The impact of the timer method accuracy and invocation on the measured values has been discussed in Section 3.3. Thus, this section is presented under the assumption that the accuracy/invocation cost of the considered timer method can be ignored as the time interval to be measured is significantly (at least two orders of magnitude) larger than the accuracy and the invocation cost.

The quantification of timer stability is shown in Algorithms 3.5 and 3.6. The approach uses the correlation principle of Algorithm 3.3, but with the difference that the units of t1() and t2() are already known and converted to the same unit.

In Algorithm 3.5, $aboveExpectationThreshold$ and $belowExpectationThreshold$ quantify *how far* the measurement can deviate from the expected value before it qualifies as an outlier.

Both $aboveExpectationThreshold$ and $belowExpectationThreshold$ are positive values which are interpreted as shares of the expected measurement result. For example, $aboveExpectationThreshold$ set to 0.45 means that values which are 45 % and more above the expected measurement result are outliers. $outlierFrequency$-$Threshold$ is the maximum percentage of outliers among the measured values, before a timer is considered unstable on the basis of analysed experiment.

Of course, the outcome of an experiment depends on the execution platform's state (e.g. load, CPU utilisation etc.), and several experiment runs should be carried out under varying condition. Additionally, it is possible to use a more elaborate formula, e.g. by weighting how far off the measured value is compared to the expectation, rather than treating each outlier equally. This would allow expressing the stability of a timer as a floating point value, rather than as a boolean value in Algorithm 3.5.

In Algorithm 3.5, apart from the time whose stability is to be analysed, an additional timer t1() is used because, as explained in Section 3.4.1, the actual sleep time resulting from the invocation of sleep() can be different from the requested sleep time. So instead of comparing the requested sleep time to the measurements of t2(), the requested sleep time is compared to both t1() and t2(). If possible, t1() should be a timer which has been analysed for stability with positive result. Then, the conclusions about t2()'s stability are trivial.

If both the stability of `t1()` and `t2()` is unknown, several outcomes for `m_1` and for `m_2` in Algorithm 3.5 are possible and all of their combinations should be analysed:

- for `t1()`: either
  (i) `m_1` is within *aboveExpectationThreshold* / *belowExpectationThreshold* of `r` or
  (ii) it is not

- for `t2()`: either
  (iii) `m_2` is within *aboveExpectationThreshold* / *belowExpectationThreshold* of `r` or
  (iv) it is not

The combination (i)/(iii) is good: the considered measurement is not an outlier, neither for `t1()` nor for `t2()`. The combination (i)/(iv) hints to an outlier for `t2()`, while the combination (ii)/(iii) hints to an outlier for `t1()`. Finally, the combination (ii)/(iv) can mean that either (a) both `t1()` and `t2()` produced an outlier, or (b) both produced non-outliers but the effective sleep time was different from the requested sleep time.

There are several possibilities to deal with the combination (ii)/(iv), the possibility chosen in this thesis is to consider both `m_1` and `m_2` as non-outliers if $|m_1 - m_2| < min(m_1, m_2) \cdot min(aboveExpectationThreshold, belowExpectationThreshold)$, and consider both of them as outliers otherwise.

In Section 7.2, the stability of serveral frequently-used timers will be evaluated using the presented approach.

3.5. Computing the Maximum Measurable Time Interval and the Epochs

The *overflow behaviour* of a counter/timer describes what happens once the maximum value of the counter is reached, and the date of this event (which is different from the next epoch).

An example that motivated the work described in this section is the Java API timer method `System.nanoTime()`: its official documentation [164] states that "the value returned represents nanoseconds since some fixed but arbitrary time (perhaps in the future, so values may be negative)". Clearly, the value of "fixed but arbitrary time" impacts the overflow behaviour of this method, and must be determined. Furthermore, it is unclear how "fixed" that value is: for example, for a multi-JVM application residing on a single computer with a multi-core CPU, is the above value really "fixed" across cores and JVMs, even in the light of CPU sleep management and when JVMs are started up at different times? Thus, what is needed here is a scientifically sound approach for obtaining the value of the "fixed but arbitrary time", and a study of whether it changes between JVM products, application runs, operating systems etc. A further question is: when will the values of `System.nanoTime()` overflow? It is also interesting to know the overflow behaviour, i.e. whether the timer method will start returning negative values, or start again from 0.

In this section, `<TYPE>.MAX_VALUE` refers to the maximum value for a numeric primitive data type `<TYPE>`, and `<TYPE>.MIN_VALUE` to its minimum value. To shorten the notation, $Type_{min}$ is used instead of `<Type>.MIN_VALUE`, and $Type_{max}$ is used instead of `<Type>.MAX_VALUE`.

The numeric range is usually fixed for a given type, but some languages provide integer (i.e. non-decimal) data types with dynamically growing numeric range. In Java, for example, the class `BigInteger` has a quasi-arbitrary value range, though its runtime instances are immutable (i.e. the memory requirement of each instance is computed at its creation, and remains unchanged over the lifetime of the instance). Therefore, `BigInteger` is rather rarely used due to its memory demand, as each operation (even additions or subtractions) results in a new `BigInteger` instance. In this section, we consider only integer (non-decimal) types with a fixed numeric range, as all known timer methods (cf. Section 7.2) return timing value as fixed-value types.

The *arithmetic overflow* (hereafter simply called the overflow) occurs when an arithmetic calculation leads to a result that is greater than $Type_{max}$. Overflows form an object of intense research in the areas of verification research, security and robustness [172, 173, 174], as unhandled overflows can lead to unexpected behaviour and immense costs (e.g. Ariane rocket failure, cf. [175]).

Prevention, prediction or at least detection of an overflow is important because an overflow changes the results of a measurement in an undesirable way. In the broader context of software engineering, a number of costly or compromising failures stem from undetected overflows, e.g. the failure of the Ariane rocket [175]. Therefore, though the potential risks in performance engineering may be lower, a sound scientific approach is needed to understand this issue.

This section addresses these challenges using a general and platform-independent approach. It also formalises the computation of the *maximum correctly measurable time interval*, which depends on the overflow behaviour of timer methods.

3.5.1. Foundations

A few programming languages and execution platforms provide special arithmetical operators to detect overflows [176], e.g. C# operation "+" throws an `OverflowException` in certain cases. In the majority of the cases, however, users have to deal with overflow themselves (which increases the complexity of the code and decreases the performance of the application).

A *wraparound* is observed when an integer type overflows with no mechanisms in place to detect it, to handle it, or to throw an exception. More formally, the following overflow types exist:

1. a wraparound uses the entire numeric range of the value type:

   $Type_{max} + 1 = Type_{min}$ and

   $Type_{min} - 1 = Type_{max}$

2. *saturation* stops modifying the value once it reaches one of the bounds:

   $Type_{max} + 1 = Type_{max}$ and $Type_{min} - 1 = Type_{min}$

3. *nulling* "resets" the value to 0 if an overflow occurs:

   $Type_{max} + 1 = 0$ and $Type_{min} - 1 = 0$

115

In all three cases, it holds that $Type_{max} - 1 < Type_{max}$ and $Type_{min} + 1 > Type_{min}$. In this section, we only consider wraparound because saturation and nulling are not used for primitive numeric types in modern object-oriented programming languages, such as Java.

This method returns `long`-typed timing values, i.e. it will overflow once it reaches `long`'s $Type_{max}$ (which is defined in the corresponding `java.lang.Long` class). Whether the reaction to the overflow will be a wraparound, a nulling or even a saturation remains unknown from the (textual) documentation of the method. However, assuming that a wraparound to `long`'s $Type_{min}$ occurs and assuming that `currentTimeMillis()` will continue to return monotonically increasing values, there will be a next epoch once the value returned by `currentTimeMillis()` again reaches 0.

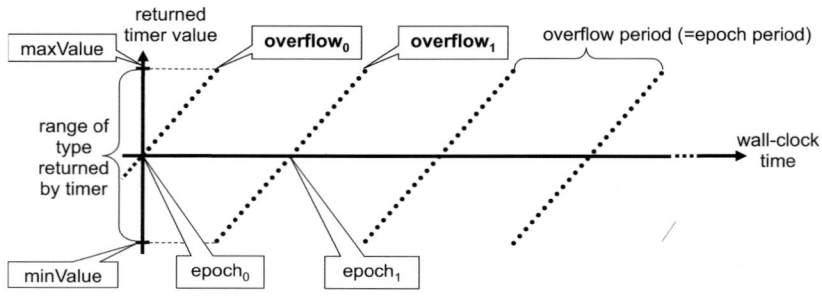

Figure 3.11.: Overflow of range-limited values

An *overflow period* is the timespan between two subsequent overflows of a counter (or timer) which returns monotonically increasing integer-typed values and which does not handle arithmetic overflows. Under these conditions, the overflow period is finite and it is determined by the numeric range of the used numeric type. Figure 3.11 illustrates such a case (using wraparound as overflow consequence), and features indexed epochs ($epoch_i$, ...) and indexed overflows ($overflow_i$, ...). In Figure 3.11, $epoch_0$ denotes the most recent epoch from an analyst's point of view, i.e. at the time of drawing the diagram, the analyst's "now" is in the interval $[epoch_0, epoch_1)$. Note that the x-axis (with wall-clock time) continues to the left to account for the (hypothetical) case that the timer method may have had previous epochs $epoch_{-1}$, $epoch_{-2}$, etc.

The *most recent epoch*, called $epoch_0$ in this section, is not standardised across platforms and languages, as many timer methods choose between system time, computer startup time etc. as the value for $epoch_0$. For example, the epoch of Windows NT is 00:00:00 UT on January 1st, **1601**, while the system time on Unix is 00:00:00 UT on January 1st, **1970**. On the other hand, plat-form-independent APIs often select a platform-independent epoch, such as the `System.currentTimeMillis()` method of Java Platform API, which uses 00:00:00 UT on January 1st, 1970 on *all* supported platforms.

3.5.2. Impact of Overflow on Timer Methods with High Precision

The impact of overflow issues in security-related software warrants a closer look on the impact of overflow on timer measurements. It also reveals why timer methods with certain characteristics (high resolution, early epoch) are not avail-able in particular languages/execution platforms.

Assume that a programmer is requested on April, 1st 2009 to implement a `long`-returning Java timer method with the fixed epoch of Windows sys-tem time, and a unit of 1 ns. That is, the timer must return the number of nanoseconds which have passed since January 1st, 1601 00:00:00 UTC. Re-calling that a `long` in Java ranges from -2^{63} to $2^{63} - 1$, the programmer decides to study the overflow period. The programmer takes $2^{63} - 1 = 9,223,372,036,854,775,807 \approx 9.223 \cdot 10^{18}$ ns, which, converted to years, is $\frac{2^{63}-1}{10^9 \cdot 60 \cdot 60 \cdot 24 \cdot 365} \approx \frac{9.223 \cdot 10^{18}}{31.536 \cdot 10^{15}} \approx 292.22$ years. This means that $overflow_0$ (i.e. the first overflow after $epoch_0$) would happen at a timer method value corresponding to a wall-clock date during the year 1893 (=1601+292).

No matter which of the three overflow scenarios described in Section 3.5.1 will apply, the overflow has very negative effects and reveals the flaw in the request to the programmer:

1. For a wraparound, the timer method will return negative values for $\approx$ 292.22 years after 1893, i.e. until ca. 2185, which means that the request given to the programmer cannot be fulfilled (and, of course, negative timing values are not very intuitive). Note that the overflow period is 2^{64} ns, i.e. 584 years – the next overflow from $Type_{max}$ to $Type_{min}$ will happen during the year 2477 (=1893+584).

2. For saturation, the timer method would be "stuck" at long's $Type_{max}$ since the moment that the programmer obtains the request, prohibiting any meaningful use of the timer since after saturation, since measurement of time intervals would always return 0.

3. For nulling, the timer would return increasing positive values at the time of writing – however, its last epoch $epoch_0$ would be in the year 1893, not in the year 1601 as requested.

These considerations explain why Windows' system time is counted in ticks, where each tick corresponds to 100 ns – this way, the overflow will take place after 29222 years, which is more than enough. In contrast to Windows, several popular operating systems have relatively imminent system time overflows: September 17th 2042 for IBM's z/OS, and 19 January 2038 for certain implementation of the `time()` function in Unix [177, 178, 179].

Dates *before* the (most recent) epoch form a further challenge in conjunction with overflow. For example, consider the case where a programmer is requested to use the class `java.sql.Date` from the Java platform API. The documentation states that `java.sql.Date` is a "thin wrapper around a millisecond value [...] [which] represents the number of milliseconds that have passed since January 1, 1970 00:00:00.000 GMT" (the official documentation uses GMT and UT almost synonymously, differences are explained in the documentation for the `java.util.Date` class). If the application that the programmer is working on also needs to save dates before 1970, and use them for the computation of time intervals, `java.sql.Date` will have to be used with negative values. At this point the programmer has to think about timing values and timestamps with different signs, and look into classes such as `java.sql.Timestamp`, `java.util.Date`, etc.

3.5.3. Impact of Overflow on Measuring Time Intervals

A further overflow-related issue is signalled by the documentation of `System.-nanoTime()` method in the Java platform API, which says that "Differences in successive calls that span greater than approximately 292 years (2^{63} nanoseconds) will not accurately compute elapsed time due to numerical overflow" [164]. It is unclear, however, what "accurately" means, and whether the problem is specific for the `nanoTime()` method but not other timer methods. From the findings in the previous subsection, however, the statement "2^{63} nanoseconds" points to an issue with the type of values that `nanoTime()` returns, which is again `long`.

The issue of this subsection, which we called *Maximum Correctly Measurable Time Interval* (MCMTI), depends on (i) the numeric range of the used data type (which is expressed by $Type_{max}$ and $Type_{min}$) and (ii) the overflow behaviour. Here, we consider the most common case ($Type_{min} \leq 0$, $Type_{max} > 0$, overflow behaviour is "wraparound") – other cases can be analysed in a very similar way. Recall that for the considered case, it holds that $Type_{max} + 1 = Type_{min}$ and $Type_{min} - 1 = Type_{max}$.

Let t_1 be the first value returned by a timer method and let the second, later value be t_2; the trivial case of $t_1 = t_2$ is excluded. Let $bound(t_x)$ be the value of t_x which fits into the numeric range of the data type `<TYPE>` which is to store t_x. In particular, $Type_{min} \leq bound(t_x) \leq Type_{max}$, even if $t_x > Type_{max}$ or $t_x < Type_{min}$. Therefore, due to overflow it may happen that $bound(t_2) < bound(t_1)$ even if t_2 is later than t_1. Also note that t_1 and t_2 need not be wall-clock time values – they can be timestamps referring to a timepoint in future or in the past.

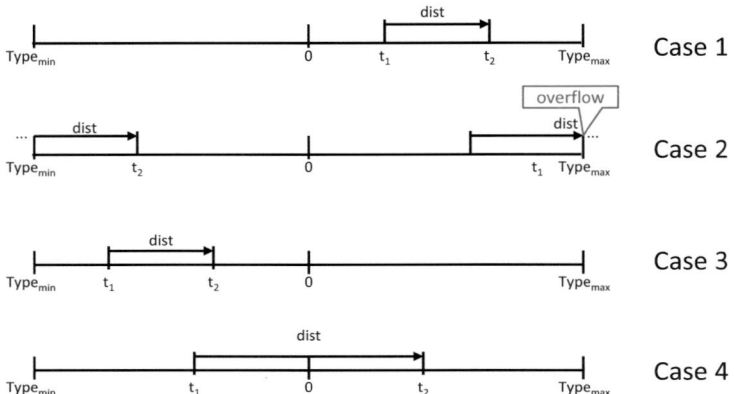

Figure 3.12.: The impact of numeric ranges on measuring time intervals between t_1 and t_2

First, consider a simple example for `nanoTime()` which reveals the problem: $Type_{min} = -2^{63}$, $Type_{max} = 2^{63} - 1$, $t_2 = 2^{62} + 5 < Type_{max}$, $t_1 = -2^{62} > Type_{min}$. $bound(t_2) - bound(t_1) = t_2 - t_1 = 2^{62} + 5 - (-2^{62}) = 2^{63} + 5$, which is larger than $Type_{max}$ and thus overflows to $Type_{max} + 5 = (Type_{max} + 1) + 4 = (Type_{min}) + 4 = -2^{63} + 4 < 0$. The negative result means that t_2 is earlier than t_1 – a clear contradiction to the value of t_1 and t_2.

In a more systematic way , the following cases can occur (all of them with $t_2 > t_1$, see Figure 3.12):

1. $0 \leq t_1 \leq Type_{max}$, $0 \leq t_2 \leq Type_{max}$
   $\Rightarrow bound(t_2) - bound(t_1) = t_2 - t_1 > 0$
   $\Rightarrow$ no overflow happens and the time interval is measured correctly

2. $0 \leq t_1 \leq Type_{max}$, $Type_{min} \leq t_2 \leq 0$
   (i.e. an overflow occurred between t_1 and t_2)
   $\Rightarrow bound(t_2) - bound(t_1) = ((t_2 - Type_{max} - 1) + Type_{min}) - t_1 = t_2 - t_1 - (Type_{max} + 1) + Type_{min} = t_2 - t_1$ (since $Type_{max} + 1 = min$)
   $\Rightarrow$ if $t_2 - t_1 > Type_{max}$, the value of $bound(t_2) - bound(t_1)$ will overflow into the

negative (which means that t_2 came before t_1), contradicting the assumptions.

3. $Type_{min} \leq t_1 \leq 0, Type_{min} \leq t_2 \leq 0$
   $\Rightarrow |t_2| < |t_1|$ and $bound(t_2) - bound(t_1) = t_2 - t_1 = (-|t_2|) - (-|t_1|) = |t_1| - |t_2| > 0$
   $\Rightarrow$ no overflow happens and the time interval is measured correctly even though both t_2 and t_1 are negative

4. $Type_{min} \leq t_1 \leq 0, 0 \leq t_2 \leq Type_{max}$
   $\Rightarrow bound(t_2) - bound(t_1) = t_2 + |t_1|$
   $\Rightarrow$ if $t_2 + |t_1| > Type_{max}$, the value of $bound(t_2) - bound(t_1)$ will overflow into the negative (which means that t_2 came before t_1), contradicting the assumptions.

This analysis shows how overflow affects the computation of time intervals, and explains in detail the comment in the documentation of `System.nanoTime()` method, which motivated the analysis in this section by stating that "differences in successive calls that span greater than approximately 292 years (2^{63} nanoseconds) will not accurately compute elapsed time due to numerical overflow" [164].

3.5.4. Computing the Last and Next Epochs

For the time method with the signature `<Type> m()`, we can compute the last epoch e_0 (as observed from timepoint t_{now} with $epoch_0 < t_{now} \leq epoch_1$) from the following input values

- `m()`'s unit u_t in seconds (see Section 3.4.1 for unit computation)

- the minimum value $Type_{min}$ of the returned value's `<Type>`

- the maximum value $Type_{max}$ of the returned value's `<Type>`

- the value m_{now} returned by the method `m()` at the timepoint t_{now}

Then, it holds that

$$epoch_0 = t_{now} - m_{now} \cdot u_t \tag{3.15}$$

and $\forall i \in \mathbb{N}, x \in \mathbb{N}$,

$$epoch_{i+x} = epoch_i + x \cdot u_t \cdot (|Type_{min}| + Type_{max}) \tag{3.16}$$

This implies that the epoch period can be computed as

$$epoch_{i+1} - epoch_i = u_t \cdot (|Type_{min}| + Type_{max}) \tag{3.17}$$

and the next epoch following t_{now}, denoted as $nextepoch(t_{now})$, will occur at

$$u_t \cdot (|Type_{min}| + Type_{max} - m_{now}) \tag{3.18}$$

seconds after m_{now} (i.e., after t_{now}).

3.6. A Unified Quality Metric for Timer Methods

In Sections 3.3, 3.4 and 3.5, the algorithms to compute the individual quality properties of a timer method have been presented and they result in a *set* of metrics. However, most users prefer a *single* metric as a simple way to compare things, instead of using multidimensional metric sets. Therefore, the individual quality properties such as accuracy, invocation cost etc. should be composed to form a new unified and pragmatic metric. Additionally, the new metric should reflect how much spread (i.e. variance) the invocation cost of the timer method exhibits.

A timer method is only usable if it is monotonic, stable and thread-safe. In the following, we assume that all three of these quality requirements are fulfilled – otherwise, the quality metric defined below should be set to 0.

3.6.1. Accounting for Different CPU Processing Speeds

Quality properties of timer methods are computed from measurements collected at runtime under specific circumstances such as system load, CPU core affinity etc. Therefore, the quality properties are valid for the specific execution platform and the settings in which the measurements were performed. A unified timer quality metric should reflect the properties of the execution platform, in particular its processing speed.

For example, consider two execution platforms: platform P1 has a 1.0 GHz CPU and platform P2 has a CPU with 2.0 GHz. A timer method that is available on both platforms has an accuracy of 100 ns on platform P1 and an accuracy of 80 ns on platform P2. At the first glance, the timer method is more accurate on platform P2. However, consider an algorithm implementation which takes a largely constant (but unknown) number of cycles to execute, independent of a concrete CPU and platform- For this algorithm, the choice between P1 and P2 looks different: the timer method accuracy on platform P1 corresponds to 100 cycles but on platform P2, the timer method accuracy corresponds to 160 cycles.

Thus, the algorithm implementation should be measured on platform P1 rather than on platform P2, as the timer accuracy there will account for lesser measurement error on P1 than on P2. In a similar way, the timer method invocation cost should be expressed in CPU cycles, rather than in time units. Based the fact that the smallest unit of time-related measurements is 1 CPU cycle, the following discussion presumes that the minimum value of accuracy and invocation cost is 1 CPU cycle. We assume that the CPU frequency of the execution platform on which the measurements were performed remained constant over the course of the measurements, and therefore the effective CPU processing speed remained constant as well.

3.6.2. Factors Contributing to the Unified Timer Quality Metric

The first element of the formula is based on timer method accuracy, for which it holds that "smaller value is better" while $Quality_{timer}$ is a metric for which "bigger value is better" applies. The accuracy value is expressed in CPU cycles (with the minimum value being 1) and not in conventional time units such as nanoseconds for above reasons; the unit is dropped because $Quality_{timer}$ is unitless.

The second element of the formula is based on the timer method invocation cost, again with minimum value of 1 CPU cycle. For the same reasons as for accuracy, invocation costs are expressed in CPU cycles (again, the units are dropped to make $Quality_{timer}$ is unitless). As with accuracy, "smaller value is better" applies to invocation cost.

As Section 7.2 will show, there is a *minimal* invocation cost but very often, the invocation cost varies from invocation to invocation by one or more values of timer method accuracy. When the invocation cost varies in such a way, the *median* invocation cost is a more realistic measure for the majority of samples (see Section 7.2 for a more detailed analysis of the distribution of invocation cost values). Therefore, the second element of the formula uses the median invocation cost, which leads to the need to express in Formula (3.19) how the entirety of all recorded invocation cost values are spread around the median invocation cost. This need is addressed by the next element in Formula (3.19).

The third element of Formula (3.19) is called $invocationCostSpread$ and based on the percentage of invocation cost values (samples) within ± 1 $accuracy$ of the median invocation cost. To make $invocationCostSpread$ have the value range $[0.0, 1.0]$, the percentage values are divided by 100%. For $invocationCostSpread$, it holds that "larger value is better", since the less invocation cost samples are too far away from the median, the easier it is to capture the timer method overhead. $invocationCostSpread$ will never become 0 as long as there is at least one sample invocation value and therefore also a median invocation cost which makes the aforementioned percentage non-zero.

The definition of $invocationCostSpread$ allows it to become 1.0 even if the invocation cost varies between samples – as long as it all samples remain within ± 1 $accuracy$. The motivation for the definition of $invocationCostSpread$ is the consideration of the case pictured in Figure 3.10 in Section 3.4.3. Note the difference between the definition of $invocationCostSpread$ and the relation between the median and standard deviation in the context of Gaussian distributions: there is no established relation between accuracy and standard deviation in our case.

3.6.3. Designing the Unified Timer Quality Metric

The formula for the new unified timer method quality metric is given in Equation (3.19). $Quality_{timer}$ has no unit and its values are in the range $(0.0, 1.0]$; its design and details are explained in the remainder of this section. For convenience purposes, $Quality_{timer}$ can be expressed as percentage value, in the range $(0\,\%, 100\,\%]$.

$$Quality_{timer} := accuracy^{-0.1} \cdot invocationCost_{median}^{-0.1} \cdot invocationCostSpread^{0.5}$$

$$(3.19)$$

The elements of Equation (3.19) (mathematical operations and values of the exponents) have been chosen to fit two requirements:

- The range of $Quality_{timer}$ should be $(0.0, 1.0]$ so that $Quality_{timer}$ would work as a normalised metric (the $Quality_{timer}$ value is 0.0 iff the timer method is non-monotonic, unstable, not thread-safe or a combination thereof)

- The values of $Quality_{timer}$ for real-life measurements and timer methods should be expressible in four decimal places, i.e. the smallest realistically expected value (after rounding) should be 0.0001 (i.e. the calculated value should be at least 0.00005).

The first requirement was solved by devising a *product* of three contributions as described below, and by designing the contributions so that the value range of every contribution is within $(0.0, 1.0]$. The exponents $(-0.1, -0.1$ and $0.5)$ of the contributions are explained and justified in the next section.

The fulfilling of the second requirement is based on the worst-case scenario where a timer has an accuracy of 15 ms (i.e. 15,000,000 ns) and a median invocation cost of 16 μs, with the CPU running at 4.0 GHz. Such a coarse accuracy was in fact observed for `java.lang.System.currentTimeMillis()`

on Windows XP computes, though with invocation costs significantly below 16 μs. An invocation cost of 16 μs would correspond to 64,000
CPU cycles on a given CPU, which is also a rather high value, though
invocation costs of 47,709 CPU cycles have in fact been found for
`java.lang.management.ThreadMXBean.currentThreadCpuTime()` on
modern machines (Core 2 Duo CPU) running Linux (see Table 7.19, platform
T400b, row `CTCT`).

The worst-case scenario assumes an invocation spread of 0.3, although in
practice, values below 0.5 did not occur during the validation of the presented
approach (cf. Section 7.2). The value of $Quality_{timer}$ for the worst case scenario is
calculated from timing values using the relation that 1 ns correspond to 4 CPU
cycles on a 4 GHz CPU. Thus, $Quality_{timer} = (4 * (15 * 10^6))^{-0.1} \cdot (4 * (16 * 10^3))^{-0.1} \cdot$
$0.3^{0.5} \approx 0.1668 \cdot 0.3307 \cdot 0.5477 \approx 0.03021 \equiv 3.02\%$. Thus, the second requirement is
fulfilled by the above formula.

3.6.4. Choice of the Exponents for the Unified Timer Quality Metric

The contribution of accuracy is set to $accuracy^{-0.1}$, and since $accuracy \geq 1$, one obtains for $accuracy^{-0.1}$ ($= \frac{1}{accuracy^{0.1}}$) the range estimation $0 < accuracy^{-0.1} \leq 1$. The
contribution of invocation cost is set to $invocationCost_{median}^{-0.1}$, and it means that
$0 < invocationCost_{median}^{-0.1} \leq 1$. The median value has been chosen to decrease
the impact of outliers, and since the invocation cost spread already captures the
fact that the invocation cost is a stochastically distributed rather than a constant
value.

The choice of non-trivial exponents for the first two contributions is motivated
by the range of the raw values $accuracy$ and $invocationCost_{median}$. The initial solution for the metric was $accuracy^{-1} \cdot invocationCost_{median}^{-1} \cdot invocationCostSpread$,
and it fulfilled the first requirement, since $0 < accuracy^{-1} \leq 1$ and
$0 < \cdot invocationCost_{median} \leq 1$. However, for timer methods which return value in
ms (1 ms=1,000,000 ns), the first contribution of the formula would be too small,
in particular since modern CPUs execute more than 1 cycle in 1 ns.

For example, on a CPU running at 2 GHz, a timer method with 1 ms accuracy, 100 ns invocation cost and invocation cost spread of 1.0 would have resulted in a metric value of $\frac{1}{2,000,000} \cdot \frac{200}{.} 1.0 = 0.0000000025 \equiv 0.00000025\,\%$, which is a very small value compared to the range $(0.0, 1.0]$. For an other timer method with a smaller invocation cost of 100 ns (and same values otherwise, on the same machine), the formula with the trivial exponents would yield 0.000000005. While the values are clearly different (by the factor of 2), they are hard to compare because they are too small, and the do not fulfil the second requirement stated above.

With the exponents in Formula (3.19), things look differently and better for these two timers: quality is ≈ 0.1379 (i.e. $\approx 13.79\%$) for the first timer and ≈ 0.1479 (i.e. $\approx 14.79\%$) for the second timer. The quality values no more differ by the factor of two, but this is an advantage: since the (identical) accuracy is rather poor, the differences in invocation cost are no so important anymore, which is made clear by the quality values. In Section 7.2, the quality values for different timer methods on different platforms will be compared, which will add further empirical justification to the choice of exponents in Equation (3.19).

For the invocation spread, the contribution is set to $invocationCostSpread^{0.5}$, to decrease its impact onto the total result (note that $0 < invocationCostSpread \leq 1$). To see the reasons for the adjusting the impact of the spread, consider the following two results (which are real-life values, taken from Table 7.19 and obtained on the same execution platform **T400b**, rows HRC and JETM):

- Timer **a** has an accuracy of 2400 CPU cycles, an invocation cost of 4800 CPU cycles, and an invocation cost spread of 0.993.

- Timer **b** has an accuracy of 168 CPU cycles, invocation cost of 1680 CPU cycles and a spread of 0.578;

For **a**, the resulting quality metric value (in %) is ≈ 19.60 for spread's exponent being 0.5 and would be ≈ 19.53 if the exponent were 1.0. For **b**, the quality metric value (in %) is ≈ 21.67 for exponent 0.5 but would be ≈ 16.48 for exponent 1.0. Despite its higher spread, **b** is more accurate and causes less overhead: thus, its quality should be *higher* than that of **a** – this is the case when the exponent if

127

the spread's contribution is 0.5 but is not the case when the exponent is 1.0. This small example illustrates the need to decrease the impact of the spread – still, note that the choice of the concrete exponent value has no formal underpinning. Given that $x^{0.5} = \sqrt{x}$, $0 < invocationCostSpread^{0.5} \leq 1$ means that the range of the spread's contribution is $(0.0, 1.0]$.

3.7. Summary

In this chapter, timer method quality attributes have been identified and their impact on the accuracy of measurements has been explained. In addition to accuracy and invocation cost, further important properties such as stability, monotonicity and epochs have been analysed. Platform-independent algorithms for quantification of these properties have been developed, and these algorithms do not require any analysis of the implementation of the timer method: they are designed to work on black-box implementations of timer methods.

After considering the timer method quality attributes individually, a new unified metric has been devised which aggregates these attributes into one value. Since a one-valued metric is easier to perceive for human users, it simplifies analysis and comparison of timer methods. The new metric allows expressing the timer method quality as a value between 0 % and 100 %, making comparisons between timer methods more intuitive.

The algorithms and metrics developed in this chapter will be studied and validated in Section 7.2. In the next chapter, resource demand quantification is addressed as the first part of cross-platform performance prediction.

Algorithm 3.5: Analysing timer stability, Part 1

Data: numberOfIncreases, numberOfIterations, initialSleepDuration, sleepDurationIncrease, aboveOutlierThreshold (as percentage), belowOutlierThreshold (as percentage), outlierFrequencyThreshold (as percentage)

Result: counter unit

for $i = 1 \dots nrOfIncreases$ **do**
$\quad\mid\quad sleepTime_i \leftarrow initialSleepDuration + i \cdot sleepDurationIncrease$
end

for $j = 1 \dots numberOfIterations$ **do**
$\quad$**for** $k = 1 \dots numberOfIncreases$ **do**
$\qquad\mid\quad$ t1start $\leftarrow$ t1();
$\qquad\mid\quad$ t2start $\leftarrow$ t2();
$\qquad\mid\quad$ sleep($sleepTime_k$);
$\qquad\mid\quad m1_{k+j \cdot numberOfIncreases} \leftarrow$ (t1() - t1start);
$\qquad\mid\quad m2_{k+j \cdot numberOfIncreases} \leftarrow$ (t2() - t2start);
$\quad$**end**
end

outlierFrequency1 $\leftarrow$ 0
outlierFrequency2 $\leftarrow$ 0

for $j = 1 \dots numberOfIterations*numberOfIncreases$ **do**
$\quad$**if** $m1_j \geq aboveOutlierThreshold \cdot sleepTime_j$ **then**
$\qquad\mid\quad m1_j$ is an above-outlier
$\quad$**end**
$\quad$**if** $m1_j \leq belowOutlierThreshold \cdot sleepTime_j$ **then**
$\qquad\mid\quad m1_j$ is a below-outlier
$\quad$**end**
$\quad$**if** $m2_j \geq aboveOutlierThreshold \cdot sleepTime_j$ **then**
$\qquad\mid\quad m2_j$ is an above-outlier
$\quad$**end**
$\quad$**if** $m2_j \leq belowOutlierThreshold \cdot sleepTime_j$ **then**
$\qquad\mid\quad m2_j$ is a below-outlier
$\quad$**end**

$\quad$**if** $|m1_j - m2_j| <$
$\quad min(m1_j, m2_j) \cdot min(aboveExpectationThreshold, belowExpectationThreshold)$
$\quad$**then**
$\qquad\mid\quad similarity_j \leftarrow$ true
$\quad$**else**
$\qquad\mid\quad similarity_j \leftarrow$ false
$\quad$**end**
end

Algorithm 3.6: Analysing timer stability, Part 2

Data: numberOfIncreases, numberOfIterations, initialSleepDuration, sleepDurationIncrease, aboveOutlierThreshold (as percentage), belowOutlierThreshold (ditto), outlierFrequencyThreshold (ditto)

Result: counter unit

for $j = 1 \ldots$ *numberOfIterations·numberOfIncreases* **do**

    if $m1_j$ *is an above-outlier* **then**

        if $m2_j$ *is an above-outlier* $\wedge$ *similarity$_j$==true* **then**

            | neither $m1_j$ nor $m2_j$ are outliers

        end

        if $m2_j$ *is a below-outlier* **then**

            `/* both` $m1_j$ `and` $m2_j$ `are outliers */`

            outlierFrequency1++, outlierFrequency2++;

        end

        `/* only` $m1_j$ `is an outlier */`

        outlierFrequency1++;

    end

    if $m1_j$ *is a below-outlier* **then**

        if $m2_j$ *is an below-outlier* $\wedge$ *similarity$_j$==true* **then**

            `/* neither` $m1_j$ `nor` $m2_j$ `are outliers */`

        end

        if $m2_j$ *is a above-outlier* **then**

            `/* both` $m1_j$ `and` $m2_j$ `are outliers */`

            outlierFrequency1++, outlierFrequency2++;

        end

        `/* only` $m1_j$ `is an outlier */`

        outlierFrequency1++;

    end

    if $m1_j$ *is not an outlier* **then**

        if $m2_j$ *is not an outlier* **then**

            `/* neither` $m1_j$ `nor` $m2_j$ `are outliers */`

        end

        `/* only` $m2_j$ `is an outlier */`

        outlierFrequency2++;

    end

end

if *outlierFrequency1 > outlierFrequencyThreshold* **then**

  | t1() is an unstable timer

end

if *outlierFrequency2 > outlierFrequencyThreshold* **then**

  | t2() is an unstable timer

end

Chapter 4.

Quantifying Resource Demands for Performance Prediction

The bytecode-based performance prediction presented in this thesis is implemented as a tool suite called BYSUITE. This chapter describes how BYSUITE quantifies resource demands for the subsequent use in performance evaluation and performance prediction.

In devising an approach for resource demand quantification, this chapter addresses following **scientific challenges**:

- no special (purpose-built or modified) execution platform shall be needed to run resource demand quantification

- the starting point of the approach is *black-box bytecode* of an application, i.e. no source code should be needed

- the approach should require a minimum of execution platform performance indicators and monitoring facilities (to increase the applicability of the approach to execution platform implementations)

- the approach should be applicable to complex, multi-threaded applications and transparent non-explicit background resource demands

- the resulting demands should form an abstraction-raising aggregation of individual resource usages, rather than a trace of them

The high-level view of the work performed by BYSUITE is shown in Figure 4.1: the input consists of black-box bytecode application classes, the application

workload plus the BYSUITE settings, and its output consists of aggregated resource demands which are valid for a given workload.

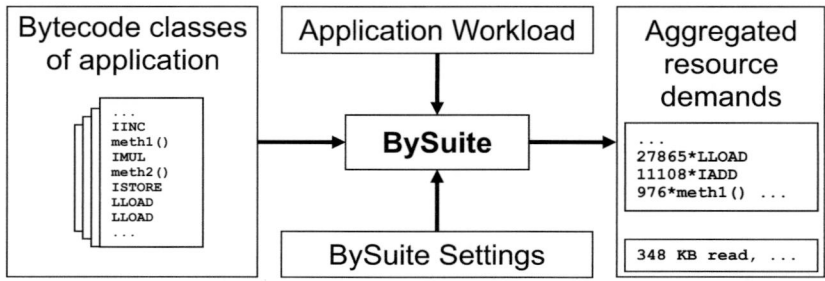

Figure 4.1.: High-level overview of Resource Demand Quantification in BYCOUNTER

In general, resource demands of an application depend on its runtime usage
profile, because control flow constructs such as loops or branches depend on the
values of input variables. In the PCM, the state of an application is (currently)
not modelled explicitly, and case studies have shown that this does not prevent the PCM and its tooling from delivering a very good accuracy for performance prediction. Instead, the variability of performance behaviour is captured
by measuring and predicting probability distributions of performance metrics,
which offers more information than just one value, be it worst case, median or
the mean.

Therefore, this thesis considers neither the state of the application nor the state
of execution platform and its resources in an explicit way. When quantifying
resource demands, the BYSUITE users need to make sure that the considered
application runs in the same state as intended (alternatively, different states of
the application or of the execution platform should be compared to each other
in terms of resource demands).

The **contribution** of this chapter is described in Section 4.4: using transparent instrumentation of the application's bytecode,platform-independent resource demands are quantified accurately yet with a conveniently low overhead. This solution runs on any standard-compliant Java Virtual Machine, and requires no performance indicators since the executed bytecode instructions and methods are the quantified resource demands.

This chapter starts with discussing the notion of resource demands (Section 4.1), which is followed by the derivation of requirements for the process to quantify resource demands in the scope of PCM (Section 4.2). Foundations of Java bytecode and challenges for taking it as the basis for platform-independent resource demands are discussed in Section 4.3.

4.1. Timing Values versus Resource Demands

"Why resource demands?" is a question often heard from practitioners when the subject of a conversation is software performance. Indeed, time (and sometimes utilization or throughput) is the favourite performance metric as it is familiar, comparable, universal and (apparently) easy to measure. Another objection often heard is that it is sufficient to *rank* several alternatives (be it applications or platforms), and that concrete performance metrics are not needed, or need not be precise: even if the value of a metric is off by a given factor, it is sufficient for ranking as long as the other alternatives are off by the same factor.

In this section, time as the base metric for performance evaluation is demystified and the issues with platform-specific nature of timing values are explained. From these findings, requirements for a better performance metric are derived, and platform-independent resource demands are proposed as an alternative which has several advantages over timing values and which can serve as (partial) replacement for timing values.

4.1.1. Effects on Preemption on Response Time Measurements

The most requested performance metric is the execution time of a request (a request is a component service call, class method invocation, etc.). However, simply measuring the timestamps at request start and request stop is not sufficient and in general incorrect, as illustrated by Figure 4.2. If the request R_1

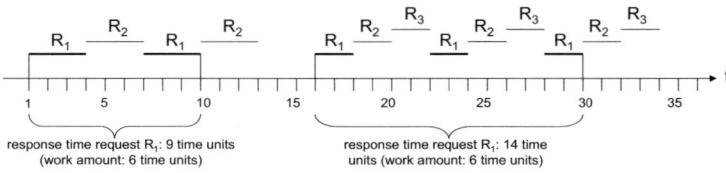

Figure 4.2.: Effects of preemption on relating response demands to execution time

is executed in parallel with other requests and activities (R_2, R_3), the preemption employed by the execution platform will mean that the timespan between the start and the end of the request R_1 will include phases where the request is paused and other requests are executed. In a setting with different number and behaviour of concurrent requests (or with different preemption behaviour of the execution platform), the measured timespan between the start and stop timestamps will be significantly different even if the actual request (and the resulting resource demands) are the same.

4.1.2. Addressing Preemption during Time Measurements

Off-the-shelf performance evaluation tools such as profilers attempt to account for preemption using *sampling*, *application instrumentation* or platform-provided *monitoring and instrumentation interfaces*.

When using *sampling*, a profiler records (at short, regular intervals) which thread and method are currently executed. From the recorded samples, the profiler interpolates the approximate time that is spent executing a particular method by a given thread. The limitations of sampling are its inability to grasp the actions that happen between samples, and the need of the execution platform to support the sampling technique itself. Additionally, the interval between samples influences the accuracy of the results, and must be set accordingly.

Application instrumentation works by inserting code for querying and saving of the performance indicators values (values of instruments), for example at method entry and method exit. The performance indicators can be time, memory state etc., and vary from platform to platform in availability, accuracy and overhead. Even though application instrumentation promises a better accuracy than sampling, it requires appropriate performance indicators to fulfil that promise. For example, if the instrumentation is inserted only at method entry and method exit, any preemption-caused execution pauses between will only be captured properly is the recorded timestamps are thread-time and not wall-clock time. As preemption is transparent to the executed application, it must rely on the execution platform to provide timing information that accounts for preemption, by providing thread time or process time performance indicators.

However, as has been shown in Chapter 3, accuracy of thread time performance indicators is far too coarse (e.g. 15 ms in the Java VM running on Windows) to be useful for measurements on today's systems. A rather large task, such as sorting of an array with 4096 (!) random `Integer` elements takes 4 ms on a computer with 1.6 GHz single-core CPU running the 32 bit Sun JVM on 32-bit Windows XP computer with just 1 GB of main memory. 4 ms is less than the accuracy of the thread time performance indicator on that platform, making that indicator unusable for even such large tasks. With computers becoming faster and the number of cores increasing, the conventional timer-based instrumentation becomes even less usable.

Monitoring and instrumentation interfaces cover a large spectrum of performance metrics and execution events, such as memory allocation, method entry, disk access, etc. Their availability, accuracy and overhead vary strongly across operating systems, execution platforms and hardware. Examples of monitoring interfaces provided by Java virtual machines include JMX (Java Management Extensions) and JVMTI (JVM Tooling Interface), and the latter one is is a native (i.e. non-Java) interface which requires manual implementation of JNI wrappers to access the interface.

What can be seen from the discussion of sampling, instrumentation and monitoring/instrumentation interfaces is that there are significant drawbacks when focusing on timing values as primary performance evaluation results. To answer the question "what are the alternatives?", the mechanisms and actions that lead to response time and other externally visible work effort quantifiers need to be analysed.

4.1.3. Resource Demands

Resource demands are issued by applications and are executed by software resources (e.g. operating system) and hardware resources (e.g. CPU and hard disks). In addition to processing resources such as the CPU, there are passive resources (e.g. monitors, barriers or instance of a pool) which influence the performance of an application through waiting times that occur when a passive resource to be acquired is not available immediately. This thesis focuses on processing resources because the usage of passive resources is highly dependent on the state and the usage profile of the application, and a PhD thesis on usage profile ([160]) has dealt with these issues. Passive resources are outside the scope of this thesis, but their influence of the approach described in this chapter will be covered in Section 4.3.10.

From an application's view, a resource demand results in time spent in different resources (resources can in turn use other resources, and resources can work concurrently), plus some waiting times due to data flow or resource contention. For example, the operating system processes a request to save data onto the hard disk by performing CPU work (e.g. calculation of metadata), using the main memory (to cache data) and the hard disk itself. Additionally, the resulting execution times are platform-dependent: the CPUs across platforms differ in quantity and speed, memory sizes vary, etc. Thus, a timing value from one CPU is not valid on another CPU; converting times into corresponding number of CPU cycles is not a remedy since pipelining and other resources do not behave in a way that can be described by a linear factor.

Decomposing a resource demand into a demand tree (to quantify individual resource demands) is a very complicated task which significantly increases the complexity of performance evaluation. The resulting resource demand tree is also platform-dependent and in the worst case, the level of detail becomes prohibitively expensive: the CPU and other resources need to be simulated (or emulated) down to a single work step, and a single work step is very hard to time due to CPU pipelining and other issues. Additionally, the same resource demand can be executed differently depending on the *state* of the execution platform and the application itself: for example, when reading the data that is stored on a hard disk, the presence of the data in the disk cache has a significant influence.

In some execution platforms, the resource demands are not issued explicitly (i.e. through actions of the application), but the required work is determined and performed by the execution platform in a more transparent way. For example, in Java EE, the Enterprise Java Beans (EJBs) carry annotations in source code which determine persistence, transactionality and other runtime behaviour properties. The Java EE execution platform (i.e. an application server running on top of a Java Virtual Machine) uses annotations that it finds inside the compiled bytecode to perform the needed runtime actions (e.g. persistence) without the need for the application to call these actions explicitly, let alone to know their signature. Such background resource demands pose an additional challenge for performance prediction, not least because even for the same technology or standard (e.g. Java EE), the background actions differ among implementors of the standard.

4.2. Requirements for Resource Demand Usage in the PCM

For performing architecture-level performance evaluation, the aforementioned disadvantages of timing values and precise trees of resource demands call for a trade-off solution which balances universality, precision and quantification effort. The performance metric(s) constituting the sought solution should fulfil the following requirements:

1. be suitable for performance modelling and performance prediction using the Palladio Component Model

2. support the resources offered by the Palladio Component Model (in particular, active resources such as CPU or hard disks, see Section 2)

3. be platform-independent, but convertible into platform-dependent performance metrics (e.g. timing values) in a systematic way with reasonable overhead

4. be suitable for business application running on a managed execution platform (i.e. where the memory management is the responsibility of the platform, and not of the application)

5. incur a low effort to quantify the performance metric values (in particular, the application should not be rewritten just to quantify resource demands)

6. reflect the parametric performance dependencies w.r.t. application workload

7. be applicable to complex, multi-threaded applications and transparent non-explicit background resource demands

8. form an abstraction-raising aggregation of individual resource demands (rather than a trace of resource demands)

9. require a minimum of execution platform performance indicators and monitoring facilities (to increase the applicability of the metric to execution platform implementations)

10. account for future application of PCM and its tooling to other application categories (such as embedded platforms)

The first requirement (suitability for the PCM) is of particular interest, because the PCM already encourages platform-independent resource demands by distinguishing resource types (e.g. "CPU") from concrete resource instances (e.g. "Intel T7200"). The PCM as it was before this thesis required to specify the number of CPU cycles needed to execute an internal action (of course, single-threaded uninterrupted execution was assumed as the valid setting for the number of CPU cycles). However, quantifying the number of CPU cycles in a static way is not a viable option not only because of control flow and data flow dependencies, but also because of CPU-specific pipelining-caused speedups.

Additionally, the executable form of today's application is often not binary machine code, but rather platform-independent, higher-level bytecode which is executed by a virtual machine that sits on top of the operating system (CPUs that have native support for bytecode are scarce and limited to embedded applications, thus being out of scope for this thesis). Execution platforms that are used for today's applications often modify the application executables, as it is the case when using aspect orientation (AOP) that employs bytecode weaving or binary instrumentation.

Determining CPU cycle counts in a dynamic way requires support from the execution platform, but the TSC counter which was discussed in Chapter 3 has been shown to be unreliable and unsuitable for multi-core operation (see Section 7.2). Taking timing measurements for later conversion into CPU cycle counts suffers from the drawbacks (outlined above in Section 4.1 in this chapter as well as in Chapter 3), such as accuracy, reliability, influence of preemption etc. Finally, modern CPUs feature load-dependent CPU frequency adjustment mechanisms.

A universally applicable pattern for analysis of large, complex system is analysis of the system into its *building blocks*, e.g. components. The expectation behind decomposing a system into its building blocks is that analysis of smaller problems is simpler and more effective – but it is also implied that the results

139

can be mapped back to the original system. In software engineering, breaking a large application into components (or classes, modules, packages etc.) is done with the same aim.

So far, the smallest (i.e. atomic) behaviour building blocks available in the PCM were `InternalActions`, `ExternalActions` etc. – for a given atomic building block, its resource demands (number of CPU cycles, etc.) had to be determined using estimation, platform-specific measurements etc.

4.3. Using Java Bytecode for Resource Demand Quantification

Based on above requirements and observations, the solution chosen in this thesis is to *consider bytecode instructions and bytecode-level method invocations as building blocks*. These building blocks are platform-independent "by design", as bytecode is platform-independent and not specific for a given operating system, hardware architecture or system type (bytecode is use on a wide range of computers, from mainframes to mobile phones). In the remainder of this chapter, the bytecode resource counting part of BYSUITE will be referred to as BYCOUNTER.

To obtain the number of executed bytecode-level building blocks for a given component service request, transparent instrumentation of application bytecode will be used. The design and details if the instrumentation mechanism will be described in Section 4.4, but first, the foundations must be discussed, starting with the bytecode itself. At a later step, these platform-independent resource demands must be translated into platform-specific timing values (this challenge is the subject of Chapter 5).

As a bytecode-based solution alone cannot be sufficient in all cases (i.e. when a native method is called), this thesis devises a novel, hybrid approach which is capable of measuring *both* platform-independent resource demands (on the basis of bytecode) *and* platform-dependent timing values and resource demands.

Before the proposed solution and the hybrid approach using it are explained, the following section presents an introduction to bytecode, which is a prerequisite for understanding the remainder of this thesis. In this thesis, Java bytecode is used as it is a very widely used, hardware-independent bytecode format to which many programming languages beyond Java itself are compiled (e.g. Scala, Clojure, JRuby and many others). Java bytecode is also the executables format for enterprise applications and frameworks such as Java EE, Spring, Grails, JBoss Seam etc. Even *grid computing* and *cloud computing* providers (e.g. Google App Engine and others) execute applications supplied as Java bytecode, where grid/cloud computing means virtualised multi-server execution platforms which make the actual resources transparent and provide dynamic runtime redeployment to support scalability, while still ensuring application isolation and end-user satisfaction.

4.3.1. Foundations of Java Bytecode

Java bytecode is a hardware-independent and OS-independent format for executables, and it includes both instructions and data. Java bytecode is executed on the *Java Virtual Machine* (JVM), which abstracts the specific details of the underlying software/hardware platform. The JVM specification [110] sets the JVM, the Java programming language and the Java bytecode into relation. It includes a description of the semantics of bytecode execution, an explanation of the format of bytecode classfiles, and discusses the compilation of programming languages to Java bytecode. However, the JVM specification neither mandates nor clarifies how Java bytecode is executed on particular hardware/software of a given execution platform.

Java bytecode is more abstract and higher-level than machine code (which is executed directly by a computer's CPU): for example, Java bytecode does not contain instructions to allocate or free memory, since the JVM manages memory for applications that it executes. On the other hand, Java bytecode contains constructs which are not found in machine code: bytecode contains classes, objects and methods as visible, first-class entities (whereas machine code is not aware of functions but only uses jumps and stack-based saving of instruction points for function returns). The names of variables/fields (and methods) are also visible in bytecode (unless obfuscated), and even line numbers are visible by default (for debugging purposes).

Java bytecode is stack-oriented, but it also provides up to 65536 *local variables* that methods can use to store value-typed data as well as pointers to objects. The executable elements of Java bytecode fall in two categories: methods and primitive instructions (the primitive instructions form the bodies of methods; primitive instructions used for invoking methods will be described further below). Other elements of a classfile, such as the constant pool, attributes, fields, access flags etc. are not executable.

There can be at most 2^8 primitive instructions (where 8 is the bitsize of 1 byte) – the name *byte*code stems from the 1 byte needed to store primitive instructions, not taking into account instruction parameters. Currently, only 203 instructions are defined and implemented, with the remainder being reserved for future purposes (and thus unavailable for programmer-driven extensions of the instruction set). Rather than referring to bytecode instruction by their numerical values, the JVM specification and other bytecode publications and tools make use of textual *mnemonics* which convey the semantic of the instruction.

For example, consider the allocation of object arrays: the Java bytecode features an own instruction with hexadecimal opcode $0xBC$ for this task, which corresponds to decimal opcode 188. The textual mnemonic for it is NEWARRAY, a self-described name which is more suitable for documentation – the remainder of this thesis prefers mnemonics over opcodes. Note that the primitive type of the array to create is stored directly in the bytecode of the method which includes NEWARRAY. At runtime, NEWARRAY expects the size of the array to create to be located on the top of the JVM stack – when executing NEWARRAY, the JVM pops the stack's topmost element, uses it as the size of the array, and pushes a reference to the created array onto the stack. From the performance point of view, the execution duration of NEWARRAY is influenced by the size of the array and by the type of the array (e.g. a a primitive double needs twice as much bits as a primitive int on 32-bit hardware) [180]. The performance of NEWARRAY may also depend on the JVM configuration and other factors – Chapter 5 will address this question in more detail. Note that a separate instruction, ANEWARRAY, is used for creating arrays with non-primitive elements.

Direct dealing with bytecode is cumbersome and error-prone, but neither the Java Development Kits (JDKs) nor the JVMs are providing bytecode construction tooling beyond source code compilers. As a consequence, bytecode engineering frameworks such as BCEL [115] or ASM [114] have been created to allow analysis, instrumentation, direct creation and verification of Java bytecode. However, these tools often introduce simplifications that hide some aspects of bytecode from the programmer.

For example, consider loading of primitive integer values from local variables onto the stack. In Java bytecode, this is accomplished by the ILOAD instruction that pops its sole parameter (the index of a local variable storing a primitive integer) from the stack and pushes the primitive integer (read from the local variable) onto the stack. There exist four additional instructions that serve as shortcuts for ILOAD: ILOAD_0, ILOAD_1, ILOAD_2, ILOAD_3, where the local variable index is signalled by the digit in the opcode's mnemonic. The shortcuts do not expect a parameter on the stack, and the JVM may execute a ILOAD_0 faster than ILOAD with 0 on the stack (or faster than ILOAD preceded by an operation such as ICONST_0 to push 0 onto the stack).

However, the ASM framework does not distinguish between ILOAD_0 and ILOAD 0 when parsing the bytecode of classfiles, and similar simplifications are applied to other cases, incl. the WIDE instruction. The effect of this simplification will be studied later by comparing the performance of ILOAD_0 vs. ILOAD, and for similar constellations. In the following two subsections, the role of methods and method invocations in bytecode is studied, followed by the usage of passive resources in bytecode.

4.3.2. Black-box Java Bytecode

A *black-box Java bytecode component* (hereafter called BBBC) is a set of Java classes which are present only as bytecode without further information about their internals. In particular, a BBBC comes without source code, without static or dynamic models (architectural, performance or other), and without human-readable documentation about its internal working.

As it is possible to modify bytecode after compilation in several ways: by applying post-compilation AOP (rather than using AOP inside source code), using load-time instrumentation (e.g. using `java.lang.instrument` package of the Java Platform API), at runtime using JVM's Hotswap technique [181] or using JRebel [182], etc. However, using bytecode for resource usage quantification must be applied to the bytecode as it is executed. Thus, we assume that during analysis presented in this thesis, a BBBC is *final* in the sense that its bytecode will not be changed for execution. However, as the implementation of the presented approach itself supports and uses load-time instrumentation, it is nonetheless possible to apply it even in scenarios where third-party load-time instrumentation is taking place: by assuring that BYCOUNTER instrumentation is the last part of the instrumentation chain, resource demands will be quantified properly.

The only artefacts which are exposed by BBBC are its provided and required interfaces (we follow Szyperski's definition of a component [183]), and a BBBC cannot directly access the fields of classes that belong to other BBBCs. Since the BBBC is black box, there is also no behaviour model and thus no description on how and when externals calls to other components are performed. Note that the calls to the Java Platform API which are present in Java bytecode are not considered as calls to external components, but rather as calls to the underlying infrastructure.

While some programming languages offer constructs and concepts of components, there are no components at bytecode level – only classes and (object-oriented) interfaces. Therefore, to apply component-oriented approaches (such as performance prediction in the Palladio Component Model context) on black-box bytecode, the semantic gap between bytecode and components must be bridged, by mapping bytecode-level artefacts to component-level modelling artefacts.

For example, a black-box component that implements sorting can consist of several classes (dictionary, buffer, main logic etc.), and it provides one or several interfaces to access its functionality. The sorting component may use classes and methods of the Java Platform API (e.g. collection classes). Creating performance models for BBBC is needed in reverse engineering, as well as in scenarios where legacy or IP-protected third party components are used: without source code or when decompilation is not allowed, bytecode and the publicly visible interfaces are the only artefacts available for model creation.

BBBCs are also important even when the source code is available: the source code does not provide enough information on the performance and the source code cannot be executed to observe its dynamic (runtime) behaviour. To the best of our knowledge, there is no tool that analyses the performance of a component on the basis of its source code. Additionally, the results of translating source code into executable bytecode also depend on the used compiler, and the Java compilation is not standardized.

In the next section, bytecode instructions are subjected to a more detailed analysis which will help in explaining the design and implementation of BY-COUNTER.

4.3.3. Bytecode Instructions with Special Roles and Properties

The majority of Java bytecode instructions are rather straightforward to understand and to analyse, as they perform stack loading and clearing, mathematical operations, comparisons, conversions, control flow and similar tasks. Some instructions, however, require more attention from the performance point of view, e.g. when their parameters have a strong impact on their performance.

The ATHROW instruction throws an error or an exception, which results in a rather costly chain of operations by the JVM. However, as exceptions/errors should not be a part of conventional program execution, their influence on component performance under normal conditions is expected to be negligible in this thesis. Note that both PCM and Beagle neither consider nor model exceptions/errors for the same reasons.

CHECKCAST is another instruction of special interest : it pops an object instance from the stack, tries to cast it into an instance of a type given by
CHECKCAST's bytecode-stored argument, and pushes the result of the cast onto
the stack (if the cast operation is illegal or fails, an exception is thrown). Consider the following sequence of statements:

```
float floatA = 0f;
double doubleB = (double) floatA;
java.lang.Number numberC = new java.lang.Float(0);
java.lang.Number numberD = (java.lang.Double) numberC;
```

While the cast from floatA to doubleB is performed via the primitive bytecode instruction with the mnemonic F2D (float to double), the cast from
numberC to numberD is performed via the CHECKCAST instruction. Note that
at runtime, a java.lang.- ClassCastException will be thrown because a
Float cannot be casted into a Double *despite* the fact that both are floating-
point values and the range of Double fully includes (and extends) the range of
Float.

The instruction INSTANCEOF is similar to CHECKCAST: it returns int values
0/1 as false/true if the object on the stack is instance of its in-bytecode parameter (which designates the class type to perform the check against). Note tat
INSTANCEOF does not throw runtime exceptions.

The instruction WIDE is an optional immediate predecessor for instructions
such as ILOAD, istore etc. [110]. The WIDE instruction is used to allow the
immediately following instruction the access to local variables beyond indexes
0...255 (stored in 1 byte) by using WIDE addressing. Wide addressing means that
the index of the local variable is stored in two bytes (16 bits), which allows up
to $2^{16} = 65,536$ local variables to be addressed. Note that the JVM specification
does not mandate the bytecode creator's choice of used local variable indexes:
an index ≥ 256 can be used even if local variables with indexes ≤ 255 haven't
been used up. In practice, however, methods which required more than 256
local variables are extremely infrequent, and possible performance implications
of the WIDE instruction can be considered negligible.

4.3.4. Parameters of Bytecode Instructions

Java methods have *explicit* input parameters (i.e. the parameters are listed in the method's signature) – any other values that a method needs can be accessed from inside the method's body, adhering to the Java access modifiers and inheritance rules.

In contrast to methods, arguments of Java bytecode instructions come from three locations: bytecode of the class, the stack and the JVM local variables. For example, consider the NEWARRAY instruction: it creates a new primitive-typed array, where the new array's type is compiled into bytecode (i.e. it is fixed after compilation) and the new array's size is passed over the stack.

To used bytecode instructions as resource demand metric for performance prediction, bytecode instructions' input parameters which are relevant for performance must be identified. The majority of bytecode instructions has no parametric dependencies: for example, the execution duration of adding 1 and 2 using IADD should be the same as adding 10 and 20. Even for "border cases" (such as adding Integer.MAX_VALUE to Integer.MAX_VALUE, which leads to an overflow), IADD should have the same performance: the IADD operation does not signal the overflow in any way (i.e., not exception is thrown and no flag is set).

Among the Java bytecode instructions, the following instructions have input parameters which *could* be performance-relevant, or *could* influence other instruction in a performance-relevant way:

1. WIDE

2. NEW

3. DDIV/LDIV/IDIV/LDIV and DREM/LREM/IREM/LREM

4. MONITORENTER, MONITOREXIT

5. LOOKUPSWITCH and TABLESWITCH

6. MULTIANEWARRAY, NEWARRAY, ANEWARRAY

147

The NEW instruction ensures that "memory for a new instance of that class is allocated from the garbage-collected heap, and the instance variables of the new object are initialized to their default initial values" [110]. This definition implies that the type for which NEW is executed is relevant for NEW's performance: after all, the time to initialise an object instance depends on that object's type. Note, however, that the bytecode-level NEW instruction does not correspond to source-level new keyword: in bytecode, a NEW is followed by the invocation of a constructor (the equivalent of source code construct new <Type>(...) or a method which creates an instance of the desired type. BYCOUNTER approaches the NEW bytecode instruction in the following way: it does not separate the time spent calling a constructor/factory method from the time spent executing NEW and thus the performance of NEW on its own does not have to be quantified.

For DDIV and similar mathematical operations, it *may* be the case that the division is performed iteratively and finishes faster if the result is an integer number: for example, 4.0 divided by 2.0 *may* be faster than 2.9 divided by 7.9. To study if such an effect is indeed observable, two experiments were performed, where each experiment contained 500 repetitions of a measurement containing 4000 divisions. Each repetition started by filling an array of dividends (4000 elements) and the divisors into another array of 4000 elements. In the first experiment, all divisions had integer-typed results while the second experiment had exclusively floating-point results. For each of the repetitions of the first experiment, this was achieved by randomly generating the dividends dd_i and divisors ds_i ($0 \leq i < 4000$) in the following way ($nextInt(val)$ returns a random integer r with $0 \leq r < val$):

$$exp_{ds,i} := nextInt(30) \tag{4.1}$$

$$ds_i := 2^{exp_{ds,i}} \tag{4.2}$$

$$dd_i := 2^{exp_{ds,i}+1+nextInt(30-1-exp_{ds,i})} \tag{4.3}$$

For each of the repetitions of the second experiment, the dividend and the divisor were created in a random way (where the division result would be an integer, the random generation was repeated until the results of the division would be non-integer). Comparing the results of the first and the second experiment (after capping the outliers, i.e. the largest 10% of the repetitions), the significant statistics computed from the 500 repetitions are within 5% of each other. Therefore, DDIV does not show *significant* parametric performance dependencies, and its parameters can be disregarded. Since the parameters of LDIV, etc. behave in a similar way, they can be disregarded as well.

For MONITORENTER and MONITOREXIT, see the discussion in Section 4.3.10: the parameters may be relevant, but they refer to runtime object instances, which may or may not be recorded persistently. Therefore, the parameter of the MONITORENTER and MONITOREXIT can e.g. be a String representation of the object instance (e.g. a concatenation of the class type and the int value returned by java.lang.Object.hashCode() method).

4.3.4.1. LOOKUPSWITCH and TABLESWITCH

The instructions LOOKUPSWITCH and TABLESWITCH are used to implement the switch-case Java construct in bytecode, where switch supports a *variable* number of *cases* (0 cases are also supported). The "control variable" of switch must be integer-typed, but byte, char, short, their boxed object types (Integer etc.) and enums are also supported. The switch construct requires that all case conditions are constant expressions; optionally, an explicit default case can be specified.

To demonstrate the intricacies of switch, an example of switch is given in Listing 4.3 alongside the corresponding bytecode, as created by the default compiler in Eclipse 3.5 and shown by the Bytecode Outline Plugin [184] using ASM-oriented mnemonics. The switcher variable is an int, as is the incremented variable. Note that the source-level keyword break plays an important role for switch: if case that applies does *not* terminate with break (e.g. switcher==1), *all* subsequent case(s) are executed, regardless of whether their case check returns true or false. In Listing 4.3, replacing the constant expression 100 in the last case check with 3 leads to the replacement of LOOKUPSWITCH with TABLESWITCH.

```
switch (switcher) {      L2    ILOAD 3
  case 1:                      LOOKUPSWITCH
  case 0:                          0: L3
    variable += 1;               1: L3
    break;                       2: L4
  case 2:                      100: L5
    variable += 2;             101: L5
    break;                 default: L6
  case 100:            L3    LLOAD 1    LCONST_1  LADD    LSTORE 1
  case 101:            L7    GOTO L8
    variable += 100;   L4    LLOAD 1    LDC 2     LADD    LSTORE 1
    break;             L9    GOTO L8
  default:             L5    LLOAD 1    LDC 100   LADD    LSTORE 1
    variable += 256;   L10   GOTO L8
}                      L6    LLOAD 1    LDC 256   LADD    LSTORE 1
                       L8    RETURN
                       L11
```

Figure 4.3.: Implementation of switch Java construct in Java bytecode

The performance of TABLESWITCH/LOOKUPSWITCH depends on the number of checks (case comparisons) that must be performed, all other work is explicit in the form of GOTO statements. To study whether TABLESWITCH and LOOKUPSWITCH indeed have significant parametric dependencies on the number of checks, a series of four experiments was created for each of these two opcodes: $Exper_1,\ldots,Exper_4$ and $Exper_5,\ldots,Exper_8$.

Each experiment consists of m measurements, and each measurement consists of c "chainings" of switch statement executions, i.e. the time interval retrieved by one measurement corresponds to c switch statement executions. The measured switch statements are designed so that the experiments $Exper_1$ through $Exper_4$ use TABLESWITCH and $Exper_5$ through $Exper_8$ use LOOKUPSWITCH.

The experiments are designed as follows:

1. $Exper_1$ and $Exper_5$: such a constant value is passed to the switch statement that exactly 1 case check is required

2. $Exper_2$ and $Exper_6$: such a constant value is passed to the switch statement that exactly n ($n > 1$) case checks are required

3. $Exper_3$ and $Exper_7$: such a randomly generated value is passed to the switch statement that 1 case check is required in 50% of the cases and 2 case checks are required in remaining 50% of the cases (the duration of value generation is included in the measurement and the generation repeated for each of the c chainings)

4. $Exper_4$ and $Exper_8$: such a randomly generated value is passed to the switch statement that n ($n > 1$) case checks are *always* requireds in all 100% of the cases (the duration of value generation is included in the measurement and repeated for each of the c chainings)

Table 4.4 presents the results of the experiments, run on a computer with a single-core Intel N270 CPU (1.60 GHz) and 1 GB of main memory. The used JVM was Sun's Java SE JDK with JRE 1.6.0_18 with default settings, i.e. with JIT turned on. The timer method was java.lang.System.nanoTime(), and the results in Table 4.4 are values *after* nanoTime()'s median invocation cost on the used platform were substracted from the actual measurements. All eight experiments were run with $m = 1000$, $c = 200$ and $n = 7$, and the values in Table 4.4 are median values (across 1000 measurements) for 200 chainings of the switch statement.

m=100, c=200, n=7, medians:	1 comparison, fixed case	n comparisons, fixed case	1 comparison, random case	n comparisons, random case
			incl. random case generation	
TABLESWITCH	E_1 1118 ns	E_2 2514 ns	E_3 20674 ns	E_4 21512 ns
LOOKUPSWITCH	E_5 1118 ns	E_6 2236 ns	E_7 20674 ns	E_8 21791 ns

Figure 4.4.: Parametric performance dependencies of LOOKUPSWITCH and TABLE-SWITCH

As can be seen from Table 4.4, the number of checks influences the execution duration of the instruction by the factor of two: compare $Exper_1$ ($\frac{1118}{200} \approx 5.5$ ns per instruction) with $Exper_2$ ($\frac{2514}{200} \approx 11.5$ ns per instruction). Is is also plausible that the execution scales approximately linearly with the number of performed comparisons. Yet to evaluate the *actual* number of checks performed by LOOKUPSWITCH/TABLESWITCH, a complicated runtime monitoring and analysis of cases would be necessary.

Instead, BYCOUNTER assumes that for a given switch statement that has n checks, the runtime number of performed checks is equally distibuted between 1 and n (incl.). Then, it suffices to record how often a particular switch statement is executed, given that its maximum number of checks (n) is parsed statically and given that its execution duration is parametrised over the number of performed checks (see Section 5 for how this is accomplished during benchmarking phase in BYCOUNTER).

4.3.4.2. ANEWARRAY, NEWARRAY and MULTIANEWARRAY

The last group of instructions (NEWARRAY, ANEWARRAY and MULTIANEWARRAY) are the most interesting one from the performance point of view. For one-dimensional arrays, NEWARRAY is used for primitive data types (int, long etc.), while ANEWARRAY is used for object-typed arrays (Integer, Long etc.). MULTIANEWARRAY is used for multi-dimensional arrays, both primitive and object-typed – it distinguishes between a primitive short and an object-typed Short.

As shown in [180], array creation performance depends on the array type and array size. For the primitive types (i.e. NEWARRAY), a possible simplification would be to abstract from the concrete types and to concentrate on the performance: than, it would be better to see NEWARRAY as depending on the *bytesize* of the array type. However, the bytesize of primitive types differs across platforms (e.g.. between 32 bit and 64 bit).

ANEWARRAY allocates the memory of (initially unresolved/null) *references* to the objects, which are created and stored separately. ANEWARRAY does *not* allocate the memory for the elements of the array it creates – therefore, the performance of ANEWARRAY depends only on the size of the array to create.

Finally, `MULTIANEWARRAY` must be addressed. In source code, a multidimensional primitive typed array declaration such as `int[][] arr = new int[2][4]` is translated to bytecode as a *single* `MULTIANEWARRAY` instruction – the sub-arrays are not created explicitly. An alternative to considering the individual dimensions would be to consider `totalNumberOfElements`, which would be a product of individual dimensions (in the above example, `totalNumberOfElements` would be 8). This alternative would also invite a simplification to enable performance-oriented comparison and aggregation: `new int[3][5]` would be treated the same as `new int[5][3]`, and the same as `new int[15]`.

4.3.5. Methods in Bytecode and Java Platform API

In Java bytecode, four instructions are used to invoke Java methods, including those of the Java API: `INVOKEINTERFACE`, `INVOKESPECIAL`, `INVOKE-STATIC` and `INVOKEVIRTUAL` (hereafter called `INVOKE*`). The signature of the invoked method (callee) appears as the parameter of the `INVOKE*` instruction executed by the caller, while the parameters of the invoked method are prepared on the stack before method invocation.

While the extent (package, classes/interface, methods) of the Java Platform API is known, each JVM is supplied with a set of Java classes that form the *vendor-specific implementation* of the Java API. At bytecode level, no distinction is made between methods that are part of the Java Platform API and non-API methods, even though the extent of the Platform API is known. Furthermore, from a caller's side, it is impossible to detect whether the implementation of a callee is native except by analysing the callee's implementation (native methods will be addressed in Section 4.3.6).

These facts raise the question of how to deal with a callee when quantifying resource demands of the caller, with the following options being available:

- treat a callee as an atomic entity and do not decompose it into the constituent bytecode instructions (and possibly method invocations)

153

- decompose every callee as far as possible into bytecode instructions, skipping native methods and accepting that at runtime, a polymorphic call may land at a callee method that hasn't been decomposed

- specify which callees should be decomposed (e.g. callees that belong to the considered application's implementation) from those callees which shouldn't be decomposed (e.g. the Java Platform API methods or native methods), with the latter being regarded as atomic resource demands which must be translated at platform-specific timing values at a later stage

For a considered method (either a "direct" callee of the considered caller, or a "child callee" of a callee down the calling context tree), these three options boil down to a binary decision: *decompose* or *leave atomic*.

For a method implementation which is *"left atomic"*, its (platform-specific) execution duration depends on its input parameters. For non-static methods, the execution duration also depends on the state of the invocation target- the state of the execution platform beyond this will be ignored due to complexity and lack of support in the PCM. To simplify the wording, from now on *method parameters* refers both to method input parameters and to the invocation target (for non-static methods).

To understand the impact of polymorphism on bytecode analysis, consider the example in Listing 4.1 which helps with analysing the invocation targets of non-static methods, and the bytecode instructions used for invoke these methods.

```
1  public class GettingObjectRuntimeType {
2      private static void callPolymorphically (MyClassInterface
           myClassInterface) {
3          myClassInterface.stdPrintln();
4          System.out.println(myClassInterface.getClass().getCanonicalName())
           ;
5      }

7      public static void main(String[] args) {
8          // 1.
9          MyClassParent parent = new MyClassParent();
```

```
10      parent.stdPrintln();
11      System.out.println(parent.getClass().getCanonicalName());

13      //2.
14      MyClassParent childMaskingAsParent = new MyClassChild();
15      childMaskingAsParent.stdPrintln();
16      System.out.println(childMaskingAsParent.getClass().
            getCanonicalName());

18      //3.
19      MyClassChild child = new MyClassChild();
20      child.stdPrintln();
21      System.out.println(child.getClass().getCanonicalName());

23      //4.
24      MyClassInterface parentMaskingAsInterface = new MyClassParent();
25      parentMaskingAsInterface.stdPrintln();// invokeinterface on
            MyClassInterface
26      System.out.println(parentMaskingAsInterface.getClass().
            getCanonicalName());

28      //5.
29      MyClassInterface childMaskingAsInterface = new MyClassChild();
30      childMaskingAsInterface.stdPrintln();// invokeinterface on
            MyClassInterface
31      System.out.println(childMaskingAsInterface.getClass().
            getCanonicalName());

33      //6.
34      callPolymorphically(new MyClassParent());

36      //7.
37      callPolymorphically(new MyClassChild());
38    }
39  }
```

```
43  interface MyClassInterface {
44    public void stdPrintln();
45  }

47  class MyClassChild extends MyClassParent {
48    public void stdPrintln() {
49      System.err.println("Child");
50    }
51  }

53  class MyClassParent implements MyClassInterface {
54    public void stdPrintln() {
55      System.out.println("Parent");
56    }
57  }
```

Listing 4.1: Effect of polymorphism on method invocation in bytecode

For case 1., the INVOKEVIRTUAL instruction is used to invoke the signature MyClassParent.stdPrintln() – this is well expected, and the output on standard out is Parent. For case 2., the INVOKEVIRTUAL instruction is used to invoke the *same* signature MyClassParent.stdPrintln(), and this means that the declared type of childMaskingAsParent is used – still, the output on standard out is Child, i.e. the correct implementation of the method (the one in MyClassChild, the runtime type of childMaskingAsParent) is used. As these two cases show, one must analyse the invocation target type to correctly account for the actually executed method – note that the reference to the invocation target is placed onto the JVM stack during execution, and can be analysed by BYCOUNTER, using the java.lang.Object.getClass() method.

The fact that the declared type of the invocation target decides which signature will be inserted into bytecode is visible from cases 4. and 5.: in both, INVOKEINTERFACE of MyClassInterface.stdPrintln() is found in bytecode. Still, of course, the right method implementation is resolved by the JVM, and the runtime type of the invocation target can be retrieved using getClass(), which works for Interface-typed variables. For case

156

6., `INVOKEINTERFACE` is found in the bytecode of `callPolymorphically`, which is expected.

Due to polymorphism, the implementation of a callee may change between invocations and thus the callee's performance changes between invocations. Even for a fixed callee implementation, the parameters of the callee can vary from invocation to invocation and they can have crucial impact on the method's performance, which then also differs among invocations. Thus, the parameters of atomic, non-decomposed methods must be recorded during resource demand quantification as a prerequisite for correct translation to timing values at a later stage. Consequently, translation of callee invocations to time values must also be parameter-aware.

Often, the parameter *values* are not needed in their entirety, but the parameter *characteristics* are sufficient: for example, if a method takes an `int` array as input parameter, it is sufficient to record the array's size instead of recording all the values in the array. Such an abstraction (discussed in more detail in Section 4.4) helps to raise the abstraction of resource demand quantification, and simplifies/streamlines the quantification itself.

On the other hand, an abstraction may miss the point: if the method is sorting the array elements, the entropy ("un-sortedness") of the array may be important as well, though it is hard to quantify in an effective way. Additionally, as Java bytecode instructions or methods can have parameters of arbitrary object types (incl. `transient` ones), persistent parameter recording by simply saving the parameter value may be not only irrational, but also technically impossible. Hence, to allow for flexibility in parameter characterisation treatment, hooks (insertion points, "callbacks") should be provided so that third parties *can* "plug in" external methods for computing parameter characterisations.

For *"decompose"*, the question arises on how to deal with the method invocations found in a given method implementation: should they be decomposed as well (and possibly in a recursive way)? It also remains questionable whether decomposing a method into a large number of fine-grained bytecode instructions leads to higher precision during performance prediction. This question will be addressed later in Chapter 5, in the context of benchmarking of API methods, where the benchmarking of an API method as an atomic entity will be contrasted with predicting its performance from the constituent bytecode instructions.

From a practitioner's point of view, the resource demand of a method is easy to understand when it is specified as (platform-specific) timing value (possibly with a parametric dependency on the method's input parameter). In contrast to that, if the practitioner is confronted with (aggregated) counts of bytecode instructions (and possibly some indecomposable native methods), the method's performance is harder to judge and to compare.

Note, however, that it is still possible to turn the aggregated instruction counts into a platform-specific timing value if there is a mapping from instructions to their platform-specific execution durations (Chapter 5 shows how to obtain such a mapping using virtual machine benchmarking).

Parameters of non-`INVOKE`∗ bytecode instructions can be significant, because they influence the execution speed of the instruction [185]. Hence, in order to describe the bytecode-based resource demands of applications as precisely as possible, it must be possible to record bytecode parameters. However, parameter recording slows down the execution of the instrumented methods, and parameters may be relevant only in specific cases and only for some instructions or methods.

4.3.6. Native Methods in Java Bytecode

Because native methods cannot be decomposed into bytecode instructions, they must be treated as atomic entities and should not be instrumented – this means that native methods must be recognised as such by BYCOUNTER. In bytecode, a native method implementation is visible by the access flag `ACC_NATIVE` (see [110], Section 4.1), though this flag is not part of the method's signature and thus not visible to the method's caller.

The JVM Tooling Interface (JVMTI) supports dealing with native methods, and Binder et al. [92] have performed a study on the quantitative evaluation of the contribution of native code to Java workloads inside SPECjvm98 benchmarks. According to [92], the quantitative contribution was below 6% for all SPECjvm98 parts except for the Java compiler javac and for "Jack", a Java parser generator.

Native method detection can be implemented using JVMTI following the guidelines of [92], but a JVM is not required to implement JVMTI and JVMTI is missing from Jikes RVM and other Java Virtual Machines. Therefore, a simpler but equally effective approach was chosen for BYCOUNTER that performs bytecode analysis using the ASM framework without using JVMTI. Not requiring JVMTI (which must be accessed using native C/C++ code) ensures that BYCOUNTER itself does not use native code and remains a truly platform-independent approach.

In Java bytecode, it is not possible to recognise whether a called method is native or not just by looking at the method's invocation in caller's bytecode: the signature does not expose a method's nativeness, and all four INVOKE* opcodes are used to invoke native methods, and none of them is exclusive to native methods. Though there are no methods declared as native in interfaces (JVM specification[110], Section 2.13.3.2), still "a method declared in an interface may be implemented by a method that is declared native [...] in a class that implements the interface".

Thus, the callee's method bytecode *implementation* must be inspected to check for the ACC_NATIVE flag, which can be detected statically by ASM (but also by bytecode engineering frameworks or through direct bytecode analysis, so using ASM is not a restriction) Note that there are no native constructors (JVM specification [110], Section 2.12.1), so constructors (which are very similar to methods at bytecode level) *can* be treated as non-native methods without further inspection.

Thus, if *before execution* it is known which methods will be invoked during an application's execution, it is possible to detect which ones of them are native. In the case where it cannot be known which methods will be invoked during an application's execution (e.g. due to polymorphism), approaches such as the one introduced in this thesis (using load-time bytecode instrumentation, see Section 4.4) need to analyse the method's access flags on the fly.

4.3.7. Static Methods in Java Bytecode

Static methods are invoked at bytecode level only using the INVOKESTATIC instruction – other INVOKE* instructions cannot be used. This is particularly interesting in the context of polymorphism: static methods cannot be abstract and therefore interfaces cannot contain static methods. abstract classes can contain static methods but cannot contain abstract static methods.

At the level of Java programming language, it is allowed (though discouraged) to invoke static methods on instances of declaring classes. For example, consider Listing 4.2: running the class MyClass will output true, false and true.

```
1  public class MyClass {
2    public static void main(String[] args) {
3      MyClass myClassA = new MyClass();
4      System.out.println(myClassA.doSmthg());

6      ExtendingMyClass myClassB = new ExtendingMyClass();
7      System.out.println(myClassB.doSmthg());

9      MyClass myClassC = (MyClass) myClassB;
10     System.out.println(myClassC.doSmthg());
11   }

13   public static boolean doSmthg() { return true; }
14 }

16 public class ExtendingMyClass extends MyClass {
17   public static boolean doSmthg() { return false; }
18 }
```

Listing 4.2: Static methods in declared and runtime classes

While the first two outputs are expected, the third output shows that when using the (discouraged) source code style for calling static methods on a class instance, the instance's *declared* type is deciding (here, it is `MyClass`) – not the instance's runtime type (which is `ExtendingMyClass` for `myClassC`, even despite the cast to `MyClass`).

Another executable `static` element of Java classes are static initialisers, expressed at source code level as `static{...}`. Inside bytecode, they are implemented using a special static method, called `<clinit>` by ASM. `<clinit>` is not invoked explicitly inside bytecode when its class is used – instead, the JVM invokes `<clinit>` when the class is loaded by the ClassLoader. However, as `<clinit>` contributes to the total performance of an application, it must be instrumented as well.

A related concern are constructors: at bytecode level, they are represented as non-static special methods. Even when the source code of a non-abstract class does not contain an explicit constructor, a default constructor (ASM signature `public <init>()V`) is created. As for static initialisers, the bytecode of constructors must be instrumented to account for the resource demands created by class instance construction. Note that when instrumenting transitively, constructor implementation will be instrumented once their invocations (through the `INVOKESPECIAL` opcode) is detected. As `<clinit>` is never called explicitly inside bytecode, it will be instrumented for all application classes to make sure its performance impact is not missed.

4.3.8. Working with Calling Context Trees

When a method invokes another method, the invoked method can itself invoke other methods. Rather than just the signatures of the callees, their parameters are also significant, and a *calling context* encompasses a concrete invocation case incl. the caller and the callee. At runtime, *calling context trees* describe the method invocations starting with the root node of the tree, i.e. the initial invoked method (e.g. `public static void main` in conventional Java programs). For a given calling context tree node $CCTN_i$, its resource demands include the resource demands of all the nodes in the subtree which has $CCTN_i$ as its root.

Thus, the nodes of the subtree must be analysed as well, and the dealing with calling context trees is the subject of this section.

In the remainder of this section, the example in Listing 4.3 will be used as a running example. In Listing 4.3, some methods of `MyClass` are omitted in source code to shorten the example, and because they are not relevant for the following discussion.

```java
1   long methodExample(InterfaceA param, int inputValue){
2     long start = java.lang.System.nanoTime();
3     this.performPreparations(inputValue);
4     for(int i=0; i < java.lang.Math.pow(inputValue,2); i++){
5       this.arrayOfElements[i%inputValue] = param.performWork();
6     }

8     // static method, OtherClass belongs to another component
9     OtherClass.doService(this.arrayOfElements);

11    long stop = java.lang.System.nanoTime();
12    this.record(start,stop); // sets this.startTime and this.stopTime
13    return this.performCleanup();
14  }

16  void performPreparations(int input){
17    // ... some other work
18    this.arrayOfElements = new int[input];
19  }

21  long performCleanup(){
22    long ret;
23    ret = this.stopTime − this.startTime;
24    return ret;
25  }
26 }
```

Listing 4.3: Example of a Java class

Consider the method `performCleanup()` in Listing 4.3: its implementation (and, consequently, the corresponding bytecode) are *invariant*: it contains neither control flow constructs nor calls of other methods. Speaking with compiler construction terminology, the entire method body is a single basic block. Therefore, the bytecode-level resource demands can be analysed in a static way: 2· ALOAD, 2· GETFIELD, 1· LSUB, 1· LSTORE, 1· LLOAD and 1· LRET. Note that the corresponding bytecode contains further elements (linenumber, localvariable, maxstack and maxlocals), but these are not executable instructions.

For the performPreparations method, the situation is slightly more interesting: since the performance of the NEWARRAY instruction is parametric, the individual invocations of performPreparations must be distinguished as long as input varies between invocations. Consequently, a runtime analysis (dynamic analysis) of the bytecode execution is needed. But as long as performPreparations does not call other methods (in the listing, it is indicated that it may perform some other work), it suffices to consider only it and other methods can be ignored.

The method methodExample is significantly more complex: it includes loops, nested statements and runtime polymorphism (using param). The expected result of BYCOUNTER when applied to methodExample (with values of input variables) is the number of bytecode instructions executed for a given methodExample invocation with the used input values. The number of bytecode instructions should include the bytecode instructions executed by all method invocations inside it (java.lang.System.nanoTime, java.lang.Math.pow, etc.). Consequently, the resource demands of the invoked methods must be quantified as well, incl. the runtime instance(s) of param and the doService method of OtherClass.

The first method invoked from inside methodExample is Java Platform API method java.lang.System.nanoTime(). The implementation of BY-COUNTER is based on the instrumentation of *application's* bytecode, and by default, API methods are treated as atomic entities which are not further decomposed (cf. 4.3.5). Section 5.3 presents API benchmarking as a novel technique to quantify platform-specific timing values of API methods.

However, BYCOUNTER is capable of instrumenting `java.lang.System.-`
`nanoTime()` for obtaining its (dynamic) bytecode counts as resource demands.
Due to the security-motivated restrictions of the Java Platform, load-time (or
runtime) instrumentation of classes that belong to the Java Platform API is not
allowed. Therefore, instrumenting the Platform API methods with BYCOUNTER
needs to be performed statically (before execution and before loading, i.e. "offline"), and the instrumented classes must replace the original classes on the
classpath. The Platform API method `java.lang.Math.pow` is treated in the
same way as `nanoTime`.

The invocation of the polymorphic method `performWork` (declared in
`InterfaceA`) can have one or different runtime invocation target. However,
in general, the invocation target's classtype is not known at compile time and
in general needs not to be known at load time, since runtime classloading (e.g.
over an `URLClassLoader`) is supported in Java. But even given this complexity, treating `performWork` as an atomic method just to avoid instrumenting
it (for obtaining bytecode-level resource demands) does not constitute a good
solution.

Instead, instrumenting the classtypes of `param` instances (i.e. runtime invocation targets) should be used, and several opportunities exist for this task.

Load-time instrumentation is the first opportunity, and it means that the instrumentation is delayed until loadtime. In load-time instrumentation, each loaded
class that implements `InterfaceA` is checked for whether it is a Platform API
class. If a loaded class is not part of the Platform API, `performWork` (and possibly other methods whose bytecode resource demands are needed) are instrumented on the fly, except when a method is abstract, has a native implementation or is already instrumented. Section 4.4 describes how load-time instrumentation works, and how BYCOUNTER marks instrumented methods and detects
alredy instrumented methods.

One disadvantage of load-time instrumentation is its runtime impact incurred
by class checking *on each execution* of a virtual method, plus the runtime instrumentation overhead. Additionally, the complexity of load-time instrumentation

is high (dealing with classloading in Java is error-prone), and each application run repeats the instrumentation because the instrumented classes are not persisted and do not overwrite the original classes.

Offline instrumentation of virtual methods is a (partial) remedy for problems incurred by load-time instrumentation. Offline instrumentation attempts to discover all known implementations of `InterfaceA` *before* load time, and instruments the found implementations of `performWork`. Of course, offline instrumentation cannot guarantee that all runtime instances of `InterfaceA` will be found. Furthermore, it only removes the overhead of load-time instrumentation – the overhead of load-time checking remains. Offline instrumentation may also instrument those implementations of `InterfaceA.performWork` that will actually never be used at runtime.

To find all implementers of a given interface, offline instrumentation needs to to an extensive search as it there is no such functionality in the Java Reflection API or other platform facilities. Some application (e.g. the Eclipse IDE) maintain an internal index by parsing the entire classpath, which could be a possible solution for BYCOUNTER.

For the remaining methods in Listing 4.3 (`doService`, `record`, `performCleanup`), the same considerations apply. However, an open question remains: should the resource demands of the methods invoked by `methodExample` ("callees" of the "caller") be considered individually (i.e. the structure of the calling context tree is fully preserved), or should they just be inlined into the resource demands of methodExample (i.e. the subtree is replaced by one node with aggregated resource demands)? Note that after inlining, the resource demands of the caller do not expose any hint that a callee resource demand existed and was inlined. With other words, inlining is a one-way operation (as it is in compiler construction from which the term was borrowed). The general disadvantage of inlining is that after it is performed, it is impossible to quantify the resource demand contribution of the callee towards the caller.

For inlining of the callee's resource demands, both "online" inlining (at execution time) and "offline" inlining (after the execution of the caller has finished) are possible candidates. Online inlining has the advantage that less storage is needed, and that the "so far" resource demands are available at any execution step of the caller. The disadvantages of online inlining is runtime overhead of the inlining-caused calculations. Offline inlining has the advantage that it preserves the original tree of resource demands, and can be performed in a selective way.

4.3.9. Considering Subtrees of Calling Context Trees

In a multi-threaded platform, a method such as `methodExample` from Listing 4.3 can be invoked concurrently, which means that invocations of `methodExample`'s callees (`performPreparations` and others) must be mapped to the correct CCT node representing a given `methodExample` invocation. That is, information needed to construct a CCT must be made available – however, from inside an executed Java method, it is not possible to query for its caller. While a method can find out the thread ID of the thread that is executing it, the calling relations needed to create a CCT also need the caller method.

While some JVMs support an event-based notification mechanism that signals both the callee *and* the caller of a method invocation, request IDs are a more general technique to collect data for CCT construction. A request ID is passed from the caller to the callee, which requires the signatures of the callees to be extended (e.g. by introducing wrappers) and also requires that the callee invocations be replaced by the wrappers/extended signatures.

However, there are scenarios where a single request ID is not sufficient, as it is the case when for a given considered CCT, one or several CCT subtrees are also requested. Figure 4.5 shows an example which needs more than one request ID: assume that that the aggregated resource demands of both `method1()` and `method2()` are sought. `method1` runs in Thread A and invokes `method2` asynchronously, which runs in a separate thread (Thread B). After `method2` starts, `method1` invokes `method3` in a synchronous way, and `method1` continues to run after method3 terminates. After some time, method2 invokes method4 in a synchronous way – note that method3 runs at the same time in parallel (in Thread A).

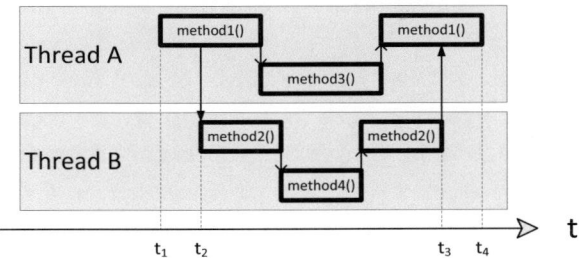

Figure 4.5.: Subtrees of Calling Context Trees

The resource demands of method1 include those of method2, method3 and method4 – but the resource demand of method2 (which includes the resource demands of method4) does *not* include the resource demands of method3. The resource demands of method1 can be aggregated (both online and off-line) by propagating a *request ID* to method2 (which propagates it to method4) and to method3, thus identifying their resource demands as sub-demands of method1.

However, judging just by the request ID that method2 *receives*, it is not clear which sub-demands belong to it. It is also not possible to deduce the resource demand aggregation relations using the timestamps and "contains" relation: while method2 starts before method3 and ends after it, the resource demands of method3 do not belong to method2.

A possible solution would be to create a *separate* request ID for method2 and propagate it to method4 together with the request ID from method1. However, each nesting level would add one request ID to the list of request IDs, and the resulting hierarchy of IDs adds to the management and instrumentation overhead. Section 4.4.6 describes how BYCOUNTER costructs CCTs and CCT subtrees in an efficient and scalable way.

4.3.10. Usage of Passive Resources from Java Bytecode

As explained above, the focus of this thesis is the quantification of processing resource demands for PCM-level `InternalActions` and `ExternalActions` – the identification of RDSEFF elements incl. control flow constructs such as `LoopAction` or `BranchAction` (e.g. using reverse engineering) is a separate task which is covered by Klaus Krogmann's dissertation [42] and Heiko Koziolek's dissertation [186]. For passive resources, the identification of `AcquireResource` and `ReleaseResource` actions for building PCM RD-SEFFs is also outside the focus of this thesis and the assumption taken in this chapter is that BYCOUNTER does not need to be aware of passive resources.

However, the following brief discussion of the bytecode methods/instructions that can correspond to `AcquireResource` and `ReleaseResource` is warranted for the following two reasons: (i) BYCOUNTER can check whether bytecode sections that should correspond to internal actions contain unexpected (or undesired) usages of passive resources and (ii) future versions of BYCOUNTER and a PCM-independent usage of BYCOUNTER may need a bytecode-level understanding of passive resources usage. Additionally, the following discussion shows which bytecode instructions carry potential performance implications because they affect the acquisitions and releases of passive resources.

The keyword `synchronized` in Java marks a method or a code section which can be used by at most one thread at a time; a second thread that wishes to enter the `synchronized` method/section must wait until the first thread leaves it. At bytecode level, `synchronized` source code keyword in the signature of methods results in the `ACC_SYNCHRONIZED` flag, which can be used to detect whether a given method is `synchronized`. Since the JVM implementation must ensure that a monitor is acquired at method entry and released at method exit (both normal and with exception), there are no further traces of synchronized in the bytecode of methods which carry synchronized in their signature.

For entirely synchronized methods, the JVM specification does not clarify which monitor is acquired; for modelling in a PCM RDSEFF, a synchronized method should be preceded by an AcquireAction and followed by a ReleaseAction (on the same passive resource). The cardinality of the PassiveResource that is acquired/released to model the synchronization should be 1, and the PassiveResource should not be acquired/released in other SEFFs or AcquireActions/ReleaseActions. A proper treatment of synchronized methods implies that if the InternalAction that contains the considered synchronized method contains additional methods, the considered InternalAction must be broken into several parts.

When the keyword synchronized is applied to code sections and not to the entire method, it has a different source code syntax: synchronized(obj), where obj is any initialised object instance. At bytecode level, the bytecode instructions MONITORENTER and MONITOREXIT are used to implement the beginning ({) and the end (}) of a synchronized(obj) statement. The used obj object instance is the only parameter needed by MONITORENTER and MONITOREXIT , it is expected to be found on the stack and is consumed by MONITORENTER /MONITOREXIT from the stack. The presence of MONITORENTER /MONITOREXIT in bytecode can be used to reconstruct (reverse engineer) acquire/release actions for PCM model instances.

Usage of any other passive resources (locks, barriers etc.) from Java bytecode happens over method calls, with the Java Platform API already providing a significant set of passive resources. For example, the java.util.concurrent package and its subpackages provide a CyclicBarrier, a Semaphore, a mechanism for locks and a thread pool mechanism etc. Therefore, purely at bytecode level, only MONITORENTER and MONITOREXIT are visible, while to properly account for method invocations accessing barriers, locks etc., an understanding of the *patterns* involved in using CyclicBarrier etc. is needed. Consequently, only when there is a mapping from bytecode to PCM, BYCOUNTER analyses the presence of MONITORENTER /MONITOREXIT in bytecode sections which are declared to correspond to InternalActions, and reports violations that it finds.

4.3.11. Bytecode Instruction Equivalence Classes

As discussed above, the Java bytecode instruction set is not orthogonal: it contains instructions which duplicate the effect of other instructions (or sequences thereof). For example, ILOAD_0 (which occupies one byte in the classfile) is *equivalent* to ILOAD 0 (which occupies two bytes because the parameter 0 is stored explicitly). Similarly, I2D (integer to double conversion) is equivalent to I2F followed by F2D (F stands for float), without loss of precision.

But from the performance perspective, *performance* equivalence is even more interesting. A trivial performance equivalence classification only aggregates semantically close instructions such as ILOAD variants in the above example, but there is potential for more. For example, DDIV (double division) and FDIV (float division) are likely to be mapped to the same CPU instruction(s) as they are both floating-point operations, and are likely to expose the same performance.

Instruction grouping has been explored in the performance community on several occasions: [187] has introduced incremental grouping based on criteria such as operation type, data type, etc. However, the grouping relations do not address performance equivalence, and haven't been validated empirically.

In the following, the performance equivalence classes are suggested which simplify the identification of performance invariants. The presented classes will be empirically validated by benchmarking results in Section 5, and are different from equivalence classes introduced by Dujmovic in [187]. For the discussion on performance equivalence classes, it is important to highlight the differences and the mismatches between the primitive Java programming language types and the primitive Java bytecode types.

Unlike for int or long, there is no support for booleans in Java bytecode, and only a limited support for bytes, chars and shorts (the last two types occupy 2 bytes, i.e. chars support UTF-16). These types are mainly represented as `integer`s (occupying 4 bytes, i.e. 32 bits): for example, the source code statement `byte b = 120;` is translated to `BIPUSH 120, ISTORE <index>` by the Eclipse compiler. Note that depending on an `integer`'s size, a source code compiler can use different instructions to push an `integer` value onto the stack: `BIPUSH` (as long as the integer value fits into one byte) or `SIPUSH` otherwise – the `S` stands for `signed`, not for `short`.

The data types `byte`s, `char`s and `short`s only become visible when they are targets of a conversion (e.g. `I2B` (for `byte`), `I2C`, `I2S` – note that there is no inverse conversion), or when creating arrays (e.g. `BALOAD`, etc.). Figure 4.6 gives an overview on the conversion and array support of the Java bytecode instruction set – note that other instructions types (such as `ISUB` etc.) are not listed.

	byte	char	double	float	int	long	short
byte	–	–	–	–	–	–	–
char	–	–	–	–	–	–	–
double	–	–	–	D2F	D2I	D2L	–
float	–	–	F2D	–	F2I	F2L	–
int	I2B	I2C	I2D	I2F	–	I2L	I2S
long	–	–	L2D	L2F	L2I	–	–
short	–	–	–	–	–	–	–
array operations	BALOAD BASTORE	CALOAD CASTORE	DALOAD DASTORE	FALOAD FASTORE	IALOAD IASTORE	LALOAD LASTORE	SALOAD SASTORE

Figure 4.6.: Overview of Conversion-oriented Java Bytecode Instructions

Appendix A.1 contains a detailed list of the identified performance equivalence clases for Java bytecode instructions. The equivalence of these classes will be analysed using benchmarks, as described in Section 5.

4.4. Using Transparent Application Instrumentation for Bytecode Counting

In Section 4.3, the number of executed bytecode instructions and methods invocations has been identified as a platform-independent resource demand metric. In the course of Section 4.3, it was mentioned that BYCOUNTER uses *transparent instrumentation of application's bytecode* to quantify this metric. In this section, the design and implementation of this mechanism are discussed in more detail. Since this part of BYSUITE can also be used as a stand-alone tool (independent of the remaining parts of BYSUITE), it is referred to as BYCOUNTER in the remainder of this section.

BYCOUNTER proceeds in two steps, shown in Figure 4.7: after the instrumentation is carried out, the instrumented classes are executed with a workload to obtain the counting results. The results of the first step (the instrumented classes) can be persisted and are reused with several workloads. The instrumentation phase identifies performance invariants in the application to instrument (to minimize the instrumentation overhead) and that inserts counters into the bytecode which will be incremented and evaluated at runtime, when the instrumented application is executed. A detailed description of the instrumentation phase will be provided in Section 4.4.4.

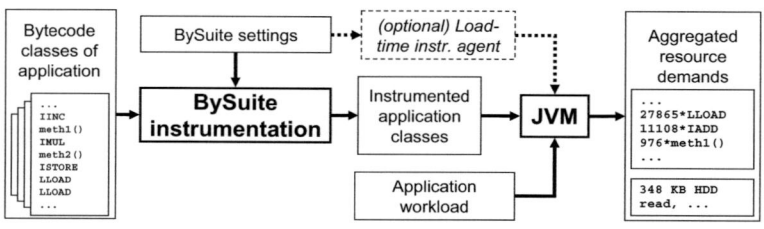

Figure 4.7.: Overview of BYCOUNTER instrumentation and phases

In the situations where methods are called polymorphically, the runtime type of the invocation target is unknown before instrumentation starts. Thus, to account for dynamic method dispatching, BYCOUNTER offers *load-time instru- mentation* that is implemented as an agent hooked to the JVM. In BYCOUNTER, load-time instrumentation can be configured to either complement static instru- mentation (when new classes are loaded which were not known during static implementation), or to replace it entirely. Load-time instrumentation can also persist the classes containing instrumented methods for later re-use.

As different instruction types have different execution durations, they must be counted separately, and the parametric dependencies of the array-creating instructions (see Section 4.3.4) must be considered as well. Method invocations should be recorded, with their parameters (or characterisations) where appro- priate – BYCOUNTER should provide ways to configure which methods need parameter analysis and which don't. Calling Context Trees (cf. Sections 4.3 8 and 4.3.9) should be considered as well.

To obtain *runtime* counts of instructions and methods, static analysis (i.e. ana- lysis without executing the application) could be used, but it would have to be augmented to evaluate runtime effects of control flow constructs like loops or branches. Even if control flow consideration is attempted with advanced tech- niques such as symbolic execution, additional effort is required for handling infinite symbolic execution trees [188, pp. 27-31]. Hence, it is imperative to use dynamic (i.e. runtime) analysis for counting executed instructions and invoked methods.

However, dynamic counting of executed Java bytecode instructions is not offered by Java profilers or conventional Java Virtual Machines (JVMs). Ex- isting program behaviour analysis frameworks for Java applications (such as JRAF [28]) do not differentiate between bytecode instruction types, do not iden- tify method invocations performed from bytecode, or do not work at the level of bytecode instructions at all. These frameworks frequently rely on the instru- mentation of the JVM, however, such instrumentation requires substantial effort and must be reimplemented for different JVMs.

4.4.1. Requirements for the Instrumentation Process

Bytecode instrumentation performed by BYCOUNTER has to fulfil the following requirements:

1. the instrumentation has to account for each instruction type *individually* and return precise counts for each instruction type and each method signature, but also be configurable to support bytecode instruction equivalence classes (e.g. those described in Section 4.3.11)

2. the instrumentation has to count how often a concrete method implementation is invoked (for polymorphic calls, e.g. over an interface, BYCOUNTER should record *both* the polymorphic, in-bytecode method's signature *and* the concrete method's signature – see the examples in Section 4.3.5)

3. BYCOUNTER should recognise native methods and skip instrumenting them (cf. Section 4.3.6)

4. BYCOUNTER should recognise Java Platform API methods and skip instrumenting them during load-time instrumentation (for static instrumentation of Java Platform API classes, it is the BYCOUNTER user's responsibility to replace the uninstrumented Java Platform API classes on the classpath through the instrumented ones)

5. *PCM awareness*: PCM constructs such as internal actions often correspond to sections of *non-abstract* methods rather than to entire non-abstract methods – thus, BYCOUNTER must support quantifying bytecode resource demands for one or several method sections (with the requirement that the specified method sections are non-overlapping)

6. *resource demand quantification targets*: the methods and CCTs for which the resource demands have to be obtained should be configurable in a convenient way, and should support CCT subtrees as well as separate quantification of callees' resource demands

7. *instrumentation scope*: it should be possible to configure the instrumenta-tion scope with minimal effort, where the default implicit instrumentation behaviour is "instrument all method in all application classes" (of course, excluding native methods and abstract methods which lack an implemen-ation body), but the instrumentation scope can also be specified at the level of packages, classes and methods

8. *parameter analysis*: it should be configurable for which instructions and which methods parameter analysis should be performed (incl. input para-meters or characterisations thereof, and invocations targets or characterisa-tions thereof for non-static methods)

9. *controlling class size increase*: the instrumentation should introduce as few additional instructions into the classfile as possible (and the bytesize of classes and methods must be controlled to remain within the JVM specific-ation)

10. *minimizing runtime overhead*: the runtime overhead of the instrumentation (incl. results collection) should be minimized, both in terms of execution time and memory

11. *deactivatable resource demand quantification for instrumented classes*: even a class is instrumented, it should be possible to switch off the metric col-lection and metric reporting as far as possible, to minimize the overhead of BYCOUNTER when metric collection is unneeded but it is not appropriate/-possible to replace the instrumented class back with the uninstrumented one

12. *transparency*: BYCOUNTER must not unnecessarily change the existing fields, variables, method signatures, class structure and execution se-mantics

13. *method wrappers for CCT support*: method wrappers are only introduced if *concurrency-safe* CCT construction is required explicitly (by default, it is suf-ficient to have CCT support which is potentially thread-unsafe)

14. *precision*: for methods with control flow constructs (loops, ...) that depend on the input parameters, counts must be reported correctly for any execution path, i.e. for all allowed values of input parameters

15. *self-awareness*: BYCOUNTER should mark instrumented classes in such a way that it can recognise already instrumented classes to prevent erroneous/unintended double-instrumentation (no matter from where the candidate classes are loaded)

16. *storage* of metric results: storing all collected bytecode metrics in memory may slow down the execution of BYCOUNTER, so the options of (background) serialisation to HDD or a database should be available

17. *aggregation*: for CCTs, the aggregation should happen offline (i.e. after the CCT root's execution has terminated), but an option should be available to enable online aggregation, since online aggregation offers up-to-date resource demands of a method incl. the resource demands of that method's callees, even while that method is still executing

18. *passive resources usage checking*: optional checking of `MONITORENTER` and `MONITOREXIT` (see Section 4.3.10)

4.4.2. Evaluating and Storing Counting Results

In BYCOUNTER, there are several possibilities to deal with counting result trees (where each tree node corresponds to a CCT node). Consider the example where method A makes a synchronous calls to method B and afterwards to the method C, while method B calls the method D. Assume that the resource demand of A is required, i.e. the resource demands of B, C and D count towards it.

In the simplest case which is called *offline inlining*, the full resource demands of A are calculated once B, C and D have terminated. This means that these results must be kept (either in main memory or in a persisted storage) until A has terminated. This storage requires effort and space, and it would be sufficient to add the resource demands of B to those of A once B has terminated – this is called *online inlining*. Of course, a counting result must indicate whether inlining of its sub-demands has already been performed or not – this is supported by BYCOUNTER implementation.

For both online and offline inlining, the inlined counting results can be discarded once they have been evaluated – however, BYCOUNTER can be configured to keep these intermediate results after inlining, e.g. for analysing them offline.

To see what this means for (in)transparent inlining of resource demands, again consider the above example with methods A, B, C and D, but now assume that the resource demands of both A and B are needed. Figure 4.8 illustrates the two different options available for online inlining – note the difference between the counting results available at the end.

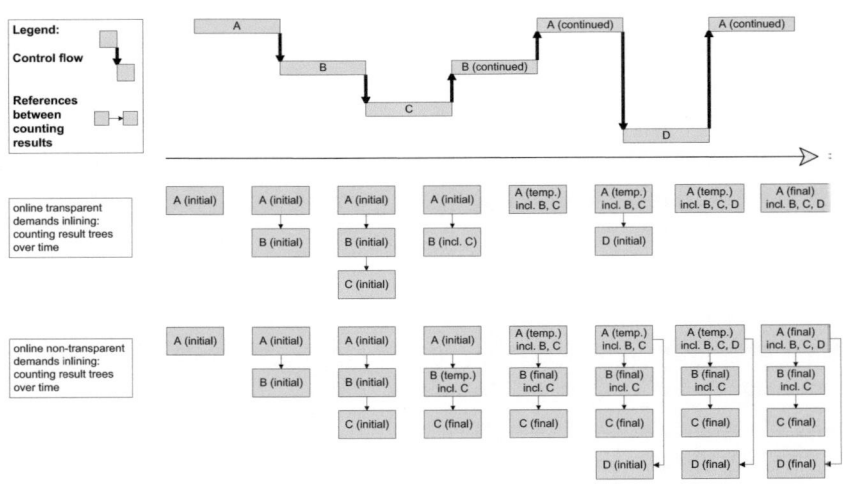

Figure 4.8.: Different Options for Online Inlining of Counting Results in BYCOUNTER

To prevent heap memory from being flooded by counting results, at most a predefined threshold number of counting results is kept in memory by BY-COUNTER. Since the reporting of counts is currently implemented using a synchronous method, the counting result collector (described in Section 4.4.7) can be implemented to block until the result serialisation backlog is resolved when capacity of memory storage for counting results is depleted.

Another issue encountered during the implementation was the overflow of counters: initially, `int`-typed counter were used. After refactoring, BY-COUNTER now uses `long`-typed counters (see Section 4.4.4 for more details). This means that counter incrementation needs several instruction: `LLOAD` for on-stack loading, `LCONST` for putting increment onto the stack, `LADD` for the addition and `LSTORE` for storing the actual results.

While these instruction sequence may be replaced by one processor instruction on some platforms, executing the instrumented code in interpretation (i.e. non-JITted) modus still incurs more overhead than if `int`-based counters are used since a single `IINC` instruction would be sufficient for `int` counters. In scenarios where the range-limited `int` counters are sufficient, the BYCOUNTER user can switch back to them. Note, however, that only *plausibility checking* (counter results must always be positive), but no counter overflow checking is implemented in BYCOUNTER.

To judge how soon (i.e. in the worst case) it is possible to obtain an undetected overflow using `int` counters, consider the following: positive values of `int` are in the interval [0 , 2147483647]. Ignoring all but one (the most often executed) instruction in the method, and assuming that this instruction takes $\frac{1}{12}$ CPU cycle to execute (which is well possible given JIT compilation being followed by CPU pipelining), on a 2 GHz CPU (which would execute $2 \cdot 10^9$ CPU cycles per second), we obtain $\frac{2,147,483,647}{12 \cdot 2 \cdot 10^9} \approx 89.48$ seconds. This computation shows that for long-running methods, `int` counters may indeed be insufficient.

4.4.3. Analysis of Bytecode Invariants and Basic Blocks

A basic block is not necessarily invariant with respect to performance: even though it does not contain any control flow branches, loops etc, it can contain parameter-dependent instruction, whose parameter change between basic block executions. In BYCOUNTER, this means that for a *performance-invariant* basic block, one counter is sufficient: the actual bytecode-oriented resource demands of a *performance-invariant* basic clock can be identified statically. If a basic block contains an instruction with parametric performance dependencies, that basic block must be split into three parts, unless analysis of instruction parameters reveals that they are always the same (e.g. the array size is fixed).

To minimize the counting-caused overhead, it is tempting to check whether *performance invariants* can be found beyond single performance-invariant basic blocks. We define a performance invariant as a consecutive bytecode section (but possibly including branches and other non-linear control flow) which has performance-equivalent bytecode counts independent of the input parameters of the method which contains the bytecode section.

As an example, consider the method `example()` which contains a performance-invariant call of method `meth()`. The call to `meth()` is performed between two basic blocks B_1 and B_2, and the particular invocation of `meth()` is indexed as `meth()`$_{idx}$. The index is used to distinguish a particular invocation from other calls to `meth()`, and the index $_{idx}$ can be the bytecode offset from the beginning of `example()` or any other unique index. As B_1 and B_2 are performance invariants, they are refered to as PI_1 and PI_2, and since `meth()` is performance-invariant (i.e. $PI_3 :=$ `meth()`$_{idx}$), the three can be merged into one performance invariant: $PI_4 := PI_1 PI_3 PI_2$.

Real-world examples of performance-invariant methods are `CodeTable.set(int i, int v)`, `CompBase.getMaxCode()`, `DeStack.isEmpty()`, `DeStack.pop()` from SPECjvm2008's `compress` benchmark, and others. While performance-invariant methods are often short (e.g. `getters` and `setters`), they are often called very often, and invariant detection leads to valuable speedup at runtime: in the above example, only one counter (for PI_4) is needed and used, instead of creating and incrementing three counters (for PI_1, PI_2 and PI_3), instrumenting meth() $_{idx}$, collecting its counting results, etc.

Requiring absolute bytecode counts to be identical (after "normalisation" using the above equivalence classes and parameter erasure) may be too "strong" and leaves room for relaxation. Consider the following example of a suggested performance invariant: the source code if(condition){a=b+2;}else{c=d+2;} would be translated to the bytecode in Listing 4.4:

```
1    ...
2        L5
3            ILOAD  5
4            IFEQ  L6
5            ILOAD  2
6            ICONST_2
7            IADD
8            ISTORE  1
9            GOTO  L7
10       L6
11           ILOAD  4
12           ICONST_3
13           IADD
14           ISTORE  3
15       L7
```

Listing 4.4: Branch Invariant In Java Bytecode

Note that the condition checking is done using IFEQ instruction, that is the boolean condition value is treated as an integer that is compared to 0. The IFEQ instruction performs two tasks: the comparison and (depending on the outcome) a jump to label L6. Also note that the labelblock between L5 and L6 is *not* a basic block since it includes a conditional jump caused by IFEQ that is only taken if condition is false (i.e. the variable stored at index 5 is 0).

The branch path which is taken if the condition is false consists of an ILOAD, ICONST, IADD and ISTORE. The branch path taken if condition is true also consists of an ILOAD, ICONST, IADD and ISTORE, but with different parameters – yet assuming that these four instructions do not have a parametric performance behaviour, the two branch pathes are almost equivalent. If it can be assumed that the IFEQ with jump *but without* GOTO is performance-equivalent to "jump-less" IFEQ *plus* GOTO, the two pathes are indeed performance-equivalent and the entire bytecode in Listing 4.4 is performance-invariant.

Another example of performance invariants are loops whose conditions are independent from their input and the state of the executing class. For example, for(int i=0; i<10; i++){arr[i]=i*i;} (where arr is an array of integers) is a performance-invariant loop. In fact, detecting performance invariants is related to inlining performed by source code compilers and JIT compilers, but the novel contribution of performance invariant detection as introduced by this thesis is the use of hard, platform-independent performance equivalence classes for bytecode instructions.

In BYCOUNTER, the performance invariant detection is implemented for basic blocks (which are detected by BYCOUNTER on the basis of bytecode) and for simple if-then-else structures. Performance invariant detection would additionally benefit from method-level analysis and semantic invariant detection as performed by Daikon [189]. A platform-specific invariant detection may also be possible if platform-specific performance equivalence classes are known (e.g. on some platforms, LDIV and DDIV may end up in the same performance class). However, using platform-specific performance invariants for instrumentation optimization would results in platform-specific bytecode resource demands, and contradict the design goal of BYCOUNTER.

In this thesis, the performance invariant analysis is not carried out further than discussed above for the following reasons: (i) the speedup of executing the instrumented application (achieved through less instrumentation code) is not significant enough to warrant performance invariant analysis beyond branch comparisons, e.g. using point-to analysis and data flow analysis (ii) the approaches that create parametrised performance models with bytecode resource demands (such as BEAGLE) carry out performance abstractions and model simplifications that have an even stronger influence than the relaxation of the equivalence classes.

Another research area is related to performance invariants is worst-case performance analysis: in the above example on the `if` branch, the "worst case" would include `GOTO` as if it would be executed in both of the to branches ("then" and "else"). The resulting deviation would be small enough to accept it given the simplification of instrumentation and counting. However, BYCOUNTER is designed to yield *precise* bytecode counts, and worst-case analysis lies outside of this thesis' scope.

4.4.4. Inserting Bytecode Infrastructure for Runtime Counting

After parsing the instrumentation settings, BYCOUNTER analyses the bytecode to instrument and inserts the counting infrastructure, incl. result reporting infrastructure. It does so in two passes: the first one performs the analysis, while the second one inserts the counting infrastructure into bytecode.

In the first pass, BYCOUNTER parses the existing bytecode class file into a navigable, structured representation, because direct manipulation of bytecode is very complex and error-prone. BYCOUNTER uses the ASM bytecode engineering framework [114], which offers a bytecode class representation that includes semantic details (method signatures, fields, etc.). ASM's bytecode representation can be accessed and changed through the ASM API, which follows the visitor pattern and allows creating custom visitors to add, change or delete the elements of the class representation down to the level of individual bytecode instructions.

During the first pass, BYCOUNTER identifies performance-invariants (e.g. basic blocks without parametric bytecode instructions, performance-invariant methods, etc.). It also detects which methods are invoked from the parsed method, and analyses which invocations are polymorphic.

During the second pass, BYCOUNTER inserts counting instrumentation into the bytecode representation using a special ASM class visitor that is part of the BYCOUNTER implementation. The basic principle behind the visitor is to add

182

new counters to existing bytecode instructions and method invocations, and to add parameter-analysing bytecode, invocation target analysis bytecode as well as bytecode that reports the counting results. Later, during the execution the instrumented method, these counters will be initialised, incremented, evaluated and finally reported.

A suitable data structure must be selected for the counters, which should be both effective, occupy a reasonable amount of space, and should be specification-compliant. The JVM specification [110] and recent official additions (such as INVOKEDYNAMIC opcode) result in 203 valid bytecode instructions, including four INVOKE* instructions. Hence, these instructions require a fixed number of counters (one per instruction). Note that the "discovery" pass could identify bytecode instructions that *really* occur in the considered bytecode to initialise less than 203 counters (one for each officially defined opcode). However, this enhancement ultimately results in more overhead than simply creating counters for all 203 instructions.

In contrast to bytecode instruction, the number of the different runtime *methods* (including application's own methods and API methods) which will be invoked using INVOKE* in the instrumented method depends on the concrete application which is considered. Hence, in principle, method invocations inside the instrumented bytecode should be counted using a data structure which allows a *dynamic* addition of new counters for found method signatures. For BYCOUNTER, the counters for method invocations could be stored in a java.util.Map-like data structure. At runtime, this structure can be easily extended, however, each access to a Map-like structure for incrementing a counter is very expensive.

Thus, a more efficient technique is used in BYCOUNTER by creating long counters for *both* polymorphic *and* non-polymorphic method invocations, and of course "primitive" bytecode instructions. For each polymorphically invoked signature (i.e. which is called using INVOKEVIRTUAL), an additional dynamically extending structure is maintained, which counts how often a given invocation target runtime type is used. This allows keeping track of the actual methods executed at runtime.

The list of found signatures might contain some methods that will not (or not always) be executed at runtime, because the execution path does not reach them for some values of input parameters passed to the instrumented method. The case-specific non-execution of these methods is not problematic, as the corresponding counts will simply maintain their initial value of 0.

Potentially, other bytecode-instrumenting operations (e.g. advice and pointcut insertion from AOP programming) could take place *after* BYCOUNTER instrumentation. These insertions could add new method invocations to bytecode, and runtime counting of BYCOUNTER would not capture them. Yet when no bytecode modification happens after BYCOUNTER instrumentation, the list of callee method signatures used inside bytecode of a given caller method will not grow at runtime. Hence, for correct counting results, we require that BYCOUNTER is the last tool in the bytecode instrumentation chain.

After the list of found method signatures has been populated in the "discovery" pass, BYCOUNTER performs its "instrumentation" pass over bytecode. In the "instrumentation" pass, counters of type `long` are added to bytecode through ASM-based instrumentation. From the bytecode view, these counters are "local variables". The maximum number of "local variables" in the bytecode of a Java method is 65536 (incl. those variables that existed before instrumentation), and this number does not constitute a limitation in realistic cases. After creating the counters, BYCOUNTER adds instrumentation to update (i.e. increment) them when the corresponding instructions and methods are executed.

So far, the instrumentation inserted by BYCOUNTER into the application bytecode was transparent in the sense that no method signatures were changed, and the functional behaviour of the application remained unchanged as well. Only if recording calling context trees is enable, BYCOUNTER must apply changes to method signatures, which is needed to support caller ID propagation required for CCT construction. The details of this step are described in the next section, before Section 4.4.7 describes how results are reported and collected.

4.4.5. Quantifying the Impact of the Instrumentation

The BYCOUNTER instrumentation has *static overhead*: it impacts the size of classes and methods of the instrumented application as it inserts additional instrumentation instructions into the application. Even more important, the BY-COUNTER instrumentation leads to *runtime overhead* since extra execution time is spend on the instrumentation itself and because larger classfiles lead to longer classloading times for the JVM.

In the following, we discuss both types of overhead by considering three BY-COUNTER phases: (i) counter creation and initialisation, (ii) counter incrementation and (iii) reporting of counter values. It is important to remember that the overhead can decrease significantly when performance-invariant bytecode instruction sequences (PIBISes) are identified and used, as will be shown during the validation in Section 7.1.6. In the following, we only consider the "worst case scenario" which does not benefit from the use of PIBISes.

The dynamic overhead of counter creation/initialisation depends on the number of building blocks (instructions and called methods) in the implementation of the instrumented method. Per building block, about 20 instructions need to be executed for initialisation. Even for a large number of building blocks, this overhead is not critical when compared to the overhead of the counter incrementation and reporting, which are given in the following.

The dynamic overhead of counter incrementation depends on the chosen counter type, as was already explained in Section 4.4.2 on page 177: incrementation of an `int`-typed counter only needs one `IINC` instruction, while `long`-typed counters need four instructions (even six instructions if counters are allocated in JVM local variables which have high indexes accessible only with the `wide` addressing instruction). Thus, in the *worst* case, the counter incrementation *can* lead to a slowdown factor of 6 – or even more if the counter incrementation operations are costlier than the counted operation itself.

The dynamic overhead of counter reporting is that of the call to the reporting method. The reporting method writing to the console will be delayed by the console's performance, and providing exact numbers for this operation is not possible – however, as a rule of thumb, reporting to the console takes in excess of 1 millisecond, and should therefore be avoided. Instead, reporting of the result can be cached in memory or written to a series of files: once a reporting file is complete it can be saved to permanent storage by a background operation.

The more performance-heavy building blocks (e.g. costly API methods) appear in the instrumented method and the more often they are executed, the lesser is the runtime overhead of BYCOUNTER, since the counter incrementing overhead remains constant and thus has a smaller share of the overall execution time of the instrumented application. In some cases where a large number of very short methods had to be instrumented and the reporting of each execution of such methods overweights the duration of the actual method, the dynamic overhead of instrumentation can be as high as a factor of 27 (i.e. 2700 %). While this appears to be a heavy burden, it should be kept in mind that BYCOUNTER delivers instruction-precise bytecode counts, and many applications exhibit a significantly smaller BYCOUNTER overhead. The use of PIBISes reduces the overhead as well.

For the static overhead, it should be noted that for non-trivial applications, classloading (even from slow storage) usually has a very minuscule share of execution time compared to the actual work performed by the program. The static overhead of BYCOUNTER includes BYCOUNTER's own classes (which have a total size of 130 KB) – this bytecode which must be verified and loaded.

In each instrumented method, counter creation and initialisation is done by a method which consists of 647 bytecode instructions with a bytesize of 1505 bytes. When `int`-typed counters are used, each counter incrementation consists of 1 parameterless instruction which fits into 1 byte; when `long`-typed counters are used, each counter incrementation consists of up to 6 instructions with a total size of up to 10 bytes. The code to do the reporting of results is a rather compact operation: 227 bytecode instructions that occupy 511 bytes (this is a static count, as we only consider classloading-related overhead).

Overall, the overhead of BYCOUNTER depends on the structure of the instrumented application and on the instrumentation settings. The runtime overhead (which caused by counter usage and reporting) overweights the "static" overhead caused by increased classfile sizes and the addition of BYCOUNTER-own classes. In general, the largest share of the dynamic overhead is taken by counter incrementation and reporting – counter initialization is a rather low-effort task.

4.4.6. Recording Calling Context Details

The approach taken by BYCOUNTER for supporting Calling Context Trees is both simple and powerful: it needs to pass just *one* ID from caller to callee and allows reconstructing a thread-aware execution trace from the counting results. The approach works as follows: for each instrumented method, the instrumentation code is inserted that generates a unique invocation ID – a new invocation ID is generated for *each* invocation. Each time an instrumented method calls another instrumented method, the caller's invocation ID is passed to the callee, which reports its caller's invocation ID in addition to its own (i.e. callee's) invocation ID.

In the example from Section 4.3.9, `method3` knows that it has been called by `method1`, but `method4` only knows that it has been called by `method2` – it is not directly aware that it is part of a request originating in `method1`. However, having the invocation relations `method1→method2` and `method2→method4`, the transitive relation `method1→method4` can be reconstructed. Thus, it is possible to construct an entire CCT from binary relations. The inserted instrumentation for invocation ID generation is customisable to allow for invocation IDs that embed the executing thread's ID or other details (e.g. JVM instance ID, etc.). One restriction of this simple and effective approach is caused by calling context trees that include uninstrumented methods, e.g. API methods: if `method2` is not being instrumented, it is not possible to establish the (transitive) relation `method1→method4`.

To trace CCTs through ID passing, the signatures of instrumented methods must be enhanced with an additional input parameter, for receiving the caller's ID. Figure 4.9 shows a simplified example of the additional changes performed by BYCOUNTER – the counting instrumentation is omitted for brevity and clarity.

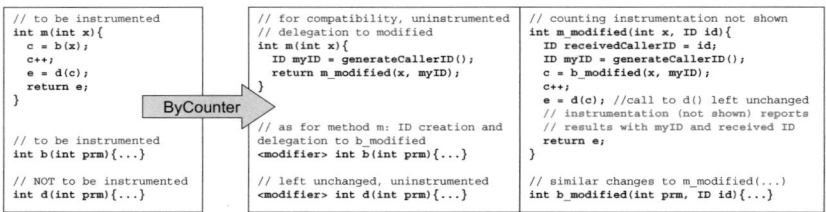

```
// to be instrumented          // for compatibility, uninstrumented    // counting instrumentation not shown
int m(int x){                  // delegation to modified                int m_modified(int x, ID id){
   c = b(x);                    int m(int x){                              ID receivedCallerID = id;
   c++;                            ID myID = generateCallerID();           ID myID = generateCallerID();
   e = d(c);                       return m_modified(x, myID);             c = b_modified(x, myID);
   return e;                    }                                          c++;
}                                                                          e = d(c); //call to d() left unchanged
                               // as for method m: ID creation and         // instrumentation (not shown) reports
                               delegation to b_modified                    // results with myID and received ID
// to be instrumented          <modifier> int b(int prm){...}             return e;
int b(int prm){...}                                                      }

// NOT to be instrumented      // left unchanged, uninstrumented          // similar changes to m_modified(...)
int d(int prm){...}            <modifier> int d(int prm){...}             int b_modified(int prm, ID id){...}
```

ByCounter

Figure 4.9.: Effects of preemption on relating response demands to execution time

Several precautions are taken to ensure that the application remains in a consistent state despite these changes:

1. the suffix added to the newly created method (e.g. b_modified in Figure 4.9) is chosen in such a way that no naming collisions in class that contains the method is created, which also means that b_modified may not exist in superclasses of the class holding b_modified

2. the access modifiers of the original method meth to be modified (e.g. b in Figure 4.9) is preserved for its both the "renewed" meth and the new meth_modified

3. in all *instrumented* methods that call a method meth, if meth is instrumented, the invocation of meth is replaced by the invocation of meth_suffix, where the caller's invocation ID is passed as an input parameter to meth_suffix

4.4.7. Reporting and Aggregating Counting Results

For reporting of counting results, two alternatives have been implemented in BYCOUNTER. The first alternative instruments the method with code to directly write a log file with the counting results; for this, no additional classes must be loaded manually into the JVM. Details of the log file writing, such as the log file path, can be configured by the BYCOUNTER user before the instrumentation starts. The second alternative is based on BYCOUNTER's `ResultCollector` class, and has the advantage that it can aggregate and reference counts of different methods. In order to report the state of counters using `ResultCollector`, a call to its `collectResults` method is inserted by the instrumentation.

BYCOUNTER is implemented to report the complete results immediately before the instrumented method exits. However, if a method declares possible *uncaught* exceptions in its signature (instead properly handling them with `try`/`catch` and the resulting exception table), there is no way to foresee from the bytecode where and when method execution will exit due to an exception. At the same time, caught exceptions declared using `try`/`catch`/`finally` are handled properly in BYCOUNTER, as they are a part of the "normal" control flow. Thus, the BYCOUNTER implementation ensures that the counting results are reported if and only if the method exits properly (i.e. if it returns without an uncaught exception).

To achieve this, for both reporting alternatives (log file and `ResultCollector`), BYCOUNTER adds instructions that report the result immediately preceding *every* "return"-like bytecode instruction. These instructions include `areturn`, `dreturn` etc., depending on the type of returned value (bytecode of methods returning `void` also uses a `return` instruction). As the proper execution of a method always terminates with exactly one `*return` instruction, any such `*return` instruction is accounted for properly by pre-initialising the corresponding counter with 1.

For the interpretation of the counting results, it can be important to have knowledge about the runtime parameters of the instrumented method itself. Hence, BYCOUNTER is designed to store the *characterisations* of these parameters at the beginning of the method's execution and can report them together with the counting results. These characterisations can be the length of a `String`, size of an array etc.

After the instrumentation has been completed, BYCOUNTER converts the instrumented ASM bytecode representation into a Java class which is to substitute the original, uninstrumented class. The instrumented class can be saved as a class file, or passed to a suitable `ClassLoader` for immediate, reflection-based invocation.

4.5. Assumptions and Limitations

We assume that it is possible to pass the final class bytecode that will be executed to BYCOUNTER for instrumentation. For applications where bytecode is generated on the fly and not by the Java compiler (for example in Java EE application servers), additional provisions must be taken. We also assume that the bytecode to instrument conforms to the JVM specification, even if it has been protected using obfuscation.

The ASM library that is used in BYCOUNTER has one small limitation: ASM does not generate a 1:1 representation of parsed bytecode in a few cases. For example, ASM visitors consider the parameterless `LLOAD_0` bytecode instruction to be the same as the (different) `LLOAD` instruction with parameter 0. Hence, BYCOUNTER reports the four `LLOAD_*` instructions and the `LLOAD` instruction using *one* counter, and their execution durations are considered to be the same. However, as there is no semantic difference between the two instructions in the above example, it does not invalidate the semantic accuracy of BYCOUNTER. If needed, this small limitation can be overcome by modifying the ASM library.

Finally, superfluous bytecode instructions can exist in an application, i.e. bytecode which can be optimized away by Just-In-Time (JIT) compiler of the JVM without effects on execution results. These instructions are instrumented by BYCOUNTER as it cannot anticipate later JIT optimisations. The instrumentation instructions cannot be optimised away by JIT, with the effect that they increment counters even for those (superfluous) instructions that have been removed by JIT.

4.6. Summary

This chapter presented a novel approach for dynamic resource demand quantification on the basis of executed instructions and method invocations in bytecode-based applications. The approach works by instrumenting the application bytecode, without the need to instrument or modify the JVM or the Java API implementation. By instrumenting the application bytecode and not the JVM, BYCOUNTER simplifies the entire counting process and becomes truly portable across JVMs.

The instrumentation added by BYCOUNTER is designed to be as lightweight as possible to keep the runtime overhead of counting low despite instruction-level accuracy. In addition to being portable, the presented approach has been designed for easy use: no understanding of bytecode internals is needed to use it, and the application methods available for instrumentation are automatically identified and proposed to the user.

To minimise disruptions, BYCOUNTER instrumentation preserves the signatures of methods and constructors, and it also preserves the application architecture. It supports request For reporting of counting results, BYCOUNTER offers two alternatives: either using structured log files or using a result collector framework (the latter can aggregate counting results across methods and classes).

In the course of this chapter, an in-depth discussion of Java bytecode was used to motivate the design decisions for BYCOUNTER. The discussion included such topics as treatment of native methods during instrumentation, analysing parameters of bytecode instructions, working with calling context trees, etc.

By identifying and using performance equivalence classes of Java bytecode instructions, the presented approach simplifies instrumentation and decreases the runtime counting overhead. An additional novel feature is the identification of performance-invariant bytecode instruction sequences and performance-invariant methods. In the future, extending the presented approach to other virtual machines and their bytecode languages (for example .NET runtime and its CIL bytecode) would allow the use BYCOUNTER in heterogeneous systems.

In Chapter 7, the Java implementation of the presented approach will be evaluated, and will be used to supply resource demands for bytecode-based cross-platform performance prediction. To perform this prediction, platform-specific timing values of the application-agnostic resource demand elements (bytecode instructions and methods) are needed. The next chapter presents novel approaches for JVM benchmarking and API benchmarking, which provide the sought timing values.

Chapter 5.

Benchmarking the Java Virtual Machine Operations for Performance Prediction

To translate platform-independent resource demands into platform-specific timing values, the resource demands must be measured on the execution platform. For the bytecode-based performance prediction approach presented in this thesis, this means that bytecode instructions and methods must be benchmarked.

Response time and other platform-specific timing values are the desired result metrics in the scope of performance evaluation and performance prediction. So far in this thesis, quantifying platform-*independent* application resource demands has been presented in Chapter 4: runtime counts of executed low-level *building blocks* (bytecode instructions and method invocations) were quantified using a platform-independent technique. Now, to obtain platform-*specific* timing values (e.g. for performance prediction) on the basis of these resource demands, platform-specific *timings* (i.e. execution durations) of all building blocks are needed.

However, such timings for bytecode instructions (let alone API methods) are not provided by the execution platform. Whereas real-time systems and JVMs [190, 191] offer a guarantee on the *worst-case* execution durations, they do not provide expected or average or median execution durations. As most business applications do not make use of real-time JVMs, even worst-case execution times are not available and cannot be used for predicting realistic (average or median) application performance.

Significant challenges concerning the measurement of bytecode-level building blocks remain unsolved, especially due to the shortness of the measured operations and the impact of runtime optimisations, such as Just-in-Time compilation (cf. Section 2). Further challenges are described in the following section, and they have served as guidelines for developing a new approach, since existing attempts to quantify the execution durations of bytecode-level building blocks provide no solution to these approaches, e.g. by ignoring the impact of Just-in-Time compilation.

The contribution of this chapter is a novel approach for automated *construction* and execution of microbenchmark suites which fulfil the identified requirements and decrease the amount of human involvement in benchmarking. The microbenchmark suite provides timing values for *all* bytecode-level building blocks – it is not just a conventional benchmark suite (e.g. SPECjvm2008) which provides a *limited* set of metrics which characterise the execution platform as a whole. The suite addresses both fine-grained, low-level bytecode instructions and high-level, complex and parametric API methods.

Before the details of these benchmarks are explained, Section 5.1 details the challenges that are solved by the benchmark suite. The remainder of this chapter is structured as follows: Section 5.2 presents the benchmarking of elementary bytecode instructions, while Section 5.3 describes benchmarking of Java methods and entire APIs.

5.1. Challenges of Translating Resource Demands into Timing Values

The scientific challenges addressed and solved in this chapter are the following:

- finding an approach for benchmarking of fine-granular virtual machine operations so that the results can be used for performance prediction

- quantifying the duration of operations that are orders of magnitude shorter than timer resolution and which cannot be executed repeatedly in isolation, but require additional operations for ensuring preconditions and postconditions

- automated finding of pre- and postconditions for complex operations, such as Java Platform API methods

- automated construction of benchmarks out of semi-formal definition of preconditions and postcondition of benchmarked elements

- dealing with JIT compilation and other optimisations in the scope of benchmarking

From the implementation point of view, the execution duration of a bytecode instruction or of a group of instructions heavily depends on the concrete JVM and the hardware/software of the underlying execution platform. The same is true for methods, especially for Java Platform API methods which are considered as atomic basic blocks in this thesis (cf. Section 2).

In particular, the *capabilities* of the JVM (such as JIT optimizations), the JVM *configuration* (settings such as the heap memory usage) and the *state* of the JVM are relevant. The measurement itself depends on the granularity of the measured instruction(s), on the accuracy of the used timer methods, and is subject to non-determinism (CPU scheduling, interference from other CPU processes, etc.).

A measurement must be repeated several times to control systematic errors due to garbage collection, CPU scheduling etc. The number of repetitions also depends on the precision/accuracy of the used timer method (see Chapter 3), the amplitude of measurement errors, and the desired confidence level or other statistical measures. However, repeating too many measurements in a row may exhibit unexpected side effects (e.g. garbage collection interruptions that did not occur for a smaller number of repetitions).

The most precise Java platform API timer (`System.nanoTime()`) has a accuracy of more than hundred CPU cycles (see Section 7.2). This means that the timer method accuracy is more than *two orders of magnitude* larger than it takes to execute a simple CPU instruction such as a subtraction of two integer values, and instruction pipelining of the CPU further increases the instruction throughput. This means that a single bytecode instruction such as `IADD` (integer

195

addition) cannot be measured in isolation. Additionally, the invocation cost of the timer methods also needs to be considered.

The **JVM configuration** (and, in a broader sense, the configuration of the execution platform) plays a significant quantitative role. For example, switching between the interpretation-only and optimising JVM modes results in performance differences in the order of a magnitude, as we show in Section 2. Ideally, a sensitivity analysis should be run to study the impact of the individual configuration parameters and also of their combination. This chapter provides the infrastructure for performing a sensitivity analysis, which is left for future work.

The **JVM optimization capabilities** of current JVM implementations provide several techniques for optimising bytecode execution and performance. For example, just-in-time compilation (JIT) is monitoring the execution of bytecode for some time before it decides that some "hot spots" (frequently-executed or performance-heavy) methods need to be optimised.

The JIT can then optimise these "hot spots" using a variety of techniques, such as loop unrolling, method inlining, but also the partial or full translation of (interpreted) bytecode methods into native machine code. The scope, time point, scale and performance effect of JIT optimizations exhibit strong variances across components, usage profiles, JVM implementations and even JVM settings, as we have shown in Section 2.

Even if we assume business systems where only the "steady state" is relevant (which is reached after JIT optimization have taken place), the speedup achieved by JIT can vary among JVMs, and also among applications. Existing approaches to bytecode instruction benchmarking disregard the speedup introduced by JIT despite the fact that JIT introduces speedups at the order of one magnitude and even more.

5.2. Bytecode Instruction Benchmarking

The contribution of this section is a novel approach for benchmarking the bytecode instruction set of a virtual machine, by automatically generating a set of valid executable microbenchmarks from which a uniquely solvable system of linear equations is derived and solved to yield the execution duration of each instruction type. This approach pioneers the use of bytecode-level generative programming for benchmark creation, and its results will be validated in Chapter 7 by predicting the performance of real-world programs.

The contributions described in this section have been designed and implemented for Java bytecode, which is the target of many programming languages beyond Java itself, e.g. Scala, JRuby and others. At the same time, the underlying ideas and design decisions are likely to be applicable to other bytecode formats, such as the Common Intermediate Language of the .NET platform. Some challenges might even be simpler to solve for other platforms than Java: for example, .NET runtimes usually utilise Ahead-of-Time compilation (AOT) instead of Just-in-Time compilation or bytecode interpretation, so the resulting native code may be simpler to quantify, in contrast to the *runtime* indeterministic effects and scope of Java JIT (de-optimisation, on-stack-replacement).

In general, the performance of a bytecode instruction is the result of instruction's usage of underlying software layers and hardware resources. For example, a Java bytecode instruction that initialises an array is processed by the JVM which in turn uses the CPU, but also allocates logical memory and may include accesses to the hard disk. Such a detailed, low-level consideration of an instruction's execution is not needed at all if its total execution duration is already sufficient to predict the response time of the entire component service [192]. In our approach, we consider the execution platform as a black box and consider the time that this black box spends executing the bytecode instructions as the desired performance metric.

Four Java bytecode instructions (`INVOKEINTERFACE`, `INVOKESPECIAL`, `INVOKESTATIC` and `INVOKEVIRTUAL`) are responsible for calls to Java methods. Using these instructions, bytecode classes can call other classes' methods, including the Java platform API methods. The called method, the target class instance (for non-static methods), and the method's parameters are passed using the stack which need to be set up accordingly before the method is invoked.

The performance of these four INVOKE* instructions hence strongly depends on the implementation of the called method, which may include native methods, etc. Therefore, in this section, we consider the performance of these four instructions as being part of the called methods' performance. Method benchmarking is a separate task which needs to deal with parameter generation, exception handling, target class instance setup and other issues that are not relevant for primitive bytecode instructions. In addition, there is a potentially infinite number of methods, while there can be at most $2^8 = 256$ *bytecode* instructions (1 *byte* = 8 bits). Method benchmarking will be addressed in Section 5.3.

If an invoked method is itself provided by a Java bytecode class, it can be analysed using tools such as BYCOUNTER (see Chapter 4) to analyse its composition from elementary bytecode instruction. Then, the results of this section can be applied to the "decomposed" method to obtain its performance. Alternatively, the method can be benchmarked as an atomic entity, which will be the focus of Section 5.3. Native methods must be considered as atomic entities, since their implementation does not consist of bytecode instructions. the execution of an instruction cannot

The following subsections address the following hypotheses, which form a logical chain leading to the solution adopted in this thesis. The hypotheses are:

1. It is not possible to write *source code* for benchmarks that measure the duration of an individual bytecode instruction type.

2. It is not feasible to write *source code* for a system of benchmarks ("kernels") that measure the duration of *several* bytecode instruction types, so that the set of kernels leads to a system of linear equations which can be solved to yield the (approximate) duration of each existing bytecode instruction.

3. It is possible to *bytecode-engineer* valid executable classes (which cannot be created from source code), so that the engineered classes attempt to measure the duration of a single instruction.

4. It is not feasible to employ brute-force *random* generation of bytecode in an attempt to create executable benchmarks.

5. It is in general not possible to write a single benchmark for a given instruction by *chaining several instructions of the same type between timer method invocations* (to overcome the issues of timer method accuracy), as the preconditions and postconditions of the instructions do not match and require additional helper instructions which are then co-measured and need to be benchmarked separately.

6. It is possible to bytecode-engineer a set of benchmarks which accounts for all instructions with their preconditions and postconditions as well as the timer resolution, and can be represented as a system of linear equations that is uniquely solvable without approximating.

7. To bytecode-engineer a set of valid benchmarks with a corresponding solvable linear equations system, the preconditions and postconditions of the bytecode instructions must be checked.

8. It is beneficial to separate the *semantics* of bytecode-engineered benchmarks (what is being benchmarked) from their *syntax* (concrete contents of the executed classes) to simplify human understanding of the benchmarks.

9. The separation of benchmark semantics and benchmark syntax can be solved by applying *generative programming*: the benchmark semantics are represented as textual scenarios, and a benchmark generator takes the scenarios as inputs and generates the valid bytecode classes for them, as well as the corresponding system of linear equations.

10. Usage of benchmark scenarios facilitates creation of benchmarks that explore the instruction parameter space.

11. The advantage of textual scenarios is that new benchmarks can be created efficiently for multi-instruction tuples (e.g. basic blocks), and also existing scenarios can be re-generated quickly and new instruction types can be covered efficiently.

12. As the benchmark scenarios are meant to be provided, modified and added by human users and humans can make errors, the set of scenarios must be machine-checked for correctness, completeness (instruction set coverage), redundancies and contradictions, cycles and whether it is underdetermined (i.e. no unique equation solution can be computed); the human user should be provided with feedback and suggestions on how to fix the set of scenarios.

13. While the textual benchmark scenarios are initially provided by humans, it is possible to generate valid scenarios *automatically* when an explicit, executable instruction sequence generator is created which incorporates the analysis and fulfilment of instructions' preconditions and postconditions.

14. The set of scenarios can be used for analysing instruction equivalence classes w.r.t. execution durations, and to analyse the parametric dependencies.

5.2.1. Unsuitability of Source Code for Bytecode Instruction Benchmarking

To measure the execution duration of a Java bytecode instruction, it must be executed by the JVM, which requires a complete and standard-compliant Java bytecode class (as a classfile) and a method which contains the considered instruction. The conventional way to create an executable Java classfile is to write source code and to compile it. The source code of the method would read a performance counter (e.g. by invoking a timer method) immediately before and after the instruction execution, and compute the execution duration from their distance.

In practice, however, it is not feasible to measure the execution duration at source code level: consider for example the IADD instruction: at source code level, it corresponds to the "+" operator. This operator can only be used together with an assignment, e.g. a=b+1 (we assume a and b to be integers – otherwise, additional instructions for casting or boxing/unboxing would be needed). Note that even for this example, the current value of a needs to be loaded onto the stack, as well as the constant value 1. Also note that a=a+1 is semantically equivalent to a++, and a compiler may deliberately choose the IINC instruction to increment the value directly in the JVM register ("local variable" in Java terminology). The IINC instruction does not load the values onto the stack; thus, the performance bytecode that is the result of source code statement a=a+1 may be different from the bytecode corresponding to a=b+1.

Omitting the assignment (e.g. by writing an expression like a+2; is valid, but most JVMs will simply skip its execution after detecting its uselessness as the addition on its own has no durable side effects in this example. Measuring a+2; would then in fact measure only the timer overhead and nothing else. Thus, writing source code to measure the duration of a=a+2; (with assignment) means unintentionally co-measuring the assignment (which will result in an ISTORE or similar bytecode instruction), plus the loading of the summands onto the stack using two additional bytecode instructions.

To subtract the duration of the assignment and the loading operations, additional separate measurements need to be written and performed. However, this leads to similar problems: e.g. an assignment *at source code level* (such as d=1) is compiled to several bytecode instructions. To summarise, writing and compiling source code to measure the execution durations of bytecode instructions is not feasible, even more so if time method resolution is taken into account.

5.2.2. Unsuitability of Kernel Collections for Bytecode Instruction Benchmarking

Instead of directly writing the programs for measuring the execution durations of bytecode instructions, several researchers (e.g. Meyerhöfer [158]) have used a set of existing programs (called "kernels"). Each distinct kernel k_i contains several different bytecode instructions, and the execution duration $s_i > 0$ of the kernel k_i is measured, which corresponds to the total (aggregated) duration of the kernel's executed instructions.

In the following, the indexes of bytecode instructions range from 1 to 256, although only 203 bytecode instructions are currently defined and valid according to the JVM specification; the remaining 53 are reserved for internal JVM use and for future extensions.

A given bytecode instruction type t_i ($1 \leq i \leq 256$) occurs in several of the existing kernels $k_1, \ldots, k_n$, and the kernel-based approaches assume that the duration d_i of the instruction t_i is the same across all kernels.

Then, each kernel can be mapped to a linear equation when $f_{i,j} \geq 0$ denotes the runtime frequency of instruction type t_i in kernel k_j:

$$\sum_{i=1}^{256} f_{i,j} \cdot d_i = s_j \tag{5.1}$$

When the kernel set cardinality denoted as c, the measurement data (all the s_k with $1 \leq k \leq c$) results in a system of c linear equations, which needs to be set up and solved to derive individual instruction durations d_i from the execution durations s_k of the "kernels". To quantify the execution durations individually for each instruction, the equation system needs to have a unique solution, which is hard to achieve due to runtime measurement imprecision (timer method accuracy, OS scheduling, CPU interrupts, etc.). Even assuming that the equation system can be solved *approximately*, the rank of the execution system (i.e. the number of linearly independent equations) must be equal to or greater than the number of unknowns (here, the number of currently defined bytecode instructions, i.e. 203).

None of the kernel-based approaches for bytecode instruction benchmarking provides enough kernels to yield this number of linearly independent equations. Even if the bytecode instruction equivalence classes were used, which reduce the number of bytecode instructions to 87 (cf. Section 4), kernel-based approaches are still short of sufficient. Additionally, none of them has been validated by *predicting* the performance of applications, let alone in a scenario where JIT compilation leads to a speedup over the interpreted bytecode execution. An additional problem with kernel-based approaches is that they are not able to explicitly explore the parameter space of bytecode instructions, and that they are not suitable for exploring the performance of *instruction tuples* (e.g. basic blocks).

The conclusion that we have drawn from analysing the existing kernel-based approaches was that we needed to construct benchmarks that purposefully benchmark bytecode instructions individually or as *configurable* instruction tuples, while leaving us full control over the structure of the benchmarks. In the next section, a novel approach is introduced that separates the *semantics* of benchmarks from their *syntax*, by directly generating executable bytecode to measure bytecode instruction performance, with textual, human-understandable scenarios as the input for the generator.

An additional problem with existing approaches is that they often require specialised or instrumented JVMs to work (e.g. [33]).

5.2.3. Attempting to Measure Bytecode Instructions using Bytecode Engineering

Beyond creation of benchmarks through source code writing or kernel-based analysis, *bytecode engineering* allows programmatic creation of executable bytecode with the control over individual instructions. Bytecode engineering means direct creation and modification of bytecode, in contrast to compiler-based creation of bytecode from source code. Frameworks such as BCEL [115] or ASM [114] facilitate this task by providing programmatic access to (or even transparent administration of) the constant pool and other complicated parts of the classfile. Bytecode engineering allows an engineer to create bytecode which is valid but cannot be created by writing source code and compiling it.

Measuring the execution duration of a *single* bytecode instruction does not make any sense when considering the accuracy of API-provided timer methods (cf. Chapter 3): even for most accurate and precise timer methods the accuracy amounts to at least 100 CPU cycles, which is orders of magnitude larger than a single bytecode instruction. But as this section aims at explaining the advantages of bytecode engineering for benchmark creation, the single-instruction case is taken – to serve for demonstration purposes only.

As an example, consider the following Java method: `public void add(){a+b;}`, where `a` and `b` are `int`-typed fields defined outside of the method. The (rather conventional) compiler of Eclipse 3.6 complies this method to the following bytecode (line number information, local variable mapping and stack administration definitions omitted for brevity):

```
ALOAD 0
ALOAD 0
GETFIELD Test.a :    I
ALOAD 0
GETFIELD Test.b :    I
IADD
PUTFIELD Test.c :    I
RETURN
```

Bytecode engineering makes it possible to rewrite this instruction sequence, which will remain executable as long as the resulting sequence is valid (specification-compliant) w.r.t. stack usage, pre- and postconditions, local variable usage, etc. In particular, it is possible to write a similar method which attempts at measuring the execution duration of IADD *in isolation*, and returns the measured value, replacing the `void` return type.

While doing so, the inserted measurement infrastructure must not endanger the correct execution of the PUTFIELD instruction, i.e. the `int`-typed addition result must be on top of the stack at the moment when the execution of PUTFIELD starts. The following bytecode is valid – note that the method now returns the `long`-valued result, and the local variables 1 and 2 are used to store the results of the invocation to the timer method `java.lang.System.nanoTime()`.

Still, note that while the timer methods have been placed as close to IADD as possible, it is still needed to store the timing values using LSTORE, which is consequently co-measured by the timers. All API-provided timer method have non-`void` return types – rather than storing the value internally, it is returned to the caller which is than able to analyse it.

```
ALOAD 0
ALOAD 0
GETFIELD Test.a :   I
ALOAD 0
GETFIELD Test.b :   I
INVOKESTATIC java/lang/System.nanoTime()J
LSTORE 1
IADD
INVOKESTATIC java/lang/System.nanoTime()J
LSTORE 3
PUTFIELD Test.c :   I
LLOAD 3
LLOAD 1
LSUB
LRETURN
```

Note that after the execution of `INVOKESTATIC` followed by `LSTORE`, the JVM stack is in the same state as before – this instruction tuple is thus *stack-neutral*. Yet as it has other side effects (writing to local variables which are used later on), this tuple is not dead code and won't be skipped by the JVM.

Returning to the issue of measuring just single `IADD`, it would make sense to measure several (or, better, several *hundreds*) of them. However, it is not possible to simply insert an arbitrary number of `IADD`s between the timer method invocations. To see why, consider the fact that `IADD` is not stack-neutral: it consumes two `integer` values from the stack, but pushes just a single one (the result) back onto the stack. Inserting even a single additional `IADD` into the above bytecode sequence would lead to invalid code which will be detected by the verifier of the JVM: the *preconditions* of the second `IADD` instructions do not match the *postconditions* of the execution of the first `IADD`.

Thus, to measure a custom-created bytecode instruction sequence, the pre- and postconditions of the sequence's elements must be analysed and fulfilled. This analysis and the subsequent fulfilment are a central challenge addressed by this thesis, and the following section describes the pre- and postconditions in more depth.

5.2.4. Attempting to Create Bytecode Benchmarks Randomly

A brute-force approach to bytecode benchmarking would be to create the measured bytecode sections (i.e. methods) randomly. It could be hoped that by generating many different methods, a linear equation system could be derived from them, and that solving the equation system would yield the execution durations of individual instructions. However, this is a rather unrealistic hope: the preconditions and postconditions of bytecode instructions rarely fit together.

To see this in numbers, consider the (very simple) instruction ICONST_0, which has not preconditions whatsoever: it simply puts a constant int value 0 onto the JVM stack. Let's now quantify the likelihood that randomly choosing the next instruction (with equal probability of choosing any of the instructions) will lead to a mismatch between the postconditions of ICONST_0 and the preconditions of the randomly chosen instructions. Note that it would make sense to let the computer test whether this measured sequence is already ill-fated, before adding further instructions to the sequence.

If made by hand, the identification of the instructions whose preconditions are met incurs a considerable effort, even for a single instruction (note that later in this chapter, we describe an automated approach for doing this kind of tedious work). There are 32 instructions that can potentially follow an ICONST_0:

- ACONST_NULL, BIPUSH, DCONST_0, DCONST_1,

- FCONST_0, FCONST_1, FCONST_2 LCONST_0, LCONST_1,

- DUP, NOP, POP, I2B, I2C, I2D, I2F, I2L, I2S, INEG,

- ICONST_M1, ICONST_0, ICONST_1, ICONST_2, ICONST_3, ICONST_4, ICONST_5,

- `RETURN`, `ISTORE`, `ISTORE_0`, `ISTORE_1`, `ISTORE_2`, `ISTORE_3`.

Note that for the last group (starting with `RETURN`), the insertion must be made carefully: `RETURN` is only admissible if the method's return type is `void`, and effectively terminates the method. The `ISTORE*` instructions may overwrite an existing local variable when it's not desired: for example, in non-static methods, the local variable with index 0 holds the reference to the invocation target (referenced as `this` in Java source code).

The probability of randomly correcting a suitable successor to `IADD` is thus $\frac{32}{203} \approx 0.158$ – and it's even less when one considers the fact that for many instructions, in-bytecode parameters need to be generated as well (e.g. for `ISTORE*`). The probability of 0.158 means that on average, more than 6 random guesses will be needed per instruction. For instruction sequence of length 2000 (a realistic value given the accuracy of timer methods), at least 12000 trials for creating a *single* benchmarking class will be needed when benchmark is constructed one instruction at a time.

Note that it is still possible that after 1999 valid instructions have been found, the last (2000th) instruction cannot be created at all so that the stack is in the same state as before the instruction sequence. For example, 1999 `ICONST_0`s result in 1999 `int`s on the stack – there is no bytecode instruction that would wipe all of them off the stack in a single step. It is also likely that the successful results of random bytecode generation will tend to include simpler (less demanding) instructions, and instructions whose postcondition are less significant.

Taking into account the complexity of control flow instructions such as `IF_ICMPLE` (jump to a given label if the `int` on top of the stack is less or equal to 0), it is very hard to randomly create valid classes that include `IF_ICMPLE`, as the corresponding label must be generated correctly as well. Introducing constraints on random generation of bytecode would ease the situation, but could not qualify as random generation anymore. Even if it would succeed, a minimum of 203 correct different benchmarks (corresponding to the number of opcodes currently used in Java bytecode, out of 256 available slots) would have to be generated so that the resulting equations in the linear equation system would be *linearly independent*.

One of the future work ideas that emerged in the scope of this thesis was to use `bytecode mutation` to generate benchmarks out of existing, valid application. However, the conventional use of bytecode mutation lies in the field of fuzzying and robustness testing, where the task is to generate *invalid* programs for testing whether the JVM will indeed reject them. Contrary to that, benchmarking requires *valid*, correct benchmarks, and generating them through bytecode mutation is unlikely to yield satisfactory results quickly.

Overall, randomly generating bytecode benchmarking is not a feasible option.

5.2.5. Preconditions and Postconditions of Bytecode Instructions

As stated in the previous section, bytecode engineering offers a technical possibility for goal-oriented creating and measuring of custom instruction sequences, and it allows us to control the instructions which are actually measured. Yet to measure the duration of a bytecode instruction sequence (i.e. to benchmark it), that instruction sequence must be executable. To be executable, an instruction sequence must be valid and part of a valid method which is located in an executable class (classfile) that complies to the Java Virtual Machine specification.

An instruction sequence is valid when its preconditions and postconditions are fulfilled, which in turn means that the preconditions and postconditions of individual classes are valid (i.e. comply to the virtual machine specification). This leads to the need to analyse pre- and postconditions of individual bytecode instructions. A special case are the pre- and postconditions of the four method-invoking instructions `INVOKEDYNAMIC`, `INVOKESPECIAL`, `INVOKESTATIC`, `INVOKEDYNAMIC`. As their pre- and postconditions depend not on the instructions themselves but on the invoked methods, the `INVOKE*` instructions are not considered in this section. The performance of these instructions is an inseparable part of the method invocation and execution, which is benchmarked in a different way, as described in Section 5.3.

For the remaining (non-INVOKE*) instructions, a JVM executes a given single bytecode instruction atomically and deterministically, unless when an exception is thrown. Even though instructions have no signature and thus do not declare exceptions, the JVM specification explains which exceptions are thrown and under which conditions. However, in the context of benchmarking bytecode instructions, exceptions and associated instruction types (e.g. ATHROW) don't need to be considered. Consequently, it is always the case that for a given non-INVOKE* instruction, same precondition lead to the same postcondition since none of the Java bytecode instructions performs activities with randomness.

To see what pre- and postconditions are possible for Java bytecode instructions, the use of input and output parameters must be studied as well as the places where the JVM keeps the execution state. The parameters of a bytecode instruction and the values it uses can be passed over or stored in the JVM local variables, JVM stack, class variables and instance fields, but some parameters are specified directly in bytecode. For example, the NEWARRAY instruction expects the array's size on the stack (as it is a dynamic parameter), and the stack's type is found directly in bytecode (as it is a static parameter, which can already be set by the compiler). The reference to the NEWARRAY-created array is pushed onto the stack after execution, i.e. the stack also contains the returned value.

The pre- and postconditions of all Java bytecode instructions are described informally using human language in the Java Virtual Machine specification [110]. Additionally, many tools (e.g. JVM verifiers and compilers) analyse pre- and postconditions of instructions as they generate or parse classes, and *symbolic execution* provide an alternative to direct bytecode execution by the virtual machine. Finally, formalisations of Java bytecode have been developed for reasoning and conducting security and another analyses, e.g. the KeY approach [193].

However, there exists no published API or tool which would allow dealing with preconditions and postconditions explicitly and in an analytic way, as required by the bytecode benchmark presented in this thesis. In particular, no API or tool which is capable of generating *valid* instruction sequences from the scratch is available publicly. Similarly, no tool is capable of deciding *which* of the Java bytecode instructions can be appended to an *existing* valid bytecode sequence $instruction_1, \ldots, instruction_n$ the sequence so that the extended sequence is still valid. Note that the appended instruction's preconditions must match the postconditions of the existing instruction sequence.

Also, the choice of the appended instruction includes the *non-deterministic* choice of its parameters: for example, if the result of IADD is to be stored using ISTORE (which is not the only possibility), the local variable index for ISTORE needs to be selected. The index should be chosen so that the storing does not overwrite an already occupied local variable which may be needed later – and if the "base" 256 local variables (8-bit addressing) are full, wide addressing needs to be used to access the local variables with indexes 256 through 65535 (16-bit addressing).

The challenge of checking or even fulfilling preconditions and postconditions becomes even harder to solve when the extension of an existing bytecode sequence is subject to constraints, and more than one instruction is allowed to be appended. Examples of constraints may be "use a minimum of additional instructions", "the stack must be empty after the execution of the entire extended sequence" or "the extended sequence may not contain instruction(s) $t_i, \ldots$".

Some instructions, such as INVOKESPECIAL, require proper classes to be loaded in the background by the classloader [110] – this is managed by the JVM and does not need to be addressed in the scope of this section. Even then, for instructions other than the rather simple IADD, it is not trivial to create pre- and postconditions in accordance with the Java bytecode specification.

The approach presented in this chapter checks valid bytecode benchmarking scenarios (explained in the next Section) and generates bytecode benchmarks as executable classes from them. As preparation for explaining (in Section 5.2.6) how these steps work, the remainder of this section explains the analysis and treatment of pre- and postconditions of bytecode instructions. The analysis utilises symbolic interpretation of bytecode instructions, i.e. of executing the instructions in a real JVM, the state of the JVM is simulated.

The instructions of the sequence are represented in an intermediate format (implemented by an own Java API), and the instruction-representing types of the API can be instantiated by parsing existing bytecode, or by parsing the benchmarked scenarios (which will be described in the next section). This enables the identification in-bytecode parameters of instructions, and abstracts away from the concrete representation of bytecode instructions.

An instruction is represented by its opcode, plus an array of `in-bytecode` instruction parameters (stack-passed instruction parameters do not appear in the bytecode of a method, and correspondingly do not appear in the instruction sequence representation). As it is required to distinguish between primitive-typed parameters (e.g. *int*) and the corresponding "boxing" object types (e.g. *Integer*), the instruction parameters must be stored in a way that allows the approach to infer their types. The solution for this requirement is based on the design decision to store the parameters in an array of generic `Objects`, and to store the parameter types in a separate array of `Strings`. This mirrors the fact that in-bytecode parameter types can be arbitrary.

The analysis itself (i.e. the symbolic execution) simulates the JVM state: the stack, the local variables and the class variables. Before an instruction is executed, its preconditions are checked carefully and detailed information is provided when a mismatch is identified. For example, when checking the `IADD` instruction, if a `float` is discovered on top of the stack, the error message describes the mismatch, as the top element of the stack should be an `int`. If an instruction can be executed successfully, its postconditions are applied to the JVM state, and the instruction pointer shifts to the next instruction.

5.2.6. Bytecode Benchmarking Scenarios

As a motivating example for bytecode benchmarking scenarios, let's study how `IADD` instruction can be measured. To account for timer meter accuracy, a significant number of `IADD`s ($\gg 1000$) needs to be measured. At the same time, since "helper" instructions may be needed because `IADD` instructions cannot be simply chained as explained above, the number and diversity of "helper" instructions should be minimised to reduce the density of the linear equation system. Note that while this example focuses on a single instruction, similar principles apply for benchmarking scenarios when instruction tuples (e.g. basic blocks) are to be benchmarked.

Let <T1> denote a timer method invocation (or reading of any other, possibly several, performance indicators), and assume that <T1> does not have any preconditions, in particular regarding the stack. Assume that <T1> also includes instructions to store the read value(s) in local variable(s) so that the *post*condition of <T1> only concerns the local variable, in the sense that <T1> is stack-neutral. In particular, this means that if the bytecode instruction sequence $instr_1, \ldots, instr_i, instr_{i+1}, \ldots, instr_n$ exists and is valid, inserting <T1> between $instr_i$ and $instr_{i+1}$ preserves the validity of the resulting sequence, as long as storing the results of <T1> does not overwrite a value which is already stored in a local variable and which will be needed by the instructions following the inserted <T1>.

An IADD instruction cannot be directly followed by another IADD unless the stack is prepared with additional integer value required by the second addition. Hence, either (i) the stack must be replenished *between* the two IADD calls, or (ii) a sufficient "inventory" of integers must be stored on the stack *before* the sequence/loop of IADDs starts executing. For the alternative (i), the stack replenishment (e.g. using an instruction such as ICONST_1 which loads the integer value 1 onto the stack) will be co-measured with the actual focus of the microbenchmark (i.e. IADD). The measured instruction(s) can be repeated using chaining (concatenation) or in a loop.

A simple example for alternative (i) (i.e. in-between stack replenishment) is the following:

$$\text{ICONST\_0, ICONST\_1, <T1>, } \underbrace{\text{IADD, ICONST\_1,}}_{n \ times} \text{ IADD, <T2>, ISTORE 123}$$

In this scenario, with <T1> is the first performance indicator value recording (recall that it is stack-neutral) and <T2> is the second recording. They are distinguished because <T2> saves the values to different local variables than <T1>, as the values saved by <T1> would otherwise be overwritten. The ICONST_1 instruction (which pushes an int value 1 onto the stack) is used for stack replenishment. In this scenario, repeating the execution of IADD plus its helper ICONST_1 is performed n times by concatenating n repetitions; the concrete syntax for expressing "n repetitions", as well as the alternatives for concatenation (e.g. loop-based repetitions) will be discussed later.

Looking at the scenario more closely, it becomes clear that the instructions preceding <T1> are the *scenario preconditions*, while the instruction following <T2> is the *scenario postcondition*. The measured value (<T2>-<T1>) thus includes the performance of $(n + 1)\cdot$IADD and $n\cdot$ICONST_1 instructions, and the performance contribution of the latter must be quantified using a separate microbenchmark. Additionally, <T2>-<T1> includes the invocation cost of the second performance indicator reading, which can significantly contribute to the measured value (cf. Chapter 3 for the overhead of timer methods). Also note that the scenario postcondition stores the scenario result into local variable 123, which should be used (e.g. printed on standard output stream) so that the computation is not considered superfluous. This serves to prevent purity analysis from inferring that the additions can be skipped without side effects, which may lead to measuring "nothing".

Now, instead of in-between stack replenishment as in alternative (i), consider the aforementioned alternative (ii), which creates the "inventory" of integers on the stack. The following scenario implements alternative (ii):

$$\underbrace{\text{ICONST\_1}}_{(n+1)\ times}, \text{<T1>}, \underbrace{\text{IADD}}_{n\ times}, \text{<T2>}, \text{ISTORE 123}$$

This scenario seems straightforward and more appealing, as the scenario is shorter and as ICONST_1 is no longer co-measured with IADD.

However, this scenario has its disadvantages. For example, the value of n is limited, as the maximum stack height permitted in a method is limited by the JVM specification to 65536 slots (double-wide types such as long and double occupy two slots). Experiments conducted to study the *real-life* working upper bound on stack height have shown that when using even substantially lower stack heights (less than 30000), severe errors in mature JVM implementations (such as the Sun JVM on 32-bit Windows) occur despite the fact that the byte-code is correct and has passed the verifier. Additionally, pre-allocating such a large collection of values on the stack is different from the "normal" stack usage behaviour, where stack heights beyond 100 are very seldom. Unusually high stack heights are likely to lead to memory access overhead which would render benchmarking results for IADD higher than normal.

The current implementation uses simple unformatted textual scenarios, whose syntax contains useful shortcuts and macros to express scenarios easily and effectively. For example, the variable n in the above scenarios can be referenced, so it is not needed to manually type the repeated instruction n types. Thus, the second example scenario from above is written as

$$(n + 1) * \texttt{ICONST\_1}, \texttt{<T1>}, n * \texttt{IADD}, \texttt{<T2>}, \texttt{ISTORE } 123$$

Additionally, it is possible to inject randomness into the scenarios. For example, on each visit of the scenario token ICONST_any, the benchmark generator will insert one of the following instructions: ICONST_M1 (pushes -1 onto the stack), ICONST_0, ..., ICONST_5. This allows us to vary the (performance-equivalent) instructions to make the scenario less susceptible to inlining and other optimisations. The benchmark scenario parser supports parentheses for grouping instructions together, which allows repeating instruction sequences: for example, the above scenario for the alternative (i) can be written as

$$\texttt{ICONST\_0}, \texttt{ICONST\_1}, \texttt{<T1>}, n * (\texttt{IADD}, \texttt{ICONST\_1}), \texttt{IADD}, \texttt{<T2>}, \texttt{ISTORE}$$
$$123$$

So far, the syntax and semantics of the textual scenarios has been described. Before the generation of executable bytecode benchmarks from the scenarios and other workflow steps are addressed in more detail, the following section provides an overview over the workflow.

214

5.2.7. Overview of Scenario-driven Automated Bytecode Benchmarking

Figure 5.1 summarises the inputs, workflow and the outputs of BYBENCH. The are two phases, separated by the dashed line: the generation phase (which is run once on *any* platform, and yields executable benchmarks), and the benchmarking phase, which is run on *every* platform where the execution durations of bytecode instructions are needed.

The inputs for the first phase (generation of benchmarks) consist of the textual benchmarking scenarios as discussed in Section 5.2.6 and a configuration for the generation, e.g. the methods to read performance indicators (timer methods etc. – refered to as `<T1>` and `<T2>` in textual scenarios). The output of the first phase consists of the executable benchmark plus the infrastructure to execute them, as well as collect and evaluate results (which includes the solving of the linear equation system). Additionally, details about the generation are available (both interactively and as a summary at the end), e.g. when cycles in scenarios are identified (see next section for detail).

The second phase consists of invoking the benchmark management infrastructure, which executes benchmarks, analyses their results, and stores them for later use, e.g. in the scope of performance prediction. The inputs in this phase are a run configuration (incl. an option to override the default value for how often a benchmark is executed), and the JVM configuration (e.g. the size of heap memory, etc.). The benchmarking results record the details about execution platform in which the benchmarks were executed, so that the benchmark results from different platforms can be collected and compared.

A scenario is translated into an executable bytecode sequence and inserted into a generic bytecode template, which contains performance indicator infrastructure, output of values to prevent unwanted purity analysis optimisations, etc. The inserted bytecode sequence should not expect anything on the stack or in the local variables, should not modify the existing stack contents (if any), and should not use the local variables with the index higher than 10000, as the performance indicator values are stored there. After the execution, the inserted bytecode sequence should have pushed a single new `java.lang.Object` in-

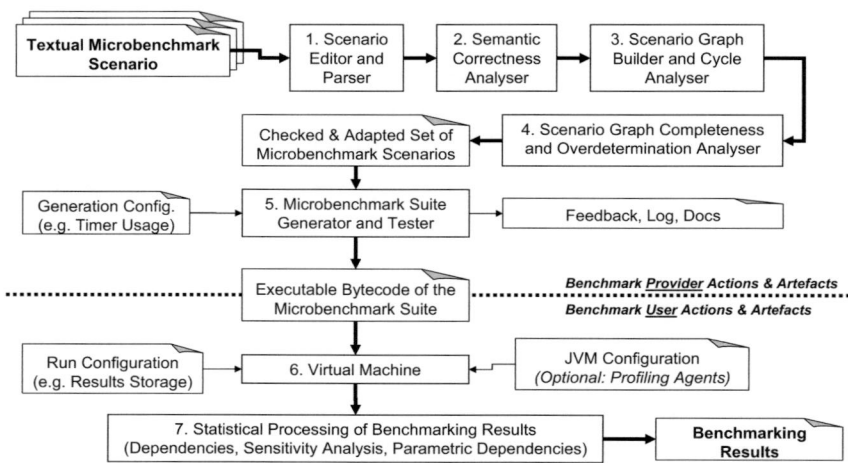

Figure 5.1.: ByBench Overview

stance onto the stack, which is treated by the template as a purity-related value which must be printed to prevent unwanted optimisation based on purity analysis.

But these requirements also mean that the (human) scenario author must know the bytecode language semantic and these requirements – still, humans can make errors, and human input must be checked. So after parsing their textual representation into an object-oriented structure (Step 1), the analysis for semantic correctness is performed in Step 2, which checks whether the pre- and postconditions are met as described above.

Still, even if each scenario is individually correct (semantically and syntactically), the collection of scenarios can have significant problems. For example, the resulting linear equation system can be under-determined (i.e. the set of scenarios is incomplete). Step 3 builds a graph, with nodes being scenarios and a directed edge from node N_i to N_k if the benchmarking result of N_i includes the duration of a helper instruction which is the target instruction of scenario N_k.

Every benchmarking scenario has a specific instruction op_t (or a sequence of instructions) that is the target of the benchmark, i.e. the instruction(s) that the scenario author intends to measure. However, there are often co-measured "helper" instructions, which are needed to fulfil the preconditions of op_t and to keep the timed block *stack-neutral*, since the timed block is repeated many times between <T1> and <T2>. This means that the measured time <T2>−<T1> contains not only the execution duration of op_t, but also the execution duration of all other instructions in the timed block.

It is important to note that N_i is connected with *all* candidates N_k, even though only one of the candidates is needed to compute the duration of N_i's target instruction. During the graph construction, Step 3 detects cycles and under-determination, but does not fix them – these problems are addressed by Step 4.

5.3. Method and API benchmarking

This section addresses the next constituent of the platform-independent metric, the methods. Of course, only non-abstract methods and constructors can be benchmarked, as abstract methods have no implementation body and only non-abstract methods are executed at runtime. The mechanisms and principles described in this section apply to both the methods of the application itself and to external methods, such as API methods and other components' methods (cf. Section 4.3.5 for usage of methods in Java bytecode).

One possibility for quantifying the performance of methods would be to decompose them into bytecode instructions, and use instruction timing values to compute the method's performance. However, this would not be applicable to native methods, and would become very complex for methods with parametric dependencies, as instruction counts *for every occurring instruction* would have to be parametrised over the method's inputs.

Method benchmarking as described in this section should not study the internals of the method's implementation – still, analysing the bytecode of the method's implementation would not violate the black-box nature, as long as the bytecode is not decompiled into source code. However, as discussed in Sec-

217

tion 4.3, it is often impossible to decompose a method into its implementation's bytecode instructions (e.g. when a method is native). Even when such as decomposition is technically possible, considering and analysing a method as an atomic entity has several advantages:

- programmers and software engineers think at level of methods and service, rather than at the level of bytecode

- parametric dependencies should be studied and expressed at method level, using method input parameters

- for non-static methods, the invocation target can play a significant role for the method's performance – such information is hard to capture at the level of bytecode instructions

- method-level benchmarking enables performance characterisation of large APIs that often contain thousands of methods

A simpler alternative is to use just one performance metric, i.e. the (platform-specific) execution time, eventually parametrised over the method inputs. This means that benchmarked methods are considered as atomic entities, and this allows treating methods as black boxes. In particular, the approach presented in this sections permits to benchmark third-party methods which come without source code and without functional specification or interface contracts – only externally visible artefacts of a method (signature incl. parameters and their types) are allowed to be used.

5.3.1. Scientific Challenges

Writing a method benchmark (even for a single method) is a non-trivial task: consider, for example, the method `valueOf(char[] data, int offset, int count)` in the Java Platform API class `java.lang.String`. For a human programmer, it is obvious that the `offset` parameter should be non-negative and the `count` parameter should match the `data`'s length and `offset` so that `offset+count≤data.length`. Also, `data` should be non-`null`, etc – but this understanding and reasoning are not available to a computer due to lack of formal specification and due to the fuzzy, human-oriented documentation.

Different from testing, where the target is to find a test case where a method behaves differently than expected, parameter generation for benchmarking needs to find one (or, for parametric dependencies, several) cases (=parameter assignments) which are valid, i.e. suitable. The `IndexOutOfBounds` exception that the above method `valueOf` would throw if wrong parameters are passed contains information about the problem, which can help the human programmer – using such information during parameter finding for benchmark creation would be helpful. Even if the programmer is unsure how the method behaves (e.g. when `offset>data.length`), the API documentation can be consulted, or a trial-and-error approach can be followed. Also, the parametric dependency should be studied by experimenting with `data` of different length, different `counts`, etc.

For benchmarking many methods (e.g. large components, or complete APIs), an automated solution is needed because manual benchmarking does not scale to the size of production-level APIs: for example, the Java platform API is comprised of thousands of methods. Even if it is known which external methods an application will use, benchmarking only the used methods by manually writing and executing benchmarks incurs a high effort. But due to the complexity of method benchmarking w.r.t. parameter finding etc., there exists no standard automated API benchmarking tool or strategy, even for a particular language such as Java.

Developers and researchers often manually create microbenchmarks that cover only tiny portions of the APIs (e.g. 30 "popular" methods [32]). While profiling tools such as VTune [194] help with finding performance issues and "hot spots", they are not suitable for performance testing of many methods or of entire APIs: suitable parameters must be specified by humans, who have to create a workload with suitable method parameters.

Also, the statistical impact of measurements error is ignored and the developers must manually adapt their (micro)benchmarks when the API changes.

Additionally, modern execution platforms such as the Java Virtual Machine perform extensive non-deterministic runtime optimisations, which need to be considered and quantified for realistic benchmarking. To obtain realistic results, extensive runtime optimisations such as Just-in-Time compilation (JIT) that are provided by the JVM and the CLR need to be induced during benchmarking and quantified.

The resulting **scientific challenges** are the following:

- How to automate benchmark creation and benchmark evaluation, scaling to thousands of methods and to future methods (e.g. API extensions)?

- How to automate the finding of suitable input parameters for methods, while performing better than the trivial, brute-force parameter finding?

- How to automate the finding of parametric dependencies of the benchmarked methods, including parametric dependencies on invocation targets of non-static methods?

- Devise an approach to create dependable, realistic benchmarks for methods that execute in less than a microsecond, while accounting for runtime optimisations (e.g. JIT compilation, method inlining, dead code elimination, invariant detection)?

- How to combine several source of information on suitable method parameters, e.g. from human specification, application execution monitoring and the suggested automated parameter finding?

- When methods are grouped into APIs: how to make use of the API structure (e.g. inheritance trees) while constructing the benchmarks?

The **contribution** of this section is an automated solution for benchmarking not only single methods in isolation (on their own), but also in the context of APIs, since APIs provide additional context such as inheritance trees, usage patterns, etc. The central novel idea of this section is to use heuristics during finding of suitable parameters: by analysing the method's signature and exceptions thrown by trying unsuitable parameters, the search for suitable parameters is accelerated. For each method, a set of directly executable microbenchmarks is created as a set of bytecode classes, enabling automated execution of benchmarks. When a method implementation or an API changes, the benchmarks can be regenerated quickly, e.g. to be used for regression benchmarking.

The solution is called APIBENCHJ and it requires neither the source code of the API, nor a formal model of method input parameters. The approach presented in this section has been implemented for methods and (arbitrary) APIs that are available as Java bytecode, and an evaluation for several large packages of the Java Platform API is given in Chapter 7. Among other capabilities, the implementation induces the optimisations of the Just-In-Time compiler to obtain realistic benchmarking results.

5.3.2. Foundations

In the remainder of this section, *API benchmarking* is used as a synonym to *method benchmarking*. While the described principles and mechanisms apply not only to entire APIs but also to arbitrary sets of methods and to single methods, benchmarking entire APIs (such as the Java Platform API) poses additional challenges and chances that the presented work addresses.

Benchmarking a method means systematically measuring its execution duration as it is executed, i.e. measuring the response time from the view of the method's caller. To execute a method, it must be called by some custom-written Java class, i.e. the bytecode of such a suitable caller class must be loaded and executed by the JVM (in addition to the callee bytecode). There are three different techniques for caller construction:

1. using the *Java Reflection API* to dynamically call methods at runtime,

2. using *code generation* to create caller source code that is compiled to executable caller classes, and

3. using *bytecode engineering* techniques to directly construct the binary Java classes that call the benchmarked methods

All these three techniques differ with respect to their scalability and their impact on the behaviour of the JVM (just-in-time compilation, etc.). They also differ with respect to the measurement itself (e.g., whether the overhead of Java Reflection API usage can be clearly separated from the execution duration of the benchmarked method). The measurements have to be carried out with respect to statistical validity, which is influenced by the resolution of the used timer (cf. Chapter 3) and the duration of the benchmarked method.

JIT compiler optimisations can cause significant problems when benchmarking: for example, the constant folding algorithm implemented in JIT can identify a simplification possibility by replacing successive calls to an arithmetic operation by a constant node in the dependency graph of the JIT compiler [195]. In order to avoid constant folding during benchmarking, the JIT compiler should not identify input parameters of the benchmarked methods as constants.

Purity analysis and dead code elimination pose a further challenge: if the benchmarked piece of code is repeated n times with the same outcome and the same inputs, $n - 1$ repetitions will be eliminated when they have no side effects. Such challenges have to be met in order to avoid misleading benchmarking results.

During benchmarking, in order to execute a method that has one or several input parameters, these parameters *must* be supplied by the caller and they must be *appropriate*. In general, method parameters can be of several types: primitive types (`int`, `long` etc.), object types that are 'boxed' versions of primitive types (e.g. `Integer`), array types (e.g. `int[]` or `Object[]`) and finally of general object or interface types (e.g. `StringBuffer`, `List`, etc.)

For primitive parameter types, often only specific values are accepted, and if a 'wrong' parameter value is used, the invoked method will throw an exception – either a documented or an undocumented runtime exception. Very often, runtime exceptions do not appear in method signatures, and are also undocumented in the API documentation.

Even for a single `int` parameter, randomly guessing a value (until no runtime exception is thrown) is not recommended: the parameter can assume 2^{32} different values. For parameters of types extending `java.lang.Object`, additional challenges arise [168].

Unfortunately, almost all APIs provide no formal specification of parameter value information, and also provide no suitable (functional) test suites or annotations from which parameters suitable for benchmarking could be extracted. The same also holds for individual methods of classes and components, since a formal description of their input parameter ranges is very infrequent.

To see why parameter finding benefits from considering the surrounding API, consider the method `append(java.lang.CharSequence s, int start, int end)` in the class `java.lang.String`. The type of parameter s is an interface, and to initialise an instance of s, a class implementing `CharSequence` must be found. Unfortunately, the Java Platform API (and in particular its Reflection API) do not provide facilities for querying types implementing a given interface, or types extending a given type. Furthermore, some methods such as for example `Long.parseLong(String s)` require specific parameter types to be cast into `String`s or `Object`s.

To collect and use this information, indexing of the API implementation (i.e. the type hierarchy) is employed by Javadoc utility, by the Eclipse IDE and also by the presented approach. Collecting such information by querying *all* classes available at the classpath can lead to incompatibilities when the classpath contains classes outside the benchmarked scope, and such classes may not be available on the platform different from the one where the benchmarks were generated.

Due to the size of APIs, manual specification of parameters is extremely work-intensive, and only a minor alleviation in comparison with completely manual benchmarking. Hence, manual specification of parameters should only be used where it is indispensable, and automated specification/generation of parameters should be used otherwise.

An API can cover a vast range of functionalities, ranging from simple data operations and analysis up to network and database access, security-related settings, hardware access, and even system settings. Hence, the first consideration in the context of automated benchmarking is to set the limits of what is admissible for automated benchmarking.

For example, an automated approach should be barred from benchmarking the method `java.lang.System.exit`, which shuts down the Java Virtual Machine. Likewise, benchmarking the Java Database Connectivity (JDBC) API would report the performance of accessed database, not the performance of the JDBC API, and it is likely to induce damage on database data. Thus, JDBC as part of the Java Platform API is an example of an API part that should be excluded from automated benchmarking – APIBENCHJ handles exclusion using patterns that can be specified by its users.

From the elements of an API that are *allowed* for automated benchmarking, the only two element types that can be executed and measured are non-abstract methods (both static and non-static) and constructors (which are represented in bytecode as special methods). Opposed to that, neither class fields nor interface methods (which are unimplemented) can be benchmarked.

5.3.3. Overview of the APIBENCHJ Framework

Figure 5.2 summarises the main steps of control flow in APIBENCHJ, and we explain it in the following – relevant details of its implementation will be described in the following Sections. The output for APIBENCHJ is a platform-independent suite of executable microbenchmarks for the considered API which runs on any Java SE JVM. While the approach has been tailored to methods executing on the Java Virtual Machine, the novel, heuristics-based parameter generation and other contributions of this section can be applied on the .NET execution platform which also offers the exception mechanism and a reflection API.

Note that all but the last step can performed on *any* execution platform, and the generated microbenchmarks are persisted so that they can be readily run on any platform. Also note that when not an entire API needs to be benchmarked, a knowledge of the surrounding API is useful or even essential, as explained above.

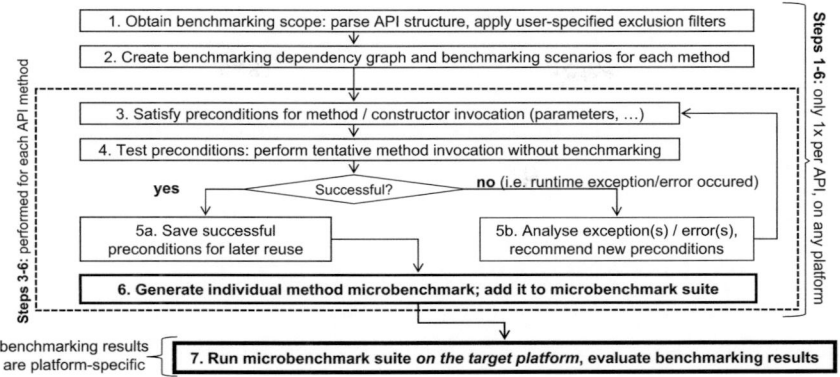

Figure 5.2.: APIBENCHJ : overview of automated API benchmarking

Step 1 starts with *parsing and storing the API structure* to identify the relations between API elements, e.g. inheritance relations and package structure. APIBENCHJ can operate directly on bytecode and does not requires source code, i.e. it is suitable for black-box APIs whose implementation is not exposed. The Java platform and its Reflection API do not provide sufficient functionality for this task, e.g. one cannot programmatically retrieve all implementers of an interface. Thus, APIBENCHJ has its additional tools to parse the API structure using the bytecode classfiles of its implementation. Step 1 also applies *user-specified exclusion filters* to exclude entities that must not be benchmarked automatically. The exclusion filters are specified beforehand by users (i.e. APIBENCHJ does not try to exclude such entities itself). Filters can be package names, classes implementing a specific interface or extending a given class, etc.

Step 2 in Figure 5.2 creates *benchmarking scenario(s)* for each method. Scenarios describe the *requirements* for benchmarking, e.g. which parameters are needed and which classes must be instantiated *before* the considered method can be benchmarked. Actual runtime *values and objects* are created/instantiated later, in steps 3 through 7. In APIBENCHJ, a scenario consists of *preconditions*, the actual *benchmarked operation* and the *postconditions* for a method invocation. At the beginning, step 2 creates a *benchmarking dependency graph*, which holds relations such as "`String.contentEquals` must be preceded by initialisation of a `String` instance", or "the constructor `String()` has no preconditions". As several constructors for `String` and `StringBuffer` exist, several scenarios can be created which differ in the choice of constructors used to satisfy preconditions, and which allow the quantitative comparison of these choices. Step 2 can also compute metrics for the complexity of benchmarking methods, so that step 3 can start with the methods having lowest complexity.

Step 3 starts with *trying to satisfy the precondition requirements* of a benchmarking scenario. Satisfying benchmarking requirements from Step 2 means generating appropriate method parameters, invocation targets, etc. A precondition may have its own preconditions, which APIBENCHJ must then satisfy first. As discussed in Sections 5.3.1 and 5.3.2 as well as in author's previous work [168], automating of these tasks is challenging due to runtime exceptions and the complexity of the Java type hierarchy/polymorphism. APIBENCHJ incorporates a combined approach to this challenge by providing a plug-in mechanism with different precondition sources which can be ranked by their usefulness. For example, *manual specification* has a higher rank than *heuristic search*, with *directed brute-force search* having the lowest ranking of the three. If, for example, APIBENCHJ finds that no manual plug-in exists for a precondition type, it could choose the heuristic search plug-in described in [168]. The generated preconditions can lead to runtime exceptions – hence, before they are accepted as benchmarking-ready, they must be tested.

Step 4 performs a *tentative method invocation* to test that using the generated preconditions does not lead to runtime exceptions (if such an exception occurs APIBENCHJ proceeds with **step 5b**). The error handler in step 5b triggers a new attempt to satisfy preconditions of the considered benchmarking scenario, or gives up the scenario if a repetition threshold is surpassed (this threshold serves to prevent infinite or overly long occupation with one scenario, especially if using brute-force parameter search).

Step 5a is entered if the tentative invocation succeeds, and the information on successful precondition values are internally saved for future reuse. The saved information may be a pointer to the successful heuristic, pointer to a code section that has been manually specified by a human, or a serialised parameter value.

Step 6 generates an executable microbenchmark for the considered scenario, using successfully tested precondition values. The generated microbenchmark implementation explicitly addresses measurement details such as timer resolution (cf. Section 3), JVM optimisations, etc. The *execution* of the resulting microbenchmark does not require the APIBENCHJ infrastructure that implements steps 1 through 6 – each microbenchmark is a portable Java class that forms a part of the final *microbenchmark suite*. The microbenchmark suite includes the microbenchmarks plus additional infrastructure for collecting microbenchmark results and evaluating them.

In the following Sections 5.3.4 and 5.3.6, we describe the implementation of APIBENCHJ.

5.3.4. Satisfying Preconditions using Heuristics

In this section, we present the heuristic parameter generator (HPG) which is used in step 3 of APIBENCHJ (cf. Figure 5.2) to generate appropriate parameter values for method and constructors. The following algorithm descriptions denote the signature of an invokable $\mathcal{I}$ (i.e., a method or a constructor) as $\mathcal{SG}$. The declaring class of an invokable $\mathcal{I}$ is referred to as $\mathcal{DC}$ and the instance of $\mathcal{DC}$ as $\mathcal{DCI}$.

APIBENCHJ operates in a context which offers a set of types (classes) that can be used by APIBENCHJ . As any other Java SE, APIBENCHJ has access to the types of the Java Platform API, but additional types can be available on the classpath, e.g. when external libraries are used or benchmarked. For a given classpath context, *container types*, denoted as $\mathcal{CT}$, is the set of static types whose instance has a length or a capacity, for example arrays, collections or maps. In

Java, `Strings` are also contained types (they contain `characters` and have a `length` attribute), as are buffers and similar structures.

The following discussion is split into several parts: first, the generation of primitive-typed parameters is described in Section 5.3.4.1, followed by container types (Section 5.3.4.2) and generic object types (Section 5.3.4.3). Afterwards, the treatment of runtime exceptions which occur if the initial parameter values are inappropriate is detailed (Section 5.3.5).

5.3.4.1. Generation of Primitives

The choice of heuristics for the generation of primitives is motivated by two observations:

- often, the constants declared in $\mathcal{DC}$ and/or its superclasses are the input parameters which are more likely (or even exclusively) accepted by the considered method: for example, the method `java.util.Calendar.set(int year, int month, int date)` should make use of static `int` fields `JANUARY` etc. in that class

- if one of the method parameters is container-typed (e.g. an array or a `List`), the `int`-typed parameters in the method signature are likely to refer to that container, e.g. as 'from' or 'to' indexes: an example is the method `java.lang.String.getChars(int srcBegin, int srcEnd, char[] dst, int dstBegin)`

Accordingly, we describe here the two most important heuristic strategies that HPG defines for generating instances of primitive types as input parameters for an invokable $\mathcal{I}$.

The **first heuristic** of HPG is to use the constants (i.e. static final variables, if available) defined in $\mathcal{DC}$. The constants in the superclasses of $\mathcal{DC}$ are also considered (the set of superclasses is denoted $\mathcal{S.DC}$). These constants may well be negative; the order of selecting them is randomised. If no declared constants are available (or if there are less declared constants than primitive parameters in the signature), the primitive values are generated randomly and may be negative as well. A random number generator with uniform distribution is currently used, but distributions that favour smaller positive and larger negative values (i.e. values around zero) should be considered as a replacement, because it appears that these values are more frequent in practice.

The HPG needs to accounts for the fact that `int` parameter values are often used as indexes and thus are the only primitives likely to throw `IndexOutOfBoundsExceptions`.

Therefore, a **second heuristic** has been defined for `int`-typed parameter values: a lower and an upper bound are imposed on `int`-typed parameter values *if* container-typed parameters are present in the signature, or if $\mathcal{DC}$ is itself container-typed. For example, for generating the parameters for the method `String.getChars(int srcBegin, int srcEnd, char[] dst, int dstBegin)`, the `dst` array of `chars` should be generated first, and then the `int` values `srcBegin`, `srcEnd` and `dstBegin` should be generated afterwards, as they have an obvious, important relation to `dst`. Hence, the second heuristic is applied after generating all other parameters in $\mathcal{SG}$.

A simple constraint that is used by the second heuristic is to set the lower bound of `int` values to 0. It should be stressed that this restrictive constraint is only applied if either $\mathcal{DC}$ is of container type, or if at least one of parameters in the signature of $\mathcal{I}$ is container-typed. In other cases, `int` parameters may be negative.

After the lower bound has been calculated, the heuristic calculation of the upper bound $\mathcal{BOUND}$ for the `int` values is carried out, as specified in the Algorithm 5.1. In the case of the above method `String.getChars(int srcBegin, int srcEnd, char[] dst, int dstBegin)`, the upper bound that HPG will find is `dst.length` which means that the following three conditions should be true: (i) $0 \leq srcBegin \leq dst.length$, (ii) $0 \leq srcEnd \leq dst.length$ and (iii) $0 \leq dstBegin \leq dst.length$.

In the Algorithm 5.1, if the signature of the target method has container-typed parameters, parameter generation of `int`-typed values does not consider the length or the size of the target class instance on which the method will be invoked. Thus is because it assumes that container-typed parameters used in Algorithm 5.1 have been already generated with consideration to the class instance, as we will demonstrate in the next section while generating container types.

Algorithm 5.1: Finding the Upper Bound for Integer Arguments

/* $\mathcal{S}_{INT}$ is the set of int constants declared by $\mathcal{S}.\mathcal{DC}$ */
Data: Method $\mathcal{I}$
Result: $\mathcal{BOUND}$: upper bound for generating int parameter values in
        $\mathcal{SG}(\mathcal{I})$
$\mathcal{CTS} \leftarrow \{\{param | param \in \mathcal{SG}\} \cap \{param | param.TYPE \in \mathcal{CT}\}\}$;
if $\mathcal{CTS} \neq \emptyset$ **then**
    | /* $\mathcal{SG}$ declares container types */
    | $\mathcal{BOUND} \leftarrow min((param.VALUE).LENGTH | \forall param \in \mathcal{CTS})$;
else
    if ($\mathcal{I}$ *is not static*) $\cap (\mathcal{DCI}.TYPE \in \mathcal{CT})$ **then**
        | /* $\mathcal{DCI}$ is of container type */
        | $\mathcal{BOUND} \leftarrow \mathcal{DCI}.LENGTH$;
    else
        if $\mathcal{S}_{INT} \neq \emptyset$ **then**
            | $\mathcal{BOUND} \leftarrow x \in \mathcal{S}_{INT}$;
        else
            | $\mathcal{BOUND} \leftarrow$ random positive int value;
        end
    end
end
return $\mathcal{BOUND}$;

5.3.4.2. Generation of Container Types

During the generation of container-typed parameters, HPG must decide on the length of the container and the type and values of its elements. The static type of the container's elements is called *component type* in convention with the Java programming language specification For computing the length of the container parameter to generate, HPG selects the *first available* value from the following list as an upper inclusive bound for the container size: (i) if the type of the $\mathcal{DC}$ is a container type: the length of $\mathcal{DCI}$ on which $\mathcal{I}$ is invoked, (ii) a positive non-zero int constant value declared in $\mathcal{DC}$ or (iii) a random positive non-zero int value.

'Non-zero' condition is imposed because containers of size zero (i.e. empty containers) will not allow the benchmark to call methods like elementAt. Currently, APIBENCHJ sets an upper bound for case (iii) to 10^5 to limit the size of containers to realistic values. Of course, if the benchmarking framework that uses APIBENCHJ needs larger containers, this restriction may be overridden by that framework by specifying larger containers, or by adding elements to the container that APIBENCHJ has generated. The length $\mathcal{L}$ of the generated container should satisfy $1 \leq \mathcal{L} \leq \mathcal{BOUND}$, if $\mathcal{BOUND} > 0$ and $1 \leq \mathcal{L}$ otherwise.

According to the declared component type of the container, HPG *randomly* generates $\mathcal{L}$ elements of the declared component type, except where the component type is Object. When the component type is Object, HPG generates Object values having the same dynamic type as $\mathcal{DC}$.

Details about the generation of reference component types (i.e. Object and its subclasses) are described in the next section in the scope of generation of non-primitive, non-container type instances.

5.3.4.3. Generation of Objects

The parameters for which Object-typed parameters need to be generated can have different static types: *interface* static type (e.g. java.util.List), *abstract class* static type (e.g. java.util.AbstractList), or non-abstract class static type (e.g. java.util. ArrayList). The Java API does not contain facilities to query which (non-abstract) subclasses of an interface exist. APIBENCHJ collects such information and creates a parameter graph, which indicates for an interface-typed or abstract-typed parameter which concrete types (to instantiate a parameter) are available. However, when several candidates exist,

APIBENCHJ still needs to decide which subclass to choose, and which constructor to take.

Interface static types are instantiated by first retrieving the public non-abstract classes implementing the interface, and then instantiating one of them as explained below. For *abstract-class* static types, the subclasses of the type's declaring class are retrieved and one of them is instantiated. If this doesn't work, factory methods returning the interface type/abstract type are tried, and the dynamic type they return is identified and stored.

To generate a parameter whose static type is declared as a *non-abstract class*, HPG first chooses the simplest constructor/factory method based on complexity of its signature. For example, the constructor `String(byte[] bytes, String charsetName)` is complexer than the constructor `String(int[] codePoints,int offset,int count)`. The complexity of a constructor's signature is judged on both the number of parameters it declares and their static type. From the perspective of HPG, signatures that declares only primitive parameters are less complex than the ones that declare fewer but reference type parameters.

The simplest constructor can turn out to be inappropriate, e.g. runtime exceptions may occur when the generated parameters are used. Similarly, the simplest constructor can return `null` objects, or empty objects such as a `String` of length 0. In such cases, other constructors or factory methods will be tried.

Preferring the simplest constructor means that APIBENCHJ is more likely to be successful in constructing the parameter value (type instance), because a more complex constructor intuitively offers more 'chances' to fail. At the same time, simpler constructors often sufficiently cover the parameter space: `String(byte[] bytes)` is as powerful as the more complex constructor `String(byte[] bytes, int offset, int length)`. A study to quantify the impact of preference of simpler constructors can be performed in future work.

Some API methods declare parameters of `java.lang.Object` type, a generic non-abstract type. As we have observed that the use of objects that implement the interface `java.lang.Comparable` reduces the likelihood of exceptions (because sorting and administration of collections are easier), we prefer `java.lang.Comparable`-implementing subclasses of `java.lang.Object`, e.g. classes such as `String` and its subclasses.

HPG pays special attention to the generation of *reference* container types (e.g. collections, maps, strings, buffers). Container types are very similar to arrays, hence HPG computes the length of reference container types in the same way as for arrays (cf. Section 5.3.4.2). Another heuristic strategy is used for initialisation of such types: APIBENCHJ prefers constructors whose input parameters are arrays, for example `String(char[])`.

For collections such as classes implementing `Lists` and `Maps`, HPG constructs empty instances and then fills them with n objects (n smaller than the above fixed capacity/length). The filling proceeds with respect to the type parameter bounds which the collections declare. For example, in order to generate a `List<E extends Number>`, HPG constructs an empty `java.util.ArrayList` instance and fills it with objects having a dynamic type that is a subtype of the type parameter bound `Number` (`Long` is such a subtype of `Number`).

5.3.4.4. Impact of Java Generics on Parameter Finding

Generics in Java were introduced with Java 5, and allow programmers to impose type restrictions on method parameters, method return types and even class types (in particular container types). Java generics are similar to template libraries and parametrised types in other programming languages.

As an example, consider the Java Platform API class `java.lang.ArrayList`. Since Java 5, it is denoted as `java.lang.ArrayList<E>`, where the *type parameter* E denotes the type of elements stored in the `ArrayList`. E can be any type that is subtype of `java.lang.Object`. Correspondingly, the methods of `ArrayList` also feature E in their signature: for example, `add(E)` means that only elements of type E (or a subtype thereof) can be added to the `ArrayList`. The parameter of the method `addAll(Collection<? extends E> c)` must be a collection whose component type is type-compatible with the type of the invocation target `ArrayList` instance. Note that primitive types (e.g. `int` etc.) are not permitted as type arguments.

While Java generics are a great way to support programmers at source code levels, they do not appear at bytecode level: a source compiler translates generics into bytecode using a mechanism called *type erasure*. In particular, for the above example, an `ArrayList<Integer>` would be translated to bytecode which does *not* feature any information about the `Integer` generic type. At the same time, generics allow for a transparent type casting: invoking `Collections.min()` on a `ArrayList<Integer>` will result in bytecode which performs the conversion from `Collections.min()`-returned `java.lang.Object` to `java.lang.Integer`, without having to write the casting step manually.

Generics present an additional challenge APIBENCHJ , but their benchmarking is fully supported by APIBENCHJ , as is their usage in parameter types. APIBENCHJ also supports wildcards usage in Java generics: e.g. `do(List<?> a)`, where `<?>` denotes *any* type as well as polymorphism expressions such as `do(List<? extends SomeType>)` and `do(List<? super SomeType>)` During the generation of the type parameters for generic types, APIBENCHJ relies on the type information delivered after type erasure.

5.3.5. Heuristic Exception Handler

The heuristically generated argument values still can cause runtime exceptions, as heuristics generally offer no guarantee of success. Consequently, in steps 6 and 7 of our approach (cf. Figure 5.2), the caught exceptions are analysed and handled by the Heuristic Exception Handler (HEH), which devises new input for the heuristic parameter generator.

The handler (HEH) and the generator (HEG) interact closely, but are separate entities to allow for better extendability. The HEH is modular and creates feedback for the HEG to repeat parameter generation (as described below). The

HEG can be modified without an effect on the HEG as long as the interfaces between them are kept constant.

First, it needs to be clarified which exceptions will be analysed and reacted upon by the HEH. In the Java SE 6 Platform API, the `java.lang.Exception` class has almost 80 *direct* subclasses, some of which in turn have their own subclasses. From our initial benchmarking experience, the vast majority of exceptions that occur in case of inappropriate method parameters are the 38 subclasses of `java.lang.RuntimeException`.

From these, APIBENCHJ currently covers 19 which are both general-purpose and frequent. APIBENCHJ currently does not address exceptions which relate to GUIs (AWT and Swing), annotations, XML processing, CORBA calls, security permissions as well as I/O and concurrency/multi-threading. In particular, the assumption holds that the benchmarked methods are executed in a single-threaded fashion.

In the future, the principles of APIBENCHJ can be extended to the currently unaddressed exceptions, as well as runtime `Errors`. Note that it is still possible to tun APIBENCHJ on methods which may throw `RuntimeException` not covered by APIBENCHJ .

Even if a `RuntimeException` is thrown for which HEH does not have a heuristic, APIBENCHJ will try to generate other input parameters and/or (for non-static methods) other invocation target and will re-run the method. Thus, even when there is no heuristic to handle a particular `RuntimeException`, APIBENCHJ is still more sophisticated than pure brute-force search, because it starts with parameters generated by HEG, which already takes care to generate meaningful parameters.

In the following subsections, several heuristics will be covered in more detail.

5.3.5.1. Handling `IndexOutOfBoundsExceptions`

An `IndexOutOfBoundsException` is thrown when an index is out of range for a container class (e.g. `List`, `Queue`, etc.), for an array, or for a `String`. The heuristics of APIBENCHJ handle `IndexOutOfBoundsExceptions` as well as its subclasses `ArrayIndexOutOfBoundsExceptions` and `StringIndexOutOfBoundsExceptions`. Indexes are `int`-typed parameters, and as discussed in Section 5.3.4.1, they are generated *after* other parameters have been generated. In particular, all container-typed parameters have already been generated before generation of `int`-typed parameters starts.

Let the range $\mathcal{R}$ be the local minimum of positive (non-zero) lengths of container-typed elements in the method signature. These elements include the (already generated) container-typed method parameters as well as (when the $\mathcal{DC}$ is container-typed and where the considered method $\mathcal{I}$ is non-static) the invocation target instance $\mathcal{DC}$ itself. Suppose that $\mathcal{I}$ declares n `int` arguments and that the discrete value of argument a_i is v_i ($1 \leq i \leq n$). Let $\mathcal{A} = \{a_1, a_2, ..., a_n\}$ denote the set of `int` arguments, and let $\mathcal{V} = \{v_1, v_2, ..., v_n\}$ denote the value set of $\mathcal{A}$ which should be generated.

APIBENCHJ imposes three conditions for the generation of $\mathcal{V}$, as described in equations 5.2, 5.3 and 5.4:

$$\forall v_i \in \mathcal{V} : v_i \geq 0 \tag{5.2}$$

$$\sum_{v_i \in \mathcal{V}} v_i < \mathcal{R} \tag{5.3}$$

$$\forall i \in \{2, ..., |\mathcal{A}|\} : v_{i-1} \leq v_i \tag{5.4}$$

According to the equation 5.3, the (positive) `int` values that have to be generated should have a sum that is smaller than the range $\mathcal{R}$. This restriction and the sorting order imposed by equation 5.4 are designed to correspond to many method signatures where the "from" index appears before the "to" index, and where the indexes (which start with 0) should not reach beyond the collection's first or last element.

To define an individual value interval for each `int` parameter, the heuristic uses equation 5.5 and proceeds starting with $i = 1$ up to $i = n$, with $\mathcal{R}$ being the aforementioned range and $\mathcal{L}_i$ defined as follows:

$$\mathcal{L}_i = \begin{cases} 0 & \text{if } i = 0 \\ v_i & \text{if } 0 < i \leq n \end{cases}$$

$$\mathcal{L}_{i-1} \leq v_i \leq \frac{(\mathcal{R} - \sum_{k=1}^{|\mathcal{A}|} \mathcal{L}_{k-1})}{(|\mathcal{A}| - i + 1)}. \tag{5.5}$$

The algorithm tries the generated `int` values by invoking the considered method $\mathcal{I}$ and recording any eventual exceptions. If the generated values still cause an instance `IndexOutOfBoundsException` or one of its subtypes, the algorithm permutates the generated `int` values.

The algorithm terminates if no `IndexOutOfBoundsException` is thrown, or if all possible permutations have been tested. The possible number of permutations are defined as follows: for n `int` parameters in a method signature, the algorithm can perform maximal $n!$ parameter value permutations (in general, this is an acceptable value, with $4! = 24$ permutations for a method that has 4 `int`-typed parameters, 24 ranging orders of magnitude below the range of an `int` value in Java).

5.3.5.2. Handling `ClassCastExceptions`

`ClassCastExceptions` are thrown to indicate that the code has attempted to cast an object to a class type of which that object is not an instance. In order to handle `ClassCastExceptions`, APIBENCHJ includes a heuristic that attempts to determine the appropriate dynamic type of the parameter. If several `Object`-typed parameters exist, the heuristic is applied to all of them.

`ClassCastExceptions` often occur when the $\mathcal{I}$ and/or $\mathcal{DC}$ are generic, since the parameters must be of appropriate types, even though this is not directly visible from the signature. For example, when executing the method `java.util.concurrent.DelayQueue.add(Object)`, a

`ClassCast Exception` can be thrown. The exception indicates that the `Object` parameter cannot be cast to `java.util.concurrent.Delayed`, the latter being an interface. A heuristic thus has to deduce from the declaration of the class `DelayQueue` (`DelayQueue<E extends Delayed>`) that it accepts `Delayed`-implementing parameters only.

The `extends` keyword thus signals an *upper bound* w.r.t. type hierarchy, (a lower bound would be signalled by the `super` keyword). So in the case of $\mathcal{DC}$ being generic, the heuristic creates $\mathcal{S}_{\mathcal{CUIF}}$ so that it contains (depending on the keyword in the $\mathcal{DC}$ signature) either all *sub*classes of the upper bound (incl. the bound itself), or all *super*classes of the lower bound (including the lower bound itself, but excluding `Object`).

Then, for each static type $\mathbf{T} \in \mathcal{S}_{\mathcal{CUIF}}$, the heuristic generates new parameter value of type $\mathbf{T}$ and tests it by invoking the target method with the new parameter value. The algorithm terminates when no `ClassCastExceptions` are thrown, or when all possible types from $\mathcal{S}_{\mathcal{CUIF}}$ have been used. Similar techniques are used for casting instances from `String`s.

If the $\mathcal{DC}$ that declares the considered method is not generic, the heuristic generates the set $\mathcal{S}_{\mathcal{CUIF}}$ of candidate static types for the parameter as follows: $\mathcal{S}_{\mathcal{CUIF}}$ includes $\mathcal{DC}$ and all its subclasses/subinterfaces. Interface-typed or abstract $\mathbf{T}$s are skipped in favor of their non-abstract subtypes (if any). Then, elements of $\mathcal{S}_{\mathcal{CUIF}}$ are processed as just described.

If the generated parameter values still lead to exceptions, their handling is delegated to other exception handlers, which can access the execution history stored in the repository. Note that here, too, the heuristic is more purposeful than a brute-force search.

5.3.5.3. Handling `NumberFormatExceptions`

A significant number of Java Platform API methods (many of them static) take numeric parameters which are encoded in `String` instances. For example, the method `Integer.valueOf(String s)` will throw a `NumberFormatException` when the passed `s` is `1.00`, i.e. a `double`. The scope of methods which throw `NumberFormatExceptions` is not limited to numeric classtypes such as `Byte`, `Integer` or `Long` – `java.lang.Package.isCompatibleWith(String desired)` expects a numeric value encoded in `desired`, too.

APIBENCHJ handles `NumberFormatExceptions` by generating instances of the considered method's declared type, and converting them to a `String`. The creation of instances is tried until a predefined threshold is reached, after which other heuristics are tried, such as the more generic heuristic defined in the next section.

A particular challenge in the context of `NumberFormatExceptions` arises when dealing with radix-converting methods such as `Integer.parseInt(String s, int radix)`. The meaning of the radix is best illustrated with an example: `parseInt("FF", 16)` returns `255`, i.e. the characters in the parsed `String` are interpreted as hexadecimal digits ranging from 0 to F. Consequently, `parseInt("33", 2)` would throw a `NumberFormatException`.

Thus, if there are one (or several) `int`-typed parameters in the signature of the method which has thrown an `NumberFormatException`, the `String` is generated from the chars reaching from 0 to the smallest value of the `int`-typed parameters. The String is generated by (randomly) deciding on the sign of the number to encode (as long as the number type permits both positive and negative values), and then by randomly creating the digits (i.e. the `characters` of the `String`) one-by-one.

Note that the heuristic pays attention to the `MAX_VALUE` and `MIN_VALUE` fields of the declaring type, as long as the declaring type is a subtype of `java.lang.Number`. In fact, all numeric types of the Java Platform API inherit from it: `AtomicInteger`, `AtomicLong`, `BigDecimal`, `BigInteger`, `Byte`, `Double`, `Float`, `Integer`, `Long` and `Short`.

5.3.5.4. Handling State Exceptions for Collections

Collections contain a set or a list of elements, and include queues, maps, iterators and other structures. Some collections in Java allow duplicate elements and others do not; some are ordered and others unordered. Most collections have capacity-restricted implementations, which means that exceptions are thrown if the collection capacity is exceeded after an `add` or similar operation, or if a `remove` or a similar operation cannot be performed because the collection is empty.

There are several runtime exceptions that can be thrown by a collection operation, depending on the actual problem. The `java.nio.BufferOverflowException` is thrown when the `put` operation reaches the limit of the invocation target buffer, the `java.nio.BufferUnderflowException` happens when the `get` operations fails. The `java.util.EmptyStackException` and the `java.util.No-SuchElementException` are thrown if there are no more elements in the collection.

In order to handle a collection state exception thrown by a collection operation OP, the relative operation of OP has to be called before OP. The relative operation changes the state of the collection and prepares it for the target operation OP. For example, in order to handle a `java.util.NoSuchElementException` thrown for example by the `element` operation on a `Queue`, APIBENCHJ should fill the queue by calling the relative operation `add` and then call the method `element` again.

In order to handle such exceptions, APIBENCHJ includes mappings to the relative operation for each collection operation, e.g. `add` has the relative operation `remove`). Special attention to filling the collections is paid in APIBENCHJ : capacity restrictions should not be violated, and the number of elements to add in a collection should not exceed its declared capacity.

240

5.3.5.5. Handling Exceptions Based on the Class Variables

One generic opportunity for handling runtime exceptions is the heuristic use of the static and non-static (instance) class variables of the class declaring the method that threw the exception.   For example, the class `java.util.zip.Deflater` declares the constructor `Deflater(int level)` which throws an `IllegalArgumentException` if the specified compression `level` is invalid.   The same class also declares methods like `setStrategy(int strategy)` which throws an `IllegalArgumentException` if the compression strategy is invalid.

In order to handle such an exceptions thrown by the `Deflater` constructor, APIBENCHJ heuristically selects the compression level/strategy from the class variables of `Deflater`. Thus, `public static final int DEFLATED 8` and the other seven variables are used for the constructors of the constants-declaring class, but also for its methods when initial parameters lead to an exception.

This heuristic is one of the most generic ones and is widely used in APIBENCHJ when the more specialised heuristics (outlined in previous sections) do not apply or do not lead to successful parameters. The constants are retrieved from both the declared class of the considered method, but also from the superclasses/superinterfaces of the declared class, as well as (for object-typed parameters) from the types of the parameters.

5.3.5.6. Handling EncodingExceptions

`EncodingExceptions` are thrown to indicate that an API operation has attempted to specify an unsupported encoding.   For example, the method `String.getBytes(String charsetName)` throws an `UnsupportedEncodingException` if the given `charsetName` is not supported.

In order to handle such exceptions, APIBENCHJ includes a heuristic that addresses both the data to convert (i.e. to encode) and the name of the encoding. Initially, the heuristic assumes that `String`-typed parameters designate encodings, and fills these parameters with values specifying the standard `charset` names. The standard charset names (cf. the definitions in the Java Platform API class `java.nio.charset.Charset` for the minimum set of supported charsets) are `US-ASCII`, `ISO-8859-1`, `UTF-8`, etc.

For the data to encode, the heuristic generates new invocation targets by avoiding special characters. For primitive parameters such as characters or bytes, the algorithm makes use of the *American Standard Code for Information Interchange* (ASCII) printable characters. Such ASCII characters are usually supported by each encoding.

If the found parameter values repeatedly lead to encoding exceptions, the heuristic starts to consider the `String`-typed parameters as the data to convert, rather than as the charset designation. If this also fails, APIBENCHJ resorts to more generic heuristics.

5.3.6. Generating and Executing Microbenchmarks

In this section, we assume that appropriate method parameters are known, and it is known how to obtain the invocation targets for non-static methods (see steps 1-5 in Section 5.3.3). Using the results of Chapter 3, we know the accuracy and invocation cost of the timer method used for measurements, and thus can compute the number of measurements needed for a given confidence level (see [196] for details).

The remaining steps 6 (generating individual microbenchmarks) and 7 (executing the benchmarks) are discussed in this section. First, we discuss the runtime JVM optimisations and how they are addressed (Section 5.3.6.1), followed by the discussion in Section 5.3.6.2 on why bytecode engineering is used to construct the microbenchmarks.

5.3.6.1. JIT and other JVM Runtime Optimisations

Java bytecode is platform-independent, but it is executed using interpretation which is significantly slower than execution of equivalent native code. Therefore, modern JVMs monitor the execution of bytecode to find out which methods are executed frequently and are computationally intensive ("hot"), and optimise these methods.

The most significant optimisation is Just-in-Time compilation (JIT), which translates the hot method(s) into native methods *on the fly*, parallel to the running interpretation of the "hot" method(s). To make benchmarked methods "hot" and eligible for JIT compilation, they must be executed a significant number of times (10,000 and more, depending on the JIT compiler), before the actual measurements start. JIT optimisations lead to speedups surpassing one order of magnitude (See Chapter 2), and an automated benchmarking approach has to obtain measurements for the unoptimised *and* the optimised execution, as both are relevant.

Different objectives lead to different JIT compilation strategies, e.g. the Sun Microsystems Server JIT Compiler spends more initial effort on optimisations because it assumes long-running applications, while the Client JIT Compiler is geared towards faster startup times. We have observed that the Sun Server JIT Compiler performs multi-stage JIT compilation, where a "hot" method may be repeatedly JIT-compiled to achieve even higher speedup if it is detected that the method is even "hotter" that originally judged.

Therefore, the benchmarks generated by APIBENCHJ can be configured with the *platform-specific* threshold number of executions ("warmup") after which a method is considered as "hot" and JITted by that platform's JIT compiler. To achieve this, APIBENCHJ implements a calibrator which uses the -XX:+PrintCompilation JVM flag to find out a platform's calibration threshold, which is then passed to the generated benchmarks.

APIBENCHJ must also ensure that JIT does not "optimise away" the benchmarked operations, which it can do if a method call has no effect. To have *any* visible functional effect, a method must either return a value, change the value(s) of its input parameter(s), or it must have side effects which not visible in its signature. These effects can be either *deterministic* (same effect for the same combination of input parameters and the state of the invocation target in case of non-static methods) or *non-deterministic* (e.g. random number generation).

If a method has non-deterministic effects, APIBENCHJ simply has to record the effects of each method invocation to ensure that the invocation is not optimised away, and can use rare and selective logging of these values to prevent JIT from "optimising away" the invocations. But if the method has deterministic effects, the same input parameters cannot be used repeatedly, because the JVM detects the determinism and can replace *all* the method invocation(s) directly with a *single* execution (native) code sequence, e.g. using "constant folding". This forms an additional challenge that has been solved in APIBENCHJ.

Thus, APIBENCHJ needs to supply different *and* performance-equivalent parameters to methods with deterministic behaviour, and it solves this challenge by using array elements as input parameters. By referencing the ith element of the arguments array `arg` in a special way (`arg[i%arg.length]`), APIBENCHJ is able to "outwit" the JIT compiler, and also can use arrays that are significantly shorter than the number of measurements. Altogether, this prevents the JIT compiler from applying constant folding, identity optimisation and global value numbering optimisations where we do not want them to happen.

Other JVM optimisations such as Garbage Collection interfere with measurements and the resulting outliers are detected by our implementation in the context of statistical evaluation and execution control.

5.3.6.2. Generating Executable Microbenchmarks

Using the Java Reflection API, it is possible to design a common flexible microbenchmark for all methods of the benchmarked API, where the latter are invoked with the Reflection API method `method.invoke(instanceObj, params)`. However, invoking benchmarked API methods dynamically with the Reflection API is very costly [197] and will significantly bias the measured performance.

An alternative is source code generation, which is the straightforward way to construct reliable microbenchmarks. Source code is generated based on models that represent the code to render; in case of benchmarking, each microbenchmark is specific to a single method of the Java API. Hence, for each method to benchmark, a model has to be manually prepared.

However, the manual generation of the models and code templates for each API method would be extremely work-intensive and would contradict the goal of APIBENCHJ, which strives to automate the benchmarking of Java methods and APIs. In addition, if the API changes, the generation models must be manually adapted. Consequently, the scope of the benchmark would be limited to specific Java implementations.

The solution used in APIBENCHJ employs direct creation of the 'skeleton' bytecode for a microbenchmark, using the Javassist bytecode instrumentation API [198]. This 'skeleton' contains timer method invocations (e.g. calls to `nanoTime()`) for measuring the execution durations. The 'skeleton' also contains control flow for a warmup phase which is need to induce the JIT compilation (cf. Section 5.3.6.1). Thus, two benchmarking phases are performed: one for the 'cold' method (before JIT), and one for the hot (after JIT).

For each benchmarking scenario with appropriate preconditions, APIBENCHJ creates a dedicated microbenchmark that starts as a bytecode copy of the 'skeleton'. Then, the actual method invocations and preconditions are added to the 'skeleton' using Javassist instrumentation. Finally, APIBENCHJ renames the completed microbenchmark instance, so that each microbenchmark has a globally unique class name/class type, and all microbenchmarks can be loaded independently at runtime. An infrastructure to execute the microbenchmarks and to collect their results is also part of APIBENCHJ. Finally, APIBENCHJ evaluates, aggregates and persists the benchmarking results.

Chapter 6.

Bytecode-based Performance Prediction and its Integration into the Palladio Component Model

Section 1.4 described how the performance prediction proposed by this thesis is made: it works on the basis of the *application performance profile* and the *platform performance profile*. The two profiles share the same choice of application building blocks, which are seen as the resource demand units that express the workload put by the application onto the platform.

The choice of bytecode instructions and API methods as application building blocks was motivated and detailed in Section 4.2. Bytecode-based performance prediction is an alternative to performance prediction on the basis of CPU cycles. It provides the possibility to quantify the workload in a platform-independent way, and promises better prediction accuracy (the validation in Section 7.1 will show that this is indeed the case).

In bytecode-based performance prediction, the application performance profile is composed of runtime frequencies of bytecode methods and instructions. This profile is platform-independent but needs to be parametrised over the application workload. In Chapter 4, an approach for quantifying the bytecode-based application performance profile was presented, which works through transparent instrumentation of application's bytecode and does not require a specialised JVM. The developed approach itself is thus also platform-independent.

In Chapter 5, a novel approach for creating the matching platform performance profile was described, which works by benchmarking bytecode instructions and methods. The results of the benchmarks are the platform-specific performance metrics (e.g. execution durations) of these building blocks.

One notable observation from Chapter 5 was that the speedup caused by Just-In-Time compilation (JIT) by the JVM was different across applications and benchmarks: the speedup measured for bytecode microbenchmarks was significantly *lower* than for method benchmarks or for larger, non-synthetic applications. While the instruction execution durations obtained from these microbenchmarks are suitable for predicting the performance of applications in environments where JIT is not available or not activated, predicting the performance of applications in *realistic* settings requires the consideration of JIT.

As has been demonstrated in Section 2.14, the JIT-caused speedup is application-dependent. In particular, the result of a prediction made on the basis of microbenchmark results needs to be calibrated *individually* for each application. In Section 6.1, this calibration will be formulated and explained. The calculation of the calibration factor will also take into account the fact that the API method benchmarks are subject to JIT compilation to such a degree that their contribution to the performance of the considered application does not need to be calibrated. Therefore, the calibration will only be applied to the contribution of individual instructions and instruction sequences that are not part of an API method implementation.

The subject of this chapter is to describe the actual process of the prediction and the calculation of the calibration, and to introduce support for bytecode-based performance prediction into the Palladio Component Model (PCM). This task is performed in a systematic way, by defining scenarios and requirements and extending the PCM metamodel and the tooling to support them. The **scientific challenges** addressed in this chapter are the following:

- finding an approach for considering the effects of Just-In-Time compilation (cf. Sec. 2.6) and other runtime optimisations performed by the JVM, balancing prediction accuracy and simplicity

- extending the Palladio Component Model to support bytecode-based performance prediction

- design the PCM extension so that a more detailed modelling of the execution platform is possible for several benchmarking and performance prediction extensions that are currently being developed

The resulting contributions are

- a prediction model that minimises the effort and the number of inputs that
  are needed for the calibration of the prediction model

- an extension of the Palladio Component Model that balances abstraction,
  detailedness and prediction precision

The remainder of this chapter is structured as follows: Section 6.1 defines the
prediction process and explains the design rationale for it. Section 6.2 details
the integration into the Palladio Component Model. Section 6.3 concludes.

6.1. Computing the Predicted Execution Duration

The final step of bytecode-based performance prediction is calculating the
platform-specific execution duration for the considered component service. The
first input for the calculation are the platform-independent instruction/method
counts, and the second input consists of the platform-specific timing values of
instructions/methods from benchmarking. As this thesis deals with performance prediction at design time, no absolute precision is required for the prediction, as it would be the case in real-time platforms. In particular, according to
Menasce [199], performance prediction errors of 30 % are considered sufficient
in software engineering, since the used abstractions and simplifications have
their impact on the prediction accuracy.

As explained in Section 5.3, method benchmarking is designed so that it encourages just-in-time compilation – thus, the resulting timing values will be
used without calibration. For the bytecode instruction benchmarking, however,
the situation is different. While just-in-time compilation indeed takes place for
the bytecode microbenchmarks (as confirmed through the analysis of JIT logging), the resulting speedup for microbenchmarks is different from the speedup
which is observed for entire, real applications and algorithms.

The difference between speedups of bytecode microbenchmarks and of entire applications means that the prediction contribution (i.e. execution durations) of the bytecode instructions cannot be derived directly from the results of instruction microbenchmarks. Instead, these results must be *calibrated* for correct accounting during the prediction, since the JIT speedup must be reflected in the prediction.

Before devising an approach for calibration, experiments were designed and performed to study whether it depends on the considered program, on the program inputs, or even on the execution platform. Clearly, taking as much information into the calibration as possible makes the prediction precision better – however, the presented approach should not lose its advantages by requiring that the calibration factor is measured on the target platform. Indeed, performing any application-related (or even application-specific) measurements on the target platform would violate the intention to construct an approach that decreases the effort of prediction in relocation and sizing scenarios (cf. Section 1.2).

6.1.1. Selecting the Input for Prediction Calibration

For several execution platforms, algorithms and algorithm inputs, bytecode-based performance prediction was performed successfully [200] on the basis of a platform-independent yet workload-dependent *multiplicative factor*. While the calibration factor is workload-dependent, it works very well (see validation in Chapter 7) when it is fixed for a given algorithm implementation, while the algorithm input varies [138].

The fact that this multiplicative factor is used in a platform-independent way means that it only needs to be measured on the platform where the component service is already running. The validation in Chapter 7 will also investigate the impact of the execution platform choice for the calibration for the performance prediction precision for other platforms. Additionally, the differences of the calibration factor between the considered applications will be discussed.

It is important to highlight that the prediction precision generally increases when the calibration factor is more specialised, i.e. more information is made available during the computation of it. For example, the calibration factor can be computed as the average of calibration factors obtained on several, different "reference platforms". Alternatively, a set of calibration factors can be maintained, categorised by the properties of the execution platforms. For example, the calibration factor can be distinguished for platforms with an Intel CPU and with an AMD CPU, or for platform with the Oracle JVM as opposed to Apple JVM.

Another possibility for future work is identifying the correlation between the bytecode of the considered application and the calibration factor. For example, studying the basic blocks in the application's bytecode could help to establish such relationships. Additionally, a deeper understanding of native code results of JIT compilation and how they map to the bytecode could be helpful here. However, such a refinement would introduce significant complexity into the approach presented in this thesis, since the inner working of JIT compilation is highly complex, dependent on program structure and behaviour, and constantly evolving as JVM engineers optimise JIT for new processors, operating systems, and application profiles.

Considering the fact that the calibration factor is computed from executing and measuring the algorithm with *one* single algorithm input, the choice of the input itself has a strong impact on the prediction precision when the obtained calibration factor is used. In Section 7.1, the impact of this choice will be studied, by locking the reference platform as well as the algorithm, while varying the inputs to the considered algorithm.

The choice of the algorithm input used for calibration can be based on several criteria (representativeness, complexity, etc.). Another option to mirror the diversity of algorithm inputs would be to use the average of calibration factors from different inputs, or even create a library of calibration factors for a given algorithm, and (for an input not present in the library) select the most suitable one on the basis of similarity. Apart from the danger that such a library may start to resemble a "lookup table" (while still remaining a platform-independent prediction approach), a measure of similarity would be needed. Here, too, potential for future work is clearly visible.

6.1.2. Computing the Calibration Factor

After discussing the choice of the calibration factor's *nature*, its calculation and usage have to be formalised. The multiplicative calibration factor is applied to the prediction contribution of the bytecode instructions but not (as explained above) to methods that were benchmarked using the approach from Section 5.3.

The reason for choosing CPU cycles in the following definitions is that the integration into the Palladio Component Model will involve expressing platform-specific execution durations in CPU cycles rather than in timing values. Using CPU cycles is potentially more accurate than timing values for CPUs which operate at variable frequencies and thus execute a varying number of CPU cycles per unit of time.

In the remainder of this chapter, an algorithm A is employed as a running example and the following notation is used:

- $Calib(A)$ is the calibration factor which is calculated using a reference platform P_{ref} and a reference input Inp_{ref}

- $Dur(A, Inp_{ref}, P_{ref})$ is the measured duration (in CPU cycles) of the considered algorithm with reference input on the reference platform

- $Freq(Opc_i, A, Inp)$ denotes the runtime frequency of opcode Opc_i for algorithm A with input Inp

- $Freq(Meth_i, A, Inp)$ denotes the runtime frequency of method $Meth_i$ for algorithm A with input Inp

- $Perf(Opc_i, P)$ denotes the uncalibrated benchmarked duration *in CPU cycles* of Java bytecode instruction (opcode) Opc_i on platform P (it holds that $0 \leq i < 203$, since only 203 of the 256 possible Java opcodes are currently used according to the Java Virtual Machine specification [110] and recent extensions of it)

252

- $Perf(Meth_i, P)$ denotes the benchmarking duration *in CPU cycles* of method $Meth_i$ ($Perf(Meth_i, P)$ needs no calibration since method benchmarking already exercises execution platform optimisations and captures the resulting speedup, which is independent of the application that contains calls to $Meth_i$.)

Depending on the benchmarking scenario from which $Perf(Opc_i, P)$ was obtained, the value of $Perf(Opc_i, P)$ can vary *on the same platform* due to several reasons in additional to the normal nondeterminism of execution on non-realtime platforms. The first reason is that the performance of the instruction Opc_i can be parametric – this aspect has been discussed in detail in Section 4.3.4.

The second reason is that the *pipelining* effects may have an impact on the benchmarked instruction execution duration, depending on the benchmarking scenario. The pipelining effects are almost impossible to capture (and especially to predict) *at bytecode level* in the platform performance model without introducing a very detailed knowledge of the CPU and without knowing the mapping of bytecode instructions to native instructions. This mapping, however, is specific to the interpreter/JIT compiler (and possibly specific to the hardware architecture), and would require additional effort to measure the pipelining-caused speedup.

Finally, the *context* of a bytecode instruction, e.g. whether it is a part of a basic block (which is JIT-compiled into a native code) plays a role. The structure of this basic block determines how it is JIT-compiled and whether other (non-JIT) optimizations can be applied, e.g. constant folding and constant propagation.

The detailed consideration of these factors would require much more knowledge about the application and about the execution platform, while this thesis puts the emphasis on *simplicity* and easy handling of performance models. Additionally, as the validation in Section 7.1 will show, the prediction accuracy of the approach presented in this thesis is within the borders defined in the standard literature, and constitutes an improvement over the previous prediction approaches which were based on CPU cycle counts.

Unlike instructions (opcodes) which have a numbering according to a specification, the methods $Meth_i$ that contribute to the performance of the considered method can be from different APIs, libraries and components. Therefore, the indexes of $Meth_i$ in general apply only to the considered algorithm, and no globally unique numbering exists.

The calculation of the calibration factor is shown in Formula (6.1) and explained in the following

$$Calib(A) = \frac{Dur(A, Inp_{ref}, P_{ref}) - \sum_j (Freq(Meth_j, A, Inp_{ref}) \cdot Perf(Meth_j, P_{ref}))}{\sum_{i=0}^{202}(Freq(Opc_i, A, Inp_{ref}) \cdot Perf(Opc_i, P_{ref}))}$$

(6.1)

During the prediction of algorithm A's performance, methods calls which are A's building blocks are *either* considered atomically (i.e. they are not decomposed into their constituting bytecode instructions and the internally called methods), *or* they are decomposed into their own building blocks. A trivial condition for the correct working of the prediction for A is that one execution of a given building block is not counted twice. Therefore, if a method which is a building block of A has been decomposed into its own building blocks, it should not appear in Equation (6.1) as $Meth_j$ when it building blocks are counted in Equation (6.1) as well.

Equation (6.1) subtracts the contribution of the counted methods from the total duration of the considered method, thus obtaining the contribution of the counted bytecode instructions to the total duration of the method. The *measured* contribution of the instructions is than set into relation to their *predicted* contribution. In the implementation of the presented approach, this calibration is only performed on one platform, as will be detailed in the validation (Section 7.1). The resulting ratio is the multiplicative calibration factor which is applied to the contribution of the bytecode instructions towards the performance of A – and now on other platforms than P_{ref}, and/or to other inputs then $Input_{ref}$).

Note that $Calib(A)$ is useful for predicting the execution durations on the reference platform, too – it can be used for inputs other than $Input_{ref}$. Similarly, it can be used for $Input_{ref}$ on platforms other than P_{ref}. Finally, note that applying it to A on P_{ref} with $Input_{ref}$ will simply return 1 in that case.

The elements of Equation 6.1 do not need to be constant values: they can be functions or stochastic distributions. For example, $Perf(Meth_j, P_{ref})$ is the benchmarked performance of method $Meth_j$ and it can be a distribution rather than a single value. Using distributions would reflect the fact that method execution duration is rarely constant due to CPU scheduling by the operating system and due to CPU interrupts. Note that when distributions appear in Formula (6.1), the sign · should be read as convolution, which is usually denoted as $\otimes$.

Similarly, consider $Freq(Opc_i, A, Input_{ref})$, the runtime frequencies (counts) of opcode Opc_i. In general, the runtime counts depend on the algorithm input $Input_{ref}$, and can parametrised over it; the fact that the counts are already formulated as a *function* in Equation (6.1) stems from this view. For example, the bytecode-based performance prediction approach presented in this thesis has been combined with genetic algorithms in [138] to learn the dependence of bytecode counts on the input parameters of the considered algorithm. Several algorithm inputs were used in [138] as learning data, and the suitability of the obtained dependencies has been validated successfully on a separate set of algorithm inputs.

After the calibration factor has been expressed and explained, the prediction of the execution duration for algorithm implementation A on platform P with input Inp is shown in shown in Equation (6.2) (recall that there are 203 valid bytecode instructions – thus, i is in the range $[0, 202]$):

$$
\begin{aligned}
Pred(A, Inp, P) \quad = \quad & Calib(A) \cdot \sum_{i=0}^{202} (Freq(Opc_i, A, Inp) \cdot Perf(Opc_i, P)) \\
& + \sum_{j} (Freq(Meth_j, A, Inp) \cdot Perf(Meth_j, P)) \qquad (6.2)
\end{aligned}
$$

6.2. Integration into the Palladio Component Model

In this section, the integration of bytecode-based performance prediction into the Palladio Component Model is described. After revisiting the existing PCM concepts for resource demand specification in Section 6.2.1, Section 6.2.2 explains why it is not possible to realise bytecode-based performance prediction on the basis of current PCM concepts. Based on requirements and scenarios developed in Section 6.2.3, extensions of the Palladio Component Model are presented in Section 6.2.4. Section 6.2.5 details how the JVM and bytecode components are modelled, and Section 6.2.6 explains how bytecode instructions and methods are represented in the model instances of the extended PCM. Section 6.2.7 shows how the modelling expresses the platform-specific nature of benchmarking results, while Section 6.2.8 explains how the prediction calibration is modelled.

6.2.1. Existing Resource Demand Modelling in the PCM

In the Palladio Component Model, the resource demands of components are specified using annotations to internal actions (see Section 2.13). Note that in this section, the state of PCM modelling constructs is described as it existed before the extensions developed in this thesis, which will be described in Section 6.2.4.

Figure 6.1 shows such an internal action, which has a parametrised resource demand to the CPU resource. The CPU resource model does not correspond to a specific exemplar or series from a specific manufacturer. Instead, it is a generic ("abstract") CPU which is parametrised over the processing rate (with Hz as unit).

Concrete instances of CPU resource models are stored in a repository, and a component model instance can be placed in different *allocation contexts* (cf. Section 2.13.2) to run the performance prediction on different CPUs. Figure 6.2 shows a repository with several resources, as it is seen by a PCM workbench user. A `ResourceEnvironment` consists of

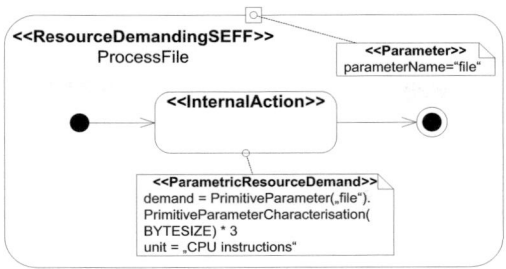

Figure 6.1.: PCM RDSEFF with one internal action

a `ResourceContainer`, which contains several resource specifications, e.g. `ProcessingResourceSpecifications`. The resource specifications refer to the `ResourceRepository` which stores resource types, and a CPU is modelled as an instance of the `ProcessingResourceType`.

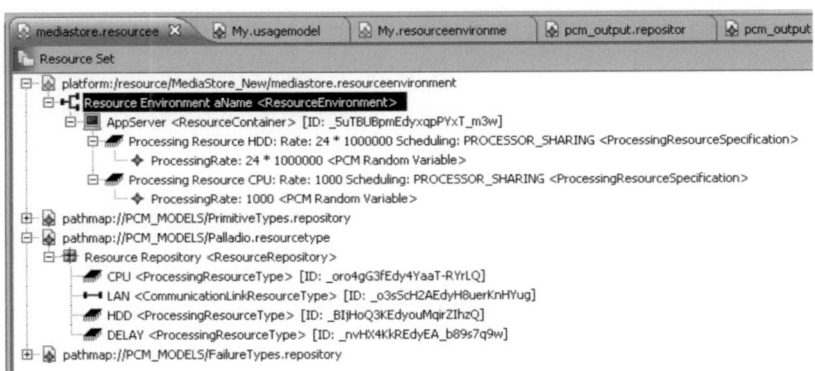

Figure 6.2.: Resource Modelling and Resource Demands in the PCM before Extending it to support Bytecode-based Performance Prediction

When setting the allocation contexts for components, the user chooses among execution platforms and assigns single components to the `ResourceContainers`. She can configure the CPUs and other processing resources (e.g. hard disks) by setting their processing rates and scheduling algorithms. The resources repositories can be stored to and loaded from XML files, which allows PCM users to share and to version model-containing files.

Note that the performance prediction results will be based on the same information for two different modelled CPUs as long as their processing rates and the scheduling policy used for modelling (e.g. PROCESSOR_SHARING, see Figure 6.2) are the same. This makes it impossible to distinguish two execution platforms that have different characteristics and capabilities (e.g. different amount of RAM and different cache sizes) as long as the CPU frequencies are identical.

When simulation is used by the PCM tooling for performance prediction, preemption and resource contention need to be simulated, too. Thus, the request scheduling can have a certain degree of non-determinism, as it is the case in real-world applications. Consequently, the simulation's internal non-determinism can lead to different performance values (i.e. predicted wall-clock times) for individual executions of one particular internal action. The different performance values for different executions of one internal action are stored as a stochastic distribution, rather than a simple average value across all occurrences, so the simulation results carry a greater detail and are more realistic.

6.2.2. Bytecode-based Performance Prediction: Unsuitability of existing PCM Resource Modelling

As has been shown in Section 2, having the processing rate as the only performance characteristic is not sufficient: the precision of cross-platform prediction on the basis of CPU cycles is often not satisfactory when dealing with bytecode-based components and applications. Thus, measuring an internal action's execution on one platform and converting the results into CPU cycles will lead to a valid model on the employed platform, but not necessarily on other platforms.

Therefore, if CPU cycles would have to be kept as the CPU resource usage metric, either the modelling of components or the modelling of resources requires adaptations to accommodate bytecode-based performance prediction.

The first option would be to devise different amounts of resource demands (in CPU cycles) for different execution platforms, and the second option would be to specify a single component model instance, and to modify the CPU model instances. In the remainder of this section, we consider both alternatives and show that they are not viable, leading to the requirement for a new resource model, which will be described in Section 6.2.3.

6.2.2.1. Considering Platform-specific Resource Demands in Internal Actions

Creating RDSEFFs with internal actions that carry *platform-specific* resource demands is not an option, and would violate the semantics of PCM and the intention of the modelling. It is not possible to encode platform dependencies (such as "only valid for CPU x") in resource demand annotations, so more than one instance of the considered business component would have to be created.

Since the interfaces of the existing and additional components would be identical, the platform-specific instances of the considered component would be interchangeable, and performance prediction would become error-prone because users would have to know exactly which component model instance to use with which CPU. Additionally, it would produce a number of additional components (which grows linearly with the number of considered platforms), and would require measurements on each considered target execution platform to obtain the platform-specific CPU cycle count.

6.2.2.2. Considering Platform-specific Resource Demands using Resource Modifications

The second option is to encode the platform-specific nature of CPU counts using the resource modelling. This alternative is even less viable, and it would also violate the semantics of application-independent processing resources in the PCM. It would mean that each measurement or prediction (i.e. each combination of an internal action's resource demand and a concrete CPU model) would require an own CPU model instance.

More formally, consider two applications, $A1$ and $A2$, and two execution plat-forms, $P1$ and $P2$. The CPU cycle count C for application a on platform p is denoted as $C(a, p)$. Even if $C(A1, P1) = C(A1, P2)$ (i.e. CPU cycle counts match between platforms $P1$ and $P2$ for $A1$), it does not have to hold that $C(A2, P1) = C(A2, P2)$.

More generally, if $\frac{C(A1,P1)}{C(A1,P2)} = x$, it does not have to hold that $\frac{C(A2,P1)}{C(A2,P2)} = x$ – the ratio describing the difference between the CPU counts on the two platforms can vary across applications. Finally, the ratios of CPU cycle counts for two dif-ferent applications on the same execution platform do not need to match across platforms: $\frac{C(A1,P1)}{C(A2,P1)} = x$ does not need to mean that $\frac{C(A1,P2)}{C(A2,P2)} = x$.

6.2.2.3. Attempting to Model the JVM as a Separate Component

Finally, modelling the JVM as a separate component with explicit provided in-terfaces is an option, which would require business components to use a *JVM interface* offered by the JVM component. The JVM component would have no required interfaces – instead, each provided interface would have a RDSEFF with internal actions only, and with CPU resource demands annotated to these internal actions.

This would mean that the JVM component could be deployed on *any* CPU, which in turn would mean that the CPU frequency would remain the con-trolling factor for the performance of bytecode-based components. However, it is known [201] that the platform-specific performance of bytecode instruc-tions does not scale linearly with the CPU frequency. With other words, the JVM benchmarking results (execution durations of bytecode instructions and method invocations) are specific to a given *combination* of JVM and execution platform – in general, they cannot be expressed so that they are valid for a given JVM on *any* execution platform.

6.2.2.4. Conclusion

The results of Sections 6.2.2.1 through 6.2.2.3 mean that modelling the JVM as a component using the current PCM metamodel is not viable, and a concept that allows expressing the dependence of benchmarking results on the *combination* of JVM and execution platform is needed. Therefore, the PCM *concepts* of modelling the active resources and components' resource demands need to be expanded to accommodate the bytecode-based resource demands. The design decision for this task and the resulting changes for the PCM meta-model are described in the next section.

6.2.3. Scenarios and Requirements for Extending the PCM Metamodel

Supporting bytecode-based performance prediction requires an extension of the modelling of resources and components, as shown in the preceding section. This extension is a wide-reaching operation, which is subject to concerns and requirements such as backward compatibility, ease of modelling, expressive power and others. The prime scenario requiring the extension was the support for bytecode-based performance prediction, but other scenarios (such as the support for layered execution environments, and third-party non-PCM performance models and simulators) have also been covered, as described in [192].

For each PCM internal action, a bytecode-based resource demand consists of instruction counts (individual for each instruction type) and method invocation counts. Of course, the method invocation counts should not contain methods of other components, but only the methods of the component itself. Calls to the Java Platform API are considered as part of component-internal work as long as they do not target other components: for example, using the Java Reflection API to invoke a method which belongs to another component is effectively an external call. As components have to be used *directly* over their provided interfaces, we assume that reflection-based calls to other components are recognised as such and are not counted towards component-internal work.

From this scenario, the following requirements have been derived:

R1 "explicit platform dependencies": Components should not make assumptions on their platform that are not stated in their required interface(s), as required by Szyperski's component definition [142]. This requirement is not fully addressed in the current PCM version, since the resources used by the component are not made explicit, but are specified indirectly (and not by the component developer), namely through the component allocation. Instead of stating platform assumptions through interfaces, the components' use of platform resources is visible only when performance annotations to internal actions are considered. At the same time, the requirement that third parties should be able to deploy a component independently is correctly mirrored in the PCM through the use of resource *types*. When extending the PCM, resource independence should me maintained: for example, a component cannot know whether it is run directly on hardware (e.g. a hard disk) or on a virtualiser of it (e.g. a RAID array). At the same time, explicit resource dependencies need to be introduced using the component's interfaces, to capture the assumptions of a component.

R2 **"support for non-hardware execution platform elements"**: so far, the PCM only considers hardware resources of the execution platform, e.g. CPU, hard disk and network connections. However, to represent those software layers that are not part of the application (e.g. the JVM or the middleware), the execution platform modelling needs to support *infrastructure components*.

R3 **"explicit interfaces for execution platform resources"**: supporting different bytecode instruction types, as well as (API) methods, requires an infrastructure component to offer several interfaces, in contrast to current modelling in the PCM where the CPU (and even the hard disk) offer just one operation. For hard disk, this current modelling restriction means that read and write operations have the same processing rate, although in reality, difference in processing speeds can be very significant, especially when file systems are used and meta-data needs to be written, too.

R4 **"third-party models"**: Existing third-party, source-code level behaviour models of complex parts of execution platforms (e.g. operating system schedulers [202]) needed to be supported. Integration of such behaviour models promises and increased precision of performance prediction.

6.2.4. Extensions of the PCM Metamodel

This section describes the extension of the PCM model to support the requirements listed in the previous section.

The extended PCM metamodel introduces explicit `ResourceInterfaces`, which contain `ResourceServices`. `ResourceInterfaces` allow the extended PCM metamodel to fulfil the requirements **R1**, **R2** and **R3** from Section 6.2.3. `ResourceInterfaces` are different from conventional component interfaces in a number of ways, as described below.

Usage of conventional (business) required interfaces is modelled in a RDSEFF as an `ExternalCallAction`: each single invocation of a service from a required interface requires one `ExternalCallAction`. For resource interfaces, the usage of required resource services is handled differently, in the same way as conventional resource demands: resource demands over resource interfaces are expressed as annotations of the internal action which issues the resource demands. In particular, each used resource interface service (i.e. with a non-zero demand) has an entry in the annotation. This entry expresses the resource demand *quantity* as a stochastic expression (StoEx, see [46] for details), and explicitly says which required resource service is used.

A resource has at least one provided resource interface, but no required resource interface and no component interfaces. A resource service of a (hardware) resource does not have an associated RDSEFF – instead, a platform-dependent fixed timing value (for non-concurrent resource usage) is associated with a resource service. Work requests to this resource service are processed directly by the PCM tooling, e.g. by the SimuCom simulation. The `ControllerScope` contains the aforementioned controllers; note that controllers are not allowed to have required or provided *component* interfaces – only resource interfaces are permitted, and a controller must have at least one provided and one required resource interface. An infrastructure component can provide and require both component and resource interfaces; a given interface can be both provided and required. This allows the implementation to forward a work request to layers further below, and permits to model the overhead added by the forwarding layer, if such overhead is quantifiable and important for performance prediction. Note that the infrastructure components are modelled in the same way as business components, and share meta-modelling elements. In fact, a component becomes a business component by placing it in the corresponding layer/scope, and can be seen as an infrastructure component if it is placed in the infrastructure scope. A clarification of terminology is needed concerning the service-providing resource interfaces: a component issues resource demands to *roles*, not to interfaces: different instances of one interface type can only be distinguished by their role-implemented attachment to a component/resource. A role is what connects the interface to the component – therefore, in the following illustrations, it is the *role's* name which appears in internal actions as the addressee of resource demands.

Figure 6.3 [203] shows the PCM workbench view of an example RDSEFF (on the basis of PCM extensions described in this Chapter) with resource requirements over resource interfaces. The used resource service is `process`, and it is a part of the newly-introduced `ResourceInterface` called `ICpu`. Note that the resource demand is parametrised over the input `fileToMark.BYTESIZE` of the `watermark` service which is modelled by the shown RDSEFF.

Figure 6.4 [203] shows the "background" view for Figure 6.3, and illustrates the component and resource repositories.

For the `ICpu` resource interface, specifying the resource demands in the internal actions of RDSEFFs carries similar effort as specifying CPU demands using the "old" PCM resource modelling. For JVM-oriented resource interface with *hundreds* of provided resource services, the effort of manual specification of resource demands would be very high. Additionally, counting results were obtained in an automated way and an automation of PCM instance creation from bytecode-based resource demands offers itself as a missing link in the toolchain.

Therefore, the creation of PCM model artefacts has been automated to decrease the effort of bytecode-based performance prediction using the PCM. PCM artefacts which carry JVM-related information (resource instances, resource interface, components, internal actions, RDSEFFs, etc.) are created from the arte-

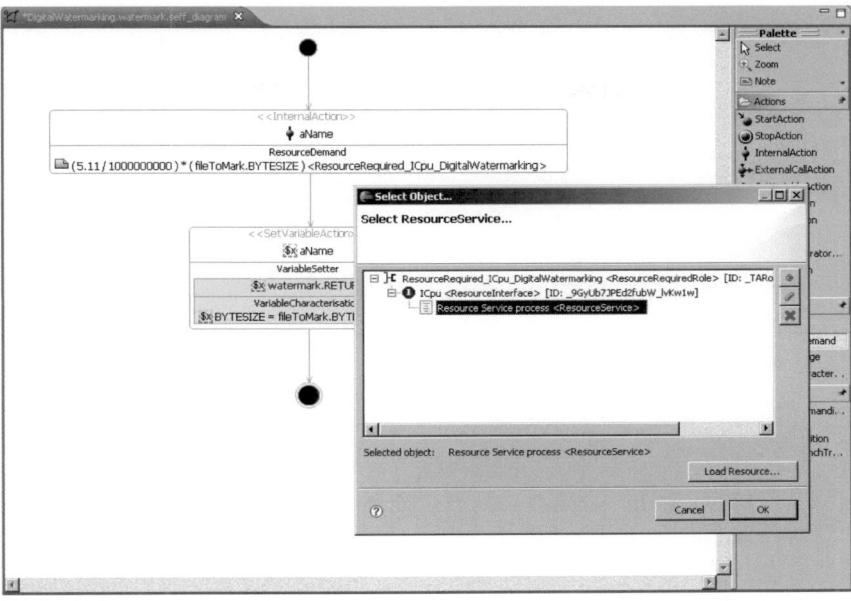

Figure 6.3.: PCM Workbench View of an RDSEFF which uses newly-introduced Explicit Resource Interfaces [203]

facts produced with approaches from Chapter 4 and Chapter 5. The created artefacts are stored in file-based repositories, in the same manner as manually created PCM artefacts are persisted. PCM users can take advantage of these artefacts when they create PCM models which consist of component models for existing and planned components. While the approach presented in this thesis focuses on the resource demands of internal actions of components, the integration with reverse engineering of static and dynamic component models by Krogmann has been demonstrated in [204, 200].

ResourceInterfaces can be offered by (hardware) resources and *controllers*, but not by infrastructure components or business components. The reason for this is that resource interfaces are meant to be tightly integrated with the performance prediction tooling of the PCM, rather than resemble conventional ser-

265

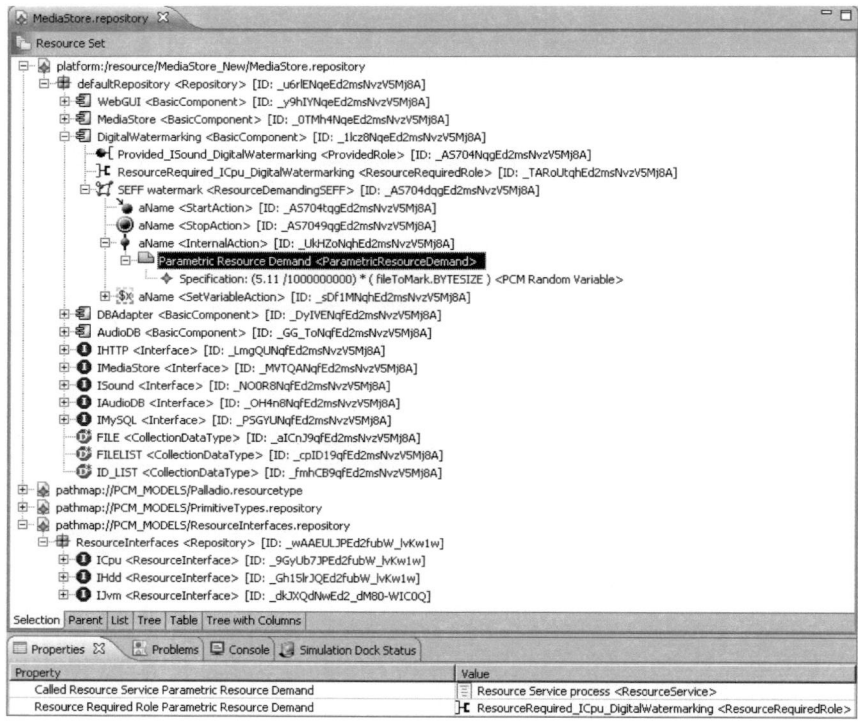

Figure 6.4.: PCM Workbench View with Component Repositories, Resource Repositories, and their Elements [203]

vices for which RDSEFFs with resource-demanding actions need to be provided. Correspondingly, no RDSEFFs are allowed to be specified for resource services.

The interface compatibility of newly introduced resource and conventional ("business") interfaces is summarised in Table 6.1. It is obvious that a required conventional business interface can be connected to a provided business interface, and a provided resource interface is compatible with a required resource interface. If need arises, a required resource interface can be connected to a provided business interface because infrastructure components may not offer resource interfaces. Finally, a required business interface cannot be connected to

Provided interface / Required interface	Business interface	Resource interface
Business interface	✓	⃠
Resource interface	(✓)	✓

Table 6.1.: Compatibility of Resource Interfaces and Business Interfaces

a provided resource interface because a resource service cannot be used from an `ExternalCallAction`.

Controllers are new constructs to fulfil the requirement **R4**: it is used to support complex existing non-PCM behaviour models, e.g. network simulations or operating system schedulers. A controller has no provided component interfaces and no required component interfaces, instead it must have at least one provided and one required resource interface. A controller contains no RDSEFFs – it can be used together with other PCM model instances because the controller's existing behaviour model (e.g. a network simulator) integrates with the PCM prediction/simulation tooling. Controllers have been introduced to support future extensions of the PCM, and are not discussed further in this thesis.

Resources can only offer resource interfaces, may not require resource interfaces, and may not offer or require business interfaces. They do not contain RDSEFFs for the provided resource services – instead, resources are integrated with the PCM toolchain at the implementation level.

Further implementation details including the metamodel extensions and the modification of PCM model transformations can be found in the diploma thesis of Michael Hauck who implemented them [203].

6.2.5. Modelling the JVM and the Bytecode Components

To predict the performance of an internal action using bytecode instruction/-method counts, their platform-dependent timing values (i.e. execution durations) are used, as detailed in Section 6.1. These timing values are specific for the combination of the JVM and the underlying parts of the execution platform, and Section 6.2.2.3 detailed why it is not viable to model the JVM as a component that can use *any* CPU. Thus, even after the PCM metamodel extension have been introduced, the question on *how* to model the benchmarking results' dependency on the used execution platform needs to be solved.

As explained in Sections 5.2 and 5.3, the benchmarking of the internal actions' building blocks (bytecode instructions and methods) returns timing values that are abstractions of resource usage during the building blocks' execution. For example, the initialisation of an array may incur RAM memory swapping to the hard disk, but such level of detail is neither predictable at architectural level, nor easy to model. On the other hand, of the hardware resources constituting the execution platform, the PCM currently models the CPU, the hard disk and the network connections.

Modelling the JVM together with the underlying layers of the execution platform as *one* big box offering both a JVM interface and hardware resource interfaces (e.g. hard disk) would contradicts the layering approach presented in the previous section. Thus, the *aggregated*, resource-abstracting timing values obtained during benchmarking must be mapped to one resource or several of them, though it is not known which of these resources are used in reality.

Since none of the bytecode instructions performs direct hard disk or network operations, only methods (including but not limited to API methods) can lead to hard disk access and network access. Consequently, it makes sense to assume that significant hard disk and network access for internal actions is captured and modelled outside of bytecode-based benchmarking. This allows the user to map the benchmarking-obtained timing values *exclusively* to the CPU, but the problem that the benchmarking values are not valid for any CPU still remains.

6.2.6. Representing JVM Instructions and Methods as Resource Services

Expressing primitive bytecode instructions as provided services of the resource interfaces (of a JVM infrastructure component) needs a few considerations. Bytecode instructions aren't methods (they have no declaring class, not signature, no body, etc.), and their treatment of parameters is significantly different as well.

To choose the *name* of the JVM infrastructure component service that mirrors a bytecode instruction, a simple mapping from the mnemonic to the method's name offers itself first. However, it works only if the mnemonic is capitalised: otherwise, e.g. the mnemonic goto collides with the Java protected token goto, while GOTO as method is permissible and treated differently then goto. Note that no naming clashes to classes of the Java platform API can occur, because all classes of the latter are located in non-default packages.

It would be tempting to reduce the number of instruction in the JVM resource interface for the PCM, e.g. to decrease its complexity. Indeed, the JVM instruction set is designed with attention to code size, rather than orthogonality, and on several occasions, two instruction can be used for the same tasks. For example, to decrease the code size, the JVM specification defines several "shortcuts" (ILOAD_0 through ILOAD_3) for the instruction ILOAD. ILOAD requires one byte and one byte for the index parameter, whereas the shortcuts occupy only one bytecode as the parameter is implicit.

In principle, ILOAD_n and similar shortcuts can be dropped from the signature of the provided interface of the JVM infrastructure component. Indeed, performance equivalence classes from Section 4.3.11 provide a good start for such an optimisation. However, for the sake of completeness, such "shortcuts" have been kept and the entire Java bytecode instruction set is represented in the interface.

For methods, the signature, is original signature is adopted for the resource service, of the IJavaPlatformApi interface, but the types are fully qualified (i.e. their package is included), both for the method's declaring type and for its parameters.

The expression of instruction and method parameters in PCM model instance is subject of future research, the currently used option is to keep the resource interface simple by permitting only one `double`-typed input parameter for a resource service. This simplification enforces performance abstractions, and simplifies the creation of models. It must be matched by the resource demand quantification and benchmarking phases.

A separate issue is the treatment of return values. The JVM specification does not allow method signatures which differ *only* at the returned value and are otherwise identical. Thus, returned values are not critical for distinguishing API method signatures. Also, returned values are not quantified BYSUITE because their influence on the performance is already captured: a returned value matters when it is used as input parameter for another method/instruction – in such a case, it is captured as the input parameter of that method/instruction. So in the current version of BYSUITE, the returned values are not included in the provided interface of the JVM infrastructure component.

Enumerations (`Enums`) are Java programming language constructs for typesafe enumerations, and a Java compiler translates an `enum` into a conventional Java class which extends the Java API class `java.lang.Enum`. For example, the declaration `enum Train{ICE,TGV,Thalys}` is translated into a class which has three `public final static` fields of type `Train`, and an array which contains all of these fields. An enum does not need `getters`/`setters` (as an `enum`'s fields are all public), but an enum can define its own methods as it extends the `java.lang.Enum` *class*. For example, the `enum Train` could define the method `public int getMaxSpeed()`. For the provided interface of the JVM infrastructure component, a component's accesses to enum values are treated as fields accesses (i.e. intro-component resource demands) regardless of the enum's location. Accesses to an enum's methods are treated as method invocation, i.e. it is a resource demand when the enum belongs to the same component or the Java Platform API, or it is an external call if the enum belong to another component.

Java *generics* are programming language constructs that are checked by the compiler/editor – inside Java bytecode, generics are not visible as they are dropped/ignored during the compilation. For example, the statements `ArrayList untypedList = new ArrayList();` and `ArrayList<Long> untypedList = new ArrayList<Long>();` result in the same bytecode. For methods, the Java treatment of generics is *erasure*, i.e. the generic types are replaced by the most common type confirming to the type required by the generic declaration (in some cases, even *erased*). Therefore, in the scope of this chapter, generics can be ignored.

6.2.7. Expressing the Platform-specific Nature of JVM Benchmarking Results

To express the platform-specific nature of JVM benchmarking results, it must be expressed that the benchmarking results are valid for a given combination of JVM and underlying layers of the execution platform. From the underlying layers, only the CPU is considered, as explained in Section 6.2.5. However, the CPU cannot be "hidden" by modelling the execution platform as one atomic entity, since for other infrastructure components (e.g. a database), direct usage of CPU may need to be modelled, as these components do not use the JVM.

Thus, the JVM needs to be modelled separately from the CPU (which has 1 resource service called `process` in the new resource model). Consequently, the only solution to express the platform-specific nature of JVM benchmarking results is to specialise the interface between the JVM and the CPU.

Pictured in Figure 6.5, the infrastructure component `JVM-Oracle1.6.20-W732-Intel-C2D` models a specific JVM and offers the generic `IJvm` interface. The name of the component (`JVM-Oracle1.6.20-W7-Intel-C2D`) expresses the fact that it models an Oracle JVM (version 1.6.20) running on Windows 7 (32-bit version), with an Intel Core 2 Duo ("C2D") CPU. `JVM-Oracle1.6.20-W7-Intel-C2D` requires a *specialised* `ICpu-Intel-C2D` resource interface, which inherits from the generic, PCM-standard `ICpu` interface. Note that other components that

271

require the CPU can access the `ICpu-Intel-C2D` interface without problems, as it offers the services of its parent type `ICpu`.

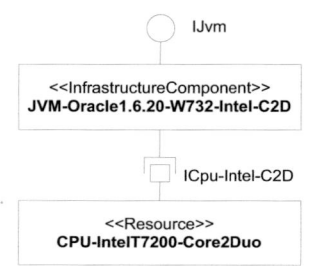

Figure 6.5.: Specialising CPU Resource Interfaces to Model Platform-Dependent JVM Benchmarking Results (the squared interface is a resource interfaces)

The specialisation of the `ICpu` interfaces makes it possible to express that the timing values in `JVM-Oracle1.6.20-W7-Intel-C2D` (which have been converted into CPU cycles) are valid not for any CPU, but only for CPUs offering certain behaviour. Here, the `ICpu-Intel-C2D` interface expresses the specialisation to the CPUs from the Intel Core 2 Duo CPU family, but the hardware resource model instance offering the `ICpu-Intel-C2D` interface can also represent other CPUs for which the resulting timing values of `Oracle1.6.20-W7-Intel-C2D`'s offered interface `IJvm` correspond to benchmarking results. The many degrees of execution platform variability found in reality (operating system, amount of main memory, etc.) are not forgotten or abstracted here: `JVM-Oracle1.6.20-W7-Intel-C2D` has been benchmarked on a *fixed* execution platform configuration.

Using the extended PCM model, it is also possible to model the execution platform in different ways. For example, a controller model instance representing an operating system scheduler could be modelled to offer the `ICpu` interface (or

a subtype thereof), and the infrastructure component model instance representing a JVM could access that interface (since it would not be allowed to access
the CPU resource model anymore, because it would be on a lower layer than
the controller). Using a controller, the dependency of benchmarking results of
the JVM-representing infrastructure component could be factored out, and the
JVM infrastructure component could be parametrised over the controller. Alternative modelling of the JVM are also possible, and the flexibility introduced
by the extension of the PCM metamodel offers both opportunities and dangers.

For instance, the creator of the `JVM-Oracle1.6.20-W7-Intel-C2D` infrastructure component in the above example cannot control the creation of
CPU resource models offering the `ICpu-Intel-C2D` resource interface. This
means that some other stakeholder could create a CPU model that offers
`ICpu-Intel-C2D` but still *violates* the validity of resulting timing values for
`JVM-Oracle1.6.20-W7-Intel-C2D`'s offered interface. In fact, it remains
the responsibility of the system deployer to ensure that the JVM infrastructure
component is connected to the matching, valid CPU resource model.

An infrastructure component model instance must be created for each considered (and benchmarked) combination of JVM and execution platform, unless
the benchmarking results (as timing values) for two *different* execution platforms
become identical when converted from timing values to CPU cycles. Note that
it is normal to expect small differences in the resulting benchmarking values
(in CPU cycles), and it is advisable to define a threshold up to which the differences are attributed to measurement errors. Above the threshold, the differences
would be attributed to substantial changes in execution platforms, and would
require a differentiation using distinct CPU interfaces, and different infrastructure component model instances.

6.2.8. Modelling the Calibration Factor

Finally, the calibration factor from Section 6.1.2 must be considered in the extended PCM model, since it is substantial for realistic performance prediction.
Initially, it was assumed that this factor would be algorithm-*independent* but,

instead, platform-dependent. Therefore, it was modelled by a separate component, as shown in Figure 6.6. Recall that t

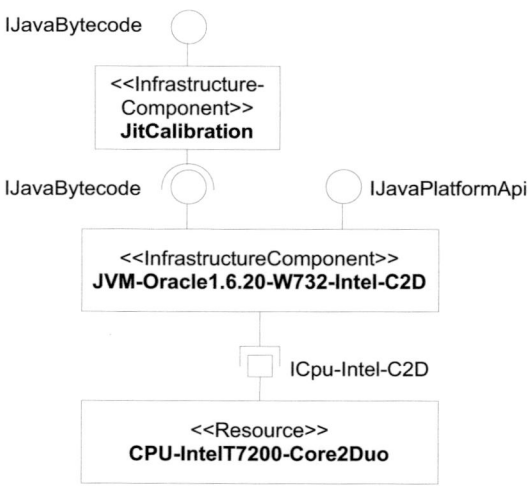

Figure 6.6.: Initial Modelling of the Calibration Factor as a Separate Infrastructure Component

However, the validation in the following Chapter 7 refuted this assumption, and instead found that a better prediction accuracy is achieved with a calibration factor that is algorithm-specific and platform-independent. Consequently, the speedup cannot be expressed in the infrastructure component that models the JVM. Instead, it must be expressed in the internal actions that constitute the algorithm whose workload has been quantified using bytecode instruction and method counting.

The currently favoured approach to do this is to introduce an attribute of the internal action, and to express the calibration factor there. The new attribute must be presented to the PCM workbench users in a way which does not irritate those PCM users who are not familiar with the JIT and its impacts. Additionally, it would have to be made clear that it applies only to the bytecode instructions, and not to atomically benchmarked methods.

The attribute would be specified in a similar way as the failure probability attribute already supported in the PCM for reliability analysis. The adaptation of the PCM simulation toolchain that is required to evaluate this new field has not been completed yet.

Since this thesis assumes that the calibration factor has been quantified for the stable state of the application (i.e. after JIT compilation and other optimisations have been applied), the performance before the stable state has been reached is not very relevant. Consequently, to provide a temporary workaround until the calibration factor is available as an attribute of the internal action, it has been integrated *transparently* into the performance prediction and resource demand quantification.

This is done by applying the calibration factor to each of the collected *instruction counts* before specifying them as resource demands in the internal action. Why it is true that this temporary solution alters the semantics of the instruction counts in the internal action's resource demands, the resulting performance prediction adheres to Equation (6.2). Recall that the method benchmarking results are already calibrated, and the calibration factors is not applied to method counts. Equation (6.2) demonstrates multiplying the instruction *counts* with $Calib(A)$, instead of calibrating the prediction contribution of the instructions:

$$
\begin{aligned}
Pred_{modif}(A, Inp, P) \;=\; & \sum_{i=0}^{202} (Calib(A) \cdot Freq(Opc_i, A, Inp)) \cdot Perf(Opc_i, P) \\
& + \sum_{j} Freq(Meth_j, A, Inp) \cdot Perf(Meth_j, P) \qquad (6.3)
\end{aligned}
$$

6.3. Summary

This chapter detailed the computation of predicted execution durations using bytecode-based performance prediction. It explained the need of a calibration factor, and how this factor is quantified. The rationale for selecting the input data for calibration factor calculation was presented, and the selected tradeoff between prediction accuracy and overfitting was explained.

To integrate bytecode-based performance prediction into the Palladio Component Model, a careful study of its concepts was undertaken to understand whether bytecode-based performance prediction can be realised with existing concepts. As it emerged that an extension of the PCM meta-model and tooling would be needed to accommodate the bytecode-based prediction approach, this extension was carried out according to a set of requirements defined in Section 6.2.3. Additionally, the task of constructing PCM model instances using bytecode-based workloads has been automated, and reusable infrastructure components representing JVMs can also be created in an automated way.

While the modelling of the calibration factor remains to be refined, the PCM tooling is already capable to use bytecode-oriented performance models for performance prediction. At the same time, bytecode-based component performance models can be combined with performance models with resource demands based on CPU cycles or other resource interfaces, and obtained in other ways. By introducing explicit resource interfaces, this chapter has brought explicit parametrisation over the execution platform to the component modelling in the PCM. Future extensions of the PCM can benefit from explicit resource interfaces when new resource types are added to it.

Chapter 7.

Validation

In this chapter, the contributions of this thesis are validated, which can be grouped into two fields: cross-platform performance prediction and quality-driven timer method selection. Cross-platform performance prediction encompasses bytecode-based resource demand quantification (Chapter 4), virtual machine benchmarking (Chapter 5), and the prediction process (Chapter 6).

Cross-platform performance prediction is validated in Section 7.1, which validates both the entire prediction process and its constituents.

Quality-driven timer method selection was presented in Chapter 3, and its results have been used during virtual machine benchmarking. Quality-driven timer method selection is validated in Section 7.2.

7.1. Bytecode-based Performance Prediction

To realise performance prediction in relocation and sizing scenarios (see Section 1.2), this thesis has introduced a bytecode-based performance prediction approach which is evaluated in this section. The approach quantifies the platform-independent performance of applications in terms of instruction and methods counts (see Chapter 4).

The platform-independent counts are translated into platform-specific timings using instruction benchmarking (Section 5.2) and method/API benchmarking (Section 5.3). Runtime optimisations of the execution platform (such as Just-In-Time compilation) are considered during prediction using an algorithm-specific but input-independent and platform-independent calibration factor (see Section 6.1 for the details).

Validating performance prediction means validating the entire approach atomically, i.e. comparing the predicted performance to the measured performance, while also studying the properties of the approach, such as scalability, overhead, effort etc. At the same time, the individual steps of the approach (resource demand quantification, benchmarking, calculation of the predicted values) need to be evaluated individually to study their strengths and limitations.

As discussed in Section 6.1, performance prediction errors of 30 % are considered sufficient in software engineering according to Menasce [199], since the used abstractions and simplifications have their impact. This prediction error sets the target for the presented approach, and it will be shown that it is achieved in almost all cases, while prediction based on CPU cycles fails this targets for the vast majority of predictions.

The remainder of this section is structured as follows: Section 7.1.1 gives an overview of the validation including the Goal-Question-Metric approach (GQM) which guides it. Section 7.1.2 presents the applications and algorithms on which the validation was performed. Section 7.1.3 details the goals, questions and metrics for the validation of the bytecode-based performance prediction which is then performed in Section 7.1.4. The GQM elements for bytecode-based resource demand quantification form the contents of Section 7.1.5, with the results following in Section 7.1.6. For JVM benchmarking, the GQM elements are given in Section 7.1.7, and the validation of JVM benchmarking follows in Section 7.1.8. Section 7.1.9 concludes with the discussion of the validation results for bytecode-based performance prediction and its sub-steps.

7.1.1. Validation Overview

Figure 7.1 provides an overview of the contributions and artefacts involved in the validation of the approach presented in this thesis. Figure 7.1 shows that the validation involves three comparisons: between predicted and measured execution durations (C1), between manually quantified and instrumentation-quantified resource demands (C2), and between manual and automated benchmarking of bytecode instructions/API methods (C3).

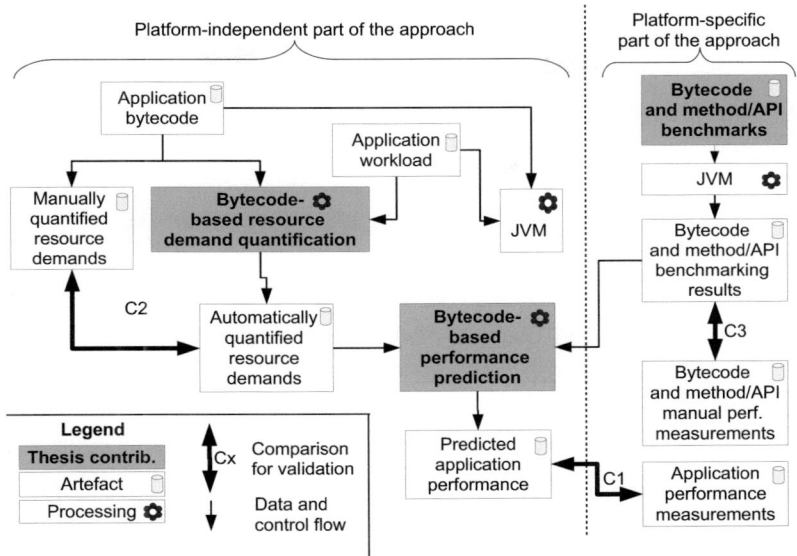

Figure 7.1.: Validation of Bytecode-based Performance Prediction (Overview)

To perform a validation in a systematic way, its goals must be made explicit, and the metrics which are measured to achieve the goals must be selected accordingly. A three-level approach by Basili et al. [205] is called GQM ("goals, questions, metrics"), and the remaining sections of this chapter follow the GQM approach. This thesis uses the following notation: **Gx** is the goal **x**, **Qy** is the question **y** and **Mz** is the metric **z**.

On the top, conceptual level, a goal is described using human language, and can be formulated using a hypothesis, e.g. "show that approach X scales". The level between the goal and the metric is taken by questions that related to a particular goal, e.g. "how many concurrent requests can be processed by the approach?". One possible metric for such a question is "number of concurrent requests per CPU core". The descriptions of GQM instances can contain details on the *purpose* of setting the goal(s)/asking the question(s), information on stakeholders, views and contexts, etc.

In this thesis, an extensive Type 1 validation that focuses on performance prediction has been performed for several Java applications (workloads) which differ in type, size, shape, complexity and age. These applications are described in Section 7.1.2, and the GQM goals for the cross-platform performance prediction are described in Section 7.1.3. The validation results are described in the Sections 7.1.4.1 through 7.1.4.6.

After successfully validating the performance prediction as an atomic mechanism, its constituents are validated on their own, to show the feasibility of the novel approaches developed in this thesis. The instruction-precise workload recording mechanism from Chapter 4 is evaluated in Section 7.1.6 following the goals that are set in Section 7.1.5, which include the demonstration of precision, low overhead, scalability and other advantages.

The method benchmarking from Section 5.3 (using parameter generation heuristics and automated generation of executable bytecode microbenchmarks) is evaluated in Section 7.1.8 following the goals set in Section 7.1.7. These goals include the precision of benchmarking, the success rate of the heuristics, the effort of benchmark generation, etc.

Bytecode instruction benchmarking can only be validated in the context of performance prediction and not be validated on its own: there are no available alternative measurement approaches for bytecode instruction duration. Therefore, it is validated indirectly, as a contributor to bytecode-based cross-platform performance prediction.

7.1.2. Subjects and Scenarios for the Validation

Seven different workloads from six applications were used for validation of the performance prediction approach, and this section describes the applications in more detail. Note that the resource demand quantification and performance prediction were performed for a number of other workloads, but the precision of the prediction accuracy was only verified for the seven workloads described below, since the validation of cross-platform prediction requires deployment and measurement on several platforms.

SPECjvm2008 [59] is an industry-grade benchmark developed by SPEC (Standard Performance Evaluation Council), and it is the successor of the SPEC-jvm98 benchmark. SPECjvm2008 measures the performance of a Java Runtime Environment (JRE) using several real-life applications and workloads that focus on core Java platform API and functionality. Its documentation states that it "has low dependence on file I/O and includes no network I/O across machines".

The workloads of SPECjvm2008 can be run in different modes, e.g. to measure the startup performance of the JVM (which, however, is of lesser significance to business applications than response time and throughput). From the workloads of SPECjvm2008, the two most complicated were selected for performance prediction validation (the complexity was judged by the number and size of classes outside of the JVM/Java Platform API that used for the implementation of the workloads). These two workloads are `compress` (13 classes) and `MPEGaudio` (35 classes), and the latter is an MP3 encoder and thus a functionality whose performance had to be measured manually in previous publications concerned with PCM validation [206].

Complexity served as the criterion because workloads should be as realistic as possible. At first, SPECjvm2008 benchmarks with the prefix `startup` were excluded from consideration, because they measure the performance of the corresponding workloads as the JVM starts up – before JIT compilation can show its benefits and before the execution reaches a "steady state". Additionally, workloads were not considered when the bulk of complexity (and execution time) was shouldered by a API methods, as it is the case with XML workloads in SPECjvm2008. Other workloads were rather "toy benchmarks" (e.g. small mathematical kernels, such as Fast Fourier Transform or the LU algorithm).

SPECjbb2005 [207] is another benchmark developed by SPEC, SPECjbb-2005 is a benchmark for evaluating the performance of execution platforms running business applications written in Java, and it designed as an order-processing application for a wholesale supplier. More than 540 publicly available SPECjbb2005 results have been published by hardware and software vendors such as IBM, Oracle, Sun Microsystems, Hewlett-Packard, SAP, AMD, Apple and others. During a SPECjbb2005 run, the degree of parallelism is gradually increasing by increasing the number of concurrently active, and the reported results allow the users to analyse how the benchmark scales, in particular on multi-core platforms.

JFreeChart is a framework for creating complex diagrams, with support for Gantt charts, histograms, time series etc. It is an open-source product that is very popular (more than 20000 downloads per month) and which is widely used in enterprise applications such as JBoss application server, Atlassian JIRA (an issue tracking and project management tool) and others. Its data processing algorithms such as regression calculation form good candidates for bytecode-based performance prediction, while the charting functionality is GUI-oriented and therefore not targeted by the Palladio Component Model and the contribution of this thesis.

Linpack is a benchmark that performs numeric linear algebra computations, originally written in Fortran by Jack Dongarra et al. (in this thesis, a Java implementation of Linpack is used [208]). Originally intended for use on supercomputers of the 1970s and 1980s, it continues to be developed and used for benchmarking supercomputers in the 21st century. The last incarnation, called High-Performance Linpack (HPL), was published in 2008 and its results are the single criterion used for ranking supercomputers in the TOP500 list [209]. Still, the core algorithm continues to be linear algebra computations.

Finally, **Whetstone** is an even older benchmark (the original version appeared in 1972 and was written in Algol60), and it focuses on floating-point performance. The validation uses a Java implementation which was retrieved from [210].

7.1.3. Performance Prediction: Goals, Questions and Metrics

Following the GQM approach described in Section 7.1.1, the following goals, questions and metrics guide the evaluation of the performance prediction:

G1: show that the approach predicts the execution durations accurately

G1-Q1: what is the difference between the predicted and manually measured execution durations?

G1-Q1-M1: the difference between prediction and measurement, calculated from the formula $\frac{predicted - measured}{measured}$

G1-Q2: is it sufficient to consider the JIT speedup factor as input-independent?

G1-Q2-M1: the dependence of **G1-Q1-M1** on the algorithm input for which the calibration was performed

G2: show that the bytecode-based approach predicts the execution durations more accurately than the approach based on CPU cycles

G2-Q1: what is the difference between the prediction errors based on bytecode instructions vs. based on CPU cycles?

G2-Q1-M1: the difference between the prediction errors obtained for the two approaches

The metric **G2-Q1-M1** deserves some attention, because the prediction error can be both positive (overprediction) and negative (underprediction). For example, if the prediction error is -5 % for one approach and 5 % for the other, it's hard to compare them because the absolute error percentage is the same. However, overprediction is better in the sense that in reality, the system will run faster than predicted, and no "undersizing" error can happen when prediction results are used for system sizing.

When comparing prediction errors x % and $-x$ %$(x \geq 0)$, the *absolute* difference between the prediction errors is $2 \cdot x$ %, although the prediction errors are of equal amplitude (but opposite signs). The absolute difference between the prediction errors 0 % and $2 \cdot x$ % is also $2 \cdot x$ % , but in this case, the first prediction error is clearly better than the second.

Therefore, the absolute difference between prediction errors is not a good formula for **G2-Q1-M1**. In this thesis, **G2-Q1-M1** for prediction errors PE_1 (from CPU cycle counts, computed in the same manner as **G1-Q1-M1**) and PE_2 (**G1-**

Q1-M1 from bytecode counts) is computed as $|PE_1| - |PE_2|$. The larger **G2-Q1-M1** is, the better is bytecode-based performance prediction when compared to prediction based on CPU cycles.

7.1.4. Performance Prediction: Results of Validation

In the following, the prediction results are presented individually for the validation subjects which were listed in Section 7.1.2, and the results are discussed. For the validation, three execution platforms were selected so that they would differ in hardware characteristics, operating system and JVM:

1. **MBP53**: a MacBook Pro notebook (model identifier "MacBookPro5,3") with 2.8 GHz Intel Core 2 Duo CPU (T9600), 4 GB of RAM, running Mac OS X 10.6.4 and Apple JVM (JDK 1.6.0_21).

2. **T60a**: a Lenovo notebook (T60, model ID 2007-49G) with 1.83 GHz Intel Core Duo T2400 CPU, 3.0 GB of RAM and Windows 7 Professional, with the JVM from Oracle (JDK 1.6.0_21)

3. **X110a**: an LG Electronics notebook (model X110-L.A7SAG) with 1.60 GHz Intel CPU (x86 Family 6 Model 28 Stepping 2), 1 GB of RAM and Windows 7 Professional, with Oracle JDK 1.6.0_20

7.1.4.1. SPECjvm2008 MPEGaudio and Compress Workloads

As described in Section 7.1.2, the MPEGaudio benchmark of SPECjvm2008 is a real-world workload concerned with decoding of compressed audio files. The evaluation has been performed on six MP3 files (of different size, duration, and bitrate) which are bundled with SPECjvm2008 and used as workloads for the MPEGaudio benchmark. In detail, the characteristics of files (referenced in Table 7.1) are as follows:

- FileA: 19,676 bytes, 20 seconds, 1 channel, 8 kbps

- FileB: 61,741 bytes, 62 seconds, 1 channel, 8 kbps

- FileC: 140,563 bytes, 12 seconds, 2 channels, 96 kbps

- FileD: 729,600 bytes, 52 seconds, 2 channels, 112 kbps

- FileE: 32,596 bytes, 2 seconds, 2 channels, 128 kbps

- FileF: 3,257,258 bytes, 204 seconds, 2 channels, 128 kbps

In addition to 9 classes of SPECjvm2008 MPEGaudio itself, the decoder library used by the benchmark have also been instrumented, to provide complete and "unfolded" bytecode instructions for the entire workload. The instrumentation of the decoder library meant instrumenting 40 classes of JLayer [211], which results in more 200 instrumented methods, and only one method needs to be treated specially (see Section 7.1.6.1 for details).

To answer question **G1-Q1** following goal **G1**, Table 7.1 presents the results of metric **G1-Q1-M1** for the performance prediction on three platforms, employing the SPECjvm2008 MPEGaudio benchmark for the six input files listed above.

For the calculation of the calibration factor, *one* platform and *one* input file (the first platform T60a and the first input file FileA) have been taken without special consideration, and without searching for the calibration basis which offers the best (smallest) prediction errors. In particular, this calibration factor is used not only for the other platforms, but also for the remaining five input files on platform T60a. Note that the files are *significantly* different both in size and in decoding complexity, which makes it particularly challenging to predict the performance on the basis of one of these files.

The prediction error for the input file FileA on platform T60a is put in parenthesis because it is not really a *prediction* error: this input is the source of calibration. For other input five files on platform T60a, the prediction error is reasonably small (<10 %). On the other platforms, the prediction error is at most 31.6 % (platform **MBP53**, FileC), and below 30 % in all but this one case.

The **MBP53** platform is also the platform exhibiting the largest prediction errors, which may be caused by a significantly different operating system (Unix-based Mac OS X, in contrast to Windows 7 on T60a and **X110a**). In all but one

Considered platform	Input	Calibration source	Calibration factor	Prediction [ns] calibrated	Measurement with JIT [ns]	G1-Q1-M1 (Prediction error)
T60a	FileA	T60a, input=FileA	0.146	55,793,369	55,793,369	(0)
X110a	FileA	T60a, input=FileA	0.146	148,917,852	163,657,995	-0.090
MBP53	FileA	T60a, input=FileA	0.146	24,000,703	21,034,000	0.141
T60a	FileB	T60a, input=FileA	0.146	174,671,876	173,301,895	0.008
X110a	FileB	T60a, input=FileA	0.146	466,466,780	429,283,365	0.087
MBP53	FileB	T60a, input=FileA	0.146	75,186,312	64,781,000	0.161
T60a	FileC	T60a, input=FileA	0.146	343,556,040	322,451,898	0.065
X110a	FileC	T60a, input=FileA	0.146	922,351,348	808,278,066	0.141
MBP53	FileC	T60a, input=FileA	0.146	145,984,146	110,904,000	0.316
T60a	FileD	T60a, input=FileA	0.146	1,595,659,664	1,478,855,755	0.079
X110a	FileD	T60a, input=FileA	0.146	4,257,424,070	3,711,015,853	0.147
MBP53	FileD	T60a, input=FileA	0.146	675,909,520	523,973,000	0.290
T60a	FileE	T60a, input=FileA	0.146	64,630,749	60,839,992	0.062
X110a	FileE	T60a, input=FileA	0.146	171,986,004	159,949,288	0.075
MBP53	FileE	T60a, input=FileA	0.146	27,302,198	21,714,000	0.257
T60a	FileF	T60a, input=FileA	0.146	6,459,242,657	5,921,457,916	0.091
X110a	FileF	T60a, input=FileA	0.146	17,195,872,763	14,978,219,424	0.148
MBP53	FileF	T60a, input=FileA	0.146	2,729,345,361	2,113,442,000	0.291

Table 7.1.: SPECjvm2008 MPEGaudio benchmark: Bytecode-based performance prediction using calibration on platform T60a and *one* input file FileA

case (platform **X110a**, FileA), the bytecode-based performance prediction *over-predicts*, and the most likely reason for this is that the runtime optimisations performed by the execution platform have more time and possibilities to become effective since all other input files are larger than FileA. The slight underprediction experienced for FileA on platform **X110a** is not surprising since the platform **X110a** is the least powerful (in terms of CPU and memory) of the studied execution platforms.

The intentionally unoptimised choice of the calibration base for SPECjvm2008 follows the discussion in Section 6.1, where it was argued that the relocation and sizing scenarios should be based on one platform, and limited application input. A better prediction could be achieved by using more information for the calibration factor, e.g. by taking an average of the calibration factors of all six files on platform T60a, possibly weighted with file sizes. Additionally, the calibration factor could be parametrised over the file size, bitrate, or other properties, and such parametrisation could be made using the least-squares technique or other approaches.

To answer question **G1-Q2**, Table 7.2 presents the results of the performance prediction for the same platforms and input files as in Table 7.1, but the calibration factor is calculated as a simple average of the calibration factors for the six input files on platform T60a. The resulting calibration factor is 0.139 ($= \frac{0.146+0.145+0.137+0.135+0.137+0.134}{6}$), i.e. it has been computed as a simple average, without weighting the contributing calibration factors by the file size or other input file properties.

The six input files used for the calculation of the calibration factor can be seen as a training set, but the approach presented in this thesis does not memorise the input files and the predictions for them. Thus, these files can be reused as part of the validation set, to see how well they are predicted. Correspondingly, in Table 7.2, the prediction error value for the different input files on platform T60a are *not* zero, because the calibration factor has been used for them, too.

From Table 7.2, it can be seen the the prediction error (**G1-Q1-M1**) improves, and Table 7.3 summarises the improvements and computes **G1-Q2-M1**: in 15 out of 18 cases, the prediction accuracy improves (by at least 5 percentage points). In the three cases where the prediction accuracy decreases, it does so by less than 5 percentage points (marked in red in Table 7.3). Of these three cases, one case (platform T60a, FileA) was the "reference case" in Table 7.1, i.e. the prediction error was 0 because the calibration factor was computed from this single reference case. As expected, using more information for the calculation of the calibration factor increases prediction accuracy, but not very dramatically. Therefore, even if only one input file is used for the calibration factor calculation, the prediction accuracy is sufficient.

Following goal **G2**, it remains to be shown that that bytecode-based performance prediction has better prediction accuracy (i.e. a smaller prediction error)

Considered platform	Input	Calibration source	Calibration factor	Prediction [ns] calibrated	Measurement with JIT [ns]	G1-Q1-M1 (Prediction error)
T60a	FileA	T60a, input=FileA	0.139	53,148,917	55,793,369	-0.047
X110a	FileA	T60a, avg over inputs	0.139	141,859,557	163,657,995	-0.133
MBP53	FileA	T60a, avg over inputs	0.139	22,863,136	21,034,000	0.087
T60a	FileB	T60a, input=FileB	0.139	166,392,912	173,301,895	-0.040
X110a	FileB	T60a, avg over inputs	0.139	444,357,543	429,283,365	0.035
MBP53	FileB	T60a, avg over inputs	0.139	71,622,689	64,781,000	0.106
T60a	FileC	T60a, input=FileC	0.139	327,272,433	322,451,898	0.015
X110a	FileC	T60a, avg over inputs	0.139	878,634,442	808,278,066	0.087
MBP53	FileC	T60a, avg over inputs	0.139	139,064,900	110,904,000	0.254
T60a	FileD	T60a, input=FileD	0.139	1,520,029,804	1,478,855,755	0.028
X110a	FileD	T60a, avg over inputs	0.139	4,055,633,930	3,711,015,853	0.093
MBP53	FileD	T60a, avg over inputs	0.139	643,873,276	523,973,000	0.229
T60a	FileE	T60a, input=FileE	0.139	61,567,430	60,839,992	0.012
X110a	FileE	T60a, avg over inputs	0.139	163,834,342	159,949,288	0.024
MBP53	FileE	T60a, avg over inputs	0.139	26,008,150	21,714,000	0.198
T60a	FileF	T60a, input=FileF	0.139	6,153,092,399	5,921,457,916	0.039
X110a	FileF	T60a, avg over inputs	0.139	16,380,835,900	14,978,219,424	0.094
MBP53	FileF	T60a, avg over inputs	0.139	2,599,981,931	2,113,442,000	0.230

Table 7.2.: SPECjvm2008 MPEGaudio benchmark: Bytecode-based performance prediction using calibration on platform T60a and *all* input files

than the prediction based on CPU cycles. To see that this is indeed the case, consider Table 7.4. It illustrates performance prediction based on CPU cycles, where the T60a platform serves as the source of CPU cycle counts.

Note that the measurement is performed individually for each of the six input files, because the cycle-based prediction approach needs to measure each workload individually. This puts the prediction based on CPU cycles in a more favourable position, because input-specific timing behaviour of the considered algorithm's implementation is captured more precisely. The calculation of CPU cycle values on T60a is performed by multiplying the measured time (in nanoseconds) with 1.83, since the CPU frequency of T60a is 1.83 GHz.

Platform	T60a	X110a	MBP53	T60a	X110a	MBP53	T60a	X110a	MBP53
Input file	FileA	FileA	FileA	FileB	FileB	FileB	FileC	FileC	FileC
Prediction error when calibration is based on one file (FileA)	0.00%	-9.00%	14.10%	0.80%	8.70%	16.10%	6.50%	14.10%	31.60%
Prediction error when calibration factor is averaged across files	-4.70%	-13.30%	8.70%	-4.00%	3.50%	10.60%	1.50%	8.70%	25.40%
G1-Q2-M1 (Change of prediction errors, in percentage points)	4.70%	4.30%	-5.40%	4.80%	-5.20%	-5.50%	-5.00%	-5.40%	-6.20%

Platform	T60a	X110a	MBP53	T60a	X110a	MBP53	T60a	X110a	MBP53
Input file	FileD	FileD	FileD	FileE	FileE	FileE	FileF	FileF	FileF
Prediction error when calibration is based on one file (FileA)	7.90%	14.70%	29.00%	6.20%	7.50%	25.70%	9.10%	14.80%	29.10%
Prediction error when calibration factor is averaged across files	2.80%	9.30%	22.90%	1.20%	2.40%	19.80%	3.90%	9.40%	23.00%
G1-Q2-M1 (Change of prediction errors, in percentage points)	-5.10%	-5.40%	-6.10%	-5.00%	-5.10%	-5.90%	-5.20%	-5.40%	-6.10%

Table 7.3.: SPECjvm2008 MPEGaudio benchmark, bytecode-based performance prediction: Comparison of prediction errors between calibration based on 1 input file and on 6 input files for bytecode-based performance prediction

The predicted CPU cycle count for a given file has the same value on all three platform and corresponds to the measured CPU cycle count on T60a. The measured CPU cycle on **X110a** is obtained by multiplying the measured timing value (cf. 7.1) with 1.6; for **MBP53**, the multiplication factor is 2.8.

From Table 7.4, it can be seen that the predicted and measured CPU cycle counts on **X110a** and **MBP53** differ significantly. Comparing the prediction errors in Tables 7.1 and 7.4, it can be seen that for the large majority of the cases, the prediction errors are significantly higher when using performance prediction on the basis of CPU cycles. Since prediction based on CPU cycles *measures* the cycle counts for all six input files on platform T60a, the prediction error is 0.0 % for these cases, whereas the bytecode-based performance prediction exhibits a small but non-zero prediction error because it is based on only one input file, namely FileA.

289

Considered platform	Input	Calibration source	CPU cycles: Prediction based on measurement on Lenovo	CPU cycles: Measurement	Prediction error for CPU cycles
T60a	FileA	T60a, input=FileA	102,101,865	102,101,865	(0)
X110a	FileA	T60a, input=FileA	102,101,865	261,852,792	-0.610
MBP53	FileA	T60a, input=FileA	102,101,865	58,895,200	0.734
T60a	FileB	T60a, input=FileB	317,142,468	317,142,468	(0)
X110a	FileB	T60a, input=FileB	317,142,468	686,853,384	-0.538
MBP53	FileB	T60a, input=FileB	317,142,468	181,386,800	0.748
T60a	FileC	T60a, input=FileC	590,086,973	590,086,973	(0)
X110a	FileC	T60a, input=FileC	590,086,973	1,293,244,906	-0.544
MBP53	FileC	T60a, input=FileC	590,086,973	310,531,200	0.900
T60a	FileD	T60a, input=FileD	2,706,306,032	2,706,306,032	(0)
X110a	FileD	T60a, input=FileD	2,706,306,032	5,937,625,365	-0.544
MBP53	FileD	T60a, input=FileD	2,706,306,032	1,467,124,400	0.845
T60a	FileE	T60a, input=FileE	111,337,185	111,337,185	(0)
X110a	FileE	T60a, input=FileE	111,337,185	255,918,861	-0.565
MBP53	FileE	T60a, input=FileE	111,337,185	60,799,200	0.831
T60a	FileF	T60a, input=FileF	10,836,267,986	10,836,267,986	(0)
X110a	FileF	T60a, input=FileF	10,836,267,986	23,965,151,078	-0.548
MBP53	FileF	T60a, input=FileF	10,836,267,986	5,917,637,600	0.831

Table 7.4.: SPECjvm2008 MPEGaudio benchmark: Performance prediction on the basis of CPU cycle counts, measured on platform T60a (to use in **G2-Q1**)

Thus, the goal **G2** is achieved successfully, as shown by the values of metric **G2-Q1-M1** in Table 7.5. Note that **G2-Q1-M1**<0 % (i.e. the prediction error seams to decrease when using CPU cycles) *only* for those cases where the CPU cycles are based on measurements. As the six measurements are individually taken on the corresponding platform (T60a) and for the corresponding files (FileA through FileF), the value of **G2-Q1-M1** for these six cases corresponds to the prediction error (**G1-Q1-M1**) values in Table 7.1 for platform T60a and files FileA, FileB etc.

Instead of having to measure CPU cycle counts individually for each input file, it could be parametrised over the attributes of the input file, such as file size. However, as Table 7.6 shows, the correlation between filesize and the number of the CPU cycles is non-linear. Thus, parametrising CPU cycles over file size

Platform	T60a	X110a	MBP53	T60a	X110a	MBP53	T60a	X110a	MBP53
Input file	FileA	FileA	FileA	FileB	FileB	FileB	FileC	FileC	FileC
Prediction error for bytecode-based prediction with calibration based on one file (FileA)	0.0%	-9.0%	14.1%	0.8%	8.7%	16.1%	6.5%	14.1%	31.6%
Prediction error for prediction based on CPU cycle counts on platform T60a	0.0%	-61.0%	73.4%	0.0%	-53.8%	74.8%	0.0%	-54.4%	90.0%
G2-Q1-M1 (Increase of prediction error when using CPU cycles, in percentage points)	0.0%	52.0%	59.3%	-0.8%	45.1%	58.7%	-6.5%	40.3%	58.4%

Platform	T60a	X110a	MBP53	T60a	X110a	MBP53	T60a	X110a	MBP53
Input file	FileD	FileD	FileD	FileE	FileE	FileE	FileF	FileF	FileF
Prediction error for bytecode-based prediction with calibration based on one file (FileA)	7.9%	14.7%	29.0%	6.2%	7.5%	25.7%	9.1%	14.8%	29.1%
Prediction error for prediction based on CPU cycle counts on platform T60a	0.0%	-54.4%	84.5%	0.0%	-56.5%	83.1%	0.0%	-54.8%	83.1%
G2-Q1-M1 (Increase of prediction error when using CPU cycles, in percentage points)	-7.9%	39.7%	55.5%	-6.2%	49.0%	57.4%	-9.1%	40.0%	54.0%

Table 7.5.: SPECjvm2008 MPEGaudio benchmark: Comparison of prediction errors between bytecode-based performance prediction and prediction based on CPU cycle counts

would further decrease the prediction accuracy of the approach based on CPU cycle counts.

In the next sections, further algorithms and components will be studied to provide further evidence for the accuracy and superiority of bytecode-based performance prediction.

7.1.4.2. SPECjbb2005 Benchmark

The SPECjbb2005 benchmark computes and reports the throughput values for a number of configurations, with varying number of warehouses and different

Considered platform	Input	File size [byte]	Measurement [CPU cycles]	CPU cycles per byte
T60a	FileA	19,676	102,101,865	5,189.16
X110a	FileA	19,676	261,852,792	13,308.23
MBP53	FileA	19,676	58,895,200	2,993.25
T60a	FileB	61,741	317,142,468	5,136.66
X110a	FileB	61,741	686,853,384	11,124.75
MBP53	FileB	61,741	181,386,800	2,937.87
T60a	FileC	14,563	590,086,973	40,519.60
X110a	FileC	14,563	1,293,244,906	88,803.47
MBP53	FileC	14,563	310,531,200	21,323.30
T60a	FileD	729,600	2,706,306,032	3,709.30
X110a	FileD	729,600	5,937,625,365	8,138.19
MBP53	FileD	729,600	1,467,124,400	2,010.86
T60a	FileE	32,596	111,337,185	3,415.67
X110a	FileE	32,596	255,918,861	7,851.24
MBP53	FileE	32,596	60,799,200	1,865.23
T60a	FileF	3,257,258	10,836,267,986	3,326.81
X110a	FileF	3,257,258	23,965,151,078	7,357.46
MBP53	FileF	3,257,258	5,917,637,600	1,816.75

Table 7.6.: SPECjvm2008 MPEGaudio benchmark: Correlation between CPU cycle counts and file sizes

workload sizes. SPECjbb2005 is a multi-threaded benchmark with one master thread and one thread per warehouse instance (the minimum number of warehouses is 1). The number of concurrently active threads/tasks increases in several phases; the throughput values are reported for each phase.

The approach presented in this thesis predicts the execution duration of a method (i.e. of an internal action of a component) for the single-threaded execution. The tooling of the Palladio Component Model then uses this execution duration (expressed as CPU resource demand) and simulates the effect of context switching, resource contention and waiting times which occur during multi-threaded execution. This functionality of the PCM tooling has been validated in several contexts and for several applications [212].

Creating a PCM model instance which captures the inner concurrency of SPECjbb2005 is outside the scope of this thesis. Still, an attempt was made to analyse whether its performance can be predicted, by analysing the design and implementation of SPECjbb2005. The results if this analysis are described in the following.

In each phase, after completing some preparatory work, the master thread of SPECjbb2005 sets a control variable that will be queried periodically by each of the warehouse threads; after that, the master thread goes to sleep for a *fixed* timespan. The work performed by a warehouse thread is implemented in a `while` loop; in the head of the loop, the aforementioned control variable is queried.

Once the master thread wakes up, it sets the control variable to a value which means "finish warehouse work"; upon reading this value of the control variable, a warehouse thread wraps up. When the last of the warehouse threads finishes, the master thread continues, prints the statistics, persists them and then terminates. This strategy means that number of loop iterations can vary across threads, and that the number of loop iteration depends on the performance of the execution platform. In particular, this strategy means that if an *bytecode-instrumented* method is run in this time-constrained manner, the number of loop iterations will be lower than for an uninstrumented method, because the instrumented method contains more instructions and method calls.

Thus, to validate the performance prediction, the number of loop iteration must be equal between the uninstrumented case and the instrumented case. However, achieving this without breaking the semantics and the code structure of SPECjbb2005 does not seem possible. Therefore, it has been decided to identify the hottest spot of SPECjbb2005 (i.e. the method which has the greatest share of the execution time of SPECjbb2005), and to validate the performance prediction for it.

The hottest method of SPECjbb2005 is `create_random_a_string(int length_lo, int length_hi, short warehouseId)` in the class `spec.jbb.JBButil`. According to JProfiler [137], it accounts for ca. 7 % of the execution duration of the entire benchmark. At the same time, it is a rather short method, but it is invoked very often. Table 7.7 shows the results of bytecode-based execution duration prediction for the `create_random_a_string` method with parameter values 20, 20 and 1. Since the prediction was calibrated on platform T60a, the prediction error for that platform is 0 per definition and has no argumentative power, it is thus put in parentheses in Table 7.7.

Considered platform	Method input parameters	Calibration source	Calib. factor	Prediction [ns] calibrated	Measurement with JIT [ns]	G1-Q1-M1 (Prediction error)
T60a	20;20;1	T60a	0.161	1,375	1,375	(0.0)
X110a	20;20;1	T60a	0.161	3,063	2,345	**0.306**
MBP53	20;20;1	T60a	0.161	689	493	**0.397**

Table 7.7.: SPECjbb2005, hot spot `create_random_a_string`: results of bytecode-based performance prediction

It can be seen that the prediction is not as good as for SPECjvm2008 MPEGaudio benchmark, but still good enough for performance prediction at design time. The execution durations for platforms **X110a** and **MBP53** are overpredicted; note that the execution duration is so short that it measuring it using timer methods at runtime would incur substantial overhead. Still, bytecode-based performance prediction is better than prediction based on CPU cycles, as Table 7.8 shows. There, for platform **X110a**, the execution duration is significantly underpredicted, while a very significant overprediction can be seen for platform **MBP53**, with the prediction error being twice the size of that using bytecode-based performance prediction.

The performance prediction and error comparison have been performed for other values of the method input that 20, 20 and 1. As the prediction accuracy

Considered platform	Method input parameters	Calibration source	CPU cycles: Prediction based on measurement on T60a	CPU cycles: Measurement	Prediction error when using CPU cycles	G1-Q1-M1 (Prediction error when using bytecode)	G2-Q1-M1 (Difference between prediction errors)
T60a	20;20;1	T60a	2,516	2,516	(0)	(0)	(0)
X110a	20;20;1	T60a	2,516	3,752	-0.329	0.306	0.023
MBP53	20;20;1	T60a	2,516	1,380	0.823	0.397	0.426

Table 7.8.: SPECjbb2005, hot spot `create_random_a_string`: results of performance prediction based on CPU cycles, and values of **G2-Q1-M1**

differs only marginally, question **G1-Q2** can be answered with "yes", and values of metric **G1-Q2-M1** are not given here in full detail.

7.1.4.3. Linpack

The prediction errors for the Linpack benchmark are given in Table 7.9 (bytecode-based prediction) and Table 7.10 (prediction based on CPU cycle counts). As the Linpack benchmark has no inputs which could be varied and studied, **G1-Q2** does not need to be addressed. Here, too, bytecode-based prediction yields much better prediction accuracy, fulfilling goal **G2**: **G2-Q1-M1** is 0.560 for platform **X110a**, and 0.579 for platform **MBP53**.

Considered platform	Calibration source	Calibration factor	Prediction [ns] calibrated	Measurement with JIT [ns]	G1-Q1-M1 (Prediction error)
T60a	T60a	0.125	2,950	2,950	(0)
X110a	T60a	0.125	8,426	9,026	-0.066
MBP53	T60a	0.125	1,296	1,093	0.185

Table 7.9.: Linpack benchmark: results of bytecode-based performance prediction

Considered platform	Method input parameters	Calibration source	CPU cycles: Prediction based on measurement on T60a	CPU cycles: Measurement	Prediction error
T60a	20;20;1	T60a	5,399	5,399	(0)
X110a	20;20;1	T60a	5,399	14,442	**-0.626**
MBP53	20;20;1	T60a	5,399	3,060	**0.764**

Table 7.10.: Linpack benchmark: results of performance prediction based on CPU cycle counts

7.1.4.4. JFreeChart Linear Regression

The performance of the linear regression calculation in JFreeChart depends on the number of inputs. Table 7.11 shows the results of bytecode-based performance prediction for three different input sizes. One difference to the results of SPECjvm2008, SPECjbb2005 and Linpack is that the calibration factor is significantly lower: 0.082 as compared to 0.146, 0.161 and 0.125, respectively.

This observation can mean that either the studied algorithm is optimised more significantly by JIT and other JVM facilities, or that the inputs of the prediction (counting results or benchmarking results) contain imprecisions. However, the latter is unlikely as the prediction results in previous section were sufficiently precise.

It can be seen that the prediction error (**G1-Q1-M1**) increases as the input parameter size increases, which means that calculating the calibration factor on more than just one input value would be beneficial in this case. Furthermore, it can be seen that the prediction error is 30 % or larger (but less than 50 %) on platforms **X110a** and **MBP53**.

However, the prediction accuracy of the bytecode-based performance prediction is still better than that of based on CPU cycles, as the last column in Table 7.12 shows. Note that the prediction based on CPU cycles has the advantage that for the input sizes 2048 and 4096 on platform T60a, *measurements* are done to obtain the number of CPU cycles, whereas the accuracy of bytecode-based performance prediction is based on the calibration, which is performed only for the input size 1024 on the platform T60a.

Therefore, the values for T60a and input sizes 2048 and 4096 are negative in the last column in Table 7.12, and they correspond to the prediction errors for these entries in Table 7.11.

Considered platform	Algor. input	Calibration source	Calibration factor	Prediction [ns] calibrated	Measurement with JIT [ns]	G1-Q1-M1 (Prediction error)
T60a	1024	T60a, input=1024	0.082	13,438	13,438	(0)
X110a	1024	T60a, input=1024	0.082	33,043	24,960	0.324
MBP53	1024	T60a, input=1024	0.082	4,419	3,418	0.293
T60a	2048	T60a, input=1024	0.082	26,839	24,637	0.089
X110a	2048	T60a, input=1024	0.082	65,983	46,079	0.432
MBP53	2048	T60a, input=1024	0.082	8,823	6,701	0.317
T60a	4096	T60a, input=1024	0.082	53,643	47,034	0.141
X110a	4096	T60a, input=1024	0.082	131,864	90,238	0.461
MBP53	4096	T60a, input=1024	0.082	17,631	12,784	0.379

Table 7.11.: JFreeChart computation of linear regression: Results of bytecode-based performance prediction

7.1.4.5. Whetstone

Table 7.13 shows the performance prediction results for the Whetstone benchmark, based on the calibration performed on the T60a platform. All of 20 methods found in the used Java implementation have been instrumented, but not all of them are executed at runtime: the implementation contains methods to run it as an applet, while the performance prediction has been applied to the execution as a conventional Java program.

The recorded workload consists of 12,840,438 instructions of 56 different types and 10 method invocations (6 from Whetstone itself and 4 from the Java API). It

Considered platform	Algor. input	Calibration source and input	CPU cycles: Prediction based on measurement on T60a	CPU cycles: Measurement	Prediction error when using CPU cycles	G2-Q1-M1 (Difference between prediction errors)
T60a	1024	T60a; 1024	24,592	24,592	(0)	(0)
X110a	1024	T60a; 1024	24,592	39,936	-0.384	0.060
MBP53	1024	T60a; 1024	24,592	9,570	1.570	1.277
T60a	2048	T60a; 2048	45,086	45,086	(0)	-0.089
X110a	2048	T60a; 2048	45,086	73,726	-0.388	-0.044
MBP53	2048	T60a; 2048	45,086	18,763	1.403	0.086
T60a	4096	T60a; 4096	86,072	86,072	(0)	-0.141
X110a	4096	T60a; 4096	86,072	144,381	-0.404	-0.057
MBP53	4096	T60a; 4096	86,072	35,795	1.405	1.026

Table 7.12.: JFreeChart computation of linear regression: Results of performance prediction based on CPU cycles

can be seen from Table 7.13 that the prediction is again within 30 %, slightly overpredicting for plaform **X110a** and underpredicting for platform **MBP53**. Table 7.14 shows that once again, bytecode-based performance prediction is more precise that that based on CPU cycles.

Considered platform	Calibration source	Calibration factor	Prediction [ns] calibrated	Measurement with JIT [ns]	G1-Q1-M1 (Prediction error)
T60a	T60a	0.089	4,340,555	4,340,555	0.000
X110a	T60a	0.089	10,790,606	10,157,186	0.062
MBP53	T60a	0.089	1,483,198	2,039,000	-0.273

Table 7.13.: Whetstone benchmark: Performance prediction on the basis of bytecode instructions, calibration performed on T60a

Considered platform	Calibration source and input	CPU cycles: Prediction based on measurement on T60a	CPU cycles: Measurement	Prediction error
T60a	T60a	7,943,216	7,943,216	(0)
X110a	T60a	7,943,216	16,251,498	**-0.511**
MBP53	T60a	7,943,216	5,709,200	**0.391**

Table 7.14.: Whetstone benchmark: Performance prediction on the basis of CPU cycles, calibration performed on T60a

7.1.4.6. Summary and Discussion

As has been demonstrated in the course of this section, bytecode-based performance prediction is vastly superior to performance prediction based on CPU cycle counting.

Bytecode-based performance prediction has been successfully applied to other applications and algorithms as well. For example, in [201], cross-platform performance prediction for a custom-written implementation of the Lempel-Ziv-Welch compression algorithm was demonstrated.

Overall, it can be stated that bytecode-based performance prediction is well-suited for design-time performance prediction in environments where runtime optimisations have a great impact on the performance of bytecode-based applications.

7.1.5. Resource Demand Quantification: Goals, Questions and Metrics for Validation

The resource demand quantification leads to a certain runtime overhead, because the instrumented applications execute slower than their uninstrumented original. Resource demand quantification needs to be run only once for each input that should be covered by the prediction, and the resulting overhead is not a critical property of the approach presented in this thesis.

Still, the overhead should be assessed for completeness' sake, alongside other properties of the approach. For validating the instrumentation-based resource demand quantification (i.e. runtime counting of bytecode instructions and method invocations), the following goals, questions and metrics have been identified:

G3: show that the BYCOUNTER-reported counting results are precise

G3-Q1: do BYCOUNTER-collected counting results (instructions and methods) correspond to manually computed counting results ?

G3-Q1-M1: what is the deviation (in percent) of BYCOUNTER-collected counting results versus manually computed counting results?

G4: quantify the overhead resulting from the instrumentation

G4-Q1: what is the overhead of the instrumentation phase?

G4-Q1-M1: how long does it take to instrument an application (in seconds)?

G4-Q2: what is the influence on the execution time (i.e. runtime overhead)?

G4-Q2-M1: how large are the increases (in percent) for the execution duration when compared to the uninstrumented application?

G4-Q2-M2: how large (in percent) is the benefit of using basic blocks, when execution times of an application instrumented with the two different modes are compared?

7.1.6. Resource Demand Quantification: Validation Results

For addressing goal **G3** by answering question **G3-Q1**, several workloads were counted by hand and using the instrumentation-based approach developed in this thesis. The workloads included benchmark from JavaGrande, Linpack and Scimark benchmark suites [201]. The results did match in all cases (**G3-Q1-M1**=0 %), and the workloads are now used as test cases for the bytecode-counting implementation.

Note that the design of the instrumentation ensures that the counting results are recorded correctly if the method terminates (returns) correctly, and when a *checked* exception is thrown. Only if an unchecked (and thus not caught) runtime exception or error are thrown, the counting results are not reported – but in such a case, the program execution is disrupted, and the counting results would be of little value anyway.

Concerning goal **G4** (the overhead of the instrumentation), different work-loads of SPECjvm2008 benchmark have been measured. It should be stressed that SPECjvm2008 benchmarks function as test subjects (i.e. the applications to instrument), not as workload drivers to evaluate the execution platform.

During all measurements, the just-in-time compilation (JIT) was monitored and it was confirmed that instrumented methods are also JITted, although at different timepoints than their uninstrumented versions. The reported execution duration values for instrumented methods include not only the execution duration of the instrumented methods, but also the effort to store the counting results and to aggregate them: if method a() calls method b(), the final (evaluated) counts of method a() must include those of b().

Of SPECjvm2008 workloads, the overhead of MPEGaudio, Crypto.AES and Derby is discussed here because the three workloads are diverse and thus offer sufficient insight into the overhead of bytecode instrumentation. The overhead of the instrumentation is compared to a conventional profiler, and the benefits of using performance-invariant bytecode instruction sequences (PIBISes) are discussed for reducing the instrumentation-caused runtime overhead.

All measurements were performed on platform **MBP53**, which is notebook with 2.8 GHz Intel Core 2 Duo CPU equipped with 4 GB of 1067 MHz DDR3 main memory, and running Mac OS X 10.6.4 (which is a 64-bit OS). The 1.6.0_20 JVM provided by the manufacturer (Apple Corp.) was used, running in the default mode for 64-bit JVMs. This default mode is equal to -server, which allows JIT compilation and favours higher optimisation degree over short compilation time). The JVM was configured to use up to 768 MB of heap memory for running the executed workload, using the -Xmx768M flag.

For each of the workloads, the median value was obtained from 21 samples, measured using `java.lang.System.nanoTime()`) timer method of the Java platform API. This method has an accuracy of 1000 ns on the used platform and average invocation costs of 1031 ns, as obtained by The profiler used for finding hotspots was JProfiler 6.0.6, started from the Eclipse Helios (3.6) IDE, run without autotuning and with instrumentation-based timing value recording.

The values are reported for each of the three following scenarios:

- *uninstrumented*: execution duration of uninstrumented workload

- *instrumented*: execution duration of instrumented workload, the instrumentation was performed *without* basic block analysis

- *instrumented-enhanced*: execution duration of instrumented benchmark *using* basic block analysis

7.1.6.1. SPECjvm2008 MPEGaudio Benchmark

The MPEGaudio benchmark of SPECjvm2008 is concerned with decoding and encoding of different MPEG audio files, incl. MP3. The benchmark-own code is relatively simple, and it relies heavily on the JLayer library that comes with SPECjvm2008.

Thus, to make the instruction counts cover more non-API methods, we have also instrumented JLayer classes, which resulted in more than 200 instrumented methods. BYCOUNTER found that the class `javazoom.jl.decoder.huffcodetab` is very large, and instrumenting all of its methods would surpass Java classfiles' mandated maximum method length and classfile length. Therefore, only the `inithuff` method is *not* instrumented in the `javazoom.jl.decoder.huffcodetab` class, yet as that method is executed only once, the ramifications for the counting results are negligible.

Uninstrumented MPEGaudio runs in 5.03 seconds (median duration of 21 measurements, all six input files decoded, JIT enabled). Profiling it with JProfiler results in a median duration of 52.8 seconds. Instrumenting it (**G4-Q1-M1**) takes 25.2 seconds conventionally and 25.5 seconds when using basic blocks – the difference is minor. Conventionally-instrumented MPEGaudio runs in 139.1 seconds (**G4-Q2-M1**=$\frac{139.1}{5.03} = 27.65$), and such a high instrumentation overhead is explained by a very high number of instructions ($> 4 \cdot 10^9$) and methods ($> 2 \cdot 10^7$): for each reported method, the counting results need to be evaluated and stored.

Using instrumentation based on performance-invariant bytecode instruction sequences unfolds its potential for MPEGaudio: the instrumented workload executes in 48.02 seconds (**G4-Q2-M1**=$\frac{48.02}{5.03} = 9.55$), which means that the speedup **G4-Q2-M2** is slightly less than 3 (=$\frac{139.1}{48.02} = 2.897$). This comparison shows that the usage of basic blocks in BYCOUNTER is indeed beneficial for long-running, counting-heavy workloads.

It also shows that identifying and using performance-invariant bytecode instructions leads to an instrumentation overhead that is comparable to that of a conventional profiler. Of course, the information collected by a profiler is different (less detailed timing results, but information about memory usage), while the presented approach returns accurate bytecode instruction counts for each instruction type. Still, it can be argued that instruction-precise resource demand quantification is viable even for large applications and large number of instrumented classes and methods.

7.1.6.2. SPECjvm2008 Crypto.AES Benchmark

The Crypto benchmark of the SPECjvm2008 suite includes the AES workload, described in the SPECjvm2008 documentation as "encrypt and decrypt using the AES and DES protocols, using CBC / PKCS5Padding and CBC / NoPadding. Input data size is 100 bytes and 713 kB". Running AES workload in -Xint mode, the execution duration is 106.13 s, while running it in the default mode takes only 5.79 s: JIT compiles and optimizes over 100 methods, though only 4 of them are from SPECjvm2008 (all in the class spec.benchmarks.crypto.Util).

Profiling AES (JVM is running in the default mode) shows that JProfiler introduces some overhead: the execution now takes 6.54 s, i.e.

303

ca. 5.1 % more. Hotspot analysis of JProfiler results shows that ca. 80 % of execution time is spent executing the Java Platform API method `javax.crypto.Cipher.update(byte[])`, although it is executed only 192 times (in contrast to `java.io.ByteArrayInputStream.read`, which is executed 182,824 times, but contributes much less to the total execution time). JProfiler does not decompose the `update` method any further, and it is hard to recognise how far JIT has been applied to this hotspot: the method itself is not listed as JITted, but a number of its callees are.

Instrumenting AES means instrumenting all methods in classes `spec.-benchmarks.crypto.Util` and `spec.benchmarks.crypto.aes.Main`. This results in the instrumentation of 17 methods, and instrumenting in the conventional way (**G4-Q1-M1**) takes 1.2 s. When executing the conventionally instrumented AES, 56 counting results are recorded (which are spread across the 17 methods), and it takes 6.09 s (=**G4-Q2-M1**), i.e. only 5.1 % more than an uninstrumented run, and less than JProfiler overhead.

This low overhead is due to the very small number of recorded counting results, which also means that the counting results include some method of SPECjvm2008 packages which have not been instrumented. When 11 additional SPECjvm2008 classes used during AES execution are instrumented as well, the instrumentation takes 12 seconds (**G4-Q1-M1**), and 221 methods are instrumented. For the resulting instrumented bytecode, the execution takes 6.47 seconds (**G4-Q2-M1**), which is still a very modest overhead of 11.7 %.

Instrumenting two main classes of AES using PIBIS analysis takes 1.22 s (**G4-Q1-M1**), but (surprisingly) results in a marginally higher execution duration of the instrumented method than for conventional instrumentation, namely 6.10 s (**G4-Q2-M1**). This is due to the fact that currently, BYCOUNTER writes and reads the definition of PIBISes using persistent storage on the hard disk, which adds disk access times to the total image and has a disproportionally impact for AES, since the instrumented methods are executed only a few dozen times. Additionally, the reported PIBIS counts must be converted back into individual instruction counts, which causes some overhead. Thus, using PIBIS-based in-strumentation may not be warranted for the AES workload.

7.1.6.3. SPECjvm2008 Derby Benchmark

The Derby benchmark "uses an open-source database written in pure Java" [59]. Derby is "synthesized with business logic to stress the BigDecimal library", while the "focus of this benchmark is on BigDecimal computations (based on telco benchmark) and database logic, especially, on locks behaviour".

The uninstrumented execution of Derby takes 84.0 s to execute. The conventional instrumentation takes 3.76 seconds (**G4-Q1-M1**) as it instruments 6 classes and 66 methods in total. The conventionally instrumented workload takes 112 4 s , i.e. 33.8 % more than uninstrumented (**G4-Q2-M1**).

But after the workload has been instrumented using performance-invariant bytecode instruction sections (**G4-Q1-M1**=5.10 seconds), the execution of the benchmark takes 84.13 seconds (**G4-Q2-M1**), i.e. less than when using conventional instrumentation. Thus, **G4-Q2-M2**=$\frac{112.4}{84.13} = 1.34$. Note that after using performance-invariant bytecode instruction sections, the execution duration is very close to that of the uninstrumented method. The reason for this is the fact the major part of execution time is spent in the methods of the Java Platform API, which are not instrumented.

7.1.6.4. Summary

The instrumentation overhead depends on the number of instrumented methods and classes, and also depends on the uninstrumented methods' contribution to the performance of the considered component/application: since library methods (e.g. Java Platform API methods) are not instrumented in the presented approach, the instrumentation-induced runtime overhead does not impact their performance.

The identification and usage of performance-invariant bytecode instruction sequences has a significant impact in cases where the instrumented methods are executed a large number of times. For example, the instrumentation overhead for the SPECjvm2008 MPEGaudio benchmark was decreased by a factor of 2.89. The instrumentation-caused overhead ranges from a few percent to a factor of 9.55, i.e. to more than 850 %. The duration of the instrumentation phase itself is a few seconds, and and is rather negligible.

Overall, instrumentation-based quantification of bytecode resource demands has an acceptable overhead, which has the same magnitude as the overhead of commercial profilers, though the collected data differs between the presented approach and the used compilers. Since there exists no profiler with the capability to collect accurate bytecode instruction counts, the presented approach can be seen as a favourable solution, especially since it is application-agnostic and platform-independent. In particular, no specialised JVM is needed to run it, and no modification of the execution platform is required.

7.1.7. Execution Platform Benchmarking: Goals, Questions and Metrics for Validation

As explained above, bytecode instruction cannot be validated in isolation, since there is no manual approach for benchmarking bytecode instruction performance. Instead, it has already been validated in the context of bytecode-based benchmark *prediction*. Thus, this section is only concerned with benchmarking methods, in particular API methods.

To validate the novel approach for method and API benchmarking (and in particular its parameter-generating heuristics), the comparison between the method execution duration returned by the benchmark and the execution duration "in reality" would be the most preferable metric. However, there exists no alternative approach which would yield the precise execution duration of Java methods, and in particular the method of the Java platform API. This means that reference execution durations must be obtained by manual benchmarking.

The following goals, questions and metrics are used for evaluating method benchmarking:

G5: show that the benchmarking results are precise

G5-Q1: how different are the results of manual and automated benchmarking?

G5-Q1-M1: difference (in %) between results of manual and automated bench-marking

G6: show that the heuristics-based approach is helpful for generating method preconditions

G6-Q1: how many methods can be benchmarked successfully?

G6-Q1-M1: effective coverage (in %) of packages/classes/methods

G6-Q1-M2: reduction (in %) of initially thrown exception after heuristic-based handling of exception reasons

G7: quantify the benchmark generation effort

G7-Q1: how long does the generation and execution of the benchmarks take?

G7-Q1-M1: time (in seconds) for generation of preconditions and microbench-marks

G7-Q1-M2: time (in seconds) for warmup and execution of microbenchmarks

Once the implementation will be complemented by a facility to detect parametric performance dependencies, a fourth GQM element (detectability of linear parametric dependencies) can be added. Of course, detecting parametric performance dependencies requires more than one input data sample to possess different parameters and different invocation targets – this aspect will be addressed in future work.

All following measurements were performed on a computer with Intel Pentium 4 2.4 GHz CPU, 1.25 GB of main memory and Windows Vista OS running Sun JRE 1.6.0_03, in `-server` JVM mode.

7.1.8. Execution Platform Benchmarking: Validation Results

To evaluate **G5** (the precision of automated method benchmarking), the validation has to compare its results to results of *manual* benchmarking, since no "reference" performance values exist. As discussed above, manual benchmarks for methods are also not readily available and had to be created manually for the validation. To enable a fair comparison, method parameters (and also method invocation targets) must be identical in both cases.

Hence, automated benchmarking was done first, and method preconditions during its execution were recorded and afterwards reused during manual benchmarking. This comparison is an indicator of whether the microbenchmark generation mechanism (cf. Section 5.3.6.2) generates microbenchmarks which will produce realistic results w.r.t JIT etc.

The method `java.lang.String.substring(int beginIndex, int endIndex)` was selected as a representative API method, because it is performance-intensive and because its declaring class is used very often. This method was benchmarked with an invocation target `String` of length 14, `beginIndex` 4 and `endIndex` 8. Since the same technique (template) is used for all microbenchmark scenarios, the application of the approach (benchmark generation, warmup, prevention of overoptimisation and measurement setup) is comparable across the methods to benchmark. Consequently, it appears that it is not necessary to repeat this evaluation for all 66 public methods of the class `String`.

The result of manual "best-effort" benchmarking performing by an experienced MSc student with profound knowledge of the JVM was 9 ns for the above parameters. On the same execution platform, the benchmarking result of automated benchmarking (after removing GC-caused outliers) had the following distribution, as shown in Figure 7.2: 7 ns for 19 % of measurements, 8 ns: 40 %, 9 ns: 22.5 %, 10 ns: 9 %, 11 ns: 4 %, and 12 ns for 5.5 % of measurements. Thus, the average result from automated benchmarking is 8.555 ns, which constitutes a deviation **G5-Q1-M1** of 5 % compared to manual benchmarking. Note that a distribution and not just a single value is returned by automated benchmarking because several measurements are run, and because the JVM execution is interrupted by the OS scheduler to allow the OS other applications to use the CPU. Note that the measured time continues to run when the JVM is interrupted because wall-clock timers are used, given the insufficient accuracy of timer

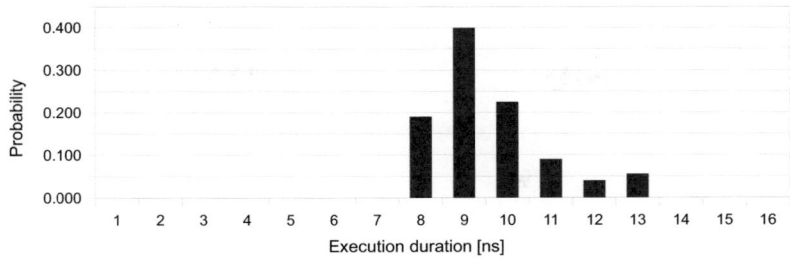

Figure 7.2.: Probabilities of benchmarked execution durations of the `java.lang.-`
`String.substring` method (parameter values: `beginIndex=4`, `endIn-`
`dex=8`; invocation target `String` length: 14)

methods which should provide thread CPU time and process CPU time (cf. Section 7.2.3).

Clearly, this is a promising result, but it does not give any guarantees for other
parameter values of `substring`, or for other API methods. At the same time,
it is seen is a strong argument for the generation mechanism described in Section 5.3.6.2. A more extended evaluation of the benchmark generation mechanism and its approach for realistic benchmarking (in particular the JIT-addressing
design) is planned for future work.

Concerning **G6** (benchmarking coverage), it should be noted that there exists
no alternative approach to compare against, so the reference coverage percentage is set to 100 %. Such a high coverage can be reached only by manual benchmarking, and only with extremely high effort – or by brute-force benchmarking
with extremely high effort.

The automated method benchmarking approach presented in this thesis can
benchmark *all* the methods for which correct (*appropriate*) and *sufficient* input
parameters are given. *Sufficient* means that the benchmarking method can be
executed *repeatedly* with the input parameters, i.e. more than just once.

For example, the `java.util.Stack` class contains the method `pop()` which
should be benchmarked, which means that the method must be called often

enough to account for timer resolution. If the `Stack` does not contain enough elements to call `pop`, an `EmptyStackException` is thrown – thus, the invocation target (the used `Stack` instance) must be sufficiently pre-filled. For non-static methods, correct invocations targets must also be found or provided externally.

If parameter generation is automated, the resulting *benchmarking coverage* (the percentage of methods for which parameters have been generated successfully) is less than 100 % because not all parameters are generated successfully. For the `java.util` package of the Java platform API, all 58 public non-classes have been considered for validation, which contain 738 public non-abstract methods. The automated approach can benchmark 645 out of 738 these methods, which is a success rate (**G6-Q1-M1**) of 87.4 %. Similarly, for the `java.lang` package, the presented approach can benchmark 790 out of 861 public non-abstract methods, which is a success rate (**G6-Q1-M1**) of 91.75%.

To see in detail where the automated benchmarking has a low coverage, we now consider those classes for which the effectiveness of heuristic-based parameter benchmarking was low (below 70 %).

In the `java.util` package, this was the case for only five classes, namely `java.util.Currency`, `java.util.Properties`, `java.util.Scanner`, `java.util.StringTokenizer` and `java.util.Timer`. The underlying issues are diverse and would require human parameter specification to work around. For example, creating instances of the `java.util.Currency` fails because currencies are identified by ISO 4217 currency codes, but the `Currency` does not declare static field from which the codes could be derived. Since automated creation of invocation targets fails, just the one static method can be benchmarked. The `java.util.Properties` class has methods with byte streams as input parameters, and automated parameter creation heuristics cannot handle such a case. The `java.util.Scanner` class requires special regular patterns (encoded as `Strings` or `java.util.regex.Pattern`), and such complex inputs need human intelligence. All but one methods of the `java.util.Timer` class require `java.util.TimerTasks` as parameters, so these methods couldn't be benchmarked. Finally, repeated invocation of the `nextToken()` method in the class `java.util.StringTokenizer` requires the considered `String` to have a large number of tokens, which currently is not ensured by automated benchmarking.

For the `java.lang` package, the coverage rate is under 70 % for three classes, namely: `java.lang.Object`, `java.lang.Runtime` and `java.lang.SecurityManager`. For the class `java.lang.Object`, five methods could not be benchmarked: `notify()`, `notifyAll()`, `wait()`, `wait(long)` and `wait(long, int)`. All of them throw an `IllegalMonitorStateException` because the thread executing these methods is not the owner of the monitor of the `Object` instance on which the five methods are executed. Such a precondition is very hard to fulfil in an automated way. The class `java.lang.Runtime` declares six convenience methods for execution of operating system commands, such as the method `exec(String[]` `cmdarray, String[] envp, File dir)`. All six methods check that a valid operating system command is passed in `cmdarray` (some methods also take the command as a single `String`). Such commands are of course platform-dependent, yet the approach presented in this thesis cannot guess the names of valid system commands and consequently a `SecurityException` is thrown. Of course, adding source code for operating system recognition and adding some valid commands is possible, but adding human intelligence to the benchmarking infrastructure would contradict the intention of measuring the success of *automated* parameter finding. None of the 34 methods declared in the class `java.lang.SecurityManager` could be executed since the creation of a `SecurityManager` invocation target is not trivial to automate. The only constructor declared by that class throws a `SecurityException` if a security manager already exists and its `checkPermission` method does not allow the creation of a new `SecurityManager` instance.

To validate the effectiveness of the heuristics for parameter generation (**G6-Q1-M2**), the number of runtime exceptions that were thrown *before* the heuristics were was applied has to be compared to the number of runtime exceptions that were thrown *after* heuristics were applied. Additionally, the duration of the entire process, including *initial* heuristic parameter generation (and including exception handling during parameter generation) needs to be considered. Since no reference implementation or approach that uses completely-random parameter generation (especially for object-typed parameters) was available, the validation cannot compare the effectiveness of the initial parameter generation to completely-random parameter generation.

The time values (**G7-Q1-M1** and **G7-Q1-M2**) given below include the effort needed for the generation of arguments and for the verification of the arguments by executing the method and observing whether runtime exceptions are thrown. The values also include the handling of runtime exceptions (if they occur), but excludes the time needed for storing the generated parameter values for subsequent reuse, because the storage process is currently not optimised (verbose XML serialisation is used). Also, it makes sense to concentrate on the core contribution of the presented approach, i.e. on the parameter-generating heuristics. The microbenchmark for which the parameters were created have been executed using the Java Reflection API.

For the methods in the package `java.lang`, 151 out of 204 thrown runtime exceptions could be successfully handled, resulting in a success rate **G6-Q1-M2** of 74.01 %. The parameter generation took about 259.44 seconds (i.e. **G7-Q1-M1** is less than 4.5 minutes).

For the methods in the package `java.util`, 95 out of 160 thrown runtime exceptions were handled successfully by the heuristics-based approach, resulting in a success rate **G6-Q1-M2** of 59.37 %. The parameter generation took about 168.67 seconds (i.e. **G7-Q1-M1** is less than 3 minutes).

The benchmarking duration (**G7-Q1-M2**) for the `java.util` was 107 minutes due to extensive warmup for inducing JIT optimisations. For the `java.util` package, the persisted input parameters (incl. parameters to create invocation targets) together with persisted benchmarking results occupy 1.15 GB on hard disk. In comparison, only 75 MB of data needed to be stored for the `java.lang` package.

The generation of individual microbenchmarks using bytecode engineering is very fast in comparison to parameter finding and the actual execution durations of the microbenchmarks. For the `String` method `contains(CharSequence s)`, the generation of the microbenchmark took less than 10 ms. The actual benchmarking took ca. 5000 ms: the microbenchmark runs were repeated until the predefined confidence interval of 0.95 was reached, which required 348 repetitions. In general, the number of repetitions depends on occurrence of outliers and on the stability of measurements, and it varies across methods and platforms.

A comprehensive validation of the total effort for automated benchmarking should be performed in the future, by comparing it to manual creation, execution and evaluation of microbenchmarks. However, to get a reliable comparison, a controlled experiment needs to be set up according to scientific standards, and this remains future work due to the size and complexity of APIs.

7.1.9. Summary and Discussion

Following the Goal-Questions-Metrics approach presented in Section 7.1.1, the bytecode-based cross-platform performance prediction and its constituents have been validated in Sections 7.1.3 through 7.1.8, using applications described in Section 7.1.2.

Validating the bytecode-based cross-platform performance prediction has shown promising results, and delivers better prediction accuracy than prediction based on CPU cycles. Despite a high abstraction and limited input, it has shown good prediction accuracy when varying the input of the predicted component service/application. In Section 7.1.4.6, the results of the validation of the bytecode-based performance prediction have been discussed in detail.

The prediction approach has been evaluated on execution platforms that differ significantly in hardware characteristics, operating system and other properties. A prediction error of less than 30 % is achieved in most cases, and a deviation of at most 50 % can be observed over all scenarios. In the overwhelming majority of the cases, the bytecode-based approach *overpredicts* the measured execution

313

duration. Overprediction is better than underprediction because for relocation and sizing scenarios, decisions made on the basis of overprediction result in (slightly) oversized systems, rather than undersized systems.

There are numerous ways in which the bytecode-based performance prediction can be enhanced in the future. It can be modified to use more information sources for the calibration, e.g. by performing calibration on several execution platforms rather than one; using multiple inputs instead of just one can also lead to a better prediction accuracy. In general, analyses of application similarity and calibrating the prediction on instruction sequences rather than on entire methods are further research directions.

An additional enhancement would be to consider the platform-independent and application-specific calibration as a function of the application input, rather than as a constant. This would allow the approach to address the effects observed in Section 7.1.4.1, where there is a certain dependency on the application input's size.

The prediction approach currently requires to perform resource demand quantification for each application input, and is not equipped to approximate resource demands for a "new" input on the basis of previously observed inputs. The derivation of parametric performance dependencies is solved by an automated approach described in [138], which calls the BYCOUNTER tooling to collect the counting results that are specific for one assignment of the input variables of the internal action. From several counting results of different assignments, the approach in [138] produces instruction/method counts expressed as *functions* parametrised over the input variables of the internal action. The prediction tooling developed in this thesis reads these functions and can evaluate them both symbolically and for concrete input values.

The validation of the resource demand quantification has shown that the overhead of the bytecode instrumentation depends on the instrumented application's architecture and implementation, and on the performance share of methods that are not instrumented by the presented approach (e.g. library method such as Java Platform API methods). It has also been shown that identifying and using performance-invariant bytecode instruction sequences speeds up the execution of the instrumented application. The speedup was as high as 2.89, as shown using an application for with the instrumentation-caused runtime overhead is particularly high.

Finally, the heuristics-based automated method and API benchmarking has been validated in Section 7.1.8, and shows promising results concerning the success of the heuristics, and the precision of the benchmarking results. Additional validation effort is needed to study representativeness of the generated parameters, and future work should add capabilities to detect parametric dependencies and performance-relevant parameters. Furthermore, sensitivity analysis should be investigated to study whether the parameter space of a given method can be divided into ranges with approximately constant performance within a given range.

In the next section, the approach from Chapter 3 for quality-driven selection of timer methods is validated.

7.2. Timer Evaluation

This section presents the evaluation of the the Java and .NET implementations of the TIMERMETER approach from Chapter 3. The evaluation is performed for the different timers methods described in Section 2.4, using the following platforms:

1. **MBP53**: a MacBook Pro notebook (model identifier "MacBookPro5,3") with 2.8 GHz Intel Core 2 Duo CPU (T9600), 4 GB of RAM, running Mac OS X 10.6.4 and Apple JVM (JDK 1.6.0_21).

2. **MBP62**: a MacBook Pro notebook (model identifier "MacBookPro6,2") with 2.66 GHz Intel Core i7 CPU, 8 GB of RAM, running Mac OS X 10.6.4 and Apple JVM (JDK 1.6.0_21).

3. **T60a**: a Lenovo notebook (T60, model ID 2007-49G) with 1.83 GHz Intel Core Duo T2400 CPU, 3 GB of RAM, running Windows 7 Professional (32 bit) and Oracle JVM (JDK 1.6.0_21)

4. **T400a**: a Lenovo notebook (T400, model ID 2767WD9) with 2.40 GHz Core 2 Duo P8600 CPU, 4 GB of RAM, running 64-Bit Windows 7 Professional and Oracle JVM (JDK 1.6.0._17)

5. **T400b**: same as T400a, but running Ubuntu 10 (Lucid Lynx) and Open-JDK Runtime Environment (IcedTea6 1.8.1 6b18-1.8.1-0ubuntu1, set to use OpenJDK 64-Bit Server VM build 16.0-b13, mixed mode)

6. **X110a**: an LG Electronics notebook (model X110-L.A7SAG) with 1.60 GHz Intel CPU (x86 Family 6 Model 28 Stepping 2), 1 GB of RAM, running Windows 7 Professional (32 bit) and Oracle JDK 1.6.0_21

7. **X110b**: same as **X110a**, but running Windows XP Professional SP3 (32bit) and Oracle JDK 1.6.0_17

8. **SAMSa**: a Samsung notebook with Intel Pentium M 1.73 GHz CPU, 1 GB of RAM, running openSUSE Linux with Kernel 2.6.34 incl. HPET support (kernel-reported HPET frequency 14,318,180 Hz, i.e. 1 tick every 69.8 ns) and Oracle JVM (JDK 1.6.0_20)

9. **SAMSb**: same as SAMSa, but running Windows XP Professional and Oracle JVM (JDK 1.6.0_21)

Mono 2.6.7 was installed on all platforms (except T400a, for which no installer is available). Additionally, .NET Framework 4.0 was installed on all platforms running Windows OS.

The studied timer methods include those provided by operating systems, Java and .NET Platform APIs, third-party libraries/tools, as well as Java methods that access hardware counters using assembler instructions in native methods. The following list recapitulates the abbreviations from Section 2.4, which are used in this section in the given, alphabetic order:

- CTCT is `java.lang.management.ThreadMXBean.getCurrentThreadCpuTime()`, a method which returns the calling thread's used CPU time in nanoseconds

- CTM is `java.lang.System.currentTimeMillis()`, a static wall-clock timer method with milliseconds as units

- CTUT is `java.lang.management.ThreadMXBean.getCurrent-ThreadUserTime()`, a method which returns only the time a thread has spent in user mode, not in system mode

- CPCT is `com.sun.management.OperatingSystemMXBean.getPro-cessCpuTime()` or `com.sun.management.UnixOperatingSystem-MXBean.getProcessCpuTime()`, depending on the JVM (see explanations on page 41 in Section 2.4.3)

- GAGE: from the GAGEtimer library, the method `getClockTicks()` in class `AdvancedTimer` is used

- HRC is `sun.misc.Perf.highResCounter()`

- JETM: the JETM library selects the "best" available timer using `bestAvailableTimer()` helper method of its class `EtmMonitorFactory`. The timer method used on the obtained timer class type/instance was `getCurrentTime()`.

- NANO is `java.lang.System.nanoTime()`, a static wall-clock timer method with nanoseconds as units

- QPC (`QueryPerformanceCounter()`) is the Windows API method returning values in ticks; the separate `QueryPerformanceFrequency()` method reports the update frequency of the counter used by the `QueryPerformanceCounter()` method.

- TSC is the Time Stamp Counter

- .DAT: .NET API's `DateTime.Now` structure in the `System` namespace

- .STO: .NET API's start/stop methods in the `StopWatch` (`System.Diagnostics` namespace)

To implement the algorithms from Chapter 3 for the .NET framework, C# was chosen as it is the most popular language for .NET – however, the language choice is not important, as the result of the compilation is CIL bytecode. The algorithms were developed and compiled using the Mono framework (Mono JIT compiler version 2.6.7) for x86 architecture, using the Monodevelop 2.4 IDE.

On Windows platforms, in addition to the two .NET timer methods described in Section 2.4.3, the algorithms from Chapter 3 were implemented for Win32 API method `QueryPerformanceCounter`. This native method is called from CIL bytecode using `System.Runtime.InteropServices` bridge facility offered by the .NET API. The update frequency of `QueryPerformanceCounter` is retrieved with a call to the native `QueryPerformanceFrequency` method. `QueryPerformanceCounter` serves as a comparison to the two API methods, and to study whether it is worthwhile to use "native" Win32 API where available.

The remainder of this section is structured as follows: Section 7.2.1 shows that stability testing is indeed an issue which requires testing by the end users, and proves that the Timestamp Counter (TSC) is not reliable. Section 7.2.2 studies the units of methods that return values in ticks, and shows that the duration of a given timer method's tick on a given platform can differ by a factor of more than 6, depending on the vendor of the bytecode-executing virtual machine. Section 7.2.3 addresses accuracy, invocation cost and invocation cost spread of timers. Section 7.2.5 shows that epochs are important for multi-threaded measurements. Section 7.2.6 presents the result of the unified timer quality metric and Section 7.2.7 concludes with a discussion of the obtained results and insights that have been won from them.

7.2.1. Stability and Monotonicity

All of the tested timers and timer methods were monotonic on all tested platforms, both in the single-threaded and in the multi-threaded cases (for multi-threading testing, up to 64 threads were started). However, the stability and reliability of some timers was unacceptable: for example, the Timestamp Counter

(TSC) exhibits jumps when the algorithm from Section 3.4 is run. In the following, these jumps and possible reasons for them are discussed.

Consider Figure 7.3, which is a reproduction of Figure 3.9 in Section 3.4.3 on page 110. The values on x axis in Figure 7.3 contain requested sleep times that are passed to `Thread.sleep` method (the values are converted to nanoseconds in Figure 7.3). The requested sleep times start at 20 ms and increase in steps of 10 ms up to and including 160 ms; for each value, 20 repetitions are made, resulting in a total of 300 measurements. The y-axis values are real sleep times measured with `System.nanoTime()` on platform **MBP53** (y-axis is labelled with "characterised timer" since the units of `System.nanoTime()` are known).

Making several measurements for one value of requested sleep time means that one value on the x axis can have several values on the y axis, and connecting them (line with round shapes in Figure 7.3) results in vertical stretches, for example at x=160 ms. The line with round shapes connects the *maximum* measured value of a given requested time with the *minimum* measured value of the next requested time.

Clearly, there is a strong linear correlation between *median* `nanoTime()` measurements and requested sleep times, the resulting line (shown in red in Figure 7.3 using square shapes, but hardly distinguishable from the line with round shapes) has a gradient of 0.9986 and a correlation coefficient of 0.9999 when outliers are removed.

In contrast, consider Figure 7.4 (which is a reproduction of Figure 3.10 in Section 3.4.3 on page 111), where the y axis contains the sleep times measured with TSC, *during the same run*. The used execution platform has a CPU frequency of 2.8 GHz, i.e. one CPU cycle takes $\frac{1}{2.8} \approx 0.557\ ns$).

In Figure 7.4, there seems to be no useful correlation between the requested and TSC-measured sleep times despite the almost-perfect correlation for `nanoTime()`-based measurements in Figure 7.3. The red line that appears in Figure 7.4 shows which values *should* appear when using TSC: its gradient is 2.8, since 1 ns corresponds to 2.8 CPU cycles on the used platform.

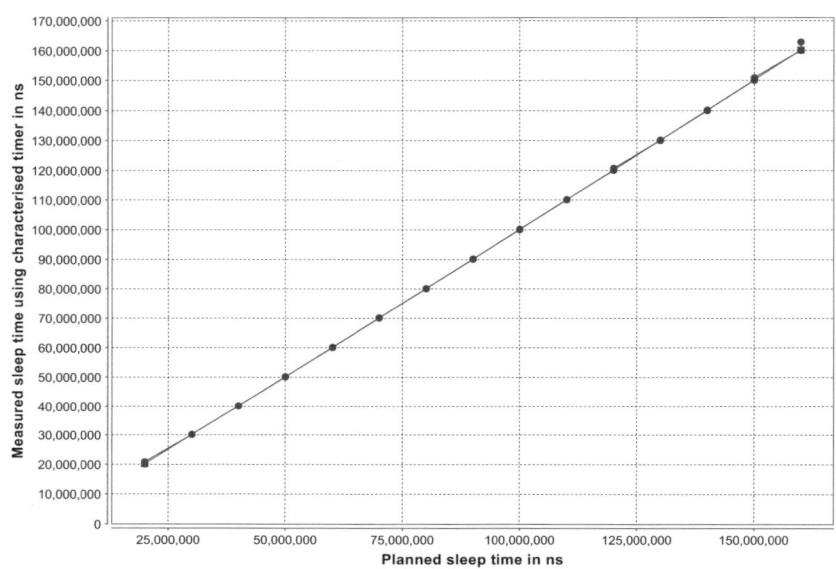

Figure 7.3.: Relation of requested sleep times (x-axis, in ns) to values measured with `nanoTime()` (y-axis, in ns) on **MBP53**

These results suggest that TSC is not a reliable, stable timer for measurements on this platform, but what are the reasons for it? And is it still possible to obtain the unit of TSC?

To answer these questions, the `Thread.sleep()` call has been replaced with a computationally intensive function, namely a Fibonacci function whose starting values and number of calculations can be parametrised. Then, the above experiment was repeated, and the problem size of Fibonacci calculation has been increased linearly. The results of the modified experiment are shown in Figure 7.5 and Figure 7.6. Additionally, Figure 7.7 shows the correlation between the `nanoTime()` measurements and TSC measurements.

The results in Figure 7.6 look better than Figure 7.4, but there are still jumps, although in a more systematic way. Note that the same jumps exist in Figure 7.5, and Figure 7.7 shows that there is an almost perfect correlation between

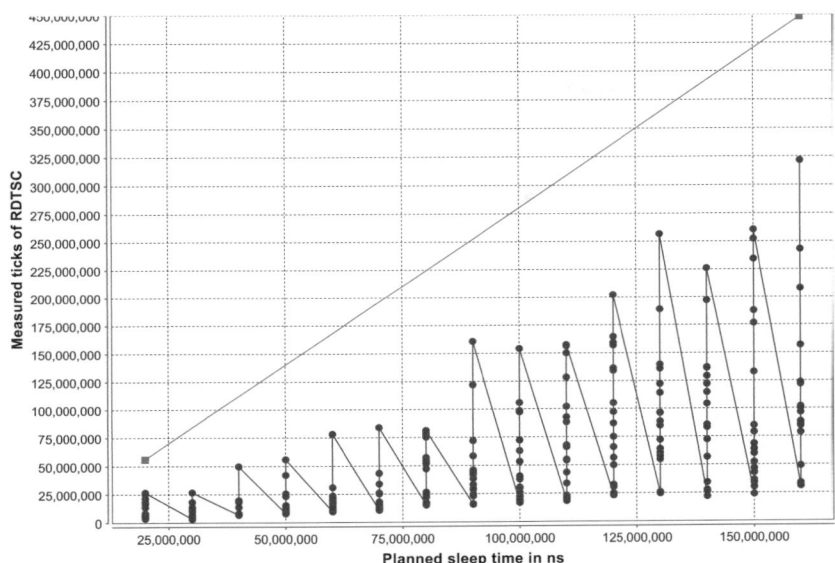

Figure 7.4.: TSC instability on **MBP53**: Zigzagged line with round shapes shows the relation between requested sleep times (x-axis, in ns) and values measured with TSC (y-axis, in ticks); straight line with two square shapes shows the number of CPU cycles (y-axis) corresponding to the requested sleep time (x-axis)

the `nanoTime()` measurements and `TSC` measurements. The jumps (and the height of vertical y "ranges" for a given value of x) mean that the Fibonacci computation for the same problem size takes different amounts of time (due to garbage collection, interruptions of the JVM by the OS, etc.) – note that the amplitude of y "ranges" increases as the problem size increases. At the same time, the TSC returns reliable measurements when `Thread.sleep` is no more used.

Thus, the thread scheduling seems to be the problem affecting TSC reading. To investigate this hypothesis, thread sleeping should be replaced with an operation that involves a different kind of thread scheduling. This effect was achieved by performing the Fibonacci computation in a parallel helper thread, and the results of the investigation are shown in Figure 7.8 and Figure 7.9. The

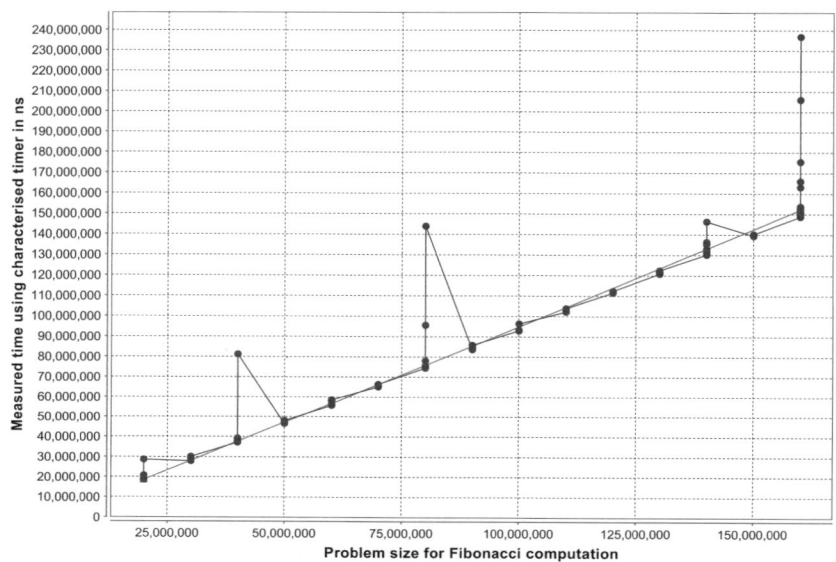

Figure 7.5.: Correlation of Fibonacci problem sizes and values measured with
nanoTime() on **MBP53**

nanoTime() and TSC measurements were taken in the main thread, not in the
helper thread; the main thread called join to wait until the helper thread com-
pletes.

It seems that Thread.sleep() causes problems, while starting and waiting
for threads does not; other techniques and calls for multi-threaded execution
(barriers, locks) have not been tested in the scope of this thesis. Still, the problems with Thread.sleep() have appeared on Linux and on Windows computers, for different JVMs and operating systems. No clear pattern could be
found, yet the application of the algorithms presented in this thesis can answer
the questions on the monotonicity and stability of a particular timer on a particular platform. As a conclusion, it can be said that TSC should be avoided in
multi-threaded scenarios if possible.

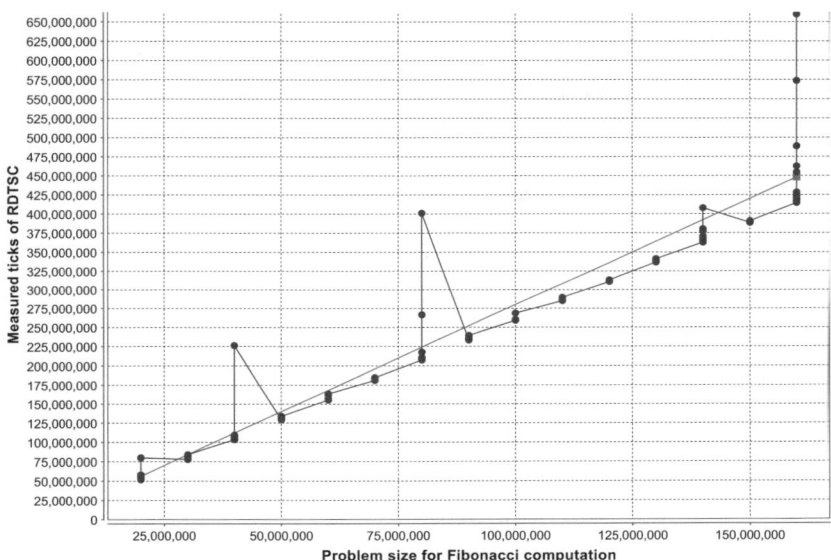

Figure 7.6.: Correlation of Fibonacci problem sizes and values measured with TSC

7.2.2. Units: Computing and Verifying

Most studied Java timer methods have a unit which is a time value (such as nanosecond or a millisecond), but there is an exception which returns its value in ticks, namely HRC (the method highResCounter in the class sun.misc.Perf). In the .NET API, both .DAT (DateTime) and .STO (StopWatch) have ticks as units, but with the advantage that either the tick duration is documented (100 ns for DateTime, at least for the official .NET implementation of Microsoft Corp.), or can be queried (for StopWatch). For the .NET API timer methods, it makes sense to check whether the tick duration in the alternative implementation (Mono) corresponds to the one specified in the official documentation provided by Microsoft Corp.

Additionally, some OS-provided timer methods and counter methods returns their values in ticks: QueryPerformanceCounter on Windows and

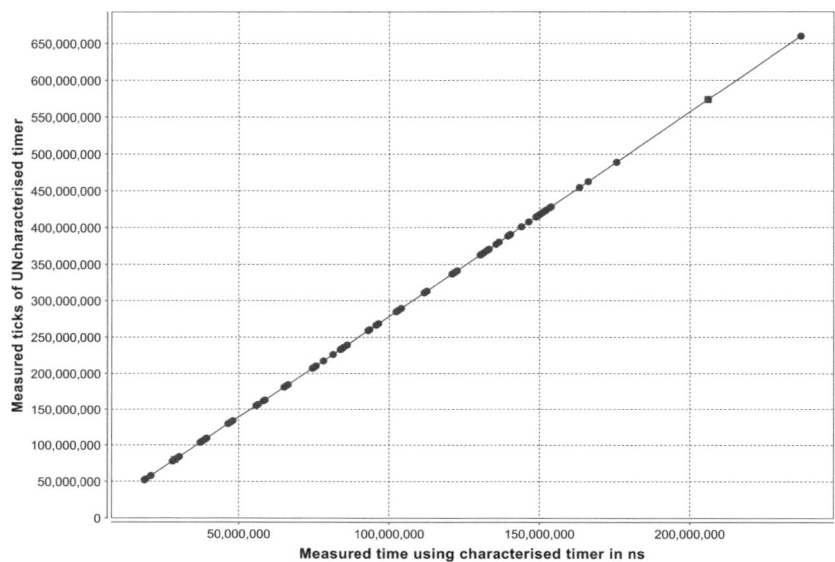

Figure 7.7.: Correlation of values measured with TSC and values measured with nanoTime for Fibonacci workload

gettimeofday on Linux (both provide methods to query the underlying update frequency). Finally, the duration of a Timestamp Counter tick needs to be quantified, as it varies across and as it is questionable whether it indeed is 1 CPU cycle.

Table 7.15 shows the results of unit value computation for the TSC timestamp counter and four timer methods (HRC, .DAT, .STO, QPC), on six different platforms. Cells marked n/a mean that the timer method is not available on a given platform. On **T60a**, two different JVMs (Oracle HotSpot and Bea JRockit) were used, but the comparison of the unit values did not reveal any differences.

There are several useful insights that can be gained from these values:

- the TSC unit is one CPU cycle on the studied considered platforms

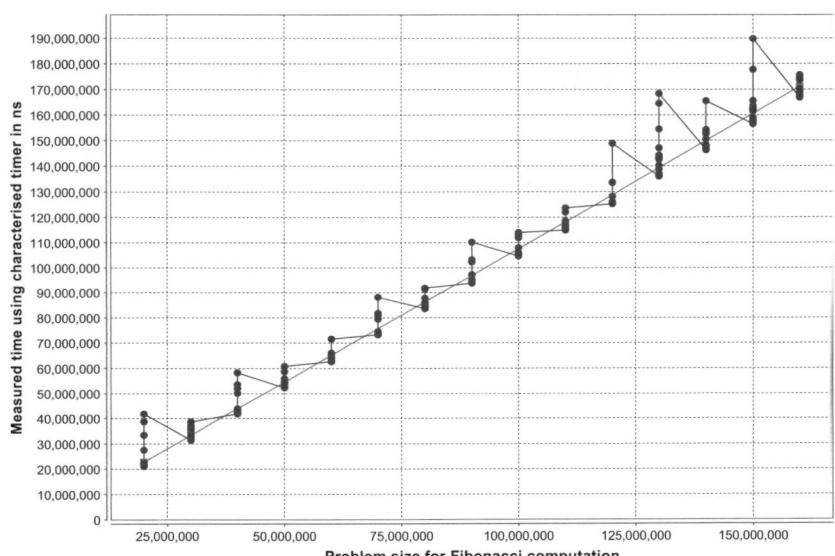

Figure 7.8.: Correlation of Fibonacci problem sizes and values measured with
nanoTime() when running Fibonacci workloads in a separate thread (master thread waits until completion of the started thread)

- when TSC is taken aside (due to multi-threading issues explained in Section 7.2.1), none of the timers has the best (smallest) units on *every* execution platform (the more important notion of acccuracy will be quantified in
  the next section)

- some units are the same on all studied platforms (TSC, .DAT), while others vary significantly (HRC, .STO), even on the same hardware (HRC on
  X110a/X110b and **SAMSa/SAMSb**)

- comparing the HRC unit values across platforms, it can be seen that their
  differences are up to three orders of magnitude (1 ns on **MBP53** vs. 1000 ns
  on **SAMSa**)

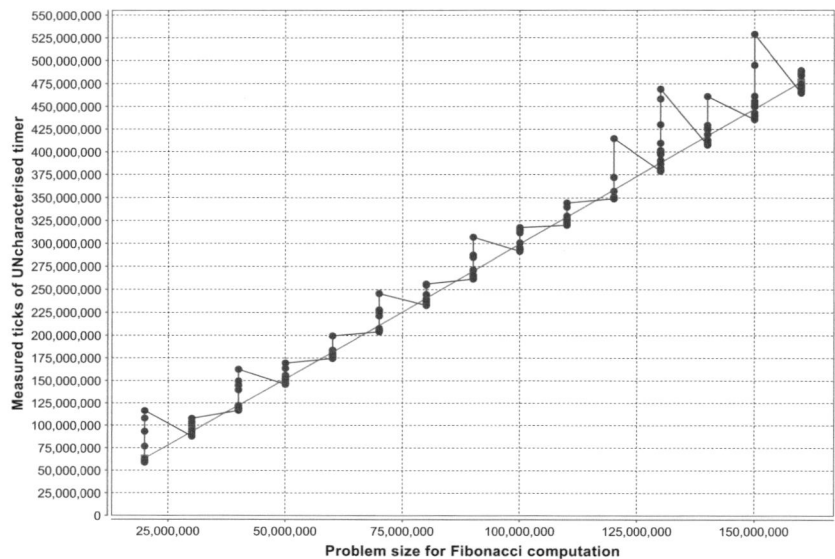

Figure 7.9.: Correlation of Fibonacci problem sizes and values measured with TSC when running Fibonacci workloads in a separate thread (master thread waits until completion of the started thread)

- for Windows platforms **T60a**, **X110a**, **X110b** and **SAMSb**, the timers HRC, .STO and QPC have the same unit value (560 ns, 279 ns, 640 ns and 279 ns, respectively); on Windows XP, the API-reported updated frequency of HRC and QPC (3,579,545 Hz) is the same for the studied platforms

- considering the API-reported frequency of HRC, one obtains 3,579,545 Hz for the **X110a** execution platform (which runs Windows XP) and 1,562,539 Hz on **X110b** (which runs Windows 7). These frequencies are returned independently of the JVM, and the latter frequency value is a few percent lower than $\frac{1}{1000}$ of the CPU frequency, which is 1.6 GHz: $\frac{1,562,539}{1,600,000} \approx 0.977$ – note that since this value is reported by the API and neither measured not changed by the presented algorithms, it is not subject to measurements errors

Timer	MBP53	T60a	X110a	X110b	SAMSa	SAMSb
TSC	0.357 ns ⋆	0.546 ns ⋆	0.625 ns ⋆	0.625 ns ⋆	0.578 ns ⋆	0.578 ns ⋆
HRC	1 ns	560 ns	279 ns	640 ns	1000 ns	279 ns
.DAT	100 ns	100 ns	100 ns	100 ns	100 ns	100 ns
.STO	100 ns	560 ns ♣	279 ns ♯	640 ns ◇	100 ns	279 ns
QPC	n/a	560 ns	279 ns	640 ns	n/a	279 ns

Table 7.15.: Units of tick-returning timers (Legend: ⋆: corresponds to 1 CPU cycle; ◇: 640 ns on .NET and 100 ns on Mono; ♣: 560 ns on .NET and 100 ns on Mono; ♯: 279 ns on .NET and 100 ns on Mono)

- the units of .STO (.NET's StopWatch) either match those of .DAT (DateTime) when the Mono is used, or match those of QPC (QueryPerformanceCounter) when the .NET framework is used

- on the same platform, the accuracy of .STO differs between .NET Framework and Mono Framework (it is important to highlight that this difference of the units does not mean that a particular VM is more favourable: it is the accuracy and the invocation cost that is deciding, and they will be addressed in the next section).

In the next section, the core quality properties of timer methods are studied, namely accuracy and invocation cost.

7.2.3. Accuracy, Invocation Cost and Invocation Cost Spread

Tables 7.16, 7.17, 7.18 and 7.19 show the values of quality attributes for eight different execution platforms. In the tables, "Accuracy" denotes accuracy (i.e. resolution), and "Cost" denotes the median invocation cost, i.e. the median execution duration of one timer method invocation. "Spread" denotes invocation cost spread, which was defined in Section 3.6 as the percentage of invocation cost values (samples) within ± 1 *accuracy* of the median invocation cost. A percentage value x % is shown as the floating-point value $\frac{x}{100}$, rounded to three decimal places.

If the accuracy of a timer is (much) larger than its invocation cost, TIMER-METER can only conclude that the invocation costs are between zero and one accuracy (cf. Section 3.2). Since this is the case for some methods (e.g. `getCurrentThreadCpuTime()`, which has a (declared) precision of 1 ns), an alternative way is needed to estimate the invocation cost. For the alternative invocation cost computation, a more precise timer is used (currently `nanoTime()`), and a large number of invocations to the considered timer is made and their *total* duration is measured.

With a (pessimistic) estimation that one invocation takes no less than 10 ns, and with the requirement that the imprecision introduced by `nanoTime()` should not account for more than 5% of the measured value, the minimum number of invocations to the considered timer method can be computed. The intermediate values returned by the considered method are used in such a way as to ensure that the invocations are not optimised away by the JVM, and the overhead of `nanoTime()` is subtracted. For .NET methods `.DAT` (`DateTime`) and `.STO` (`StopWatch`), the method itself is used instead of `nanoTime()`, after the accuracy has been quantified.

The timer method of GAGEtimer is not included in the following Tables, since it produced results that were absolutely identical to those of `nanoTime()`. A short inspection of the source code revealed that the timer class of GAGE checks for the availability of timers at initialisation, and selects either `nanoTime()` if available, and otherwise either `QueryPerformanceCounter` (if running on Windows), or the method `currentTimeMillis()` (as the "fallback default"). When `nanoTime()` is available, GAGE incorrectly states that the timer accuracy is 1 ns, while TIMERMETER returns the correct, platform-specific accuracy.

Table 7.16 provides the data for a comparison of how different the quality attributes are for the studied methods when two platforms with *different hardware* but the *same operating system* are used.

In detail, the following observations can be made in Table 7.16:

- the well-known Java Platform API timer method NANO (`System.nanoTime()`) is significantly less precise than HRC

Timer	Execution platform MBP53			Execution platform MBP62		
	Accuracy	Cost	Spread	Accuracy	Cost	Spread
CTCT	1,000 ns	2,232 ns ⋆	0.999	1,000 ns	1,756 ns ⋆	0.983
CTM	1 ms	101 ns ⋆	1.000	1 ms	70 ns ⋆	1.000
CTUT	1,000 ns	2,204 ns ⋆	0.999	1,000 ns	1,643 ns ⋆	0.984
HRC	3 ticks ⋄	51 ticks ⋄	0.778	1 tick ⋄	36 ticks ⋄	0.648
JETM	1,000 ns	92 ns ⋆	1.000	1,000 ns	70 ns	0.999
NANO	1,000 ns	97 ns ⋆	1.000	1,000 ns	70 ns	1.000
PCT	10,000,000 ns	2,298 ns ⋆	1.000	10,000,000 ns	1,712 ns ⋆	1.000
QPC	n/a	n/a	n/a	n/a	n/a	n/a
TSC	10 ticks ◇	63 ticks ◇	0.630	3 ticks ◇	33 ticks ◇	0.529
.DAT	10 ticks ♣	2 ticks ♣	1.000	10 ticks ♣	2 ticks ♣	1.000
.STO	10 ticks ♣	2 ticks ♣	1.000	10 ticks ♣	2 ticks ♣	1.000

Table 7.16.: Accuracy, Invocation Cost and Invocation Cost spread for execution platforms **MBP53** and **MBP62** (**Legend**: ⋆: invocation cost measured using `System.nanoTime()` method; ◇: 1 tick = 1 CPU cycle $=\frac{1}{2.8}$ ns ≈ 0.357 ns; ⋄: 1 tick = 1 ns; calculated from frequency; ♣: 1 tick = 100 ns; ■: 1 tick = 1000 ns.)

- the Java Platform API timer method PCT (`getProcessCpuTime()`) has a very bad accuracy (10 ms), making it useless for fine-granular measurements

- NANO and CTCT/CTUT on **MBP53** show the same accuracy, but their invocation costs differ by a factor of more than 22; the situation for **MBP62** is identical.

- CTCT/CTUT and PCT have similar intentions (obtaining measurements that are not wall clock time values), but their accuracies differ by 3 orders of magnitude on **MBP53**.

- The most accurate timer method on platform **MBP53** is NANO, the least accurate is CTM.

- NANO and JETM exhibit almost identical quality attributes, making JETM useless on **MBP53** (same situation can be observed on **MBP62**).

329

- for **MBP62**, despite lower CPU frequency than **MBP53**, the accuracy is better (or equal) and invocation cost is smaller for *all* studied methods.

- the invocation cost spread is better on **MBP53** than on **MBP62**

Table 7.17 shows the evaluation results for two different operating system running on the same hardware (in fact, the same computer was booted with the two different operating systems). Note that this allows different conclusions compared to the measurements in Table 7.16, as detailed below. Additionally, Table 7.17 shows the result for Linux and Windows XP operating systems, while Table 7.16 contained the result for Mac OS X.

Timer	Execution platform SAMSa			Execution platform SAMSb		
	Accuracy	Cost	Spread	Accuracy	Cost	Spread
CTCT	10,000,000 ns	30,000 ns ⋆	0.999	15,625,000 ns	896 ns ⋆	1.000
CTM	1 ms	1,267 ns ⋆	1.000	16 ms	127 ns ⋆	1.000
CTUT	10,000,000 ns	8,000 ns ⋆	1.000	15,625,000 ns	889 ns ⋆	1.000
HRC	1 ◇	1,283 ns ⋆	0.999	1 ■	5 ■	0.999
JETM	69 ns	1,047 ns	0.695	279 ns	1396 ns	0.996
NANO	69 ns	978 ns ⋆	0.736	279 ns	1,876 ns	0.997
PCT	10,000,000 ns	555 ns ⋆	1.000	15,625,000 ns	476 ns ⋆	1.000
QPC	n/a	n/a	n/a	1 ■	5 ■	0.999
TSC	3 ◇	86 ◇	0.994	3 ◇	84 ◇	0.896
.DAT	10 ♣	10 ♣	0.996	156,250 ♣	8 ♣	1.0
.STO	1 ♣	11 ♣	0.944	1 ♣	5 ♣	0.992

Table 7.17.: Accuracy, Invocation Cost and Invocation Cost spread for execution platforms **SAMSa** and **SAMSb** (**Legend**: ⋆: invocation cost measured using System.nanoTime() method; ◇: in ticks, 1 tick = 1 CPU cycle $=\frac{1}{1.73}$ ns ≈ 0.578 ns; ◇: in ticks, 1 tick = 1,000 ns; calculated from frequency; ♣: in ticks, 1 tick = 100 ns; ■: in ticks, 1 tick = $\frac{1}{3579545}$ s ≈ 279 ns.

Table 7.17 shows the results for one computer with two different operating systems: **SAMSa** uses openSUSE Linux with Kernel 2.6.25, while **SAMSb** uses Windows XP Professional. An analysis of the data in Table 7.17 shows that

SAMSa has better values for accuracy and invocation than SAMSb in all of the cases except HRC.

In detail, the following observations can be made in Table 7.17:

- CTCT on **SAMSa** is 10,000 less accurate than on **MBP53** or **MBP62**, and even less accurate on **SAMSb**; the same is true for CTUT

- CTM is much less accurate on Windows (**SAMSb**) than on Linux (**SAMSa**); the same is true for NANO/JETM and even for .DAT

- converting the accuracy of .DAT to nanoseconds leads to the same value as for PCT, CTCT and CTUT

- on **SAMSb**, converting the accuracy of CTM to nanoseconds returns a value that is very close to that of .DAT, PCT, CTCT and CTUT – it seams plausible that the implementation of CTM performs rounding (or truncating) internally – see Section 3.2.3 for the discussion of these effects

- on the other hand, HRC is more accurate on **SAMSb** than on **SAMSa**

- invocation cost spread is better on **SAMSb**, except for the TSC

Table 7.18 shows the evalution results for two different versions of Windows OS (both 32 bit), and provides further insights in addition to Tables 7.16 and 7.17:

- the majority of accuracy values is equal for the two operating systems – surprisingly, the (newer) Windows 7 on **X110a** has worse accuracy for HRC and NANO/JETM

- invocation cost spread is generally smaller on **SAMSb** than on **SAMSa**

- it appears that for CTM, the obtained accuracy (15 ms) is again a "victim" of method-internal rounding, so CTM is based on the same counter (or OS method) as CTCT, CTUT, PCT and .DAT.

Timer	Execution platform X110a			Execution platform X110b		
	Accuracy	Cost	Spread	Accuracy	Cost	Spread
CTCT	15,625,000 ns	2916 ns ⋆	1.000	15,625,000 ns	2289 ns ⋆	1.000
CTM	15 ms	379 ns ⋆	1.000	15 ms	423 ns ⋆	1.000
CTUT	15,625,000 ns	2653 ns ⋆	1.000	15,625,000 ns	2850 ns ⋆	1.000
JETM	640 ns	2560 ns	0.629	279 ns	1676 ns	0.796
HRC	1 ◇	3 ◇	0.851	1 ■	7 ■	0.963
NANO	640 ns	1920 ns	0.728	279 ns	1676 ns	0.797
PCT	15,625,000 ns	2778 ns ⋆	1.000	15,625,000 ns	1562 ns ⋆	1.000
QPC	1 ◇	3 ◇	0.991	1 ■	9 ■	0.991
TSC	12 ◇	108 ◇	0.859	12 ◇	108 ◇	0.858
.DAT	156,250 ♣	23 ♣	1.000	156,250 ♣	8 ♣	1.000
.STO	1 ◇	3 ◇	0.991	1 ■	13 ■	1.000

Table 7.18.: Accuracy, Invocation Cost and Invocation Cost spread for execution platforms **X110a** and **X110b** (**Legend**: ⋆: invocation cost measured using `System.nanoTime()` method; ◇: in ticks, 1 tick = 1 CPU cycle $=\frac{1}{1.6}$ ns = 0.625 ns; ◇: in ticks, 1 tick = $\frac{1}{1562539\ Hz}$ = 640 ns (i.e. calculated from frequency); ♣: in ticks, 1 tick = 100 ns; ■: in ticks, 1 tick = $\frac{1}{3579454\ Hz}$ = 279 ns (i.e. calculated from frequency).)

Table 7.19 again compares two operating system on one hardware configuration, but makes use of different hardware and operating systems than the previous Tables in this section. For the execution platforms **T400a** and **T400b** in Table 7.19, TSC was not evaluated because no 64 bit versions of the libraries for reading TSC could be obtained. For **T400b**, .DAT and .STO had to be skipped as well because the Mono framework installation failed for the used Linux operating system.

Rounding/truncating have been mentioned several times over the course of this section, and are discussed here to provide some additional clarifications. Windows-specific `QueryPerformanceCounter()` method has a precision that depends on the frequency with which the counter is updated; the Windows method `QueryPerformanceFrequency()` returns 3,579,545 (with Hz as unit) on **SAMSb** as the update frequency on both CPUs, i.e. the (rounded) time spent between the updates is 279.4 ns. Notably, this counter update frequency does not correlate in any way with the CPU frequencies. The value of 279.4 ns is identified by the presented approach as 279 (i.e. rounded with merely

	Execution platform T400a			Execution platform T400b		
Timer	Accuracy	Cost	Spread	Accuracy	Cost	Spread
CTCT	15,600,100 ns	581 ns $\star$	1.000	10,000,000 ns	19,879 ns $\star$	1.000
CTM	15 ms	64 ns $\star$	1.000	1 ms	767 ns $\star$	1.000
CTUT	15,600,100 ns	545 ns $\star$	1.000	10,000,000 ns	17,939 ns $\star$	1.000
HRC	1 $\diamond$	3 $\diamond$	0.991	1 ■	2 ■	0.993
JETM	427 ns	1283 ns $\star$	0.822	70 ns	700 ns	0.578
NANO	427 ns	1283 ns $\star$	0.824	70 ns	700 ns	0.682
PCT	15,600,100 ns	375 ns $\star$	1.000	10,000,000 ns	255 ns $\star$	1.000
QPC	1 $\diamond$	5 $\diamond$	0.993	n/a	n/a	n/a
TSC	-	-	-	-	-	-
.DAT	156,000 ♣	8 ♣ $\diamond$	1.000	-	-	-
.STO	1 $\diamond$	18 $\diamond$	1.000	-	-	-

Table 7.19.: Accuracy, Invocation Cost and Invocation Cost spread for execution platforms **MBP53** and **T400** (**Legend**: $\star$: invocation cost measured using System.nanoTime() method; $\diamond$: invocation cost measured using .STO method and chaining several .DAT invocations; $\diamond$: in ticks, 1 tick = 427.73 ns; calculated from frequency (2,337,919); ♣: in ticks, 1 tick = 100 ns; ■: in ticks, 1 tick = 1000 ns.)

0.143 % accuracy loss). Also note the similarity of accuracy values for Linux-running platforms: 70 ns for NANO/JETM on **T400b** vs. 69 ns for NANO/JETM on **SAMSa**. This accuracy corresponds to the (rounded) time interval between two successive updates of the HPET timer, whose update frequency the Linux kernel reports to be 14,318,180 Hz. Hence, this interval is $(14,318,180 Hz)^{-1} \cong 69.841\ ns$. On Windows XP, HPET is known but not used – the results of this section show that none of the analysed platforms running Windows 7 used HPET, either.

HRC, the unofficial sun.misc.Perf counter found in the JDK is not documented in the Java platform API, and does not bring any advantage except on Mac OS X (**MBP53**, **MBP62**). Its accuracy is identical to that of nanoTime() or often even worse that it (**SAMSa**).

7.2.4. Effect of Just-in-Time compilation on Timer Methods

In Java, when a timer method is used frequently, it makes sense to perform a warmup by invoking the method often enough for the JIT compiler to recognise it as popular and hot. Given that the largest invocation cost in Tables 7.16 through 7.19 is still less than 20 μs (CTCT for **T400b**), a warmup that invokes the time method 50,000 times takes less than a second, and should be performed before measurements are started.

Still, information on whether the timer method has already been optimised during the warmup phase is needed, and so is the information on whether additional optimisations are to be expected. Unfortunately, such "feedback" about optimisations is not available from today's JVMs – the only way to monitor JIT compilation from a running application is to parse the JIT logging output on the command line, or to use non-portable command-line switches [213] that create a logging file. Still, tools for *online* parsing of the logging file are not available, and the JMX-provided interfaces do not contain method-level information. Therefore, it must be studied empirically whether JIT affects timer methods, and how much warmup is *really* needed to see the effects.

Figure 7.10 shows the invocation cost of the sun.misc.Perf.highResCounter() method, which has been called 100,000 times on platform MacBookPro. The obtained values have been partitioned into 1000 bins (in the order of measurement), and the median value of each bin's 100 values have been calculated and are plotted in Figure 7.10. The partitioning into bins leads to a reduced number of samples to plot, and blends out the outliers.

It can be seen that initially, bin median of the invocation cost *increases* (until ca. 48th bin), and than decreases *in several steps*. The latter fact means that a warmup phase should not be aborted after the first durable decrease, since a stable value is reached after only after ca. 55,000 calculation. Since one calculation needed two timer method invocations, more that 110,000 timer method invocations are needed until the optimisation appears to be finished.

The initial decrease to ca. 79 ticks (after ca. 4600 measurements, i.e. 9200 invocations) can be caused by the JIT compilation or other optimisation that is applied to a separate method which is called/reused by the considered timer method. Only after the third decrease, the invocation cost reaches a stable value

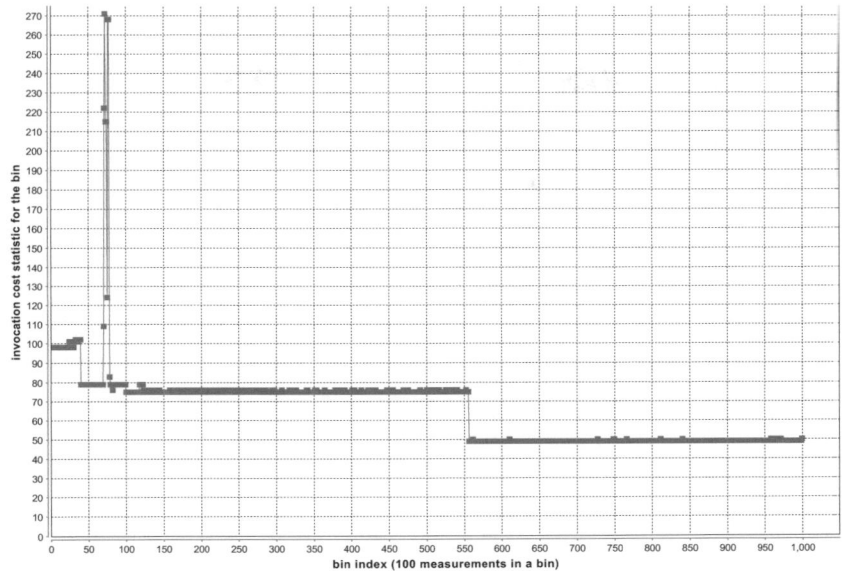

Figure 7.10.: Warmup influence on the invocation cost of `sun.misc.Perf.highRes-Counter`: medians of bins (each bin contains 100 measurements)

of 51 ticks. Similar behaviour (multiple optimisation "steps") have been observed for other methods, e.g. `System.nanoTime`. Finally, this observation confirms the fact that the optimisations performed by the JVM are highly dynamic, and rules of thumb such as "invoke a method 16,000 times to trigger JIT compilations" do not always apply.

7.2.5. Epochs and Maximum Measurable Time Intervals

Understanding epochs and maximum measurable time interval lengths is essential for dependable performance measurements, in particular in multi-threaded applications, measurements that span multiple processes, or when a thread migrates across cores or processors on a multi-core/multi-CPU execution platform. Similar to Lamport clocks [214] and vector clocks [215, 216] which are concerned with clock synchronisation and event ordering across physical machines, timing measurements that are performed by several threads/processes *on the same machine* need the security that the events and timestamps are properly ordered across threads and processes. It is usually assumed that for thread and processes running on the same machine, the last epoch (i.e. the last point in time when the value of a considered counter/timer was 0) is the same.

To study whether this is indeed the case, the last epoch must be calculated. Calculating epochs only makes sense for wall-clock timer methods with a constant *linear* increase rate, and not for timer methods such as getCurrentThreadCpuTime() for which the values may not increase linearly. Note that while the values of timers such as TSC usually increase proportionally to wall-clock time, the proportion may be linearly dependent on the CPU frequency and thus change over time, violating the requirement for a *constant* linear increase rate.

Table 7.20 shows the results of evaluating timer method epochs and maximum measurable times, performed on different computers, operating systems, and JVMs. Note that .NET timer methods were not studied, because the epochs of *DateTime* are explicitly specified and known, while the StopWatch is start by explicitly calling a method. For both .NET timer methods, the maximum measurable time interval is in excess of hundred years.

To study whether the epochs depend on process start time, thread start time, machine start time etc., the algorithms described in Section 3.5 were implemented as threads. Thus, when one (running) thread instance starts another thread instance of the algorithm, it is possible to study whether the epochs are dependent on the thread start time. To evaluate whether the epochs are dependent on the *process* start time, the Java launcher was invoked several times, so that the process which runs the algorithm implementation would be different, and feature different start times. Finally, for timer method implementations where the last epoch of the timer was identical to the startup time of the computer, the computer was restarted to study whether the epoch is indeed dependent on this time value.

MBP53 (2.8 GHz Intel Core 2 Duo CPU, Mac OS X 10.6.4, Apple JDK 1.6.0_18)					
Timer	Value type	Unit	Epoch assignment	Last / next epoch	Overflow Period and MMT
TSC	tick	1 tick = 1/2.8 ns	set at **thread** start time	thread start / ca. 208.91 years after thread start	ca. 208.91 years and ca. 104.45 years
CTM	long	1 ms	fixed across processes and threads	Jan 1st, 1970 / Jul 22nd, 2554	ca. 584.94 years and ca. 292.47 years
NANO	long	1 ns	fixed across processes and threads	Jan 1st, 1970 / Jul 22nd, 2554	ca. 584.94 years and ca. 292.47 years
HRC	tick	1 tick = 1.0 ns	set at **process** start time	process start / ca. 584.94 years after process start	ca. 584.94 years and ca. 292.47 years

T60a (1.83 GHz Core Duo CPU, Windows 7 Pro 32 bit, Oracle JDK 1.6.0_21)					
Timer	Value type	Unit	Epoch assignment	Last / next epoch	Overflow Period and MMT
TSC	tick	1 tick = 1/1.83 ns	set at last computer power up	last power up / ca. 319.64 years after last power up	ca. 319.64 years and ca. 159.82 years
QPC	long	1 tick = 560 ns	last computer restart	last computer restart / ca. 327,525 years after last epoch	ca. 327,525 years and ca. 163,763 years
NANO	long	1 ns	set at **process** start time	process start time / ca. 584.94 years after last epoch	ca. 584.94 years and ca. 292.47 years
HRC	tick	1 tick = 560 ns	set at **process** start time	process start time / ca. 327,525 years after process start	ca. 327,525 years and ca. 163,763 years

Table 7.20.: Epochs and MMT (maximum measurable time interval) of different timer methods, measured on two different platforms

From Table 7.20, several conclusions can be drawn beyond the basic observation that the measurable time intervals are sufficient in all cases. For the TSC (timestamp counter), it can be seen that it is not suitable for multi-threaded measurements on **MBP53**, at least on multi-core computers: the epoch depends on the start time of a thread, and measuring across threads needs complex synchronisation, e.g. by passing the TSC value of the calling thread to the called thread. The HRC (high-resolution counter) and System.nanoTime() can also cause problems in concurrent programs, as their epochs on some machines depend on the start time of the called process. Overall, the epoch behaviour must be evaluated on a machine-to-machine basis, e.g. using the algorithms presented in this thesis. Alternatively, timer methods with fixed epochs (such as `System.currentTimeMillis()`) can be used as reference point.

7.2.6. Unified Timer Quality Metric

The unified timer quality metric assembles quality attributes accuracy and invocation cost into one metric, and takes into account the invocation cost spread, as described in detail in Section 3.6. Table 7.21 summarises the values for this metric for the timers studied in Section 7.2.3, computed using Formula 3.19.

Platform	Timer	Quality in %	Frequency CPU [GHz]	Accuracy [CPU cycles]	Invoc. cost [CPU cycles]	Invoc. cost spread
MBP53	CTCT	**18.86**	2.800	2,800.00	6,249.60	0.9990
MBP53	CTM	**12.89**	2.800	2,800,000.00	282.80	1.0000
MBP53	CTUT	**18.88**	2.800	2,800.00	6,171.20	0.9990
MBP53	HRC	**54.08**	2.800	2.80	47.60	0.7780
MBP53	JETM	**25.95**	2.800	2,800.00	257.60	1.0000
MBP53	NANO	**25.82**	2.800	2,800.00	271.60	1.0000
MBP53	PCT	**9.43**	2.800	2,800,000.00	6,434.40	1.0000
MBP53	.DAT	**24.01**	2.800	2,800.00	560.00	1.0000
MBP53	.STO	**24.01**	2.800	2,800.00	560.00	1.0000
T400b	CTCT	**6.22**	2.400	24,000,000.00	47,709.60	1.0000
T400b	CTM	**10.85**	2.400	2,400,000.00	1,840.80	1.0000
T400b	CTUT	**6.29**	2.400	24,000,000.00	43,053.60	1.0000
T400b	HRC	**19.60**	2.400	2,400.00	4,800.00	0.9930
T400b	JETM	**21.67**	2.400	168.00	1,680.00	0.5780
T400b	NANO	**23.54**	2.400	168.00	1,680.00	0.6820
T400b	PCT	**9.62**	2.400	24,000,000.00	612.00	1.0000

Table 7.21.: Unified quality metric values for timer methods on platform **MBP53** (see Table 7.16) and **T400b** (see Table 7.19)

Several observations can be made on the basis of Table 7.21. The best timer method across the two platforms is HRC (high-res counter) on platform **MBP53**, while its quality on platform T400a is significantly lower. The worst timer method across the two platforms is CTCT (`getCurrentThreadCpuTime()`) on platform T400a, since it has a very low accuracy and very high invocation costs.

The quality metric developed in this thesis captures even fine differences between timer methods: for example, consider CTCT and CTUT on platform T400a. The value of the metric is different (6.22 % vs. 6.29 %) since the invocation cost is different, even though the accuracy is same for both timer methods and it is significantly larger than the invocation cost. The visibility of this difference is the consequence of metric design decisions outlined in Section 3.6.4.

Overall, the new unified metric allows the users to select the most suitable timer method on a given platform and across platforms.

7.2.7. Summary and Discussion

In this section, a validation of the TIMERMETER approach from Chapter 3 has been performed on a wide range of execution platforms. The TIMERMETER approach defined quality metrics for selecting timer methods, and introduced algorithms to quantify the values of these metrics. Thus, it allows developers and performance engineers to perform accurate timing measurements by selecting an accurate, low-overhead timer for a given execution platform.

First, it was demonstrated how the approach identifies unreliable and unstable timer methods, such as TSC on Linux platforms. Afterwards, units of methods which return values in ticks rather than in timing values were computed and verified. The effects of warmup and Just-In-Time compilation were studied in Section 7.2.4, and the epochs were computed and discussed in Section 7.2.5.

The results of quantifying the accuracy of timer method have lead to several interesting observations. For example, we have demonstrated that the widely used `nanoTime()` Java platform API timer method performs differently than expected, and is far from being precise down to a nanosecond. In the best case, `nanoTime()` has an accuracy of only 69 ns (e.g. on SAMSa, see Table 7.17) while in the worst case (on Mac OS X platforms), the accuracy is merely 1000 ns.

Additionally, the invocation cost overhead of `nanoTime()` is between 70 ns (MBP63 platform in Table 7.16) and 1876 ns (SAMSb platform in Table 7.17). With these large differences, obtaining accurate measurements becomes not only a question of choosing a timer methods, but also the question of choosing an execution platform. The presented approach is perfectly suited for this task, as it considers timer methods as black boxes and does not require an investigation of their implementation.

A further interesting observation is the difference between quality metric values for the same hardware but different operating systems. For example, on one of the considered computers, the accuracy of the `nanoTime()` method is four times better under Linux than under Windows (and the invocation cost is also significantly smaller).

The presented approach does not require modifications of the execution platform, and it can also be easily ported to other object-oriented or procedural languages. It is applicable to any kind of absolute and relative timer, independent of the underlying hardware or software stack. For example, the two timer methods provide by the API of the .NET execution platform have also been evaluated by implementing the TIMERMETER approach for them, and the results have been reported.

To make timer method comparisons simpler and to allow better comparisons across execution platforms, a new unified metric has been introduced. This metric combines accuracy, invocation costs and stability of timer methods into one value in the range $[0.0, 1.0]$ (larger values are better), and it accounts for different CPU clock speeds across execution platforms. The metric calculation has been carefully designed to reflect even small differences between timer method quality values, and being a single value, it can be interpreted by users as a range between 0 % and 100 %.

We have assumed that the accuracy of a timer method is stable over time, i.e. the accuracy (resolution) does not change over the course of several timer method invocations. This is a very basic requirement that is needed by any measurements, not only by TIMERMETER. In the course of evaluation, we have not encountered a setup where this assumption was violated. Interferences (such as garbage collection) will produce measurement outliers (i.e. longer time intervals than expected), which are recognised as such and filtered out.

Researchers and developers benefit from using TIMERMETER when they need to obtain accuracy and invocation cost of timer methods. This is often the case while performing reliable and statistically sound measurements, for example in microbenchmarking and during fine-granular measurements.

We have evaluated the applicability and the benefit of our approach using a Java implementation of TIMERMETER, and provide an extensive discussion of the obtained results. In the evaluation, we applied TIMERMETER to the timer methods provided by the Java SE platform API and additionally other timers accessible from Java, including hardware and software timers, as well as to third-party timing tools.

Chapter 8.

Related Work

In this chapter, related work is presented and compared to the contributions of this thesis. Section 8.1 describes work related to identifying and quantifying quality attributes for timer methods and performance indicators. Section 8.2 assesses related work on resource demand estimation. Section 8.3 studies related approaches for benchmarking the JVM. Section 8.4 presents related work for performance prediction. Section 8.5 addresses modelling of resources and the execution platforms.

8.1. Timer Methods

In [38], Buble et al. denote imprecise timing information as the first cause of imprecision in CORBA benchmarking. They also state that in their experience, the RDTSC (read Timestamp Counter) instruction is "a good source of timing information on the Intel platforms". However, they do not quantify the accuracy or other quality attributes of timers, and seem not to have experienced the reliability issues described in this thesis.

Books on performance measurement, evaluation and benchmarking (e.g. [36], [37]) discuss the importance of timer accuracy for quantifying the errors in measurements. However, these books do not provide algorithms for *computing* the accuracy or other quality metrics of counters, timers or timer methods. Also, the role of the timer method invocation costs is not discussed and no platform-specific data is provided.

Language-specific books also consider this topic. In "Java Performance Tuning" [162], Shirazi states that "[java.lang.]System.currentTimeMillis() can take up to half a millisecond to execute" (p. 15), but does not explain the origins of this (rather imprecise) statement, and no other timer methods of the Java platform API are discussed. As the 2nd edition of [162] is from 2003, newer methods such as `java.lang.System.nanoTime()` are not discussed at all. The same is true for [163], which was published in 2000.

In the "Effective Java" book [217], Bloch states that "for interval timing, always use [java.lang.]System.nanoTime in preference to [java.lang.]System.currentTimeMillis. System.nanoTime is both more accurate and more precise, and it is not affected by adjustments to the system's real-time clock" (p. 276). Also here, it is not explained how this conclusion was reached, and no concrete values are given.

In the remainder of this section, we describe further related work in a top-down manner, from application-level approaches, over third-party tools, virtual machines and operating systems down to hardware.

In [39], Holmes provides an overview of clocks, timers and scheduling events accessible from Java, but does not provide any reusable means to obtain precise characteristics of timer methods. For example, he states (in 2006) that "typically, a Windows machine has a default 10 ms timer interrupt period, but some systems have a 15 ms period". At the same time, our measurements in 2008 on a machine running Windows XP on a Intel dual-core processor show that the accuracy of Java's `nanoTime()` is better than a *micro*second, which means that "better" timers are used by the JVM in newer versions.

In [30], Meyerhoefer describes time measurements from and within Java on a variety of operating systems and platforms. He computes the accuracy of `currentTimeMillis()` in Java using an algorithm that does not consider the effects of the timer invocation cost and hence would not be applicable to the `nanoTime()` timer method or other fine-granular timers where the invocation costs are larger than the accuracy. He also does not account for the effects of just-in-time compilation.

In [40], Danzig and Melvin describe how to measure time intervals that are shorter than the precision of available timers (in their case, the precision corresponds to the accuracy of the hardware clocks they use). In [40], the authors assume that the clock accuracy/resolution (i.e. timer resolution) is known, and disregard the cost of timer invocations. They compute the number of measurements needed to achieve a given confidence level for a given number of significant digits, using statistical techniques and approximations. This thesis presents an approach to compute the timer precision on which [40] relies.

In [41], Beilner describes a stochastic measurement technique and corresponding statistical evaluation that are applied to sub-accuracy operations in a distributed, message-based system; however, Beilner has to guess the (smallest) duration of the operations to be measured. In [33], Lambert and Power build on [40] and [41] to obtain platform-independent timings of Java Virtual Machine bytecode instructions, using the RDTSC (read time stamp counter) instruction of the Intel Pentium processors. However, they also do not try to obtain the accuracy or the invocation cost of RDTSC calls.

In [105], Browne et al. introduce PAPI, a "portable programming interface for performance evaluation on modern processors". The purpose of the PAPI project is to "specify a standard application programming interface (API) for accessing hardware performance counters". However, PAPI does not offer any means to query the accuracy or the invocation cost of the timer methods it provides. Similar interfaces to hardware or operating system timers are PCL [106], JETM [107] and GAGEtimer [108], but none of them provides information on both accuracy and invocation costs.

8.2. Runtime Counting of Executed Bytecode Instructions and Method Invocations

In [218], Collberg et al. perform an empirical study of static properties on more than 1000 Java programs. In their study, they found that 98 % of methods had a method size of 699 bytes or less and contained no more than 299 instructions. This results indicate that officially specified method code length restriction (65536 bytes) does not present a critical obstacle for instruction-inserting instrumentation performed by the counting approach.

In [219], Cooper et al. describe ProfBuilder, a package for rapidly building Java Execution Profilers. However, ProfBuilder does not distinguish individual Java bytecode instruction types, and it is not capable of recording instruction parameters.

JOIE [220, 221] (Java Object Instrumentation Environment) is a framework for automatic program transformation at bytecode level. It is similar to ASM and BCEL (and precedes those by a few years), but JOIE, too, does not offer the instruction counting functionality – it is a tool which could be employed to build the instruction-counting approach presented in this thesis. However, ASM has been used instead of JOIE due to better performance, larger community and higher degree of documentation.

Unlike work that is concerned with static shape of Java programs (also called *structural* and *architectural* shape), this thesis is interested in dynamic (i.e. *runtime*) shape of Java programs. Research on the static shape of Java programs (e.g. [222]) is usually not concerned with (runtime) performance; sometimes (e.g. in [223]), the performance ramifications of decisions at architectural and implementation level are discussed (but not quantified). Deriving performance models from software architecture specifications has been researched extensively [21, 224], but the resulting approaches still have to perform estimation or to measure the performance of models' elements at runtime. Therefore, the remainder of this section only considers *runtime* (dynamic) analysis of program performance.

InsECTJ [225] is an open-source, GUI-driven customisable generic instrumentation framework for collecting dynamic information within the Eclipse IDE. It leverages bytecode instrumentation using the BCEL library, and allows users to define won probes and instrumentation tasks. However, it does not support counting bytecode instructions, and its overhead is not quantified. Additionally, the *requirement* to use a GUI means that a human user must interact with InsECTJ using an instance of Eclipse, whereas the approach presented in this thesis can be run in a headless way, by specifying a JVM agent as the bytecode-instrumenting entity.

JMT (Java Modelling Tools [226]) is an open-source tool suite of applications developed by Politecnico di Milano, and it claims to offer "a complete framework for performance evaluation, system tuning, capacity planning and workload characterization". It offers a simulator (with GUI) for Queueing Network Models, a tool for MVA (Mean Value Analysis) and other facilities. However, it requires performance data to be collected as input (the input format can be defined by the JMT user), and the data collection is not part of the tool suite. In contrast to JMT, the approach presented in this thesis focuses on performance data collection and performance prediction, none of which is covered by JMT.

Bytecode instruction counts can be considered as a dynamic bytecode metric. In [227], a collection of other metrics for Java bytecode is presented, but that collection does not include execution counts for individual bytecode instructions and method invocations.

Existing approaches for dynamic (runtime) counting of Java bytecode instructions and method invocations can be grouped into three categories, according to the technology they rely upon:

(a) using monitoring/reporting interfaces provided by the JVM

(b) by instrumenting the JVM or its API-implementing library

(c) by instrumenting the actual application bytecode or source.

For case **(a)**, different interfaces are explicitly exposed by JVMs, such as JVMTI [136], which must be programmed in a native language. These interfaces are used by standalone Java tools and profilers, such as Intel VTUNE [228]. In general, profilers measure resource usage and need manual supervision and interpretation. In contrast to that, BYCOUNTER obtains exact counts of executed instructions without human supervision of the counting process.

Since Java 6, direct access to individual bytecode instructions with Java-own means is possible only with JVMTI – for this, execution of bytecode must be single-stepped, substantially slowing down bytecode execution. JVMTI is not a mandatory part of the JVM standard, and many virtual machines (such as Jikes RVM [229]) do not implement JVMTI at all. Hence, JVMTI is not suitable as a *portable* basis for platform-independent bytecode counting when compared to bytecode instrumentation.

In category **(b)**, two parts of a JVM must be differentiated: the bytecode interpreter with its components and the JVM's Java API implementation, which consists of (partially platform-specific) Java classes. Instrumenting the first part means dealing with native (non-Java) code or binaries, which is generally a complicated, both platform-specific and JVM-specific task. Instrumenting the API implementation means instrumenting Java bytecode or source code of a very large number of Java classes. For both JVM parts, commercial JVMs usually do not provide the source code.

JVM instrumentation is done for replaying the behaviour of multi-threaded Java programs, for example in [230] and similar approaches; however, only high-level constructs and not bytecode instructions or method invocations are considered. Vertical profiling approaches such as [231], [232] or [233] also use JVM instrumentation, and only consider high-level events, too. JRAF / FERRARI [234] instruments the entire Java API, but it could not be obtained for evaluation. The available documentation shows that it does not offer counting of individual bytecode instructions and method invocations, as its instrumentation maintains only one counter for all bytecode instructions. Furthermore, FERRARI captures JVM-specific calling context trees and not an expandable "flat" view as BYCOUNTER does.

To instrument bytecode, the Java API itself does not provide any means, but only methods to read/load already instrumented bytecode. Instead, external frameworks for bytecode engineering (such as ASM [114] or SOOT [235]) can be used, as they offer rich APIs for analysing and modifying bytecode. However, they do not include bytecode-counting functionality or instrumentation templates.

For case **(c)**, the actual application code must be instrumented and then executed by the JVM. This approach is used in BYCOUNTER. Generic frameworks for bytecode manipulation, such as SOOT [235], do not offer the functionality provided by BYCOUNTER, they serve as tools to *implement* this functionality. For example, the ASM framework [114] was used for BYCOUNTER.

Aspect-oriented bytecode-analysing frameworks such as in [236] do not provide the instruction-counting functionality itself, but merely offer a different way to implement instrumentation when compared to ASM or other bytecode engineering frameworks.

In [237], Arnold and Ryder present a framework for reducing the runtime overhead of instrumented code, by using an elaborate sampling-based technique. Their approach is applied to Java bytecode using custom extensions to a particular JVM (Jalapeno), and works by maintaining one uninstrumented and one instrumented version of the program, and switching between the two. Using adaptive feedback and by adding edges between the flow control elements of instrumented and uninstrumented code, the latter is used as much as possible, since it incurs no additional overhead. The approach is evaluated using two instrumentation scenarios (call-edge recording and field access recording), and provides an accuracy in excess of 93 % (sampling mode compared to precise mode), with an overhead of 6 % and less. While [237] is an interesting and widely cited approach, it is not applicable in the scope of this thesis since precise bytecode counts and required – however, it constitutes an interesting opportunity for future research. Additionally, the approach requires a specialised JVM to work, and increases the size and complexity of instrumented bytecode more than the approach of this thesis does.

8.3. JVM Benchmarking

JVM benchmarking can focus on three different views:

1. entire virtual machine with performance-impacting aspect such as memory allocation, garbage collection, bytecode interpretation, just-in-time compilation etc.

2. performance of the individual instructions from the bytecode instruction set, e.g. for statements on individual bytecode instruction in the context of instruction set optimisation or performance prediction

3. performance of the methods constituting the Java platform API, which is implemented by the "foundation classes" bundled with the JVM

The description of related work for JVM benchmarking for these three views is given in Section 8.3.

One of the open issues at the time of publication (2005) is that the results of middleware benchmarking depend on the supporting infrastructure (hardware, operating system), but need to abstracted from to characterise only the middleware layer. They state that the lifetime of benchmarking results is short, which leads to increased cost of benchmarking, and can be understood as a factor speaking for the advantage of automated approaches presented in this thesis. Long simulation times and the need of realistic workloads are further issues discussed, but the overall focus of [238] is to characterise the middleware, rather than to *predict* the performance of applications.

A number of Java benchmarks was presented in Section 2.3.2, and it was explained why none of them can be used in the context of cross-platform performance prediction. In the following, additional benchmarks that run on the JVM are discussed.

Existing bytecode benchmarks that focus on the JVM vary in granularity and intended use. SPECjvm2008 [59] is announced as "a benchmark suite for measuring the performance of a Java [Standard Edition] Runtime Environment ([SE] JRE), containing several real life applications and benchmarks focusing on core java functionality". Granularity of the 10 benchmarks in SPECjvm2008 [59] is very large in comparison to instruction benchmarking or method benchmarking, and is not helpful in predicting the performance of Java applications, as shown in [32]. Additionally, the Java Platform API coverage of SPECjvm2008 is unknown, and the performance of individual API methods cannot be derived from SPECjvm2008 results.

Other benchmarks that execute on the Java Standard Edition are for example JavaGrande [61, 239], Linpack [208] and SciMark [240]. Additional benchmarks can be found on the JavaGrande site [61]. Benchmarks for the Java EE (enterprise edition) usually target the Java EE middleware infrastructure (application servers, Enterprise Java Beans containers) that are built on top of the JVM, instead of directly targeting the JVM. Java EE also makes extensive use of *dependency injection* mechanisms instead of direct API usage.

Comparative benchmarking yields "performance proportions" or "performance *ordering*" of alternatives. In contrast to it, method and API benchmarking needs to yield precise quantitative metrics (e.g. execution duration), parameterised over the input parameters of methods. Quantitative method benchmarking was done in HBench:Java [32], where Zhang and Seltzer have selected and manually benchmarked only 30 API methods, but they did not consider the impact of Just-In-Time compilation.

Other Java SE benchmarks such as Linpack [208] or SciMark [240] are concerned with performance of both numeric and non-numeric computational "kernels" such as Monte Carlo integration, or Sparse Matrix multiplication. Some Java SE benchmarks (e.g. from JavaWorld [65]) focus on highlighting the differences between Java platforms, determining the performance of high-level constructs such as loops, arithmetic operations, exception handling and so on. The UCSD Benchmarks for Java [64] consist of a set of low-level benchmarks that examine exception throwing, thread switching etc.

All of these benchmarks have in common that they neither attempt to benchmark atomic methods nor benchmark *any* API in its entirety (most of them benchmark mathematical kernels or a few Java platform methods). Additionally, they do not consider runtime effects of JVM optimisations (e.g. JIT) systematically and they have not been designed to support non-comparative performance evaluation or prediction.

Execution durations of individual bytecode instructions have been studied independently from performance prediction by Lambert and Brown in [33], however, their approach to *instruction timing* was applied only to a subset of the Java instruction set. Their results have not been validated for predicting the perform-ance of a real application. In the Java Resource Accounting Framework [28], performance of all bytecodes is assumed to be equal and parameters of indi-vidual instructions (incl. names of invoked methods) are ignored, which is not realistic. Hu et al. derive worst-case execution time of Java bytecode in [34], but their work is limited to real-time JVMs.

Cost analysis of bytecode-based programs is presented by Albert et al. in [35, 241], but neither bytecode benchmarks not actual realistic performance values can be obtained, since the performance is assumed to be equal for all bytecode instructions. Harkema et al. [91] monitor the performance of Java applications using a profiler interface, but do not attempt to do performance predictions.

As already described above, using benchmarks focusing on the bytecode in-struction set, execution durations of individual bytecode instructions have been studied by Lambert and Brown in [33]. However, their approach to *instruction timing* was applied only to a subset of the Java instruction set, and has not been validated for predicting the performance of a real application. In the Java Re-source Accounting Framework [28], performance of all bytecodes is assumed to be equal and parameters of individual instructions (incl. names of invoked methods) are ignored, which is not realistic.

Also focusing on the instruction set, Hu et al. derive worst-case execution time of Java bytecode in [34], but their work is limited to real-time JVMs. For .NET bytecode, a benchmark was attempted in a student thesis [242], but it failed to produce results that could be used for performance prediction. No other work about bytecode benchmarking with the focus on the instruction set is known to the authors.

In the author's own work [185], it has been shown that parameters at bytecode level are very significant, especially for operations on collections. Addition-ally, bytecode parameters specify which API methods are called from bytecode. The importance of parameters for performance prediction is a central outstand-ing contribution of Palladio Component Metamodel, and is detailed in the PhD thesis of Heiko Koziolek [46].

However, most publications in the field of bytecode performance ignore this fact; for example, in the Java Resource Accounting Framework (JRAF [28]), Binder and Hulaas use bytecode instructions counting for the estimation of CPU consumption, but all bytecodes are treated equally, and parameters of individual instructions (incl. API method names) are ignored.

In the previously mentioned HBench:Java [32], Zhang and Seltzer built the system vector by separating high-level JVM "components" (e.g. system classes implementing the platform API), memory management, JIT and control flow/primitive bytecode execution. However, the evaluation was performed by selecting and benchmarking only 30 particularly expensive API methods (some of them were found to show linear dependency on *one* parameter). Also, no absolute comparison between measured and predicted performance is provided. In HBench:Java, individual bytecode instructions haven't been considered at all.

For API benchmarking, finding appropriate parameters without knowing the constraints on their choices resembles the needs of *black-box functional testing* [243]. However, black-box testing is interested in path coverage w.r.t. control flow/data flow and in producing of unexpected errors and exceptions. In contrast to black-box testing, API benchmarking is interested in finding at least one set of appropriate method parameters so that the method executes *without* errors or exceptions.

8.4. Performance Prediction

8.4.1. Component-based Performance Prediction and Engineering

In [244, 73], Drongowski et al. describe instruction-based sampling as a performance analysis technique for a family of CPUs manufactured by AMD. However, while this technique is promising and precise, it is vendor-specific and is relevant for performance analysis at operating system (kernel) level, rather than on the level of middleware and business components. Additionally, while it is supported by tools (e.g. AMD CodeAnalyst), no performance *prediction* approach or tooling based on instruction-based sampling is provided. The approach presented in this thesis is instruction precise (at bytecode level), while sampling (as employed in [244, 73]) is only approximate.

The correlation between code and performance has been studied by many researchers, with different outcomes and subjects of analysis. In [245], Annavaram et al. focus on the Cycles per Instruction performance metric prediction, depending on the control flow behaviour of the studied program. After finding that the predictability differs strongly across studied applications, the authors propose an approach to select the sampling technique to accurately capture the program behaviour. In contrast to [245], the approach presented in this thesis operates on a higher level, and does not require extended instruction pointers and similar low-level detail as [245] does.

8.4.2. Bytecode-based Performance Prediction

In [246], Alexander et al. present a unifying approach to performance analysis in Java platforms. They suggest a single data model and a standard set of reports to simplify performance data collection, recording and reporting. However, [246] relies on vendor-specific tools, JVM extensions and kernel extensions to collect performance data, while the approach presented in this thesis is platform-independent and vendor-agnostic. Unlike existing document standards such as ODF (Open Document Format), no standard performance data exchange format is available.

Performance prediction on the basis of bytecode benchmarking has been proposed by several researchers [30, 31, 158, 32], but no working approach has been presented and no libraries or tools are available. Validation has been attempted in [32], but it was restricted to very few Java API methods, and the actual bytecode instructions were neither analysed nor benchmarked. In [185], bytecode-based performance prediction that explicitly distinguishes between method invocations and other bytecode instructions has been proposed.

In [247], Aycock presents a history of Just-In-Time compilation, including the different types and design choices in the context of Java Virtual Machines. The author states that Java revived interest in JIT, and describes research work on concurrent JIT (where the compilation runs parallel to bytecode interpretation), multi-stage compilation, and other JVM implementation techniques. However, [247] does not provide any numbers on the *speedup* achieved by JIT, and the publication date (2003) means that recent development is not covered.

8.4.3. Cross-platform Performance Prediction

Cross-platform performance prediction has been addressed by a large number of researchers, but none of the published approaches is based vendor-independent and application-independent resource demands.

In [248], Yang et al. focus on parallel applications and demonstrate performance prediction across platforms using *relative performance* between two platforms. They observe (i.e. measure) relative performance without *completely* running a parallel application. Instead, short partial executions are analysed on the target platform because the authors argue that most parallel tasks are iterative and behave predictably after a short startup period. However, the approach in [248] carries a number if limitations compared to the approach presented in this thesis: it requires application-specific measurements on the target platform, it assumes a specific application behaviour that is typical for high-performance computing but not necessarily typical in other scenarios, and it is based on timing values rather than platform-independent resource demands. The accuracy of the used timer methods and their impact on the accuracy of measurements is not discussed, either.

In [249], Sodhi et al. build a performance prediction approach on the basis of *performance skeletons*, i.e. shorter representations of existing program. They claim that the performance of these skeletons "in any scenario reflects the performance of the application it represents", but the skeletons can be executed significantly faster. The paper presents a framework for automated construction of performance skeletons and evaluates their use in performance prediction with CPU and network sharing. However, the construction of skeletons requires a full trace of the application execution, which the authors obtain from execution in a controlled testbed. This execution must be done without any competing

355

jobs, and requires a specialised profiling library developed by the authors. Additionally, timing measurement are done with Linux gettimeofday system call, for which the authors claim "microsecond granularity". Despite the fact that the skeletons are measured on the target platform, the prediction error is up to 25 %. The authors state that their approach is limited to modelling coarse computation and communication behaviour, while its implementation is limited to message-passing MPI programs. Additionally, a new skeleton must be constructed for each application input. In contrast to the skeleton-based approach of Sodhi et al., the work presented in this thesis has lesser requirements on application and execution platform and is capable of quantifying finer-grained resource demands in a platform-independent way.

In [250], Shimizu et al. present a regression-based approach for cross-platform performance prediction. The model inputs include execution platform characterisations such as front-side bus bandwidth, and requires the considered application to be profiled on *several* execution platforms with varied static resource configurations. Additionally, the approach must must model different inputs by remodelling the *entire* application, rather than changing model parameters. In contrast to [250],

Most other approaches for cross-platform performance prediction are specific for a technology such as MPI-based or Grid applications [251, 252, 253]. Some approaches use program similarity, but none of them is both platform-independent and application-independent.

In [254], Marin and Mellor-Crummey statically analyse the binary executables of application to identify the control flow in it. A dynamic analysis then parametrises the elements of the control flow model, and binary rewriting is used to instrument the application for obtaining native instructions count and low-level (cache, memory) hardware resource usage. However, the approach in [254] requires a CPU instruction level simulator to make performance prediction. Additionally, the approach requires the final native code and would not work with managed code executed by virtual machines such as JVM, since the resource usage in CPU instructions cannot be derived from bytecode instructions. Finally, the static analysis part of the approach in [254] would be unreliable on polymorphism-heavy platforms, such as Java.

Other approaches requiring *native* code and/or CPU-level simulators, such as that of Lee and Brooks [255] or PACE [256], suffer from the same drawbacks. The PACE approach [256, 257] is limited to parallel applications written in C, Fortran 77 and 90, that utilise a message passing interface (MPI or PVM). Recently [258], it has been extended to obtain input data for the performance model using application instrumentation, which makes the prediction process simpler. However, the extension utilises dynamic instrumentation of source code, while the approach presented in this thesis also works for black-box executable components which are only available as bytecode.

8.5. Resource and Execution Platform Modelling in Component Metamodels

The OMG has published UML-SPT [259], the UML Profile for Schedulability, Performance and Time. UML-SPT extends the UML standard to enable the modelling of time aspects, schedulability aspects and performance-related aspects. UML-SPT also contains a resource model including resource usage, resource management and deployment modelling. In addition to UML-SPT, the OMG develops the UML Profile for Modelling and Analysis of Real-time and Embedded Systems (MARTE) [260]. MARTE is supposed to replace the current UML-SPT profile and contains an even more sophisticated resource model. However, the UML-SPT itself does not include tools or approaches for performance prediction, and the resource modelling part of this thesis focuses on the Palladio Component Model, which is not based on UML.

In [261], Atkinson and Kuehne discuss the notion of execution platforms in the scope Model-Driven Development and conclude that the notions of "platform" and "platform model" are vaguely defined. They present a new definition of "platform" which is based on four orthogonal elements: language, types, instances and patterns. The authors also require individual characterisation of language platform, operating system platform, and hardware platform. However, their approach remains theory, as no implementation for it is provided.

The Core Scenario Model (CSM) [262] also supports modelling of resources, and it can be considered as a bridge between the UML-SPT profile and performance models like layered queueing networks. Beyond modelling capabilities for the dynamic aspects of components, CSM also provides basic resource modelling, i.e. processing resources such as CPU and passive resources such as monitors. Another approach for bridging modelling concepts and approaches is KLAPER [263], the Kernel LAnguage for PErformance and Reliability analysis. KLAPER is designed to be simple and so resources are it does not distinguish between active and passive resources. Instead, it focuses on component-based systems and provides another approach which bridges design-centric models such as UML and analysis-oriented models like queueing networks or Petri nets. However, neither CSM nor KLAPER are useful for bringing explicit parametrisation over resources and execution platform into the Palladio Component Model.

SOFA 2.0 [264] is a component model which supports code generation as well as performance prediction. Its distinguishing features are the support for dynamic component reconfiguration and controllers (controllers in SOFA are component interfaces that provide non-functional features such as lifecycle management or reconfiguration). The execution platform of SOFA components is a distributed platform called SOFAnode which contains several deployment "docks". However, SOFA does not provide explicit resource interfaces, has no support for bytecode-oriented infrastructure components, and it is not compatible with the Palladio Component Model.

Resource modelling in SPE (see Section 2.2.2) revolves around the system execution model, which is separate from the software execution model. A system execution model consists of servers and queues; jobs waiting for a service are stored in queues, while resources providing a service to the software are modelled as servers. The resulting meta-model is very generic and tied to queuing networks [46]: a resource can only be modelled as a server, which has attributes such as `quantity` and `schedulingPolicy`, `timeUnits` and `serviceTime`.

Thus, neither middleware nor bytecode-oriented resource demands can be modelled with SPE tooling.

The ROBOCOP [265, 266] project (Robust Open Component Based Software Architecture for Configurable Devices Project) focuses on embedded applications and performance prediction of them. It contains an execution framework which defines abstractions of the underlying platform [266] and aims at developing software which has to meet real-time requirements. Supported resource types include CPU, memory and data buses; the model of a component can contain resource usage specifications. However, the CPU demands must be expressed as timing values in milliseconds, and it is not possible to specify the resource demand in a platform-independent way.

Chapter 9.

Conclusion

This chapter presents a summary of this thesis (Section 9.1), followed by suggestions for future work in Section 9.2.

9.1. Summary

This thesis has introduced a new approach for cross-platform performance prediction of bytecode-based applications and components. The approach works by disentangling application performance from execution platform performance, and it offers several advantages over conventional time-based measurements. The main benefit of this approach is a decreased prediction effort, since the application does not have to be deployed and measured on *each* candidate execution platform.

The approach works by expressing the application performance using platform-independent metrics based on bytecode instructions and methods. To predict platform-specific timing values, the application performance metric is combined with platform-specific timings of the metric elements. The contributions of this thesis include a new instrumentation-based approach for quantifying the bytecode-based application performance metric, and a new benchmarking approach for obtaining the platform-specific timing values of bytecode instructions and methods.

A prediction methodology which accounts for runtime optimisations performed by modern bytecode-executing virtual machines enables the prediction of execution durations which can be used in platform sizing and application relocation scenarios. The prediction accuracy has been validated for several well-established applications and benchmarks, and has been performed for several execution platforms. The used execution platforms differ substantially in hardware resources, operating systems and middleware.

The bytecode-based application performance metrics can be quantified precisely on any platform, e.g. on a platform where the application is already running or on a different platform. These metrics consist of runtime execution frequencies of bytecode instructions and methods, and they consider parameters of instructions and methods due to their importance for performance. The individual bytecode instruction types are considered separately, since their performance is substantially different. The bytecode-based performance metric has the advantage of being application-agnostic, since it does not use application-specific building blocks found in related approaches.

To obtain platform-independent application performance metrics, the thesis utilises a new kind of application instrumentation which does not require changes to the application source code or modifications of the execution environment. By instrumenting the black-box application bytecode, it becomes possible to obtain precise runtime counts of bytecode instructions (and method invocations) without using vendor-specific platform interfaces, or even modifying the execution platform. The instrumentation is transparent in the sense that the application functionality is not impacted; the application is not aware that it has been instrumented. This application instrumentation has been implemented for the Java bytecode, and minimises overhead through usage of basic block analysis and detection of performance-invariant methods. The instrumentation does not prevent the execution platform from performing runtime optimisations, such as Just-in-Time compilation of bytecode into machine code.

To translate the platform-independent metric elements into platform-specific timing values, this thesis introduced separate approaches for bytecode instruction benchmarking and for method benchmarking. Unlike in real-time systems with predictable timing behaviour, these benchmarking approaches target bytecode-executing virtual machines which host business applications. Both benchmarking approaches are designed to automate the process of benchmarking, in order to decrease the overall effort of performance prediction and in order to encapsulate the complexity of benchmarking in tools.

Bytecode instructions are benchmarked by creating executable microbenchmarks that target individual instruction types. Since bytecode instructions execute very quickly (in a fraction of one CPU cycle when instruction pipelining is possible), they are too short for direct measurement using timer methods. The approach presented in this thesis allows handling the preconditions and postconditions (e.g. the preparation of the JVM stack) that are needed for repeated invocations of the benchmarked bytecode instructions. The number of repeated invocations depends on the timer method's accuracy, which is quantified using a novel, clustering-based algorithm as described below.

Bytecode instruction benchmarking separates the semantics of the microbenchmarks (which are saved as benchmarking scenarios) from the technical implementation of the microbenchmarks. Most bytecode instructions cannot be simply repeated an arbitrary number of times, as their preconditions must be satisfied, which requires additional helper instructions to be executed. These helper instructions need to be benchmarked separately and thus require separate microbenchmarks to be constructed.

The resulting dependencies between benchmarking scenarios are expressed using an linear equation system which captures how the benchmarking scenarios depend on each other. This thesis implements the automated creation of microbenchmarks for Java bytecode instructions, by employing bytecode engineering which allows creating benchmarks that cannot be created by a compiler from source code. The implementation of the approach ensures that the linear equation system is not underdetermined, and solves it to obtain execution durations of individual instructions.

As a high-level executable representation, bytecode contains not only "primitive" bytecode instructions, but also high-level, object-oriented method invocations. Yet decomposing all method implementations into their bytecode instructions is not possible: for example, native methods' performance cannot be quantified on the basis of bytecode instructions. Thus, it is often needed to benchmark methods as atomic entities, i.e. to treat their implementations as black boxes.

Benchmarking of methods needs to satisfy the methods' preconditions such as finding suitable input parameters and creating invocation targets for non-static methods. Satisfying semantically complex preconditions makes method benchmarking an intellectually challenging task, and makes automating it a non-trivial undertaking. Additionally, benchmarking methods in an atomic way makes it possible to capture the performance effects of runtime optimisation in a more precise way, as the effects of Just-in-Time compilation and similar optimisations can be captured better using method-level benchmarks than when using instruction-level benchmarks.

As applications make heavy use of platform APIs (such as the Java API), this thesis chooses to benchmark the performance of methods which do not belong to a component's own implementation in an atomic way, i.e. without decomposing such methods into the bytecode instructions. The reason for this choice is that platform API methods have a complex implementation which often contains platform-specific and native code. Additionally, quantifying the performance of API methods allows the programmer to compare the performance of different alternatives, for example different sorting algorithms. Finally, parametric dependencies of methods can be captured more effectively during method-level benchmarking.

The main obstacle for automating method benchmarking is the complexity of finding appropriate preconditions, i.e. input parameters and invocation targets. This thesis provides a substantial relief for this task by devising a heuristics-based approach for finding these preconditions. The heuristics are more efficient than a brute-force approach, as they take into account the information stored in the variables and constants of the class type.

Accurate time measurements are quintessential for benchmarking bytecode instructions and methods. Additionally, timing measurements have to be used in situations where bytecode-based performance prediction is not applicable, e.g. when accesses to native databases need to be measured. However, the accuracy of timer methods and performance indicators is normally not specified because it is platform-dependent and defined by the accuracy of the underlying hardware counters. This thesis contributes a new platform-independent algorithm which allows quantifying the accuracy of a timer method on any platform, without having to inspect its implementation.

The algorithm for quantifying the accuracy and other quality attributes of timer methods has been implemented in Java and C#. It was applied to all timer methods of the Java and .NET platform APIs to demonstrate the significant differences across methods on the same platform, and the differences between platforms for a given timer method. Additionally, the validation has been performed for third-party timer methods and for native access to platform-specific hardware performance counters. The algorithm implementations can be run on a concrete platform to quantify the accuracy of its timers.

Beyond accuracy, other quality attributes for timer methods have been identified in this thesis. They include method invocation cost (which often has a greater impact than the accuracy), timer stability and cross-thread epoch stability. This thesis established algorithms and techniques for analysing these quality properties, and shows why they are important for measurements in multithreaded scenarios on multicore platforms.

To compare and to select timer methods for accurate measurements, several quality properties with different ranges have to be compared, which makes the comparison complex and depends on the preferences of the user. As working with one single metric is simpler than with a set of metrics, this thesis devises a new aggregate metric for timer quality, which results in one value that can be used easily for comparisons and rankings. This new metric is normalised, i.e. the timer quality can range between 0 % and 100 % , and it aggregates such metrics as accuracy, invocation cost and stability. The metric is designed in such a way as to make even small differences between timer methods visible and takes into account the CPU characteristics of the platform on which the metric value has been obtained.

To enable the usage of bytecode-based performance prediction during early stages of software development, it has been integrated with the Palladio Component Model. This integration makes it possible to express bytecode-based resource demands in component models, and the bytecode-executing virtual machines can be modelled as infrastructure components.

Concluding, it can be said that the thesis achieved its goals.

9.2. Future Work

9.2.1. Bytecode-based Resource Demand Quantification

Future work in the area of bytecode-oriented resource demand quantification would address the runtime overhead, which offers several possibilities for improvement.

Currently, an instrumented method reports its collected instruction/method counts immediately before it returns, using a synchronous method call and blocking until that method finishes. The reported counts are processed by a central result collector – and this collector is implemented in a single-threaded fashion, running in the same thread as the reporting method. Parallelising the counting result collector could lead to performance improvements on multi-core platforms, especially where calling context tree evaluation involves significant computations. However, allowing concurrent access to the data structures that store the counting results would require measures to prevent race conditions, which could diminish the performance gains.

An additional enhancement would be the introduction of load balancing with a queue for reported counting results. Load balancing would be based on a thread pool for processing the reporting counting results, rather than having the reporting thread execute the corresponding code. This decoupling would allow making the reporting method calls asynchronous and thus increase the degree of parallelism.

Another interesting aspect of the instrumentation-based resource demand quantification is the possibility to switch dynamically between the instrumented and uninstrumented version of the application, without having to restart the application. Since the uninstrumented version does not cause any counting overhead, it would be possible to revert the execution speed to its normal value after the resource demand quantification has been finished. Such functionality could be implemented in several ways: either by class duplication or by dynamic class reloading.

Class duplication loads and maintains (at the same time) two distinct versions of the application's classes and switches between them on the basis of some control variables, i.e. without requiring the platform classloader to redefine the classes. Alternatively, method duplication can be employed, which maintains the uninstrumented and the instrumented versions of a method and allows switching between them at runtime, without reloading the class. Class/-method duplication requires the application programmer to ensure that the class state is maintained correctly when the execution switches from one class version to another, which is a non-trivial task and can introduce programming errors. It also has the disadvantage of increasing the memory footprint of the application.

Dynamic class reloading is capable of replacing the loaded class definition through a different one, while maintaining a consistent class state. This technique is offered by some (but not all) execution platforms; for Java, Oracle's HotSpot JVM offers it [181, 267, 268] and it is used by debuggers and profilers.

Another enhancement of bytecode-based resource demand quantification is concerned with a more fine-grained selection of the instrumentation scope, which is needed when a single object method contains both component-internal actions and component-external service calls. In such a case, quantifying the resource demands of an internal action means that only the corresponding part of the considered method should be instrumented.

The current Java implementation of the instrumentation-based approach is already capable of instrumenting *method ranges*, but these method ranges need to be specified by the user. These method ranges are expressed as source code ranges, which works for bytecode that is compiled using default settings since the line numbers are saved in classfiles: the JVM uses this information when printing stack traces, and debuggers uses this information for indicating the current position in source code.

However, when the bytecode does not contain such information, an alternative solution needs to be devised. One possibility to do so in future work is to use the information about component boundaries to identify method calls which are component-external. From the results of such analysis, the instrumentation ranges could be reverse engineered even for black-box bytecode of components.

A further direction of research could use purity analysis and dead code analysis to identify bytecode sections which should not be instrumented: internally, many virtual machines will perform these analyses and will not execute "useless" bytecode section which have no side effects. These kind of analysis is not performed by most source-to-bytecode compilers, but the virtual machines perform aggressive optimisation of the executed bytecode *and* machine code.

A further field of future work would be concerned with applying instrumentation-based resource demand quantification on other platforms and using other bytecode languages than Java. For example, Java EE (enterprise edition) and Java ME (micro edition, for handheld devices) could be targeted by the approach presented in this thesis. Additionally, the .NET framework and its CIL bytecode format could be addressed.

Finally, comparing the performance of the presented, instrumentation-based approach to platform-specific approaches using JVMTI and similar interfaces could be performed.

9.2.2. Benchmarking of the Java Virtual Machine

The novel bytecode instruction benchmarking presented in Section 5.2 has been applied to individual instructions, but it can be applied to instruction sequences (e.g. basic blocks), too. The number of candidate basic blocks increases exponentially with their length (with significant effects on the benchmarking duration). Also, existing research indicates that some basic blocks are more frequent than others, but the appearance of basic blocks depends on the considered application. Future work can study whether benchmarking basic blocks and using their durations leads to a better prediction accuracy.

Additionally, experiments with further benchmarking scenarios would mean that the timing values of bytecode instructions would base on a larger body of measurements. Further automation of benchmark scenario creation could help with creating benchmark scenarios for basic blocks, and with identifying valid basic blocks in an automated way.

The translation of bytecode into machine code is a further research direction of significant interest, and it would encompass both Just-in-Time compilation and Ahead-of-Time compilation. Since the resulting speedup greatly impacts the performance of applications, it is often the distinguishing factor between vendor-specific implementations of bytecode-executing virtual machines.

Understanding how a bytecode instruction (or a sequence of them) is mapped to native instructions may help with benchmarking of bytecode instructions, and thus benefit the bytecode-based performance prediction. However, as this translation is vendor-specific and platform-specific (e.g. because different CPU architectures have different native instruction sets), the knowledge gain may be moderate compared to the overhead.

The method benchmarking presented in Section 5.3 offers several opportunities for future work. For example, the heuristics-based generation of valid input parameters could be complemented by collecting valid parameters from running, real-world applications.

Additionally, valid parameters could be retrieved from a human operator, both in an interactive way (by asking the user if the heuristics fail) and in a static way (requiring the user to provide the parameters before attempting to run the benchmark). A further source of parameter information could be found in functional tests, although it would be needed to separate tests with a positive outcome from the tests with negative outcome. Additionally, method benchmarking can be extended by incorporating machine learning and other techniques of search-based software engineering for finding method parameters and parametric dependencies [138].

The method benchmarking approach can be used to express parametric dependencies and for identifying method parameters that have no (or insignificant) influence on method performance. On the other hand, it can also be used to identify "performance-dangerous" value ranges of method parameters, i.e. parameter values for which the performance degrades considerably.

In perspective, such information could be used during development to detect performance degradation, and to ensure performance testing covers the parameter range accordingly. Method benchmarking could be used for a variety of tasks beyond performance prediction of applications: for example, comparing and selecting different implementations of an interface method could be done on the basis of method benchmarking results.

In general, instruction and method benchmarking as presented in this thesis mapped the execution of an instruction or method to a timing value which comprises all resource usage that occurs during the execution. With other words, the resources beyond the CPU were not considered individually – for design-time, model-based performance prediction, such abstraction is fully warranted (because a low-level view of the execution platform would be complex to build and lead to exorbitant performance simulation duration). While other resources such as hard disk and network links are considered explicitly in the Palladio Component Model, the usage of them is only quantified when they are used explicitly.

The automated benchmarking approach developed in this thesis can be used for exploring the configuration space of the execution platform. For example, the Java Virtual Machine offers a large set of settings which impact application performance and scalability: the memory allocated to an application can be set, several garbage collection algorithms are available, etc. As many of these settings cannot be set to arbitrary values, and "more is better" does not apply to many of them, exploring the configuration space could help developers and users achieve better application performance and possibly also better execution platform utilisation.

9.2.3. Timer Methods and Performance Indicators

Quality-driven selection of timer methods can be extended to other performance indicators. For example, the utilisation of resources and system load are two important performance metric which are often exposed by the operating system. However, their accuracy and other quality attributes are usually unspecified, and no methods exist to obtain them. Future work can address this issue, and help with a more precise quantification of performance.

9.2.4. Resource Modelling and Palladio Component Model

The extension of the Palladio Component Model and the integration of bytecode-based performance prediction already have allowed to increase the accuracy of performance prediction. The introduction of explicit resource interfaces has paved the way for a more precise modelling of other existing hardware resources, such as hard disks. As it now has become possible to model read and write accesses separately, future work should create benchmarks for hard disks and approaches for quantifying hard disk accesses of components.

While performance modelling of hard disks has enjoyed attention of researchers over the past decades, most of existing performance models consider hard disks at the level of hardware accesses, and disregard the impact of software layers such as operating system and middleware. Additionally, existing hard disk performance models require very detailed information about the disk internals such as distribution of data, and a detailed model of the workload to predict the impact and scope of caching.

Future work in resource modelling should address hard disk modelling starting with a simple model and refining it until a predefined prediction accuracy is reached. Additionally, hard disk modelling should consider the impact of the software layers which are used to access hard disks, and quantify the overhead of these layers. For example, the Java platform API defines an extensive hierarchy of classes for file system access, split into categories for access in byte-oriented, character-oriented, stream-oriented and other ways. Making the performance differences between these categories explicit would benefit Java programmers since the official platform API documentation provides no performance information for these I/O classes.

This thesis extended the Palladio Component Model to support infrastructure components using explicit resource interfaces. Beyond modelling the JVM, the new concepts can be used for explicit consideration of other middleware parts, such as application servers. Until now, some support for middleware has been implemented in the PCM using declarative specification and so-called model completions [269] which are based on model transformations.

Also, the calibration factor calculation could be refined using program similarity analysis to detect the connection between the contents of methods or bytecode sequences (i.e. method parts or basic blocks) and the corresponding JIT speedup.

Appendix A.

Appendix

A.1. Performance Equivalence Classes of Java Bytecode Instructions

The following list contains the performance equivalence classes of Java bytecode instructions. These classes have been identified in Section 4.3.11 and are used in BYCOUNTER:

1. AALOAD, BALOAD, CALOAD, FALOAD, IALOAD, SALOAD

2. DALOAD, LALOAD (eventually merged with the previous class)

3. ASTORE, BASTORE, CASTORE, FASTORE, IASTORE, SASTORE

4. DASTORE, LASTORE (eventually merged with the previous class)

5. ALOAD, ALOAD_0, ALOAD_1, ALOAD_2, ALOAD_3

6. ASTORE, ASTORE_0, ASTORE_1, ASTORE_2, ASTORE_3

7. DLOAD, DLOAD_0, DLOAD_1, DLOAD_2, DLOAD_3

8. DSTORE, DSTORE_0, DSTORE_1, DSTORE_2, DSTORE_3

9. DCONST_0, DCONST_1

10. FLOAD, FLOAD_0, FLOAD_1, FLOAD_2, FLOAD_3

11. FSTORE, FSTORE_0, FSTORE_1, FSTORE_2, FSTORE_3

12. FCONST_0, FCONST_1, FCONST_2

13. ILOAD, ILOAD_0, ILOAD_1, ILOAD_2, ILOAD_3

14. ISTORE, ISTORE_0, ISTORE_1, ISTORE_2, ISTORE_3

15. ICONST_0, ICONST_1, ICONST_2, ICONST_3, ICONST_4, ICONST_5, ICONST_M1

16. BIPUSH, SIPUSH (eventually merged with the previous class)

17. LLOAD, LLOAD_0, LLOAD_1, LLOAD_2, LLOAD_3

18. LSTORE, LSTORE_0, LSTORE_1, LSTORE_2, LSTORE_3

19. LCONST_0, LCONST_1

20. ARETURN, DRETURN, FRETURN, IRETURN, LRETURN, RETURN

21. DCMPG, DCMPL

22. FCMPG, FCMPL (eventually merged with the previous class)

23. GOTO, GOTO_W

24. IFNULL, IFNONNULL

25. IF_ACMPEQ, IF_ACMPNE

26. IF_ICMPEQ, IF_ICMPGE, IF_ICMPGT, IF_ICMPLE, IF_ICMPLT, IF_ICMPNE

27. IFEQ, IFGE, IFGT, IFLE, IFLT, IFNE

28. INVOKEINTERFACE, INVOKESPECIAL, INVOKESTATIC, INVOKEVIR-TUAL

It is also plausible that the following classes are valid:

1. DUP, DUP_X1 and DUP_X2

2. DUP2, DUP2_X1 and DUP2_X2 (possibly the same as the previous class)

3. `JSR, JSR_W`

4. `LDC, LDC_W, LDC2_W`

5. `GOTO, GOTO_W POP, POP_2`

Even if the group 2, 4, 16 and 22 are not merged with groups 1, 3, 15 and 21, the groupings reduce the cardinality of the instruction set by 83, i.e. by more than 40%.

Appendix B.

List of Figures

Appendix C.

List of Tables

Appendix D.

Listings

Bibliography

[1] K. S. Trivedi and T. M. Sigmon, "A performance comparison of optimally designed computer systems with and without virtual memory," in *Proceedings of the 6th annual symposium on Computer architecture*, 1979, pp. 117–121.

[2] D. J. Roek and W. C. Emerson, "A hardware instrumentation approach to evaluation of a large scale system," in *Proceedings of the 1969 24th national ACM Annual Conference/Annual Meeting*. New York, NY, USA: ACM, 1969, pp. 351–367.

[3] Compuware Corporation, "New Survey Finds That Poor Application Performance Causes Significant Financial Losses," February 2009, http://investor.compuware.com/releasedetail.cfm?releaseid=359867, last retrieved August 31st, 2010. [Online]. Available: http://investor.compuware.com/releasedetail.cfm?releaseid=359867

[4] V. Briegleb, "Bericht: Probleme bei SAPs neuer Mittelstandssoftware," 2007, heise online news, http://www.heise.de/newsticker/meldung/88300/, last accessed on August 31st, 2010.

[5] M. Woodside, G. Franks, and D. C. Petriu, "The Future of Software Performance Engineering," in *Proceedings of ICSE 2007, Future of SE*. IEEE Computer Society, Washington, DC, USA, 2007, pp. 171–187.

[6] C. U. Smith and L. G. Williams, *Performance Solutions: A Practical Guide to Creating Responsive, Scalable Software*. Addison-Wesley, 2002.

[7] L. G. Williams and C. U. Smith, "Making the Business Case for Software Performance Engineering," in *Proceedings of the 29th International Computer Measurement Group Conference, December 7-12, 2003, Dallas, Texas, USA.* Computer Measurement Group, 2003, pp. 349–358.

[8] C. U. Smith and L. G. Williams, "Software performance engineering: A case study including performance comparison with design alternatives," *IEEE Transactions on Software Engineering,* vol. 19, no. 7, pp. 720–741, 1993.

[9] S. Becker, H. Koziolek, and R. Reussner, "The Palladio component model for model-driven performance prediction," *Journal of Systems and Software,* vol. 82, pp. 3–22, 2009. [Online]. Available: http://dx.doi.org/10.1016/j.jss.2008.03.066

[10] J. Keung, Y. Liu, K. Foster, and T. Nguyen, "A Statistical Method for Middleware System Architecture Evaluation," in *21st Australian Software Engineering Conference.* IEEE, 2010, pp. 183–191.

[11] A. Aldini, F. Corradini, and M. Bernardo, "Component-Oriented Performance Evaluation," *A Process Algebraic Approach to Software Architecture Design,* pp. 203–238, 2010.

[12] A. Pimentel, "The Artemis workbench for system-level performance evaluation of embedded systems," *International Journal of Embedded Systems,* vol. 3, no. 3, pp. 181–196, 2008.

[13] C. Smith, "Introduction to software performance engineering: origins and outstanding problems," *Formal Methods for Performance Evaluation,* pp. 395–428, 2007.

[14] H. Koziolek, "Performance evaluation of component-based software systems: A survey," *Performance Evaluation,* 2009.

[15] Oracle Corporation, "Enterprise JavaBeans Technology Homepage," 2010, last retrieved August 31st, 2010. [Online]. Available: http://www.oracle.com/technetwork/java/index-jsp-140203.html

[16] M. Kirtland, *Designing component-based applications*. Microsoft Press, 1999.

[17] K.-K. Lau, "Software Component Models," in *Proceedings of the 6th International Conference on Software Engineering (ICSE06)*. ACM Press, 2006, pp. 1081–1082.

[18] H. Koziolek, "Parameter Dependencies for Reusable Performance Specifications of Software Components," Ph.D. dissertation, Universität Oldenburg, January 2008.

[19] M. Kuperberg, M. Krogmann, and R. Reussner, "TimerMeter: Quantifying Accuracy of Software Times for System Analysis," in *Proceedings of the 6th International Conference on Quantitative Evaluation of SysTems (QEST) 2009*, 2009. [Online]. Available: http://www.qest.org/qest2009

[20] E. Lazowska, J. Zahorjan, G. S. Graham, and K. C. Sevcik, *Quantitative System Performance - Computer System Analysis Using Queueing Network Models*. Prentice-Hall, 1984.

[21] S. Balsamo, M. Bernardo, and M. Simeoni, "Performance Evaluation at the Software Architecture Level," *Formal Methods for Software Architectures*, vol. 2804, pp. 207–258, 2003.

[22] S. Kounev, "Performance Modeling and Evaluation of Distributed Component-Based Systems Using Queueing Petri Nets," *IEEE Transactions on Software Engineering*, vol. 32, no. 7, pp. 486–502, July 2006.

[23] F. Bause and P. S. Kritzinger, *Stochastic Petri Nets*, 2nd ed. Vieweg, 2002.

[24] F. Bause, "Queueing Petri Nets-A Formalism for the Combined Qualitative and Quantitative Analysis of Systems," *Petri Nets and Performance Models, 1993. Proceedings., 5th International Workshop on*, pp. 14–23, Oct 1993.

[25] Y. Liu, A. Fekete, and I. Gorton, "Design-Level Performance Prediction of Component-Based Applications," *IEEE Transactions on Software Engineering*, vol. 31, no. 11, pp. 928–941, 2005.

[26] I. Gorton and A. Liu, "Performance Evaluation of Alternative Component Architectures for Enterprise JavaBean Applications," *IEEE Internet Computing*, vol. 7, no. 3, pp. 18–23, 2003.

[27] A. Liu, Ian, Gorton, and L. Hu, "Evaluating bea systems application server technology," CSIRO Mathematical and Information Sciences, Macquarie University, Australia, Tech. Rep. 2000/241, July 2001.

[28] W. Binder and J. Hulaas, "Using Bytecode Instruction Counting as Portable CPU Consumption Metric," *Electr. Notes Theor. Comput. Sci.*, vol. 153, no. 2, pp. 57–77, 2006.

[29] M. Meyerhöfer and F. Lauterwald, "Towards Platform-Independent Component Measurement," in *Tenth International Workshop on Component-Oriented Programming*, W. Weck, J. Bosch, R. Reussner, and C. Szyperski, Eds., 2005.

[30] M. Meyerhöfer, "Messung und Verwaltung von Komponenten für die Performancevorhersage," Ph.D. dissertation, University of Erlangen-Nürnberg, Germany, 2007.

[31] C. Herder and J. J. Dujmovic, "Frequency Analysis and Timing of Java Bytecodes," Computer Science Department, San Francisco State University, Tech. Rep., 2000, technical Report SFSU-CS-TR-00.02.

[32] X. Zhang and M. Seltzer, "HBench:Java: an application-specific benchmarking framework for Java virtual machines," in *JAVA '00: Proceedings of the ACM 2000 conference on Java Grande.* New York, NY, USA: ACM Press, 2000, pp. 62–70.

[33] J. Lambert and J. F. Power, "Platform Independent Timing of Java Virtual Machine Bytecode Instructions," in *Workshop on Quantitative Aspects of Programming Languages, Budapest, Hungary, March 29-30, 2008*, 2008.

[34] E. Y.-S. Hu, A. J. Wellings, and G. Bernat, "Deriving Java Virtual Machine Timing Models for Portable Worst-Case Execution Time Analysis,"

in *OTM Workshops*, ser. LNCS, R. Meersman and Z. Tari, Eds., vol. 2889. Springer, 2003, pp. 411–424.

[35] E. Albert, P. Arenas, S. Genaim, G. Puebla, and D. Zanardini, "Experiments in Cost Analysis of Java Bytecode," *Electr. Notes Theor. Comput. Sci.*, vol. 190, no. 1, pp. 67–83, 2007.

[36] D. J. Lilja, *Measuring Computer Performance: A Practitioner's Guide.* Cambridge University Press, 2000.

[37] L. K. John and L. Eeckhout, *Performance Evaluation And Benchmarking.* CRC Press, 2006.

[38] A. Buble, L. Bulej, and P. Tuma, "CORBA benchmarking: A course with hidden obstacles," in *Parallel and Distributed Processing Symposium, 2003. Proceedings. International*, April 2003, pp. 1–6.

[39] D. Holmes, "Inside the Hotspot VM: Clocks, Timers and Scheduling Events," 2006, last retrieved August 31st, 2010. [Online]. Available: http://blogs.sun.com/dholmes/entry/inside_the_hotspot_vm_clocks

[40] P. B. Danzig and S. Melvin, "High Resolution Timing with Low Resolution Clocks and Microsecond Resolution Timer for Sun Workstations," *ACM SIGOPS Operating Systems Review*, vol. 24, no. 1, pp. 23–26, 1990.

[41] H. Beilner, "Measuring with Slow Clocks," ICSI-Technical Report-88-O03, Tech. Rep., 1988.

[42] K. Krogmann, "Reconstruction of software component architectures and behaviour models using static and dynamic analysis," Ph.D. dissertation, Karlsruhe Institute of Technology (KIT), Karlsruhe, Germany, 2010.

[43] H. Koziolek, *Dependability Metrics*, ser. LNCS. Springer Heidelberg, 2008, vol. 4909, ch. Introduction to Performance Metrics, pp. 199–203. [Online]. Available: http://www.springerlink.com/content/r66251p264177m72/fulltext.pdf

[44] T. Zheng, C. Woodside, and M. Litoiu, "Performance model estimation and tracking using optimal filters," *IEEE Transactions on Software Engineering*, vol. 34, no. 3, pp. 391–406, May-June 2008.

[45] G. Bolch, S. Greiner, H. de Meer, and K. S. Trivedi, *Queueing Networks and Markov Chains.* John Wiley & Sons Inc., 1998.

[46] H. Koziolek, "Parameter Dependencies for Reusable Performance Specifications of Software Components," Ph.D. dissertation, University of Oldenburg, 2008. [Online]. Available: http://sdqweb.ipd.uka.de/publications/pdfs/koziolek2008g.pdf

[47] C. U. Smith, *Performance Engineering of Software Systems.* Addison-Wesley, 1990.

[48] *SPE-ED User Guide*, Performance Engineering Services, Austin, TX, 2003, http://www.perfeng.com.

[49] C. U. Smith and C. M. Llado, "Performance Model Interchange Format (PMIF 2.0): XML Definition and Implementation," in *QEST '04: Proceedings of the The Quantitative Evaluation of Systems, First International Conference.* Washington, DC, USA: IEEE Computer Society, 2004, pp. 38–47.

[50] H. Curnow, "Whither Whetstone? The synthetic benchmark after 15 years," in *Evaluating supercomputers.* Chapman & Hall, Ltd., 1990, p. 266.

[51] R. Weicker, "Dhrystone: a synthetic systems programming benchmark," *Communications of the ACM*, vol. 27, no. 10, pp. 1013–1030, 1984.

[52] A. Phansalkar and L. K. John, "Analyzing Program Behavior of SPECint2000 Benchmark Suite using Principal Components Analysis," Department of Electrical and Computer Engineering The University of Texas at Austin, Austin TX 78712, Tech. Rep. TR-040122-01, 2003.

[53] Y. Chan, A. Sudarsanam, and A. Wolfe, "The effect of compiler-flag tuning on spec benchmark performance," *SIGARCH Comput. Archit. News*, vol. 22, no. 4, pp. 60–70, 1994.

[54] B. Colwell, "Benchmarketing competition," *Computer*, vol. 36, no. 12, pp. 9–11, 2003.

[55] L. Zhu, I. Gorton, Y. Liu, and N. B. Bui, "Model Driven Benchmark Generation for Web Services," in *SOSE '06: Proceedings of the 2006 International Workshop on Service-Oriented Software Engineering*. ACM, 2006, pp. 33–39.

[56] L. Gray, A. Kumar, and H. Li, "Workload Characterization of the SPEC-power_ssj2008 Benchmark," *Performance Evaluation: Metrics, Models and Benchmarks*, pp. 262–282, 2008.

[57] J. Dongarra, P. Luszczek, and A. Petitet, "The LINPACK Benchmark: past, present and future," *Concurrency and Computation: Practice and Experience*, vol. 15, no. 9, pp. 803–820, 2003.

[58] "DisCo Benchmarking Database (DBD)," 2010, http://www.cse.scitech.ac.uk/disco/database/search-parallel.php, last retrieved August 31st, 2010. [Online]. Available: http://www.cse.scitech.ac.uk/disco/database/search-parallel.php

[59] Standard Performance Evaluation Corp., "SPECjvm2008 Benchmarks," 2008, URL: http://www.spec.org/jvm2008/, last visit: October 9th, 2009. [Online]. Available: http://www.spec.org/jvm2008/

[60] S. P. E. C. (SPEC), "SPECjAppServer2004 Benchmark," 2004, uRL: http://www.spec.org/jvm2008/, last visit: June 9th, 2008. [Online]. Available: http://www.spec.org/jAppServer2004/

[61] "The Java Grande Forum Sequential Benchmarks 2.0," 2007, http://www2.epcc.ed.ac.uk/computing/research_activities/java_grande, last retrieved August 31st, 2010. [Online]. Available: http://www2.epcc.ed.ac.uk/computing/research_activities/java_grande

[62] M. Philippsen, R. F. Boisvert, V. Getov, R. Pozo, J. E. Moreira, D. Gannon, and G. Fox, "JavaGrande - High Performance Computing with Java," in *PARA*, 2000, pp. 20–36.

[63] S. Blackburn, R. Garner, C. Hoffmann, A. Khang, K. McKinley, R. Bentzur, A. Diwan, D. Feinberg, D. Frampton, S. Guyer *et al.*, "The DaCapo benchmarks: Java benchmarking development and analysis," in *Proceedings of the 21st annual ACM SIGPLAN conference on Object-oriented programming systems, languages, and applications.* ACM, 2006, p. 190.

[64] W. Griswold and P. Phillips, "UCSD Benchmarks for Java," http://cseweb.ucsd.edu/users/wgg/JavaProf, last visited October 9th, 2009. [Online]. Available: http://cseweb.ucsd.edu/users/wgg/JavaProf/javaprof.html

[65] D. Bell, "Make java fast: Optimize," *JavaWorld*, vol. 2, no. 4, 1997, http://www.javaworld.com/javaworld/jw-04-1997/jw-04-optimize.html, last visit: October 9th, 2009. [Online]. Available: http://www.javaworld.com/javaworld/jw-04-1997/jw-04-optimize.html

[66] Z. Avramov and J. Dujmović, "A NETWORK BENCHMARK FOR THE .NET FRAMEWORK," *nature*, vol. 14, p. 15, 2004.

[67] T. Kalibera and P. Tuma, "Precise regression benchmarking with random effects: Improving Mono benchmark results," *Formal Methods and Stochastic Models for Performance Evaluation*, pp. 63–77, 2006.

[68] F. Sibai, "Evaluating the performance of single and multiple core processors with PCMARK® 05 and benchmark analysis," *PERFORMANCE EVALUATION REVIEW*, vol. 35, no. 4, p. 62, 2008.

[69] ——, "Dissecting the PCMark® 05 Benchmark and Assessing Performance Scaling," *Innovations in Information Technology, 2006*, pp. 1–5, 2006.

[70] A. Phansalkar and L. John, "Performance prediction using program similarity," in *Proceedings of the 2006 SPEC Benchmark Workshop*, 2006.

[71] K. Hoste, A. Phansalkar, L. Eeckhout, A. Georges, L. John, and K. De Bosschere, "Performance prediction based on inherent program

similarity," in *Proceedings of the 15th international conference on Parallel architectures and compilation techniques.* ACM, 2006, p. 122.

[72] *Le systeme international d unites (SI) = The international system of units (SI),* 8th ed., Sevres, 2006.

[73] P. Drongowski, A. Devices, and I. Center, "Instruction-Based Sampling: A New Performance Analysis Technique for AMD Family 10h Processors," *AMD Code Analyst Project Report,* 2007.

[74] C. McCurdy and J. Vetter, "Memphis: Finding and Fixing NUMA-related Performance Problems on Multi-core Platforms," *ISPASS, IEEE Computer Society,* pp. 87–96, 2010.

[75] R. Azimi, D. Tam, L. Soares, and M. Stumm, "Enhancing operating system support for multicore processors by using hardware performance monitoring," *ACM SIGOPS Operating Systems Review,* vol. 43, no. 2, pp. 56–65, 2009.

[76] S. Eranian, "What can performance counters do for memory subsystem analysis?" in *Proceedings of the 2008 ACM SIGPLAN workshop on Memory systems performance and correctness: held in conjunction with the Thirteenth International Conference on Architectural Support for Programming Languages and Operating Systems (ASPLOS'08).* ACM, 2008, pp. 26–30.

[77] G. P. V. Venkataramani, "Low-cost and efficient architectural support for correctness and performance debugging," Ph.D. dissertation, Georgia Institute of Technology, 2009.

[78] D. Tam, "Operating System Management of Shared Caches on Multicore Processors," Ph.D. dissertation, University of Toronto, 2010.

[79] F. Schneider, "Online optimizations using hardware performance monitors," 2009.

[80] C. B. Zilles and G. S. . Sohi, "A Programmable Co-processor for Profiling," in *Proceedings of the 7th International Symposium on High-Performance Computer Architecture*, 2001, pp. 241–252.

[81] P. F. Sweeney, M. Hauswirth, B. Cahoon, P. Cheng, A. Diwan, D. Grove, and M. Hind, "Using Hardware Performance Monitors to Understand the Behavior of Java Applications," *Proceedings of the 3rd conference on Virtual Machine Research And Technology Symposium*, pp. 57–72, 2004.

[82] R. Green, "Pentium RDTSC Access using JNI," 2008, last retrieved August 31st, 2010. [Online]. Available: http://www.mindprod.com/products1.html#PENTIUM

[83] H. Mousa, C. Krintz, L. Youseff, and R. Wolski, "VIProf: Vertically integrated full-system performance profiler," in *Proceedings of the Workshop on Next-Generation Software (NGS)*. Citeseer, 2007.

[84] H. Mousa, K. Doshi, T. Sherwood, and E. Ould-Ahmed-Vall, "VrtProf: Vertical Profiling for System Virtualization," in *hicss*. IEEE Computer Society, 1899, pp. 1–10.

[85] J. Treibig, G. Hager, and G. Wellein, "LIKWID: A lightweight performance-oriented tool suite for x86 multicore environments," *Arxiv preprint arXiv:1004.4431*, 2010.

[86] B. Wylie, B. Mohr, and F. Wolf, "Holistic hardware counter performance analysis of parallel programs," *Proceedings of Parallel Computing 2005*.

[87] H. Pyla, B. Ramesh, C. Ribbens, and S. Varadarajan, "ScALPEL: A Scalable Adaptive Lightweight Performance Evaluation Library for application performance monitoring," *Arxiv preprint arXiv:0903.0035*, 2009.

[88] H. Inoue and T. Nakatani, "How a Java VM can get more from a hardware performance monitor," *ACM SIGPLAN Notices*, vol. 44, no. 10, pp. 137–154, 2009.

[89] L. Uhsadel, A. Georges, and I. Verbauwhede, "Exploiting hardware performance counters," in *5th Workshop on Fault Diagnosis and Tolerance in Cryptography, 2008. FDTC'08*, 2008, pp. 59–67.

[90] M. Curtis-Maury, D. Nikolopoulos, and C. Antonopoulos, "Dynamic Program Stirring on Multiple Cores: How Hardware Performance Monitors Can Help Regulate Performance, Power, and Temperature Simultaneously," in *Proc. of the Second Workshop on Functionality of Hardware Performance Monitors (held in conjunction with MICRO-39), Orlando, FL*. Citeseer, 2006.

[91] M. Harkema, D. A. C. Quartel, B. Gijsen, and R. D. van der Mei, "Performance Monitoring of Java Applications," in *Workshop on Software and Performance*, 2002, pp. 114–127.

[92] W. Binder, J. Hulaas, and P. Moret, "A quantitative evaluation of the contribution of native code to Java workloads," in *2006 IEEE International Symposium on Workload Characterization*, 2006, pp. 201–209.

[93] G. Ammons, T. Ball, and J. Larus, "Exploiting hardware performance counters with flow and context sensitive profiling," in *Proceedings of the ACM SIGPLAN 1997 conference on Programming language design and implementation*. ACM, 1997, pp. 85–96.

[94] R. Araiza, M. Aguilera, T. Pham, and P. Teller, "Towards a cross-platform microbenchmark suite for evaluating hardware performance counter data," in *Proceedings of the 2005 conference on Diversity in computing*. ACM, 2005, p. 39.

[95] D. Zaparanuks, M. Jovic, and M. Hauswirth, "Accuracy of performance counter measurements," Technical Report 2008/05, University of Lugano, Tech. Rep., 2008.

[96] J. Dongarra, K. London, S. Moore, P. Mucci, D. Terpstra, H. You, and M. Zhou, "Experiences and lessons learned with a portable interface to

hardware performance counters," in *Parallel and Distributed Processing Symposium, 2003. Proceedings. International*, 2003, p. 6.

[97] S. Browne, J. Dongarra, N. Garner, G. Ho, and P. Mucci, "A portable programming interface for performance evaluation on modern processors," *International Journal of High Performance Computing Applications*, vol. 14, no. 3, p. 189, 2000.

[98] D. Terpstra, H. Jagode, H. You, and J. Dongarra, "Collecting Performance Data with PAPI-C," *Tools for High Performance Computing 2009*, pp. 157–173, 2010.

[99] T. Beauchamp and D. Weston, "Dtrace: The reverse engineer's unexpected swiss army knife," *Blackhat Europe*, 2008.

[100] R. McDougall, J. Mauro, and B. Gregg, "Solaris (TM) Performance and Tools: DTrace and MDB Techniques for Solaris 10 and OpenSolaris (Solaris Series)," 2006.

[101] F. Eigler and R. Hat, "Problem solving with systemtap," in *Proceedings of the Ottawa Linux Symposium*, vol. 2006. Citeseer, 2006.

[102] *IBM AIX Version 6.1 differences guide.* Riverton, NJ, USA: IBM Corp., 2008.

[103] Bhavana Nagendra (AMD Developer Central), "AMD TSC Drift Solutions in Red Hat Enterprise Linux," 2006, last retrieved August 31st, 2010. [Online]. Available: http://developer.amd.com/pages/1214200692.aspx

[104] Microsoft Help and Support, "Computers that are running Windows XP Service Pack 2 and that are equipped with multiple processors that support processor power management features may experience decreased performance," 2007, last retrieved August 31st, 2010. [Online]. Available: http://support.microsoft.com/kb/896256/EN-US/

[105] S. Browne, J. Dongarra, N. Garner, G. Ho, and P. Mucci, "A Portable Programming Interface for Performance Evaluation on Modern Processors,"

International Journal of High Performance Computing Applications, vol. 14, no. 3, p. 189, 2000.

[106] R. Berrendorf, H. Ziegler, and B. Mohr, "PCL - the Performance Counter Library," 2003, last retrieved 2009-04-04. [Online]. Available: http://www.fz-juelich.de/jsc/PCL/

[107] JETM Team, "Java Execution Time Measurement Library," 2009, last retrieved August 31st, 2010. [Online]. Available: http://jetm.void.fm

[108] J. Banes, "GAGE - Genuine Advantage Gaming Engine," 2004, last retrieved April 4th, 2009; Website no longer online as of August 31st, 2010. [Online]. Available: http://java.dnsalias.com/

[109] K. Candar, *MONO .Net goes LINUX*, ser. Franzis professional series. Poing: Franzis-Verl., 2007, gb. : EUR 49.95 (D). [Online]. Available: http://media.obvsg.at/AC06551236-1001

[110] T. Lindholm and F. Yellin, *The Java Virtual Machine Specification*. Addison-Wesley, 1999.

[111] T. Rodriquez and K. Russel, "Client compiler for the java hotspot virtual machine," *JavaOne, Sun's 2002 Worldwide Java Developer Conference*, 2002.

[112] "Native Image Generator (Ngen.exe)," last consulted on May 5th, 2011. [Online]. Available: http://msdn.microsoft.com/de-de/library/6t9t5wcf(v=vs.80).aspx

[113] "Nanojit, a small, cross-platform C++ library that emits machine code," last consulted on May 5th, 2011. [Online]. Available: https://developer.mozilla.org/En/Nanojit

[114] E. Bruneton, R. Lenglet, and T. Coupaye, "ASM: a code manipulation tool to implement adaptable systems," *Adaptable and Extensible Component Systems*, 2002, http://asm.ow2.org. [Online]. Available: http://asm.ow2.org

[115] M. Dahm, "Byte Code Engineering with the BCEL API," Freie Universitaet Berlin, Tech. Rep. B-17-98, 2001. [Online]. Available: http://bcel.sourceforge.net/downloads/report.pdf

[116] "Retrotranslator: a tool that makes Java applications compatible with Java 1.4, Java 1.3 and other environments." 2010, last retrieved August 31st, 2010. [Online]. Available: http://retrotranslator.sourceforge.net/

[117] "AgitarOne JUnit Generator creates thorough JUnit tests on your code," 2010, http://www.agitar.com/, last retrieved August 31st, 2010. [Online]. Available: http://www.agitar.com/

[118] "Oracle WebLogic Products," 2010, http://www.oracle.com/us/products/middleware/application-server/index.htm, last retrieved August 31st, 2010. [Online]. Available: http://www.oracle.com/us/products/middleware/application-server/index.htm

[119] J. Thiel, "An overview of software performance analysis tools and techniques: From gprof to dtrace," Citeseer, Tech. Rep., 2006.

[120] C. Luk, R. Cohn, R. Muth, H. Patil, A. Klauser, G. Lowney, S. Wallace, V. Reddi, and K. Hazelwood, "Pin: building customized program analysis tools with dynamic instrumentation," in *Proceedings of the 2005 ACM SIGPLAN conference on Programming language design and implementation*. ACM, 2005, pp. 190–200.

[121] M. Dmitriev, "Design of JFluid: A profiling technology and tool based on dynamic bytecode instrumentation," *Sun Microsystems, Inc. Mountain View, CA, USA*, p. 22, 2003.

[122] H. Lee and B. Zorn, "Bytecode Instrumentation as an Aid in Understanding the Behavior of Java Persistent Stores," in *OOPSLA 1997 Workshop on Garbage Collection and Memory Management*. Citeseer.

[123] H. B. Lee and B. G. Zorn, "Bit: a tool for instrumenting java bytecodes," in *USITS'97: Proceedings of the USENIX Symposium on Internet Technologies and Systems on USENIX Symposium on Internet Technologies and Systems.* Berkeley, CA, USA: USENIX Association, 1997, pp. 7–7.

[124] A. Chander, J. Mitchell, and I. Shin, "Mobile code security by Java byte-code instrumentation," in *2001 DARPA Information Survivability Conference & Exposition (DISCEX II).* Citeseer, 2001.

[125] M. Yang, "Secure J2ME Application with Bytecode Instrumentation," 2008.

[126] P. Abercrombie and M. Karaorman, "jContractor:: Bytecode Instrumentation Techniques for Implementing Design by Contract in Java," *Electronic Notes in Theoretical Computer Science,* vol. 70, no. 4, pp. 55–79, 2002.

[127] Y. Cheng, C. Chen, and C. Hsieh, "ezcontract: Using marker library and bytecode instrumentation to support design by contract in java," 2007.

[128] H. Lee, "BIT: Bytecode instrumenting tool," 1997, bachelor Thesis at the University of Washington.

[129] W. Binder, J. Hulaas, and P. Moret, "Advanced Java bytecode instrumentation," in *Proceedings of the 5th international symposium on Principles and practice of programming in Java.* ACM, 2007, p. 144.

[130] T. Proebsting, G. Townsend, P. Bridges, J. Hartman, T. Newsham, and S. Watterson, "Toba: Java for applications a way ahead of time (wat) compiler," in *Proceedings of the 3rd conference on USENIX Conference on Object-Oriented Technologies (COOTS)-Volume 3.* USENIX Association, 1997, p. 3.

[131] G. Muller, B. Moura, F. Bellard, and C. Consel, "Harissa: A flexible and efficient Java environment mixing bytecode and compiled code," in *Proceedings of the 3rd conference on USENIX Conference on Object-Oriented Technologies (COOTS)-Volume 3.* USENIX Association, 1997, p. 1.

[132] A. Puder and S. H

"aberling, "Byte code level cross-compilation for developing web applications," *Science of Computer Programming*, vol. 74, no. 5-6, pp. 379–396, 2009.

[133] S. Kounev, F. Brosig, N. Huber, and R. Reussner, "Towards self-aware performance and resource management in modern service-oriented systems," in *Proceedings of the 7th IEEE International Conference on Services Computing (SCC 2010), July*, pp. 5–10.

[134] S. L. Graham, P. B. Kessler, and M. K. McKusick, "gprof: a call graph execution profiler," *SIGPLAN Not.*, vol. 39, no. 4, pp. 49–57, 2004.

[135] T. Mytkowicz, A. Diwan, M. Hauswirth, and P. Sweeney, "Evaluating the accuracy of Java profilers," in *Proceedings of the 2010 ACM SIGPLAN conference on Programming language design and implementation*. ACM, 2010, pp. 187–197.

[136] "Sun Microsystems, Inc., Java Virtual Machine Profiler Interface (JVMPI)," 2007, last visit: December 21st, 2007. [Online]. Available: http://java.sun.com/j2se/1.5.0/docs/guide/jvmti/

[137] "JProfiler," 2010, http://www.ej-technologies.com/products/jprofiler/overview.html, last retrieved August 27th, 2010. [Online]. Available: http://www.ej-technologies.com/products/jprofiler/overview.html

[138] K. Krogmann, M. Kuperberg, and R. Reussner, "Using Genetic Search for Reverse Engineering of Parametric Behaviour Models for Performance Prediction," *IEEE Transactions on Software Engineering*, 2009, accepted for publication, to appear.

[139] C. Hrischuk, C. Murray Woodside, and J. Rolia, "Trace-based load characterization for generating performance software models," *IEEE Transactions Software Engineering*, vol. 25, no. 1, pp. 122–135, Jan/Feb 1999.

[140] T. Israr, M. Woodside, and G. Franks, "Interaction tree algorithms to extract effective architecture and layered performance models from traces," *Journal of Systems and Software, 5th International Workshop on Software and Performance*, vol. 80, no. 4, pp. 474–492, April 2007. [Online]. Available: http://www.sciencedirect.com/science/article/B6V0N-4KSSW5C-1/2/be38c84d6892a796dc2833b6622f66d3

[141] M. D. McIlroy, "Mass Produced Software Components," in *Software Engineering*, P. Naur and B. Randell, Eds.   Brussels: Scientific Affairs Division, NATO, 1969, pp. 138–155, report of a conference sponsored by the NATO Science Committee, Garmisch, Germany, 7th to 11th October 1968.

[142] C. Szyperski, D. Gruntz, and S. Murer, *Component Software: Beyond Object-Oriented Programming*, 2nd ed.   New York, NY: ACM Press and Addison-Wesley, 2002.

[143] O. Alliance, "OSGi service platform, Core Specification release 4.1," *Draft*, *May*, 2007.

[144] J. Zhou, D. Zhao, Y. Ji, and J. Liu, "Examining OSGi from an ideal enterprise software component model," in *Software Engineering and Service Sciences (ICSESS), 2010 IEEE International Conference on*.   IEEE, 2010, pp. 119–123.

[145] Z. Durdik, "Architectural modeling in agile methods," in *WCOP2010*, B. Bühnová, R. H. Reussner, C. Szyperski, and W. Weck, Eds., vol. Technical Report 2010-14.   Karlsruhe Institue of Technology, Faculty of Informatics, June 2010, pp. 23–30. [Online]. Available: http://digbib.ubka.uni-karlsruhe.de/volltexte/1000018464

[146] Microsoft Corporation, "The DCOM homepage," 2007, last retrieved August 31st, 2010. [Online]. Available: http://www.microsoft.com/com/default.mspx

[147] J. Dietrich, C. McCartin, E. Tempero, and S. Shah, "Barriers to Modularity-An Empirical Study to Assess the Potential for Modularisation of Java Programs," *Research into Practice–Reality and Gaps*, pp. 135–150, 2010.

[148] V. Grassi, R. Mirandola, and A. Sabetta, "From Design to Analysis Models: a Kernel Language for Performance and Reliability Analysis of Component-based Systems," in *WOSP '05: Proceedings of the 5th international workshop on Software and performance*. New York, NY, USA: ACM Press, 2005, pp. 25–36.

[149] H. Koziolek, "Performance evaluation of component-based software systems: A survey," *Performance Evaluation*, vol. In Press, Corrected Proof, pp. –, 2009. [Online]. Available: http://www.sciencedirect.com/science/article/B6V13-4WXC21F-1/2/602bed8a6bd384b5516b8f84ac82c672

[150] S. Becker, L. Grunske, R. Mirandola, and S. Overhage, "Performance Prediction of Component-Based Systems: A Survey from an Engineering Perspective," in *Architecting Systems with Trustworthy Components*, ser. LNCS, R. Reussner, J. Stafford, and C. Szyperski, Eds. Springer, 2006, vol. 3938, pp. 169–192.

[151] A. Bertolino and R. Mirandola, "CB-SPE Tool: Putting Component-Based Performance Engineering into Practice," in *Proc. 7th International Symposium on Component-Based Software Engineering (CBSE 2004), Edinburgh, UK*, ser. LNCS, I. Crnkovic, J. A. Stafford, H. W. Schmidt, and K. C. Wallnau, Eds., vol. 3054. Springer Heidelberg, 2004, pp. 233–248.

[152] X. Wu and C. M. Woodside, "Performance modeling from software components," in *WOSP*, J. J. Dujmovic, V. A. F. Almeida, and D. Lea, Eds. ACM, 2004, pp. 290–301. [Online]. Available: http://doi.acm.org/10.1145/974044.974089

[153] J. Ivers and G. Moreno, "PACC starter kit: developing software with predictable behavior," in *Companion of the 30th international conference on Software engineering*. ACM, 2008, pp. 949–950.

[154] ——, "Model-driven development with predictable quality," in *Companion to the 22nd ACM SIGPLAN conference on Object-oriented programming systems and applications companion*. ACM, 2007, p. 875.

[155] S. A. Hissam, G. A. Moreno, J. A. Stafford, and K. C. Wallnau, "Packaging Predictable Assembly." in *Component Deployment, IFIP/ACM Working Conference, CD 2002, Berlin, Germany, June 20-21, 2002, Proceedings*, ser. Lecture Notes in Computer Science, J. M. Bishop, Ed., vol. 2370. Springer, 2002, pp. 108–124.

[156] R. Aigner, H. Berthold, E. Franz, S. Gbel, H. Hrtig, H. Humann, K. Meiner, K. Meyer-Wegener, M. Meyerhoefer, A. Pfitzmann, S. Rttger, A. Schill, T. Springer, and F. Wehner, "COMQUAD - Komponentenbasierte Softwaresysteme mit zusagbaren quantitativen Eigenschaften und Adaptionsfhigkeit," TU Dresden, Fakultt Informatik, Technical Report TUD-FI02-10, Nov. 2002.

[157] S. Goebel, C. Pohl, S. Roettger, and S. Zschaler, "The COMQUAD component model: enabling dynamic selection of implementations by weaving non-functional aspects," in *AOSD '04: Proceedings of the 3rd International Conference on Aspect-oriented Software Development*. New York, NY, USA: ACM Press, 2004, pp. 74–82.

[158] M. Meyerhöfer and K. Meyer-Wegener, "Estimating Non-functional Properties of Component-based Software Based on Resource Consumption," *Electr. Notes Theor. Comput. Sci.*, vol. 114, pp. 25–45, 2005.

[159] S. Becker, H. Koziolek, and R. Reussner, "The Palladio Component Model for Model-Driven Performance Prediction: Extended version," *Journal of Systems and Software*, vol. 82, pp. 3–22, 2008. [Online]. Available: http://dx.doi.org/10.1016/j.jss.2008.03.066

[160] H. Koziolek, *Parameter Dependencies for Reusable Performance Specifications of Software Components*, ser. The Karlsruhe Series on Software Design and Quality. Universitätsverlag Karlsruhe, 2008, vol. 2.

[161] S. Becker, *Coupled Model Transformations for QoS Enabled Component-Based Software Design*, ser. The Karlsruhe Series on Software Design and Quality. Universitätsverlag Karlsruhe, March 2008, vol. 1.

[162] J. Shirazi, *Java Performance Tuning*, 2nd ed. O'Reilly, 2003.

[163] C. Larman and R. Guthrie, *Java 2 Performance and Idiom Guide*. Prentice Hall PTR, 2000.

[164] "Java Platform API Documentation, java.lang.System class," 2010, http://download.oracle.com/javase/1.5.0/docs/api/java/lang/System.html, last retrieved August 31st, 2010. [Online]. Available: http://download.oracle.com/javase/1.5.0/docs/api/java/lang/System.html

[165] Chuck Walbourn, "Game Timing and Multicore Processors," http://msdn.microsoft.com/en-us/library/ee417693March 9th, 2010. [Online]. Available: http://msdn.microsoft.com/en-us/library/ee417693%28VS.85%29.aspx

[166] Intel, "Time Stamp Counter, Intel 64 and IA-32 Architectures Software Developer's Manual Volume 2B: Instruction Set Reference, N-Z, Pages 251–252," http://developer.intel.com/design/processor/manuals/253667.pdf, last visit: March 9th, 2010. [Online]. Available: http://developer.intel.com/design/processor/manuals/253667.pdf

[167] R. Richter, "Java Simon - Simple Monitoring API," http://code.google.com/p/javasimon/, last visit: March 9th, 2010. [Online]. Available: http://code.google.com/p/javasimon/

[168] M. Kuperberg, F. Omri, and R. Reussner, "Using Heuristics to Automate Parameter Generation for Benchmarking of Java Methods," in *Proceedings of the 6th International Workshop on Formal Engineering approaches to Software Components and Architectures, York, UK, 28th March 2009 (ETAPS 2009, 12th European Joint Conferences on Theory and Practice of Software)*,

2009. [Online]. Available: http://sdqweb.ipd.uka.de/publications/pdfs/kuperberg2009a.pdf

[169] M. Kuperberg and F. Omri, "Automated Benchmarking of Java APIs," in *Proceedings of Software Engineering 2010 (SE2010)*, February 2010, to appear.

[170] G. Stuer, K. Vanmechelen, J. Broeckhove, and T. Dhaene, "Sleeping in Java," in *Proceedings of the EuroMedia 2004 conference, Belgium*, vol. 10, 2004, pp. 74–78.

[171] K. S. Trivedi, *Probability and Statistics with Reliability, Queuing and Computer Science Applications*, 2nd ed. Wiley, 2001.

[172] B. Beckert and S. Schlager, "Software verification with integrated data type refinement for integer arithmetic," vol. 2999. Springer, 2004, pp. 207–226.

[173] D. Brumley, D. X. Song, T. cker Chiueh, R. Johnson, and H. Lin, "Rich: Automatically protecting against integer-based vulnerabilities," in *Proceedings of the Network and Distributed System Security Symposium, NDSS 2007, San Diego, California, USA, 28th February - 2nd March 2007*, 2007.

[174] D. Keaton, T. Plum, R. C. Seacord, D. Svoboda, A. Volkovitsky, and T. Wilson, "As-if infinitely ranged integer model," CERT Program, Software Engineering Institute (SEI), Tech. Rep. CMU/SEI-2009-TN-023, July 2009, www.cert.org/archive/pdf/09tn023.pdf.

[175] A. . I. Board, "Ariane5 flight 501 failure," Online, 1996, http://esamultimedia.esa.int/docs/esa-x-1819eng.pdf. [Online]. Available: http://esamultimedia.esa.int/docs/esa-x-1819eng.pdf

[176] S. Brunthaler, "Virtual-machine abstraction and optimization techniques," *Electr. Notes Theor. Comput. Sci.*, vol. 253, no. 5, pp. 3–14, 2009.

[177] R. Martin, "The Testing Slant on the Different Types of Y2K Errors," in *Unpublished briefing to the Intelligence Community on Year 2000 Testing Workshop, Washington, DC*, vol. 23, 1998.

405

[178] L. Prechelt, "The surprising dynamics of a simple year 2000 bug," *ACM SIGSOFT Software Engineering Notes*, vol. 24, no. 3, pp. 56–57, 1999.

[179] C. Jones, "Bad days for software," *IEEE Spectrum*, vol. 35, no. 9, pp. 47–52, 1998.

[180] M. Kuperberg, "Influence of Execution Environments on the Performance of Software Components," in *Proceedings of the 2nd International Research Training Groups Workshop, Dagstuhl, Germany, November 6 - 8, 2006*, ser. Reihe Trustworthy Software Systems, J. Happe, H. Koziolek, and M. Rohr, Eds., vol. 3, 2006. [Online]. Available: http://www.gito.de/impress/ produkte.nsf/0/81B3A5D1DBB12943C125738B00762D3C

[181] S. Chiba, Y. Sato, and M. Tatsubori, "Using HotSwap for implementing dynamic AOP systems," in *1st Workshop on Advancing the State-of-the-Art in Run-time Inspection, july*. Citeseer, 2003.

[182] J. Kabanov, "JRebel Tool Demo," *Bytecode 2010*, p. 71, 2010.

[183] C. S. Wolfgang Weck, Jan Bosch, Ed., *Proceedings of the Second International Workshop on Component-Oriented Programming (WCOP '97)*. Finnland: TUCS, Sep. 1997, general Publication No. 5.

[184] A. Loskutov, "Bytecode Outline plugin for Eclipse," last visit: October 1st, 2007. [Online]. Available: http://andrei.gmxhome.de/bytecode/index. html

[185] M. Kuperberg and S. Becker, "Predicting Software Component Performance: On the Relevance of Parameters for Benchmarking Bytecode and APIs," in *Proceedings of the 12th International Workshop on Component Oriented Programming (WCOP 2007)*, R. Reussner, C. Czyperski, and W. Weck, Eds., July 2007. [Online]. Available: http://sdqweb.ipd.uka.de/publications/pdfs/kuperberg2007a.pdf

[186] H. Koziolek and J. Happe, *Dependability Metrics*, ser. LNCS. Springer Heidelberg, 2008, vol. 4909, ch. Performance Metrics for Specific

Domains, pp. 233–240. [Online]. Available: http://www.springerlink. com/content/t13718l56531335p/fulltext.pdf

[187] C. Herder and J. J. Dujmovic, "Workload Characterization Using Metrics Based on Instruction Grouping," *International Journal of Computer and Information Science*, vol. 5, no. 1, 2004.

[188] J. Lee, "Program Validation by Symbolic and Reverse Execution," PhD thesis, BRICS Ph.D. School, Department of Computer Science, University of Aarhus, Aarhus, Denmark, November 2006. [Online]. Available: http://www.brics.dk/~jlee/papers/thesis-jooyong.pdf

[189] M. D. Ernst, J. H. Perkins, P. J. Guo, S. McCamant, C. Pacheco, M. S. Tschantz, and C. Xiao, "The Daikon system for dynamic detection of likely invariants," *Science of Computer Programming*, vol. 69, no. 1–3, pp. 35–45, Dec. 2007.

[190] F. Siebert, "Realtime garbage collection in the JamaicaVM 3.0," in *Proceedings of the 5th international workshop on Java technologies for real-time and embedded systems*. ACM, 2007, p. 103.

[191] G. Bollella, J. Gosling, B. Brosgol, P. Dibble, S. Furr, and M. Turnbull, *The real-time specification for Java*. Citeseer, 2000.

[192] M. Hauck, M. Kuperberg, K. Krogmann, and R. Reussner, "Modelling Layered Component Execution Environments for Performance Prediction," in *Proceedings of the 12th International Symposium on Component Based Software Engineering (CBSE 2009)*, ser. LNCS, no. 5582. Springer, 2009, pp. 191–208. [Online]. Available: http://www.comparch-events.org/pages/present.html

[193] B. Beckert, R. Hähnle, and P. H. Schmitt, Eds., *Verification of Object-Oriented Software: The KeY Approach*, ser. LNCS 4334. Springer-Verlag, 2007.

[194] Intel Corporation, "Intel VTune Performance Analyzer," 2009, http://software.intel.com/en-us/articles/intel-vtune-

performance-analyzer-for-windows-documentation/, last visit: October 9th, 2009. [Online]. Available: http://software.intel.com/en-us/articles/ intel-vtune-performance-analyzer-for-windows-documentation/

[195] C. Click and M. Paleczny, "A simple graph-based intermediate represent-ation," in *ACM SIGPLAN Workshop on Intermediate Representations.* ACM Press, 1995.

[196] F. Omri, "Design and Implementation of a fine-grained Benchmark for the Java API," Study thesis at chair 'Software Design and Quality' Prof. Reussner, February 2007.

[197] I. R. Forman and N. Forman, *Java Reflection in Action (In Action series).* Greenwich, CT, USA: Manning Publications Co., 2004.

[198] S. Chiba, "Javassist (Java Programming Assistant)," last retrieved August 31st, 2010. [Online]. Available: http://www.csg.is.titech.ac.jp/projects/ index.html

[199] D. A. Menasci¿½ and V. A. F. Almeida, *Capacity Planning for Web Services: metrics, models, and methods.* Prentice Hall, 2001, ch. 3.1: Basic Perform-ance Concepts: Service Times at single Disks and Disk Arrays, pp. 72–90.

[200] M. Kuperberg, K. Krogmann, and R. Reussner, "Performance Prediction for Black-Box Components using Reengineered Parametric Behaviour Models," in *Proceedings of the 11th International Symposium on Component Based Software Engineering (CBSE 2008), Karlsruhe, Germany, 14th-17th October 2008,* ser. LNCS, vol. 5282. Springer Heidelberg, October 2008, pp. 48–63. [Online]. Available: http://sdqweb.ipd.uka.de/publications/ pdfs/kuperberg2008c.pdf

[201] M. Kuperberg, M. Krogmann, and R. Reussner, "ByCounter: Portable Runtime Counting of Bytecode Instructions and Method Invocations," in *Proceedings of the 3rd International Workshop on Bytecode Semantics, Verification, Analysis and Transformation, Budapest, Hungary, 5th April*

2008 (ETAPS 2008, 11th European Joint Conferences on Theory and Practice of Software), 2008. [Online]. Available: http://sdqweb.ipd.uka. de/publications/pdfs/kuperberg2008a.pdf

[202] J. Happe, "Predicting Software Performance in Symmetric Multi-core and Multiprocessor Environments," Dissertation, University of Oldenburg, Germany, August 2008.

[203] M. Hauck, "Extending Performance-Oriented Resource Modelling in the Palladio Component Model," Master's thesis, University of Karlsruhe (TH), Germany, February 2009. [Online]. Available: http://sdqweb.ipd. uka.de/publications/pdfs/hauck2009a.pdf

[204] K. Krogmann, C. M. Schweda, S. Buckl, M. Kuperberg, A. Martens, and F. Matthes, "Improved Feedback for Architectural Performance Prediction using Software Cartography Visualizations," in *Architectures for Adaptive Systems (Proceeding of QoSA 2009)*, ser. LNCS, C. H. Raffaela Mirandola, Ian Gorton, Ed., vol. 5581.   Springer, 2009, pp. 52–69. [Online]. Available: http://www.springerlink.com/content/m0325512hl4857v1

[205] V. R. Basili, G. Caldiera, and H. D. Rombach, "The goal question metric approach," in *Encyclopedia of Software Engineering*, 2nd ed., J. J. Marciniak, Ed.   John Wiley & Sons, 2002, pp. 578–583.

[206] A. Martens, H. Koziolek, L. Prechelt, and R. Reussner, "From monolithic to component-based performance evaluation of software architectures – a series of experiments analysing accuracy and effort," *Journal of Empirical Software Engineering*, 2010, to appear in the Special Issue on Empirical Studies in Software Architecture: Opportunities, Approaches, and Challenges, edited by M. Ali Babar, Patricia Lago and Arie van Deursen.

[207] SPEC, "SPECjbb2005 - Industry-standard server-side Java benchmark (J2SE 5.0)." Standard Performance Evaluation Corporation, Jun. 2005, SPECtacular Award. [Online]. Available: http://www.spec. org/jbb2005/

[208] "Linpack Benchmark (Java Version)," 2007, uRL: http://www.netlib.org/benchmark/linpackjava/, last visit: October 9th, 2009. [Online]. Available: http://www.netlib.org/benchmark/linpackjava/

[209] "TOP500 Supercomputing Sites," 2010, http://www.top500.org/, last retrieved August 31st, 2010. [Online]. Available: http://www.top500.org/

[210] "Roy Longbottom's PC Benchmark Collection," 2010, http://www.roylongbottom.org.uk, last retrieved August 31st, 2010. [Online]. Available: http://www.roylongbottom.org.uk

[211] "The JLayer project: MP3 decoder/player/converter library for Java platform," 2010, http://www.javazoom.net/javalayer/javalayer.html, last retrieved August 31st, 2010. [Online]. Available: http://www.javazoom.net/javalayer/javalayer.html

[212] A. Martens, H. Koziolek, S. Becker, and R. H. Reussner, "Automatically improve software models for performance, reliability and cost using genetic algorithms," in *Proceedings of the 1st Joint WOSP/SIPEW International Conference on Performance Engineering (WOSP/SIPEW '10)*. New York, NY, USA: ACM, 2010. [Online]. Available: http://sdqweb.ipd.uka.de/publications/pdfs/martens2010a.pdf

[213] S. Wilson and J. Kesselman, *Java platform performance: strategies and tactics*. Prentice Hall PTR, 2000.

[214] L. Lamport, "Time, clocks, and the ordering of events in a distributed system," *Communications of the ACM*, vol. 21, no. 7, pp. 558–565, 1978.

[215] F. Mattern, "Virtual time and global states of distributed systems," *Parallel and Distributed Algorithms*, pp. 215–226, 1989.

[216] C. Fidge, "Timestamps in message-passing systems that preserve the partial ordering," in *Proceedings of the 11th Australian Computer Science Conference*, vol. 10, no. 1, 1988, pp. 56–66.

[217] J. Bloch, *Effective Java*, 2nd ed. Addison-Wesley Professional, 2008.

[218] C. Collberg, G. Myles, and M. Stepp, "An empirical study of Java bytecode programs," *Software: Practice and Experience*, vol. 37, no. 6, pp. 581–641, 2007.

[219] B. Cooper, H. Lee, and B. Zorn, "ProfBuilder: A package for rapidly building Java execution profilers," *University of Colorado, Boulder, Technical Report CU-CS-853-98*, 1998.

[220] G. Cohen and J. Chase, "An architecture for safe bytecode insertion," *Software–Practice and Experience*, vol. 34, no. 7, pp. 1–12, 2001.

[221] G. Cohen, J. Chase, and D. Kaminsky, "Automatic program transformation with JOIE," in *Proceedings of the annual conference on USENIX Annual Technical Conference*. USENIX Association, 1998, p. 14.

[222] G. Baxter, M. Frean, J. Noble, M. Rickerby, H. Smith, M. Visser, H. Melton, and E. Tempero, "Understanding the shape of Java software," *ACM SIGPLAN Notices*, vol. 41, no. 10, p. 412, 2006.

[223] E. Tempero, "How fields are used in java: An empirical study," apr. 2009, pp. 91 –100.

[224] S. Balsamo, A. Di Marco, P. Inverardi, and M. Simeoni, "Model-Based Performance Prediction in Software Development: A Survey," *IEEE Transactions on Software Engineering*, vol. 30, no. 5, pp. 295–310, May 2004.

[225] A. Seesing and A. Orso, "Insectj: a generic instrumentation framework for collecting dynamic information within eclipse," in *eclipse '05: Proceedings of the 2005 OOPSLA workshop on Eclipse technology eXchange*. New York, NY, USA: ACM, 2005, pp. 45–49.

[226] M. Bertoli, G. Casale, and G. Serazzi, "Jmt: performance engineering tools for system modeling," *SIGMETRICS Perform. Eval. Rev.*, vol. 36, no. 4, pp. 10–15, 2009.

[227] B. Dufour, K. Driesen, L. Hendren, and C. Verbrugge, "Dynamic Metrics for Java," in *OOPSLA '03: Proceedings of the 18th annual ACM SIGPLAN conference on Object-oriented programing, systems, languages, and applications.* New York, NY, USA: ACM, 2003, pp. 149–168.

[228] J. Donnell, "Java Performance Profiling using the VTune Performance Analyzer," http://software.intel.com/file/29675, 2004, last retrieved August 31st, 2010.

[229] B. Alpern, S. Augart, S. Blackburn, M. Butrico, A. Cocchi, P. Cheng, J. Dolby, S. Fink, D. Grove, M. Hind, K. McKinley, M. Mergen, J. Moss, T. Ngo, V. Sarkar, and M. Trapp, "The Jikes Research Virtual Machine project: building an open-source research community," *IBM Systems Journal*, vol. 44, no. 2, pp. 399–417, 2005.

[230] V. Schuppan, M. Baur, and A. Biere, "JVM Independent Replay in Java," *Electr. Notes Theor. Comput. Sci.*, vol. 113, pp. 85–104, 2005.

[231] J. Maebe, D. Buytaert, L. Eeckhout, and K. D. Bosschere, "Javana: a system for building customized Java program analysis tools," in *OOPSLA*, 2006, pp. 153–168.

[232] M. Hauswirth, P. F. Sweeney, A. Diwan, and M. Hin, "Vertical profiling: understanding the behavior of object-printed applications," in *OOPSLA '04: Proceedings of the 19th annual ACM SIGPLAN conference on Object-oriented programming, systems, languages, and applications.* New York, NY, USA: ACM, 2004, pp. 251–269.

[233] J. Steven, P. Chandra, B. Fleck, and A. Podgurski, "jRapture: A Capture/Replay tool for observation-based testing," in *ISSTA*, 2000, pp. 158–167.

[234] W. Binder, J. Hulaas, and P. Moret, "Advanced Java Bytecode Instrumentation," in *PPPJ 2007, Lisboa, Portugal, September 5-7, 2007.* ACM, 2007, pp. 135–144.

[235] R. Vallée-Rai, L. Hendren, V. Sundaresan, P. Lam, E. Gagnon, and P. Co, "Soot - a Java Optimization Framework," in *Proceedings of CASCON 1999*, 1999, pp. 125–135.

[236] S. Yamazaki, M. Matsumoto, T. Nakanishi, T. Kitasuka, and A. Fukuda, "A Case Study of Development of a Java Bytecode Analyzer Framework Using AspectJ," *IPSJ Digital Courier*, vol. 1, no. 0, pp. 104–116, 2005.

[237] M. Arnold and B. Ryder, "A framework for reducing the cost of instrumented code," in *Proceedings of the ACM SIGPLAN 2001 conference on Programming language design and implementation.* ACM, 2001, pp. 168–179.

[238] P. Brebner, E. Cecchet, J. Marguerite, P. Tuma, O. Ciuhandu, B. Dufour, L. Eeckhout, S. Frénot, A. S. Krishna, J. Murphy, and C. Verbrugge, "Middleware benchmarking: approaches, results, experiences," *Concurrency and Computation: Practice and Experience*, vol. 17, no. 15, pp. 1799–1805, 2005.

[239] J. M. Bull, L. A. Smith, M. D. Westhead, D. S. Henty, and R. A. Davey, "A benchmark suite for high performance java," *Concurrency - Practice and Experience*, vol. 12, no. 6, pp. 375–388, 2000.

[240] "Java SciMark 2.0," 2007, uRL: http://math.nist.gov/scimark2/, last visit: Oct. 9th, 2009. [Online]. Available: http://math.nist.gov/scimark2/

[241] E. Albert, P. Arenas, S. Genaim, G. Puebla, and D. Zanardini, "Removing useless variables in cost analysis of Java bytecode," in *Proceedings of the 2008 ACM symposium on Applied computing.* ACM, 2008, pp. 368–375.

[242] Winfried Klinker, "Analyse von MS IL Byte Code unter Performancegesichtspunkten," BSc thesis at the University of Oldenburg, 2005.

[243] B. Beizer, *Black-Box Testing.* John Wiley & Sons, Inc.; 1st Ed., 1995.

[244] P. Drongowski, L. Yu, F. Swehosky, S. Suthikulpanit, and R. Richter, "Incorporating Instruction-Based Sampling into AMD CodeAnalyst," in *2010*

413

IEEE International Symposium on Performance Analysis of Systems & Software (ISPASS), 2010, pp. 119–120.

[245] M. Annavaram, R. Rakvic, M. Polito, J. Bouguet, R. Hankins, and B. Davies, "The fuzzy correlation between code and performance predictability," in *37th International Symposium on Microarchitecture, 2004. MICRO-37 2004*, 2004, pp. 93–104.

[246] W. Alexander, R. Berry, F. Levine, and R. Urquhart, "A unifying approach to performance analysis in the Java environment," *IBM Systems Journal*, vol. 39, no. 1, pp. 118–134, 2000.

[247] J. Aycock, "A brief history of just-in-time," *ACM Computing Surveys (CSUR)*, vol. 35, no. 2, p. 113, 2003.

[248] L. Yang, X. Ma, and F. Mueller, "Cross-platform performance prediction of parallel applications using partial execution," 2005.

[249] S. Sodhi, J. Subhlok, and Q. Xu, "Performance prediction with skeletons," *Cluster Computing*, vol. 11, no. 2, pp. 151–165, 2008.

[250] S. Shimizu, R. Rangaswami, H. Duran-Limon, and M. Corona-Perez, "Platform-independent modeling and prediction of application resource usage characteristics," *Journal of Systems and Software*, vol. 82, no. 12, pp. 2117–2127, 2009.

[251] R. Badia, J. Labarta, J. Gimenez, and F. Escale, "DIMEMAS: Predicting MPI applications behavior in Grid environments," in *Workshop on Grid Applications and Programming Tools (GGF8)*, vol. 86, 2003.

[252] D. Katramatos and S. Chapin, "A cost/benefit estimating service for mapping parallel applications on heterogeneous clusters," in *IEEE International Conference on Cluster Computing*. Citeseer, 2005.

[253] S. Sadjadi, S. Shimizu, J. Figueroa, R. Rangaswami, J. Delgado, H. Duran, and X. Collazo, "A modeling approach for estimating execution time

of long-running scientific applications," in *Proceedings of the Fifth High-Performance Grid Computing Workshop.* Citeseer, 2008.

[254] G. Marin and J. Mellor-Crummey, "Cross-architecture performance predictions for scientific applications using parameterized models," in *Proceedings of the joint international conference on Measurement and modeling of computer systems.* ACM, 2004, pp. 2–13.

[255] B. Lee and D. Brooks, "Illustrative design space studies with microarchitectural regression models," in *IEEE 13th International Symposium on High Performance Computer Architecture, 2007. HPCA 2007,* 2007, pp. 340–351.

[256] G. Nudd, D. Kerbyson, E. Papaefstathiou, S. Perry, J. Harper, and D. Wilcox, "Pace–A Toolset for the Performance Prediction of Parallel and Distributed Systems," *International Journal of High Performance Computing Applications,* vol. 14, no. 3, p. 228, 2000.

[257] E. Papaefstathiou, D. Kerbyson, G. Nudd, D. Wilcox, J. Harper, and S. Perry, "A Common Workload Interface for the Performance Prediction of High Performance Systems," in *Proceedings of the IEEE International Symposium On Computer Architecture, Workshop on Performance Analysis in Design (PAID 98) Barcelona.* Citeseer, 1998.

[258] A. Alkindi, D. Kerbyson, and G. Nudd, "Dynamic instrumentation and performance prediction of application execution," in *High-Performance Computing and Networking.* Springer, 2009, pp. 513–523.

[259] Object Management Group (OMG), "UML Profile for Schedulability, Performance and Time," January 2005. [Online]. Available: http://www.omg.org/cgi-bin/doc?formal/2005-01-02

[260] ——, "UML Profile for Modeling and Analysis of Real-Time and Embedded systems (MARTE) RFP (realtime/05-02-06)," 2006. [Online]. Available: http://www.omg.org/cgi-bin/doc?realtime/2005-2-6

[261] C. Atkinson and T. Kuehne, "A generalized notion of platforms for model-driven development," *Model-driven Software Development*, pp. 119–136, 2005.

[262] D. B. Petriu and M. Woodside, "A Metamodel for Generating Performance Models from UML Designs," in *UML 2004 - The Unified Modeling Language. Model Languages and Applications. 7th International Conference, Lisbon, Portugal, October 11-15, 2004, Proceedings*, ser. LNCS, T. Baar, A. Strohmeier, A. Moreira, and S. J. Mellor, Eds., vol. 3273. Springer, 2004, pp. 41–53.

[263] V. Grassi, R. Mirandola, E. Randazzo, and A. Sabetta, "Klaper: An intermediate language for model-driven predictive analysis of performance and reliability," *The Common Component Modeling Example*, pp. 327–356, 2008.

[264] T. Bures, P. Hnetynka, and F. Plasil, "Sofa 2.0: Balancing advanced features in a hierarchical component model," in *SERA '06: Proceedings of the Fourth International Conference on Software Engineering Research, Management and Applications*. Washington, DC, USA: IEEE Computer Society, 2006, pp. 40–48.

[265] E. Bondarev, J. Muskens *et al.*, "Predicting Real-Time Properties of Component Assemblies: a Scenario-Simulation Approach," 2004.

[266] J. Gelissen and R. M. Laverty, "Robocop: Revised specification of framework and models (deliverable 1.5)," Information Technology for European Advancement, Tech. Rep., 2003.

[267] M. Dmitriev, "Application of the HotSwap technology to advanced profiling," in *Proceedings of the First Workshop on Unanticipated Software Evolution, held at ECOOP 2002 International Conference*. Citeseer.

[268] D. Kim and E. Tilevich, "Overcoming JVM HotSwap constraints via binary rewriting," in *Proceedings of the 1st International Workshop on Hot Topics in Software Upgrades*. ACM, 2008, p. 5.

[269] L. Kapova and S. Becker, "Systematic refinement of performance models for concurrent component-based systems," in *7th International Workshop on Formal Engineering approaches to Software Components and Architectures (FESCA)*, ser. Electronic Notes in Theoretical Computer Science.   Elsevier, 2010. [Online]. Available: http://sdqweb.ipd.uka.de/publications/pdfs/kapova2010a.pdf